The Ends of Freedom

The Ends of Freedom

of Freedom

Reclaiming America's Lost
Promise of Economic Rights

MARK PAUL

The University of Chicago Press

The University of Chicago Press, Chicago 60637
© 2023 by Mark Paul
All rights reserved. No part of this book may be used or reproduced
in any manner whatsoever without written permission, except in
the case of brief quotations in critical articles and reviews. For more
information, contact the University of Chicago Press, 1427 E. 60th St.,
Chicago, IL 60637.
Published 2023
Printed in the United States of America

32 31 30 29 28 27 26 25 24 23   1 2 3 4 5

ISBN-13: 978-0-226-79296-5 (cloth)
ISBN-13: 978-0-226-82629-5 (e-book)
DOI: https://doi.org/10.7208/chicago/9780226826295.001.0001

Library of Congress Cataloging-in-Publication Data

Names: Paul, Mark (Political economist), author.
Title: The ends of freedom : reclaiming America's lost promise of
    economic rights / Mark Paul.
Description: Chicago : The University of Chicago Press, 2023. |
    Includes bibliographical references and index.
Identifiers: LCCN 2022045058 | ISBN 9780226792965 (cloth) |
    ISBN 9780226826295 (ebook)
Subjects: LCSH: Economic rights—United States—History. |
    Equality—Economic aspects—United States. | United States—
    Economic conditions—20th century. | United States—
    Economic policy—20th century.
Classification: LCC HC106.84 .P38 2023 | DDC 330.973—dc23/eng/
    20221114
LC record available at https://lccn.loc.gov/2022045058

♾ This paper meets the requirements of ANSI/NISO Z39.48-1992
(Permanence of Paper).

For Chelsea and Theo

We will reach the goal of freedom . . . because the goal of America is freedom.

MARTIN LUTHER KING JR., "LETTER FROM BIRMINGHAM JAIL"

The people are what matter to government, and government should aim to give all the people under its jurisdiction the best possible life.

FRANCES PERKINS

For there is nothing mysterious about the foundations of a healthy and strong democracy. The basic things expected by our people of their political and economic system are simple. They are: Equality of opportunity for youth and for others. Jobs for those who can work. Security for those who need it. The ending of special privilege for the few. The preservation of civil liberties for all.

FRANKLIN DELANO ROOSEVELT

Contents

Introduction 1

Part I: American Freedom

1 States of America 15
2 Capitalism and Freedom 47
3 America's Other Freedom 75

Part II: Economic Rights

4 The Right to Work 113
5 The Right to Housing 135
6 The Right to an Education 153
7 The Right to Health Care 175
8 The Right to a Basic Income and Banking 189
9 The Right to a Healthy Environment 205

Part III: A Budget for the People

10 How Do We Pay for It? 227

Conclusion 249

Acknowledgments 257
Notes 261
Index 305

Introduction

I believe that virtually all the problems in the world come from
inequality of one kind or another.
AMARTYA SEN

In December 2017, Philip Alston, an Australian human rights law-
yer and the Special Rapporteur on Extreme Poverty and Human
Rights for the United Nations, was commissioned by the UN to take
a fact-finding tour of the United States. The purpose of his trip was to
determine whether "the persistence of extreme poverty in America
undermines the enjoyment of human rights by its citizens." After a
two-week tour that took him through California, Alabama, Georgia,
Puerto Rico, West Virginia, and Washington, DC, Alston described
what he observed:

> I met with many people barely surviving on Skid Row in Los Angeles,
> I witnessed a San Francisco police officer telling a group of home-
> less people to move on but having no answer when asked where
> they could move to, I heard how thousands of poor people get minor
> infraction notices which seem to be intentionally designed to quickly
> explode into unpayable debt, incarceration, and the replenishment of
> municipal coffers, I saw sewage filled yards in states where govern-
> ments don't consider sanitation facilities to be their responsibility, I
> saw people who had lost all of their teeth because adult dental care
> is not covered by the vast majority of programs available to the very

1

poor, I heard about soaring death rates and family and community destruction wrought by prescription and other drug addiction, and I met with people in the South of Puerto Rico living next to a mountain of completely unprotected coal ash which rains down upon them bringing illness, disability and death.[1]

By almost any economic measure, the United States of America is one of the richest nations ever to exist. At the same time, 65 million of its people live near or below the poverty line, struggling to feed, house, and care for themselves on a day-to-day basis. As Alston interviewed the scores of homeless occupying LA's Skid Row, he was told repeatedly that theirs is a great country: "American exceptionalism was a constant theme in my conversations." In Alston's summarizing report, he questioned whether this was still the case: "Instead of realizing its founders' admirable commitments, today's United States has proved itself to be exceptional in far more problematic ways that are shockingly at odds with its immense wealth and its founding commitment to human rights. As a result, contrasts between private wealth and public squalor abound."[2]

Alston also noted that despite its ready "naming and shaming" of other countries that are human rights violators, as well as its ratification of treaties in which human rights to sustenance and shelter are enumerated, the United States does not itself treat such economic and social conditions as rights for its citizens. Rather, the US government remains focused on defending so-called negative rights—freedoms from interventions or suppressions that could induce intimidation, coercion, or even violence.[3] The causes for this tendency are many, but one is historical. There are no more influential or important documents in the history of negative freedoms than the US Declaration of Independence and the first ten amendments of the US Constitution that followed, otherwise known as the Bill of Rights. When Americans wish to expand the list of places where they might carry a firearm, or marry a partner whom they aren't legally at liberty to marry, or erect a statue of the Ten Commandments on public property, or terminate a pregnancy, these are the texts they either appeal to or cite.

For Americans, the invocation of freedom, liberty, or rights is typically framed in the classically negative sense of "not being interfered with by others."[4]

But as Alston's account amply demonstrates, this brand of American freedom proves insufficient when it comes to the destitute and desperate. What is the value of a constitutional prohibition on laws abridging free speech to the resident of Skid Row who is without access to a toilet?[5] What good is the right to vote to the person too sick—or lacking time off from work—to get to the polls? Even the philosopher Isaiah Berlin, the first to distinguish the concept of negative freedom and a great champion of its protections, acknowledged the perversity of its bestowal on those too wretched to avail themselves of it: "To offer political rights, or safeguards against intervention by the state, to men who are half naked, illiterate, underfed, and diseased is to mock their condition."[6]

Such is the (quite literal) condition of many Americans today. And so it would seem American freedom, at least in its hegemonic form, needs a rethink.

In what follows, I offer a comprehensive prescription that aims to address the problem of persistent economic insecurity in America, one based on an expanded notion of American freedom and grounded in an alternative model of economic thought. The United States can eradicate poverty and build an economy that works for everyone— that puts, as the mantra goes, *people* over *profits*—by adopting social and economic ("positive") rights: the right to a well-paying job, the right to health care, the right to an education, the right to a home, and more.

To those who are steeped in the "negative" version of freedom, these ideas might seem radical, unrealistic, maybe even un-American. But as I show, the history of positive freedom in American thought and politics is also extensive. In fact, social and economic rights have been part of the American conversation since before there *was* an American conversation. Positive freedom is "freedom to" things— say, the right to an education through a public school system or the right to a job through direct employment programs run by the government. Positive freedom amounts to individuals' capacity to act on their free will—to live the good life and pursue happiness.[7] From Thomas Jefferson, whose Declaration of Independence asserts that all people are entitled to "life, liberty, and the pursuit of happiness"; to Thomas Paine, who first introduced the idea that a piece of the collective pie should go to each and every American as their birthright; to Franklin D. Roosevelt, who actually called for an economic bill of rights to be adopted by Congress; to Martin Luther King Jr., who argued that economic rights and civil rights were inextricably linked, many of America's most influential political and economic thinkers have recognized the importance of positive rights. For none of these figures were political and civil rights sufficient; to achieve its sacred promise of freedom, America was obliged to guarantee its citizens economic rights as well.

Of the American luminaries who have argued for economic rights, two stand out: Franklin D. Roosevelt, for his revolutionary 1944 State of the Union address, in which he called for a new—an *economic*—bill of rights; and Martin Luther King Jr., whose heroism in the fight for Black peoples' civil and political rights has obscured his equally dogged pursuit of economic equality. Drawing on Roosevelt's and King's ideas, this book proposes a new economic bill of rights, one geared to the twenty-first-century economy. That means, in addition to many of the rights Roosevelt enumerated in his 1944 address, the inclusion of the right to a healthy environment and the right to an income and basic banking services.

In detailing a contemporary bill of economic rights, I present a new vision for the role of the state in both structuring and limiting the reach of markets. Markets have long served as the de facto organizers of (and in some cases, barriers to) American capitalism and society. And while they will likely play a major role in American society for decades to come, it is increasingly essential that we recognize the merits of allowing governments to structure those markets so they support human flourishing and economic security; a society can derive all the benefits of markets while also regulating them. I argue not only that the state should implement floors and ceilings in certain markets (a *floor* being a job guarantee or social housing; a *ceiling* being maximum work hours or incomes) but also that some goods and services should simply be removed from the market entirely through decommodification (e.g., health care distributed as a matter of right rather than ability to pay).

One of the more regrettable turns in the mostly noble history of negative freedom is its co-opting and radicalization by a group of influential economists during the second half of the twentieth century. These theorists, whose primary goal was to dismantle the redistributive mechanisms of the New Deal and the Great Society, preached an extreme form of market fundamentalism—"neoliberalism"—that prescribed privatization and marketization for every economic ill. For the past sixty years, policy makers on both sides of the aisle have been held in thrall by this set of beliefs, and the results are patent: egregious levels of inequality and child poverty, persistently high unemployment and underemployment, and sickness and mortality rates higher than those of democratic countries of comparable wealth.

However, counterintuitive though it may be, there's a bright side to the neoliberal capture of America's political economy. For what it indicates is that America's social and economic crises are not obscure, unpredictable, or "natural"; rather, they stem from *intentional policy choices*. If US policy makers, at the urging of corporate CEOs and their economist enablers, can adopt a regressive tax code, they can also adopt a *progressive* one; if policy makers can choose to privatize health care, they can also choose *not* to.

In what follows, I lay out the history of and intellectual case for positive rights as an economic good. What Alston characterized as a denial of basic human rights is in practice, and for millions of people living in the United States today, a denial of dignity and a sense of being left behind by the rules that currently govern our economy. The economic rights described in this book—and by others earlier in

American history—have profound promise to smooth out the sharp, often deadly edges of the current economic system, help address critical issues of structural racism and sexism by mitigating the long-standing barriers that keep stigmatized populations from prospering, and, at long last, ensure positive freedom for all.

I begin with a discussion of where we are and how we got here. In the first chapter, I present a brisk overview of the current economic challenges faced by Main Street. I show why traditional economic indicators, like gross domestic product (GDP) and the stock market, fail to capture how the lives of everyday people like day care workers are changing. And I reveal how, despite the fact that we're in an era of extreme abundance beyond earlier generations' imaginations, policy makers continue to manufacture homelessness, poverty, and extreme economic need through conscious policy decisions.

In chapter 2, I examine the origins of neoliberalism and its disastrous influence on our economy and society—in other words, how we got here. Our current economic paradigm isn't, as Francis Fukuyama put it, the "end of history," that is, the pinnacle of a progressive historical process. Nor is there anything "natural" about where American society has landed. Rather, specific economists, including the likes of Friedrich Hayek and Milton Friedman, convinced policy makers and the wealthy that free markets were synonymous with freedom. They weaponized and radicalized freedom in its negative sense— "freedom from"—to defend markets at all costs, equating freedom with access to the market, private property rights, and little else. The result was the Reagan Revolution—tax cuts, deregulation, the crushing of the labor movement, and the neutering of non-defense public investment—which is finally being called into question today.

In chapter 3, the final chapter in part 1, I cover the long, and often untold, history of economic rights in the United States. I show that positive freedom—"freedom to"—has a rich history in this country, from the Founders to the Radical Republicans to the New Deal and Roosevelt's four freedoms to the civil rights movement. While this history has largely been pushed to the margins, it is as central to the

American story as notions of negative freedom, and it is essential to reclaim on the path to developing a richer and more meaningful understanding of freedom and to rescue American egalitarianism and prosperity.

I close chapter 3 with a brief recognition that today economic rights are in many respects back on the agenda. As self-identified democratic socialists increasingly gain political power, they are demanding that the promise of economic rights be fulfilled. However, the questions of what those economic rights look like in today's economy, how they would fundamentally reshape both markets and people's lives, and whether they are advisable from an economics standpoint are still on the table.

I take up those questions in part 2. Each chapter details a core economic right necessary to the realization of positive freedom in the United States. I start with the idea of the right to work, a refrain that has been co-opted (and corrupted) by conservatives to mean the ability to evade unions through open-shop workplaces. I aim to reorient it for progressive purposes: as an economic right, the right to work means *the right to a job at a living wage*. The intellectual case for such a policy is straightforward and, I hope, compelling. Unemployment and poverty wages are socially wasteful and personally ruinous; thus the government should put an end to them. I explain how and why the government has chosen instead to use people's livelihoods as a bargaining chip to keep wages down, workers in line, and prices more stable than necessary. But, as I show, the idea of a job guarantee— meaning the government offers everyone a job who needs one—has been part of the conversation in the United States for nearly a century. (In fact, for decades full employment was a cornerstone of the Democratic Party platform and a central demand of the civil rights movement.) I demonstrate how true full employment—meaning everyone who wants a job can get one at a living wage—can be achieved and how the fully employed will not only be made secure, but their work will help make each and every one of us better off.

The second right I discuss is the right to housing. Housing is a fundamental human need, yet a full-time worker earning minimum wage in the United States can't afford rent on a two-bedroom apartment anywhere in the country. And as the Skid Row example demonstrates, far too many go without a home entirely. The one-half of Americans who own a home enjoy a secure vehicle to build wealth, as well as a time horizon of thirty-plus years of rent control thanks to stable mortgage payments. This gives them a substantial financial benefit compared to the one-third of American households that rent, including the half of all renters who can't afford the monthly rent bill. Housing policy favors the diminishing fraction of Americans who can afford to own a home with tax breaks and special treatment, whereas housing policy for low-income Americans is riddled with not only potholes but sinkholes large enough to swallow a family whole. It is a striking example of "socialism for the rich, rugged individualism for the poor," as Martin Luther King Jr. once described it. As a result of this poor management of its housing sector, the United States has some of the highest rates of homelessness and housing insecurity among high-income nations. Not only is it a national disgrace; it is economically costly, dragging down child development and our collective capacity to flourish. But through two policies—massive investment in social housing and rent control—the United States can restructure the housing market and, instead of its current nexus of profit, create safe, stable, and green housing to meet social needs and build strong and prosperous communities.

Next, I consider the economic right that Americans are most familiar with: the right to an education. While the right to an education is already enshrined in many—though not all—state constitutions, debates persist over the ages at which this right begins and ends. Here I trace the history of the American high school movement, which helped expand the right to an education from grammar school through high school, and discuss the policy's arbitrary omission of college and pre-K today. In this chapter I lay out the economic case for free college and pre-K for all, explaining why both these measures not only provide people with greater opportunities for self-realization but also make clear economic sense.

The final chapters of part 2 explore three pressing economic rights: the right to health care, the right to a basic income and financial services, and the right to a healthy environment. In these chapters I explain how each right is a crucial piece of the puzzle as the economy is restructured *away* from a focus on short-term profits for the rich and *toward* meeting human ends. Medicare for all—which was the actual end goal of Medicare's designers in the 1960s—would save lives, save money, and sever the link between one's economic position and the care one receives. A basic income, in the form of a negative income tax, would finally eradicate American poverty. And the right to a healthy environment means taking the climate crisis seriously and rapidly decarbonizing—a goal that is eminently affordable, as programs like the Green New Deal have argued—but also providing everyone with clean air and clean water, basic necessities that far too many still lack.

Together, these seven economic rights form a comprehensive platform, a foundation, that advances the rightful goal of economic security for all. At an inflection point of American economic history, one where the divide between the upper and lower classes has never been greater, it seems that such a goal is the only one that a serious country can aspire to.

In part 3, the final chapter of the book, I address the trillion-dollar question: Can we afford it? The social goods described in this book come at a price, and in the context of the budget of the US government and the larger economy of the country and the world, how do such expenditures fit? What is their payback? Are these costs or investments?

The short, unnuanced answer is yes, the United States can afford policy programs built around positive rights. Just as important, however, the question, How do we pay for it?, should really be broken into two parts: First, where will the dollars come from? Second, where will we find the real resources—the doctors, teachers, and sustainable raw materials—to make these things a reality?

Part 3 examines how the US government can finance an economic bill of rights through substantial increases in government debt (which we should regard largely as a feature, not a bug, of our economy), a more progressive tax policy that places a ceiling on the market to combat inequality and protect democracy, and the reorganization of current government spending away from subsidizing violence and the rich and toward human needs. Then I show how the constraints that matter are not dollars and cents but rather the real resources necessary to meet national priorities. To do this, far more government coordination of the economy will be necessary. More doctors and teachers will need to be trained, and supply chains and efficiency will need to be substantially improved. But as the famous economist John Maynard Keynes once said, "Anything we can actually do, we can afford."

Some will question whether this is the time to reclaim economic freedom and mobilize around economic rights in light of how the rights Americans already have—both political and civil—are in dire jeopardy. To this I would note that America is at a unique moment in history. The tectonic plates of the country's political landscape are shifting faster than we have seen in a generation, creating gaps that are being filled by a range of political figures, from pseudofascist demagogues to working-class ideologues. During the 2016 and 2020 presidential campaigns, Senator Bernie Sanders fueled a creative ferment by envisioning what a new economy really looked like—from free college to Medicare for all to a $15 minimum wage and the Green New Deal to a wealth tax. Many of these bold economic proposals were shunned—dismissed as the pie-in-the-sky ideas of socialist utopians. In the years since, many of those same ideas have been embraced not only by a new generation of economists, whose empirical work has called into question the neoliberal assumptions that have shaped so much of our lives, but also by the general public. A program of universal health insurance now has the support of the majority of voters, including majorities in forty-two states and the majority of Republicans. A job guarantee to effectively end unemployment and poverty-level wages, a proposal I have worked tirelessly to develop and support, was endorsed by many of the 2020 Democratic presidential hopefuls. Tuition-free college, which would put an end to the current nightmare of student debt and skyrocketing tuition, is supported by 60 percent of the electorate. What the discourse has lacked thus far, however, is a unified vision—a north star—of economic reform to meet these demands. That is what an economic bill of rights offers.

Part I

American Freedom

1

States of America

(America never was America to me.)
LANGSTON HUGHES

America is a rich country. If its wealth were distributed equally, each and every adult in the United States would have roughly $400,000 to their name. If the GDP were distributed uniformly, then everyone over the age of eighteen would receive an annual injection of nearly $90,000 in their bank account—more than enough money to afford a comfortable home, a new car (including an electric car), a smart-phone, and other essentials like childcare. The good life, or at least a solvent one, would be the standard.[1]

Of course, America's wealth is not equally distributed. Its uneven-ness is so stark that narratives of an American middle class have all but disappeared, replaced by narratives of extreme wealth and pov-erty. What remains is a set of economic extremes: the proverbial haves and have-nots.

For a stark example of America's bifurcation, one need only look at the country's housing market. In a country where full-time workers earning the minimum wage can't afford a two-bedroom apartment no matter where they live, there is no option to move to an affordable neighborhood.[2] To people whose households number more than one or two individuals, there is no possibility of "tightening their belts" to get by. For 43 million working families, affordable housing just doesn't exist.

The housing shortage leaves nearly half of all American families paying more in rent than they can manage. According to the Department of Housing and Urban Development, a household is "rent burdened" if it's paying more than a quarter of its income in rent. More than half of Black and Latinx renters are rent burdened, and one in four people who rent are "severely" rent burdened, meaning they pay at least half their income for housing.[3] To some people, these proportions may not seem galling: it a common refrain among the older and affluent that paying an unwieldly rent is a rite of passage, a hardship that makes people work harder to move up in the world. In a time of skyrocketing rents and stagnant minimum wages, this is an outdated opinion. If we factor in additional costs for utilities, more than 10 million families have just a quarter of their income left for food, medicine, transportation, childcare, and the like. For the cost-burdened, there simply is not enough money to go around. Government housing assistance for the poor is even more insufficient, with only one in five people who qualify for federal rental aid actually receiving it because of systematic underfunding by Congress. Rent-burdened families aren't living beyond their means; means are being denied to them.[4]

The problem is only getting worse. Market rents have increased faster than both the cost of living and household incomes, especially in boom cities like Austin, Texas, which experienced rent inflation of 40 percent in 2021. While some cities saw rents stabilize or even decline a bit during the peak of the COVID-19 pandemic, rents rebounded beginning in the second half of 2021, surpassing pre-pandemic levels and then some. In the Boston area, where I grew up, the region was walloped by rent increases topping 22 percent in a single year, and the national average hovered at 14.1 percent in 2021 following a stronger than expected economic recovery.[5] And the affordable housing problem isn't exclusive to high-cost coastal cities: the majority—60 percent—of renters in the supposedly "affordable" city of Detroit are rent burdened, a rate that has doubled since 1990.[6]

The lack of affordable housing, combined with a generation's worth of wage stagnation and the failure to build sufficient new housing stock following the Great Recession, has created a housing crisis. Over 3 million households are experiencing homelessness in the United States, and an estimated one million families are evicted from their homes every year. (During the 2020 crisis, 40 million were in danger of eviction, though the government's pause on evictions and distribution of emergency economic impact payments helped avoid the worst catastrophe.) That amounts to millions of people—disproportionately children—being thrown into the streets on an annual basis, even during economic "boom" times. The reason? The stretching of financial feasibility in contemporary American life makes it extraordinarily challenging, and far too often infeasible, to weather unexpected (and expensive) life events.[7]

More often than not, missed rent payments are associated with major life events like job loss or illness, events economists refer to as "income shocks." According to the sociologist Matthew Desmond, author of *Evicted: Poverty and Profit in the American City* and director of Princeton's Eviction Lab, job loss, which affects one's current and future income, often sets evictions in motion. After all, without a job and with a threadbare safety net that fails to help people stay afloat during hard times, landlords become wary of tenants' ability to make up late rent and tend to push for eviction.[8]

For these people, eviction, and the homelessness that followed, wasn't about working hard or acting right. It wasn't about living within one's means. Housing, a fundamental human need, was denied to them simply because of a bump in the road called life.

While unemployment skyrocketed to 14.7 percent during the peak of the COVID-19-fueled economic crisis—nearly 50 percent higher than the peak during the Great Recession—America's wealthy upper crust saw its finances grow to dizzying new heights. Billionaires' wealth increased on average by more than 25 percent during the first year of the pandemic. Jeff Bezos, Amazon CEO and founder, added more than $70 billion to his net worth during 2020, and Tesla CEO

Elon Musk leapfrogged Bezos as the richest person in the world thanks
to a surge in wealth totaling an astonishing $140 billion (driven by
stock price increases) in the midst of the crisis. Despite his booming
fortune, Musk threatened workers, telling them they would lose their
unemployment benefits if they didn't defy government COVID-19
orders and show up at work.[9]

While the pandemic was unlocking record-breaking windfalls for
the rich, shoplifting surged amid a boom in hunger across the country. In Rhode Island, one in four households lacked adequate food.
People desperate for staples—bread, pasta, and baby formula—felt
they had no other option than to grab items off the shelves and walk
out of stores without paying.[10]

This is the reality of America.

Haves and Have-Nots in the 2010s

Before COVID-19, the economy was booming. The 2010s marked the
longest economic expansion in the history of the United States: 128
consecutive months—about 10.5 years—of nonstop economic growth.
As 2020 began, the unemployment rate sat at 3.5 percent—the lowest rate since the late 1960s, a number the Congressional Budget
Office (CBO) and many economists considered *beyond* the threshold
of "full employment." US GDP had surpassed $20 trillion in 2018;
and in early 2020, consumer FICO credit scores reached an all-time
high, fueling a rise in consumption bolstered by relatively favorable
interest rates and flexible terms on mortgages, car loans, and credit
cards.[11] In February 2020, just weeks before the crisis struck, the Dow
Jones Industrial Average reached an all-time high. That same month,
Fidelity, which manages roughly one in four retirement accounts in
the United States, reported it had a "record number of retirement
accounts containing $1 million or more."[12] Housing starts surged, and
buyers piled into the market so fast that supply simply couldn't keep
up with demand as houses flew off the market in record time.[13]

The 2010s also saw average household income surpass $90,000
a year, an all-time high.[14] American households held a record $110 tril-

lion in wealth in 2019, an average of over $700,000 per American family.[15] The average American earned over $28 an hour.[16] The average single-family house size had grown by nearly a thousand square feet—60 percent—since the early 1970s, and modern houses were over three times the size of the homes built in Levittown in the 1940s.[17] Yes, the Great Recession of 2007-9 had set the nation back, but the "great expansion"—the name given to the record economic climb of the 2010s by President Donald Trump's Council of Economic Advisers—brought the economy to levels heretofore unseen. The Trump administration told the country that "previously forgotten Americans are forgotten no more"—that economic growth (coupled with an expansion of work requirements to access public assistance programs) was delivering on the promise to end poverty and economic despair.[18]

By these measures, the economy appeared to be going gangbusters. But to understand the true state of America, one needs to go beyond the typical economic indicators—measures like GDP, headline unemployment, housing starts, the stock market—and examine the economics of Main Street. How had wages for everyday working people changed? Were preschool teachers and home health aides seeing strong wage growth? Could teachers afford to live in the communities they served? How many high-quality (as opposed to poverty-wage) jobs did the economy create? Was the country delivering on the promise of clean air and water, along with a stable climate, for all its citizens? And critically, was the nation realizing the right to "life, liberty and the pursuit of happiness," a right that entails sufficient food, housing, clothing, education, medical care, and employment—that is to say, economic security—for all?

When one digs deeper than the headline indicators, one finds that average Americans weren't any better off in the 2010s than they were a generation earlier. Not only was the growth of their wages stagnant; most people were falling further and further behind. During the forty years from 1978 to 2018, typical workers saw their compensation rise by a meager 12 percent; CEO compensation, meanwhile, ballooned by 940 percent. As of 2020, home health and personal care aides, one of the fastest-growing sectors of the economy, took home $27,080 per year on average. Other workers who provide socially necessary care, like preschool teachers, take home just over $30,500 a year. Food and service workers, meanwhile, take home just $21,250 a year. For the 7.5 million US residents who work these three jobs—and for the families dependent on them—staying afloat is a constant struggle, if not an impossibility.

I wish I could say these occupations were the anomaly, but they're not. What was once America's working class is today its working poor.[19]

The lack of economic stability experienced by millions of Americans has produced devastating downstream consequences. In their *New York Times* best seller, the economists Anne Case and Angus Deaton document how capitalism, and specifically the extreme manner of marketization practiced in the United States, is shortening people's lives. Despite life expectancy rising monotonically in the United States since World War I, it has recently reversed course, remaining flat or declining during the three years preceding the global pandemic (it will almost certainly decline further once deaths due to COVID-19 are factored in). The only times a reversal like this had been documented was the onset of World War I and the influenza epidemic of 1918. Sifting through the data, Case and Deaton find that the leading causes of the current shift are suicide, drug overdose, and alcoholic liver disease—a cluster of morbidities they term "deaths of despair." What was giving rise to this troubling upsurge? According to Case and Deaton, economic inequality, insecurity, and the general absence of opportunity. In other words, the booming economy economists were crowing about was literally killing people.

Case and Deaton also point to the growing loss of meaning in many people's lives, a loss they trace to the lack of well-paying and dignified work. As union membership collapsed, so too did the well-being of blue-collar workers. Unions not only provided a means of securing higher wages; they also provided a sense of belonging and solidarity, on top of a say in one's workplace. With the ebb of unions, workers are increasingly left to fend for themselves. The results haven't been good. As the economy grew over the past few decades, the gap between the haves and the have-nots did too. The White working class, a group that in the heyday of union membership had often been able to secure a ticket to the middle class, experienced the largest shock. White men who don't hold a bachelor's degree saw their earnings fall 13 percent from 1979 to 2017. Case and Deaton calculate that over the same period the reversal in White mortality among those ages forty-five to fifty-four resulted in an additional 600,000 deaths. For reference, they compare this number to the roughly 675,000 Americans who perished from HIV/AIDS since the start of that epidemic in the early 1980s. To be sure, the White working class still has a longer life expectancy and higher wages than the Black working class. However, the mortality gap between Black and White people without a bachelor's degree has narrowed considerably.[20]

The rich, in addition to living less precarious lives, live longer and healthier lives. The top one percent of income recipients among men live an average of fifteen years longer than the extremely poor; high-income women live about a decade longer than their low-income sisters. And a 2020 gerontological study found that the wealthiest third of Americans—when measured by wealth, as opposed to income— tend to enjoy eight or nine more healthy years than the poorest third. That is, being wealthy means you get to have almost ten extra years of *quality* life—taking care of oneself, cooking one's own meals, and staying active with friends and family.[21]

Other Main Street numbers tell similar stories. Home ownership rates have plummeted for younger Americans, leaving millennials 37 percent less likely to own a home than the two generations that came before them.[22] Some public commenters, including economists, have posited that millennials simply have a preference to rent. But this seems more a dodging of the issue than a good faith argument, or simply a palliative for boomers who recognize that home ownership—the ticket to the White middle class—is largely unattainable for a generation ravaged by two major recessions and saddled with student debt.

As the Princeton professor Keeanga-Yamahtta Taylor explains in her book *Race for Profit*, "access to appreciating homeownership" across the life span "determined whether one could afford to send one's children to college, retire, care for aging parents, and more." A home is the most important asset any American can own. It's a golden ticket to the middle class, sometimes beyond. It is also how most Americans accrue wealth, and hand it down from generation to generation, in the first place. In fact, home owners (median wealth, $255,000) have forty times more wealth on average than renters (median wealth, $6,300). And it's how housing stability—the rent one pays and the neighborhood and schools a family settles in—is achieved. Without owned homes, families have a harder time building up anything resembling a financial nest egg and are forced to watch the ever-elusive American dream slip further and further out of reach.

For Black Americans, the boon of an appreciating home has always been elusive. The twentieth-century history of Black families in American cities is characterized by their being funneled into predominantly Black neighborhoods by forces from the government, the real estate industry, and banks, each based on the racist—and notably false—assumption that the integration of neighborhoods would crush property values. For White home owners and bankers, race simply meant *risk*, so Black Americans have for more than a century found it difficult to secure mortgages or willing sellers. The economist Richard Rothstein, in his groundbreaking book *The Color of Law*, analyzes the specific government policies and actions that instantiated structural racism in the US housing market. Rothstein shows that the racism baked into US housing policy fueled residential segregation and inequality, as well as differences in the rate of return for Black and White people on their homes. From 2006 to 2016, for example, Rothstein found that White borrowers saw their homes appreciate, whereas Black borrowers saw the value of their precious asset sink into the red.[23]

Such deprivations are not limited to housing or to history, of course. Food too has become a luxury many can't afford today. As economic collapse swept the nation in the spring of 2020, the cover of the *New York Times Magazine* featured an aerial view of a line of cars waiting to receive a trunk-full of groceries from the San Antonio Food Bank. In normal times, the food bank fed thousands of people a week; as an economic collapse brought families to their knees, the same organization served two to three times that number, including up to ten thousand in a given day in the country's seventh-largest city.

Despite the fact that nearly one in six mothers with children under twelve reported that their household was food insecure before the recent crisis, many political leaders, including San Antonio's mayor, Ron Nirenberg, seemed unaware of the problem. He noted "that it took a pandemic for us to stop and assess just how precarious the economic conditions are for millions of American families." During the crisis, food insecurity climbed to levels not seen in the United States in a generation, with two-fifths of mothers with young children reporting a lack of food. At the peak of the crisis, researchers at Northeastern University reported that "nearly half [of Americans] worry they will run out of food and have no money for more." Can a society really be called "rich" if people can't put bread on the table and a stable roof over their heads?[24]

Affluence: An American Illusion

The American notion of wealth and prosperity for all can be traced to the late 1940s, the beginning of what historians call the "golden age" of capitalism. World War II had come to an end, and the factories of the United States were being retooled to produce cars, dishwashers, toasters, and other consumer products to meet the new middle class's insatiable appetite for goods. Household demand had been pent up during the war, as production efforts were focused on military needs, but soldiers were finally returning home to spend their savings, go to school, and start families. After a brief adjustment period during which the economy shifted away from war production, the factories and farms of America resumed production on overtime to meet the sudden shift in demand.

The demand didn't only come from America's burgeoning middle class. The war had reduced European factories and infrastructure to rubble, and American industry was the beneficiary of international markets with needs comparable to domestic ones. The official American response to assist in the rebuilding of Europe was encapsulated in the Marshall Plan, federal legislation that funneled billions in aid, often in the form of American exports, to European countries.

The boom in demand produced a boom in work, which was in turn accompanied by rising wages. This chain of abundance seemed to lend credence to the belief in the American dream: work hard; get ahead. Victory on the battlefield, along with victory in the economy, in turn powered the widespread conviction that the country had solved the problem that had plagued humankind since its beginning: scarcity. There was simply never enough to go around, until there was. The novelist and intellectual Mary McCarthy went so far as to argue that class distinctions in the country were vanishing and that "even segregation [was] diminishing; consumption replace[d] acquisition as an incentive." It appeared to many intellectuals that the America "of vast inequalities and dramatic contrasts is rapidly ceasing to exist."[25] The idea that American capitalism could solve American social problems, even ones as deep and thorny as racism, became an intoxicating and persisting belief.

It's important to note that the improvements in living standards that occurred during the golden age of capitalism, including those that gave rise to the great American middle class, weren't a "natural" outgrowth of markets. Rather, they were *planned*: policies were written, and public money was allocated and spent, to bring them about.

The stage had been set for these policies more than a decade earlier, when President Franklin D. Roosevelt was sworn into office in 1933. America was in the midst of the worst economic downturn in its short history, the Great Depression. One in four workers were out of a job, wages were tumbling, farmers were defaulting left and right, and the banking sector was in free fall.[26] Roosevelt was not being hyperbolic when he observed that "one-third of a nation [is] ill-housed, ill-clad, and ill-nourished."[27]

Roosevelt's solution was, famously, the New Deal, a suite of policies and spending that sought to produce two things: "a shot of adrenaline" to get people working, businesses investing, and banks lending again; and a complete restructuring of the regulatory rules to produce shared prosperity instead of the runaway inequality that had characterized the 1920s. Between March 1933 and April 1945, Roosevelt and his administration worked through Congress to craft policies that would fundamentally alter how the economy worked and who it worked for. Among these were the famous "alphabet agencies"— the Civilian Works Administration (CWA), the Civilian Conservation Corps (CCC), and the Works Progress Administration (WPA)—as well as the National Labor Relations Act (also known as the Wagner Act) and the Social Security Act, to name a few. Through these far-reaching reforms, the Roosevelt administration transformed the very nature and functioning of the American republic.

While Roosevelt and New Dealers never embraced deficit spending to the degree needed to negate the effects of the Great Depression, the economic foundation for shared prosperity laid down by the New Deal, coupled with unprecedented government spending for the war effort, put the country on a stable and prosperous path.[28] As American factories, jobs, and exports expanded with the war effort (and, later, demand from Europe), economic growth exploded. For perhaps the only time in American history, the economy came close to achieving full employment (the unemployment rate averaged just 1.7 percent between 1943 and 1945). Together with new regulations to tame the capitalist class and expand the rights of workers—bolstered most significantly by the Wagner Act and the rise of trade unionism— the country underwent a "Great Compression," a time in which economic growth led to a more equal distribution of wages and the rise of the modern American middle class.[29]

By 1961, the newly elected president, John F. Kennedy, could proclaim, "The world is very different now. For man holds in his mortal hands the power to abolish all forms of human poverty."[30] For Kennedy, as for many observers at the time, economic growth spurred by the New Deal combined with victory abroad offered real solutions to American destitution. However, the headline economic indicators of the postwar era, much like those of the 2010s, obscured the reality of living and working in America. For all the strides America had made, the postwar glory days weren't glorious for everyone.

The most influential chronicler of poverty in this era of plenty was Michael Harrington. A socialist activist and journalist—he would later become a founding member of the Democratic Socialists of America—Harrington devoted himself to the stories of those left behind by the postwar boom. Volunteering with the Catholic Workers in a home for the homeless in the Bowery, a district of New York City stricken with an appalling degree of privation and desperation, he "accepted a philosophy of voluntary poverty. We had no money and received no pay. We shared the living conditions of the people whom we were helping."[31]

During the two years he spent investigating poverty, Harrington crisscrossed the nation and talked with hundreds of people struggling under the burden of poverty. He found that poverty afflicted all races and creeds of Americans, from the poor inhabitants of Harlem, who were discriminated against time and time again, to the rural poor, or "hill folks." He came to believe that "being poor is not one aspect of a person's life in this country; it is his life." To this, "the truly human reaction can only be outrage."[32]

Harrington's firsthand account of his experiences among America's poor, published in 1962 as *The Other America*, challenged the dominant narrative that the country was on a righteous path to glory. And he was right: despite the Great Compression, some 40 to 50 million Americans—nearly one-third of the nation—still lived in poverty.[33] Incredibly, Roosevelt's famous claim, made in the thick of the Depression, that one-third of the nation was "ill-housed, ill-clad, and ill-nourished," was equally apposite almost twenty years later.

The Other America sold seventy thousand copies in its first year, influencing not only public discussion, but public policy. According to the historian Arthur Schlesinger, then an adviser to President Kennedy, *The Other America* "helped the president see the larger dimensions of poverty and resulted in poverty becoming a political issue."[34] After

Kennedy's assassination in November 1963, Lyndon Johnson took up the mantle. Seven short weeks after taking the oath of office, Johnson declared that the nation was now fighting a war at home on top of the ongoing war in Vietnam: a "war on poverty." With Johnson's declaration came more progressive reforms and programs than the country had ever seen (save with Roosevelt's New Deal). Johnson dubbed his domestic agenda, an agenda committed to racial justice and the eradication of poverty, the "Great Society."

Three landmark pieces of legislation, all signed into law in the summer of 1964, marked the first wave of the Great Society. The Civil Rights Act outlawed employment discrimination and integrated schools through the prohibition of racial segregation in public education as well as in public accommodations. The Economic Opportunity Act allowed for the creation of local Community Action Agencies in the fight against poverty, creating job training and education programs for people across the country, including the Volunteers in Service to America program. And the Food Stamp Act created the largest food assistance program in American history.

But it was Johnson's blow-out victory over the conservative presidential candidate, Barry Goldwater, in the 1964 presidential election—and the large margins liberal Democrats commanded in the Eighty-Ninth Congress—that gave Johnson his broad mandate to legislate. The resulting Elementary and Secondary Education Act of 1965—which provided much-needed federal funding to local school districts to close achievement gaps between children from well-to-do families and those from economic precarious ones—and the Social Security Act of 1965—which established Medicare and Medicaid—indeed strengthened the threadbare safety net of America. Later Johnson's Great Society would come crashing down under the pressure of the Vietnam War (pressure that would also result in Johnson removing himself from contention for reelection) and later the stagflation crisis of the 1970s.[35]

The myth of American affluence-for-all has been dogged by the realities of American poverty throughout the modern era. This reality is even starker when one traces the fortunes, literal and figurative, of Black Americans in capitalism's so-called golden age.

For one thing, many of the safety-net provisions that were instrumental in the creation of the American middle class were applied unequally. The historian Ira Katznelson has documented how government policy built the White middle class while systematically excluding Black Americans. This didn't happen organically; rather, the exclusion of Black America was part of the Faustian bargain FDR and northern Democrats struck with southern segregationists in order to pass key components of the New Deal. In his quest to reorder America's economy, the president, to his discredit, jettisoned civil rights.

To segregationists, this was welcome news. The South may have lost the Civil War, but, as the journalist Douglas A. Blackmon outlines in *Slavery by Another Name*, "forced labor remained as ubiquitous as cotton" in the region.[36] Capitalism in America has always been racialized, and Black Americans have suffered rates of destitution far greater than Whites' due to the racism built into every facet of American life. In fact, as the sociologist W. E. B. Du Bois argued, the system of racialized hierarchy that forced Black people into dire straits was "not the sole property of the South"; it manifested in the de facto experience of poor northern Black people as well.[37]

Lyndon Johnson, aware (as was anyone paying attention) of the subjugation of Black America, said in his speech launching the Great Society that the agenda rested on principles of "abundance and liberty for all. It demands an end to poverty and racial injustice, to which we are totally committed."[38] Six decades later, these causes remain works in progress.

The Death of the American Dream

A popular refrain among Americans, in particular, conservative Americans, is that being born a have-not doesn't mean a life sentence of insecurity; rather, economic mobility is possible for those who fight for it. Pulling oneself up by the bootstraps—a notion rooted in puritan ideals of responsibility, hard work, and self-control—is the American way, the path to a house, yard, and white picket fence. Even if you don't become wealthy, the American dream holds, being better off than your parents is a measure of success. A whopping 70 percent of Americans agree with the statement, "If you work hard and play by the rules, you will be able to achieve the American dream in your lifetime."[39] Most of America, it would appear, believes the dream is alive and well.

But the data reveal that the American dream is looking more and more like a pipe dream. While 92 percent of those born in the 1960s were likely to have higher earnings than their parents, only half of millennials can expect to outearn mom and dad.[40] The United States now ranks 27th on social mobility, squarely behind France, Germany, and the Scandinavian countries (which, to the surprise of some, actually lead the global economic-mobility pack).[41] Growing cash assistance and food stamp rolls, spiking suicide rates, skyrocketing incidence of opioid addiction—all indicate an American dream under duress.

Even those who have secure, steady jobs are at risk of losing ground. Many workers haven't received a raise in a generation. One in four workers don't have paid sick leave (leave that, incidentally, could have helped slow the pandemic and save lives), and nine in ten workers at the bottom don't receive paid sick days.[42] Owing to wage stagnation and rising inequality, nearly half of Americans don't have enough savings to cover a $400 economic emergency, let alone the loss of a job.[43] And of course many aren't lucky enough to have health insurance or to own a home in the first place. In twenty-first-century America, the American dream—moving up the economic ladder, doing better than one's parents, securing a comfortable and dignified life—is becoming the exception rather than the rule.

Although economists broadly agree that the American dream is under strain, they differ on how to characterize the issue. The fault lines, as one might expect, mirror the economics field's political divides more broadly. In his 2020 book, *The American Dream Is Not Dead*, Michael Strain, an economist at the conservative think tank American Enterprise Institute, argues that popular narratives about American labor and economic mobility are fundamentally false. Strain writes that "incomes aren't stagnant," "workers do enjoy the fruits of their labor," "America is clearly an upwardly mobile society," and "the game is not rigged." Tyler Cowen, another prominent conservative economist engaged in public debates, blames the breakdown of the American dream on *preferences*—as in, some people prefer having less. Cowen argues that people have become too complacent; they no longer move for jobs as frequently, they date people too similar to themselves, and they narrow their music choices, thereby reducing the dynamism and openness of US society. Strain and Cowen both enjoy large audiences, but economic data, some of which have been articulated here, don't bear out their claims about America's working poor. Nowhere was this better displayed than in the "Great Reshuffling" that occurred at the height of the COVID-19 pandemic, when record-breaking levels of workers quit their jobs, especially at the low-paid end of the labor market, in search of more meaningful, flexible, and remunerative work.

Progressive economists, meanwhile, tell a very different story, one centered on analyses of the structural inequality that continues to plague the economy. In the progressive account, the American dream amounts to a rhetorical device that has been wielded over time to keep the have-nots working low-wage jobs. While employers and the managerial class may give workers larger crumbs from time to time and while a lucky few from the working ranks are elevated to the ranks of the haves, structural inequality has been observable, even entrenched, since the founding of America. Even during periods of shared prosperity, the wealth has never trickled to the working and lower classes in the way depicted by American lore. The country has also gone through multiple gilded ages since the Roaring Twenties, and the more recent gilded age has been accompanied by levels of inequality and class rigidity similar to those of feudal Europe and the years ahead of the Revolutionary War.[44] The universal economic security and potential for upward mobility promised by the American dream has never been the lived experience of Americans. As the economists Dean Baker and Joseph E. Stiglitz, a recipient of the Nobel Prize, have argued for years, the American economy has always been rigged against working Americans.[45]

Different though they are, the progressive and the conservative analyses do have something in common. They frequently neglect the racial dynamics of the decline in economic mobility. Although it is unquestionably true that White workers have suffered a narrowing of the American dream, it is even truer that this narrowing is worse for Black and Brown workers.

In a 2015 report, "Umbrellas Don't Make it Rain: Why Studying and Working Hard Isn't Enough for Black Americans," the economists William Darity Jr., Darrick Hamilton, and colleagues found that no amount of pulling oneself up by the bootstraps could help communities of color get ahead. There are simply too many insidious, insurmountable barriers to economic security for Black and Brown workers. The data are illustrative. First, there's unemployment and underemployment, both permanent and egregious features of the economy rather than exceptions. For instance, Black unemployment was above 7 percent from the 1960s through 2018, when, for the first time in history, it dipped below that mark. A sign of economic recession is when White unemployment crests 7 percent. The Black community, in other words, has lived a permanent recession.[46]

Second, there's access to credit. Like employment, access to stable and reasonable credit is far too often dependent on one's skin color. In theory, access to credit, often guided by credit scores, is race-neutral, but the reality has shown this is simply not the case. In 2020, Wells Fargo, one of the nation's largest banks, denied more than half of mortgage refinancing applications from Black borrowers, all the while approving refinancing applications from 72 percent of White home owners.

And third, there's economic mobility. Black families whose head of household made it through college and earned a four-year degree have less wealth than White families whose head of household dropped out of high school. This isn't about saving more or working harder or acting right. And it sure isn't about *preferences*. It's about the structural racism that's baked into the economy.[47]

In Growth We Trust

When racial minorities have made economic gains, the economists William Darity Jr. and Patrick Mason find, those gains have largely stemmed from legislation rather than "the market." For instance, the narrowing of the Black-White earnings gap in the 1960s and 1970s wasn't due to market actors competing away discrimination but rather passage of the Civil Rights Act of 1964. More recently, absent additional legislation to combat discrimination, racial wage gaps have been remarkably consistent. In other words, when small pieces of the American dream were made available more broadly, including to Black Americans, it was because of the purposeful altering of the rules of the economy rather than a natural effect of capitalism and/or economic growth (though extremely tight labor markets can certainly help).[48]

Despite this historical record to the contrary, the conventional wisdom among economists remains that the only way to increase economic mobility and cure poverty is to achieve economic growth. The historical example supporting this theory is the Great Compression of the postwar era, when diminished wage disparities and reduced inequality coincided with a rapid expansion of the economy. (Of course, focusing merely on postwar GDP to the exclusion of the policy environment—a highly progressive tax code and considerable regulation of the economy—is to get the mechanisms wrong.) For the past sixty years, when faced with questions about poverty and inequality, economists have answered by quoting President Kennedy: "a rising tide lifts all the boats."[49]

The growth gospel was already entrenched when Kennedy delivered that line in 1962. Advised by a new generation of economists, he and his successors would pursue growth as the panacea to America's every economic ill. And what was the economists' preferred method of growing the economy? Tax cuts.

The economic theory was rather straightforward: taxes, in particular, those levied on "job creators" like firms and wealthy individuals, slow savings and kill investment, thereby costing the economy growth and jobs. (In econ-speak, such taxes are "distortionary," leaving the economy poorer and less efficient than it would be otherwise.) Thus, to provide a jolt to the economy and encourage wage growth, the government needs only to reduce the country's tax burden. The result was the steady reversal of the New Deal's progressive tax regime, beginning with the Kennedy-Johnson tax cut of 1964, one of the largest in American history. The policy, also known as the US Revenue Act of 1964, slashed the top marginal tax rate on the rich from 91 percent—a level unthinkable today—to 70 percent. It also pushed the corporate tax rate down from 52 percent to 48 percent and created a minimum standard deduction.[50]

Jimmy Carter, who laid the groundwork for Reaganism in many respects, contributed his own innovation: broad-based deregulation. A decade after Carter signed into law the Airline Deregulation Act of 1978, one of several efforts to increase competition and lower prices in industries like air travel, banking, and energy, a study by the Economic Policy Institute found that the measure led to more concentration in the industry, lower quality of service for customers, weaker safety protocols, and deteriorating labor-management relations. Nevertheless, Carter was committed to deregulation and to cutting government down to size. During his first State of the Union address, he proclaimed, "Bit by bit we are chopping down the thicket of unnecessary federal regulations by which government too often interferes in our personal lives and our personal business."[51]

This formula for economic growth—tax cuts for businesses and wealthy Americans, deregulation of the economy—found its most effective embodiment in Ronald Reagan. In his first inaugural address to the nation, Reagan argued that the country was "confronted with an economic affliction of great proportion." For Reagan, the continuation of deficit spending, particularly on social programs, was "to guarantee tremendous social, cultural, political, and economic upheavals." Rather than look to the government to solve the country's woes,

Reagan told his listeners, "government is not the solution to our problem; government is the problem."

The newly elected president knew better than simply to critique, however; he also offered solutions. Reagan promised a "new beginning" through the deep cutting of regulations, taxes, and government programs, together constituting an unprecedented shrinking of the federal government. In his first year as president, Reagan slashed the top marginal tax rate from 70 percent to 50 percent and cut taxes on the lowest income bracket from 14 percent to 11 percent. He also worked to slashed government spending, passing $39 billion in budget cuts in his first year alone (in reality, government spending continued to increase during the majority of Reagan's presidency; however, the rate of growth slowed markedly).[52]

Reagan too added his own innovation to the blueprint for economic growth: the crushing of the labor movement. In August 1981, Reagan dealt a devastating blow to organized labor when he arrested striking air traffic controllers and fired 11,345 workers, banishing them from federal jobs permanently.[53] But that wasn't enough. A few months later, at Reagan's urging, the Federal Labor Relations Authority voted to decertify the controllers' union, the Professional Air Traffic Controllers Organization.[54] This coupled with the "Volcker Recession," an economic and employment downturn caused by Federal Reserve chair Paul Volcker's rate hikes in his fight against inflation and labor unions, finished the job. The delicate power balance between state, labor, and capital that had given rise to the golden age of capitalism had come crashing down, with workers paying the price.

The policy trifecta championed by Reagan—deregulation, tax cuts, and the quelling of the American labor movement, a program today synonymous with the theories of neoliberalism—didn't happen together by accident. They were promoted by academics, policy makers, and businessmen in their fight to overturn the New Deal and the problem of powerful trade unions. These thought leaders were responding to a cacophony of events that had shaken the foundations of the previously stable New Deal order: the Vietnam War, the oil shock of 1973 and the ensuing stagflation, and the collapse of the Bretton Woods monetary system in which currency (and its spending) had been tied to commodities like gold. In the conservative view, too much of the economic pie was going to labor. (Labor was indeed powerful at the time: as a share of GDP, workers' wages peaked in 1970 at 65 percent.) By offering a return to stable growth and a promise to tame inflation, the trifecta was touted as a cure-all.[55]

Despite these thinkers' promises, neoliberalism's track record in achieving economic growth has not been impressive. While the economy grew at an average of 4.9 percent from 1950 to 1980, it slowed markedly in the neoliberal era, growing at just 2.6 percent from 1980 to 2018.[56] It has also been a disaster for the American working class. Until the early 1980s, when the neoliberal policy tool kit came into vogue, workers toward the bottom of the wage distribution tended to see their wages rise faster than those at the high end: from 1946 to 1980, the bottom 50 percent of Americans saw their pretax incomes more than double, while the poorest 20 percent saw their pretax income increase an average of 109 percent. When we look at post-tax income—that is, taking taxes and transfers into account—we see that the income for the bottom 20 percent increased an incredible 179 percent in just three and a half decades.

Such gains didn't come at the expense of the richest either. During the same period, 1946–80, the top 10 percent of income recipients saw their pretax incomes climb 79 percent. Which is to say, prior to the dismantlement of the New Deal order, growth was indeed leading wages toward convergence. But the arrival of Reagan and the implementation of the neoliberal program severed the link between economic growth and rising wages, especially at the lower-paid end of the distribution. Although workers have continually become more productive, their wages have stagnated for generations since.

The economists Thomas Piketty, Emmanuel Saez, and Gabriel Zucman have painstakingly documented this decoupling of economic growth and economic mobility. From 1980 to 2014, the poorest half of

Americans saw their incomes flatline. While growth during the period increased incomes in the United States by 61 percent on average, that growth bypassed one out of every two Americans. Worse, the poorest fifth of the country saw its pretax income *fall* by 25 percent. Government redistribution policies—taxes and cash transfer programs like Aid to Families with Dependent Children, Temporary Assistance for Needy Families (AFDC and TANF; commonly referred to as "welfare") and food stamps—helped keep the bottom fifth of the country whole in absolute terms, with post-tax income rising a measly 4 percent; but, when looking at relative gains, workers in America are far worse off than before.

The rich, meanwhile, have benefited handsomely from these same policies. Many analysts of inequality point to the incomes of the top 10 percent, which have jumped 121 percent over the past forty years. But to see the real rise in inequality, we need to look beyond deciles to even smaller slices of the income distribution. For example, whereas the top 10 percent saw its income a little more than double, the top 1 percent saw its income *triple*. But that's still not granular enough. If we look at the top one-tenth of 1 percent, income growth crested 320 percent; if we look at the top 0.001 percent, we find that incomes increased by an astonishing *636 percent*. The rollback of progressive taxation during the neoliberal era—taxation that had helped tame inequality from the 1930s to the 1970s—ensured that post-tax income growth for the top 0.001 percent remained off the charts: 616 percent.[57] Warren Buffet knew whereof he spoke when he said his secretary "works just as hard as I do, and she pays twice the [tax] rate I pay."[58]

These divergent patterns in income growth have led to astonishing levels of income inequality. In 1981, the year Reagan was sworn into office, the top 1 percent of income recipients took home 11.5 percent of national income—more than their fair share, to be sure, but not an unconscionable amount. The top 10 percent took home just over a third of national income (35.1 percent), while the bottom half of America received just shy of 20 percent of the income pie. The country was unequal, absolutely—more on this later—but nowhere near as much as it is now. When President Trump was inaugurated in 2017, the top 1 percent sucked up *one-fifth* of the country's income, and the top 10 percent accounted for nearly *half* the nation's annual income pie (46.8 percent). All the while, the bottom half of Americans were left to fight over relative crumbs: their share fell to just 12.4 percent of national income. And all this was before the regressive tax cuts passed later in 2017.[59]

There's a direct line running between the unequally shared prosperity of the 2010s and the changing of the economic rules wrought by the policies of the 1980s. In the name of growth and personal freedom, neoliberal thinkers and policy makers called for freer markets (read: the commodification of life's essentials and a reduction in protections for low- and middle-income people), more tax cuts, more deregulation, and more privatization. The recipe was simple. The results were profound.

Wealth Gaps

For all their faith in the American dream, America's runaway inequality isn't news to average Americans. According to the 2019 American Trends Panel Survey conducted by the Pew Research Center, six in ten Americans think there's too much inequality in the United States, including 41 percent of Republicans.[60] But studies indicate they may not know just how unequal the country has become. In 2001 the business school professor Michael Norton and the behavioral economist Dan Ariely asked people to estimate the current level of wealth distribution by estimating the percentage of wealth held across deciles, or 10 percent chunks of society. Next they asked participants to construct an ideal distribution of wealth in the United States. They found that people vastly underestimate the degree of wealth inequality in the United States: participants thought that the wealthiest quintile had about 60 percent of the country's wealth when in reality it holds nearly 85 percent. When it came to constructing their ideal America, respondents wanted the top decile to own just 32 percent of total wealth.

Participants were similarly poor judges of distribution at the low end. When asked about the bottom 40 percent, they estimated that those two quintiles held just shy of 10 percent of the wealth (in their ideal distribution, they wanted them to hold about 25 percent). In reality, the poorest 40 percent of Americans hold no wealth at all.[61]

Wealth inequality, which has always been more pervasive than income inequality, further illustrates the story of a fractured America. Income is a flow: the money a person receives for providing a good or service in the market (most often their labor, which is all that most people have to sell in the first place), interest earned on an asset, or a transfer payment from the government. Wealth, on the other hand, represents a stock of resources—the difference between the value of what one owns in assets (a house, car, savings account, etc.) and what one owes in liabilities (student debt, credit card debt, mortgage, etc.). As Piketty famously argues in his book *Capital in the Twenty-First Century*, wealth historically has tended to grow faster than the overall economy, resulting in ever increasing wealth inequality, putting yet more power in the hands of the wealthy.

In their historical review of wealth inequality in the United States, Saez and Zucman found that, like income inequality, wealth inequality was at its height right before the Great Depression. During the 1930s, wealth inequality tumbled, largely as a result of the New Deal's restructuring of the economic rules. Since 1978, however—the onset of the neoliberal era—wealth inequality has grown. Saez and Zucman report that in 1978 the richest one-tenth of one percent of Americans held 7 percent of the wealth—more than their fair share but an amount perhaps within reason. By 2012, their slice of the wealth pie had more than tripled, to 22 percent.[62]

Like all economic indicators, aggregate data tell only part of the story. When the numbers are sorted by race, ethnicity, gender, sexual orientation, and other identities, we find that current political and economic systems punish difference, giving rise to group-based inequality and economic deprivation purely on the basis of the identities people hold. In terms of wealth, Black households hold mere pennies—about a dime, actually—on the dollar compared to their White counterparts. Even those who get a degree, whether an associate's, bachelor's, or graduate degree, face an insurmountable gap, highlighting that education is no great equalizer. Black college graduates at the median have a net wealth of $70,219, whereas their White college graduate counterparts hold over a quarter of a million dollars ($268,028) in wealth. Women face a penalty too, holding just 55 cents for every dollar in wealth held by men. For those who had never been married, the gap is even larger, with women holding just 34 cents per $1 of men's wealth. As expected, race exacerbates these gaps. A 2017 report by the Samuel DuBois Cook Center on Social Equity at Duke University found that single White women who have a bachelor's degree hold seven times more wealth than their Black counterparts, though both hold markedly less than their male counterparts. In sum, wealth, like everything else in the economy, is distributed highly unequally.[63]

Insecurity Multipliers

In practice, wealth is effectively synonymous with economic security. With wealth comes the ability to weather an economic downturn, a job loss, or an unforeseen health incident. Since the late 1970s, however, with income and wealth concentrating at the top and with the bottom getting less and less, the ranks of the have-nots in America have swelled. That means scores of neighbors, friends, and family members living a hair's breadth away from economic disaster.

It also means that a massive population is vulnerable to macro-level crises like pandemics and climate change, as those without wealth are left without the means to adapt. These kinds of crises not only disproportionately affect the most desperate among us, but they throw into stark relief the inequities that prevail in contemporary America.

COVID-19 AND INEQUALITY

No event in recent history has highlighted (or exacerbated) the gulf between the haves and the have-nots in America like the COVID-19 pandemic. As the virus swept across the nation in spring 2020, the haves hunkered down, moved their work online, had their essentials delivered to their door (by workers making, at times, below minimum wage), and saw their investment accounts reach new heights. The have-nots, on the other hand, saw their livelihoods, bank accounts, and communities decimated. One could see the knock-on effects of an already deeply unequal society everywhere one looked: in who lost jobs, in infection rates, in death rates, and in vaccine distribution.

To start, low-income workers, women, and minorities experienced job losses that were literally off the charts. In part, this was because of labor market segregation. The industries and occupations that were hit the hardest—service, leisure, hospitality, and transportation—are staffed predominantly by women and people of color making below-average wages. As these industries had to shut down to prevent the pandemic from spreading even faster, low-income workers were disproportionally cast aside.

The trend in which recessions exacerbate inequality is not entirely new. (The Great Recession, of course, was responsible for a brutal hollowing out of America's middle class, as middle- and low-income workers struggled disproportionately to maintain or regain jobs and wage growth following the financial crisis.) But as former Federal Reserve chair Ben Bernanke noted of the COVID-19 recession, "It's an even more unequal recession than usual." That is, to put it mildly, an understatement.[64]

Job loss is just one way to think about the relationship between inequality and the COVID-19 crisis. Another way to slice the data is to look at who got sick. While some low-income workers and workers of color disproportionately lost their jobs during the crisis, those who kept working were less likely to be allowed to work from home and were more frequently forced to labor in unsafe conditions. The result?

Infection rates were substantially higher among these populations. In a paper published in January 2021 in the *Journal of the American Medical Association Network Open*, researchers found that a 1 percent increase in a county's Black population was associated with a 1.9 percent increase in COVID-19 infections and a 2.5 percent increase in COVID-19-related deaths. (The numbers were similar for Hispanic populations.) The same paper found that counties with higher income inequality had substantially higher infection and death rates. Inequality and racism functioned as tinder for the raging pandemic fire, and at the same time the pandemic led to a further explosion of inequality.[65]

CLIMATE AND INEQUALITY

Climate change is the greatest threat humanity has had to face. It is a problem not just for future generations, but for ours, today. The planet has already warmed by 1.1ºC and is on track to heat 3ºC above preindustrial averages this century. A warming world is an existential threat to the billions who live in coastal cities, the billions dependent on normal rain patterns for nourishing crops, the billions living in regions that will become uninhabitable hot zones, and the millions dead annually from pollution-related illness fueled by combusting fossil fuels. Humans cannot continue on their current path. As UN Secretary General António Guterres put it, "The status quo is a suicide."[66]

It's hard to overstate the destructive forces that will be—and indeed are already being—unleashed on the planet if the United States, along with other high-income countries, does not engage in a program of crash decarbonization (starting yesterday). Coastal cities, including Miami, Florida, and Charleston, South Carolina, will need to be deserted entirely. Large swaths of the American South will simply be too hot to work in for long stretches of the year. (A 2017 paper in *Science Advances* warned that by 2100, spending even a few hours outside "will result in death even for the fittest humans" in heat-prone regions of the globe.)[67] Wildfires, like the ones that ravaged California, Oregon, Washington, and Colorado in 2020, will destroy our beloved public lands, dump even more carbon and pollution into the atmosphere, and continue to cause death and destruction. In fact, scientists estimate that California's 2020 wildfire season dumped 30 million more tons of carbon dioxide into the atmosphere that year than was generated to provide electricity for the entire state in 2020.[68] And worldwide pandemics will become more frequent and more severe.

Like everything in our society, the damages—the deaths, the displacement, the pain and suffering—associated with the climate crisis will not be shared equitably. The Pentagon has called the climate crisis a "threat multiplier," a force that promises to exacerbate conflict and tensions in an already fractured global order. Resource wars will likely occur. Natural disasters will become more intense and frequent. And as the planet continues to warm, the burden will fall on those least able to carry the weight: the poor.[69]

Study after study demonstrates how climate change will exacerbate inequality both at home and abroad: by reducing children's ability to learn due to extreme heat, increasing the disproportionate burdens from natural disasters borne by poor regions, excluding the poor from access to lifesaving air-conditioning, or promoting the droughts and crop failures that threaten the very existence of those living at the margins.

While most economists have brushed aside questions of equity when it comes to environmental and climate policy, some political economists, including the University of Massachusetts's James K. Boyce, have studied the link between environmental harms and inequality. In decades of work, Boyce and his collaborators have documented the links between political and economic power and the unequal distribution of environmental harms. But they have also found something else: a link between inequality and increased environmental degradation. In other words, not only will climate change exacerbate inequality, but inequality is exacerbating climate change.[70]

No shortage of actors and entities bear the blame for the continued paralysis on the climate front. Despite the people's will—indicated by no less than a Fox News poll, televised during the evening of the 2020 presidential election, that showed 70 percent of voters wanted *more* government spending on green energy—Congress has failed to act in a meaningful way. Current policy is not responding to the needs of the people—or the planet, for that matter.[71]

The policy process has been derailed by a mistaken vision of economic scarcity. In this view, addressing the climate crisis—or poverty—must entail sacrifices to economic well-being. The argument runs something like this: The country, and the globe, simply can't afford to clean up its act. Yes, taxes and regulations may reduce emissions a bit, but they'll come at a big cost—the derailment of economic growth and, in turn, jobs—that simply isn't worth the price tag. If the government were to deploy public investment and build high-speed carbon-free public transit and massive green energy installments—a path it certainly *could* pursue—it would crowd out private investment, stifle growth, and thus make the economy, and the people in it, worse off. The days of guns or butter have yielded to solar or private jets.

Yet far from being just another input in the production function—this is how economists like to think of the planet and the bountiful natural resources it provides—the earth is the only one we have. It's not replaceable. People can't simply substitute capital for the planet, though some of America's filthy rich sure are trying: Elon Musk, for example, aims to send one million people to Mars by 2050. Despite his best attempts, there is no planet B.

Democracy in the Balance

Democracy, the late political scientist Robert Dahl wrote, is, "literally, rule by the people." The term, Dahl means, represents a joining of the Greek words *dēmos*, "the people," and *kratos*, "rule."[72] John Dewey called democracy "the idea of community life itself." But who, exactly, are *the people*? When the Founders wrote "We The People," and Lincoln spoke of a government "of the people, by the people, for the people," whom did they mean? The landless and poor? Women? People of color? The formerly or currently incarcerated? The people of American territories? The country's youth? While many Americans have clung to the idea enshrined in law in the 1960s, of "one person, one vote," others are starting to reckon with the words of the late Chief Justice Louis Brandeis: "We may have democracy, or we may have wealth concentration in the hands of a few, but we can't have both."

The tension between a democracy and an economic system that produces vast inequalities is as old as the systems themselves. Centuries ago, Aristotle wrote, "The real difference between democracy and oligarchy is poverty and wealth. . . . [W]here the poor rule, that is democracy." Many liberals believe this tension can be resolved through the extension and protection of political and civil rights—voting rights, the right to equal justice, speech rights. Armed with these rights, the argument goes, the poor can organize, agitate, and legislate to realize a more equitable economy. "One person, one vote" means an even playing field at the polls and the possibility of a democratic economy.

However, with the entrenchment of neoliberalism, the economy has become "encased" (as the historian Quinn Slobodian has characterized it) from collective action. According to neoliberal economists, in order for the economy to function properly, it must be placed squarely in the private sphere and preserved from public intervention. We the people are meant to understand concepts like private property rights as being naturally occurring—that democracy has limits, and those limits include markets. In the neoliberal conception, the economic sphere, which includes production, investment, and wage labor, must be zealously protected from democratic overreach; otherwise, we put economic growth—and its terrific powers—at risk. The end result of this policy regime? A malfunctioning economy whose central purpose seems to be the defense of the haves from the have-nots.

Choosing Inequality: Neoliberal Capitalism

In 1964, President Lyndon Johnson created the National Commission on Technology, Automation, and Economic Progress to address growing fears that rapid technological change would displace millions of

American workers. The commission's report found that automation and the economic growth that accompanied it would indeed lead to churn in the labor market—creating new jobs and obviating ones no longer useful to the country's economy—but in the end such progress would create more jobs than it would destroy. But that wasn't the commission's most important discovery. The report also noted that at the current state of technological development the country's ability to meet society's needs—quality food, shelter, water, health care, education, employment, and leisure—was satisfied. According to the authors, there was plenty to go around; the country simply needed to "decide what kind of future we want."

In other words, the authors had concluded that scarcity—scarcity that generates poverty, homelessness, unemployment, and, far too often, death—was a relic of the past. The scarcity that remained arose as a matter of *distribution* rather than *production*. By "spelling out national goals" to share the goods and services that workers produce more equitably, the authors argued, scarcity could be relegated to the dustbin of history.[73] That is, the cause of inequality wasn't capacity (or the lack thereof). It was policy.

The situation is the same today. The mess we're in—unconscionable levels of income and wealth inequality, hardworking families one raw deal away from disaster, an American dream moribund if not dead already—isn't the result of mere circumstances, a "natural" and thus inescapable outcome. Rather, our economic reality, our division into haves and have-nots, is the creation of policy makers, or perhaps just the economists on whom they've chosen to rely. Friedrich Hayek, Milton Friedman, Alan Greenspan, Gregory Mankiw, Larry Summers. To the home health aid or the McDonald's cook scraping by on the pittance that is the federal minimum wage, most if not all of these names will be meaningless. Yet it is because of them (or economists like them) that policy makers believe raising the minimum wage will shrink the economy and kill jobs, or that rent control creates deleterious "inefficiencies" in the market, or that ensuring too many workers have decent jobs results in runaway inflation. Simply put, one can trace a direct line between America's current inequality crisis and the policies that economists, for the past forty years, have advocated.

Given the starkness of the shift—before the neoliberal revolution, a country with a robust middle class and obstinate but not exceptional levels of inequality; after, a rapid hollowing out of the middle class and incredible clustering at the top and bottom of the income distribution—one could be forgiven for asking why policy makers and economists alike have continued down this path. The answer, I argue, lies in neoliberals' weaponization of America's most cherished value: freedom.

2

Capitalism and Freedom

The system of private property is the most important guarantee of freedom, not only for those who own property, but scarcely less for those who do not.
FRIEDRICH HAYEK, *THE ROAD TO SERFDOM*

Increases in economic freedom have gone hand in hand with increases in political and civil freedom and have led to increased prosperity; competitive capitalism and freedom have been inseparable.
MILTON FRIEDMAN, *CAPITALISM AND FREEDOM*

It was a hot and humid day in the nation's capital. Arrayed in front of the Jefferson Memorial, toying with the miniature Old Glories they had been given, a buzzing crowd awaited their hero. Two hundred years had passed since the Founders had descended on Philadelphia for that famously grueling summer, and there was electricity in the air, an expectation that something momentous was about to take place.

The president appeared, crossing the Memorial steps hand in hand with his wife to the fanfare of "Hail to the Chief" and rapturous cheers. Upon taking the stage, he shed his blazer and joked, "I see that the uniform of the day has already been decided on." Reagan, a former actor, demonstrated a consistent and uncanny ability to connect with people. You didn't win 525 electoral votes without charisma.

As Reagan began his remarks with the familiar paeans to liberty and self-government, it seemed like the crowd might be in for a bit of a letdown. But, as his listeners would soon discover, this was not to be a speech merely commemorating the 200th anniversary of the drafting of the Constitution or celebrating the nation's freedom from tyranny. No, this speech would be much more than that.

On July 3, the day before Independence Day, 1987, Reagan announced his plans to amend the US Constitution that the crowd had gathered to celebrate. Reagan, the only US president to ever lead a union (the Screen Actors Guild), had in his younger days been an ardent supporter of Roosevelt's New Deal. Now he had a profoundly different vision, a vision to "finish the job Jefferson began and to protect our people and their livelihoods with restrictions on government that will ensure the fundamental economic freedom of the people— the equivalent of an Economic Bill of Rights." Reagan was not the first to introduce an economic bill of rights; that honor belongs to Roosevelt. But Reagan had no intention of standing on Roosevelt's shoulders to further a progressive and inclusive vision of the state. Rather, he was seeking the precise opposite: to tear down the government, much as, weeks before, he had called on Mikhail Gorbachev to do to the Berlin Wall.

The cornerstone of Reagan's economic bill of rights was a constitutional amendment that required the federal government to balance its budget. In Reagan's mind, every family made tough decisions to live within its means; it was high time the government followed suit. And he wasn't bluffing: not only did he announce he would work with Congress to send an amendment to the states for ratification, but he also threatened the legislative branch, declaring that he would crisscross the country, taking his case directly to the people, if it failed to act.

Alongside the balanced budget amendment, Reagan outlined four economic freedoms, which together would "recognize anew the economic freedoms of our people" and deliver on the Declaration of Independence's promise of life, liberty, and the pursuit of happiness.

The first freedom was the freedom to work. For Reagan, this meant the sidelining of organized labor and its power to extract wage increases, pension benefits, and quality health care from employers, thus raising wages to levels beyond what workers would be paid in a "free" market.

The second freedom was minimal taxation. In Reagan's worldview, restricting the government's ability to spend money was essential to the preservation and growth of freedom. This was because, he averred, "freedom is not created by government"; rather, freedom is secured chiefly by *limiting* government. And the best way to tie government's hands is to reduce its capacity to spend money and collect taxes. For Reagan, minimizing taxation, and, in turn, unshackling the market, was unambiguously equated with freedom.

The third freedom, the freedom to property, amounted to a centralization of private property rights, the freedom to own and manage one's property without taking into account that these rights must often be balanced against other rights, say, the right to life. By emphasizing property rights, including the right to exchange one's property without coercion or limitation (Reagan argued that state-created patents—a form of property—were somehow natural), Reagan also provided a further rationale for the expansion of the police power—itself, of course, an arm of government—whose primary purpose is to enforce private property rights.

The fourth and final freedom, "the freedom to participate in a free market—to contract freely for goods and services and to achieve one's full potential without government limits on opportunity, economic independence, and growth," was the freedom that expressed best the neoliberals' influence on the conservative Right's (and Reagan's) agenda. Crucial to realizing Reagan's freedom to work was the privatization of government resources and programs, the elimination of government subsidies (a cause for which end he would establish a presidential commission), and a breathtaking curtailment of government regulations. Taken together, these actions would eliminate any and all unnecessary and cumbersome restrictions on people's access to markets. Because, as far as the president was concerned, free markets *were* freedom.[1]

Reagan's dogmatic laissez-faireism—his belief that markets aren't a means to realizing freedom but are rather the essence of freedom itself—led him to limit, however he could, democratic control over the economy. For example, he tacked on two additional requirements to his balanced budget amendment: Congress must have a supermajority to pass tax increases of any kind, and any new government program must be deficit-neutral and include impact statements from the private sector on potential costs to consumers and employers. (The *benefits* of the proposed government program, however, did not need to be specified.) The goal was to maximize the reach of the market, which, in Reagan's eyes, the government always and everywhere impeded.

In the area of property rights, Reagan sought to shield private interests from public interests by limiting government's ability to seize property for the public good, even with just compensation. He also aimed to strengthen intellectual property rights, rights that were already well established in the United States. The idea, quite simply, was to eliminate public rights to property, whether physical or intellectual.

Finally, to foster widespread participation in the market, the president was determined to slash the social safety net (which, in his words, "promotes dependency and destroys families and communities"), increase school choice through privatization and school vouchers, push job retraining rather than direct government job creation during economic downturns, and ensure American domination in trade. Choice in the market would deliver the freedom Reagan and his followers were in search of. But Reagan didn't just want to increase freedom within an extant system; rather, he intended to inaugurate "an economic and social revolution."[2]

Reagan didn't develop his conception of economic rights on his own. He was drawing on the newly dominant economic thinking of his time, a coherent body of concepts propounded by leading economists who had won Nobel Prizes and become household names. These thinkers idolized classical liberals (in the European sense of the word, not its more contemporary political sense) like John Locke and John Stuart Mill, early defenders of free markets and minimal government, so they had named their movement—neoliberalism—in their heroes' honor. Their project was immense. They sought not only to change how people thought about, and policy makers structured, the economy, but to promote their favored conception of freedom. Seeking to reclaim the mantle of freedom from the New Deal and the Great Society, whose policies reflected a more holistic view of freedom that included the expansion of civil, social, *and* economic rights, neoliberals drew a direct line between the reach of the market and the measure of freedom. More markets and less government—more choice and less regulation—meant greater freedom.

Freedom in the American Imagination

Part of neoliberalism's appeal was and is that it is in fact continuous with the earliest Americans' notions of freedom. Like the neoliberals, the Founders drew on Locke (Jefferson's famous turn of phrase in the Declaration of Independence can be traced back to Locke's 1689 formulation, "Life, liberty, and estate"). Both groups also conceived of freedom negatively—that is, that freedom is being free from an antagonist, whether coercion by a king or state or the impingement of one's coequals.[3] This view of freedom as freedom *from* undesirable things was the freedom that motivated Samuel Adams and the Sons of Liberty; Thomas Jefferson and the delegates to the Second Continental Congress; and James Madison, Alexander Hamilton, and the other participants in the Constitutional Convention.

In fact, it was out of that historic assembly to craft a new form of government that the most famous codification of negative freedoms would emerge. The first ten amendments to the US Constitution, the Bill of Rights, were designed to protect the members of a new nation from the coercive power of a federal state. As Jefferson put it, the original Bill of Rights "is what the people are entitled to against every government on earth." Initially many of the Founders didn't believe these amendments necessary, but, as ratification of the Constitution stumbled—due in part to allegations by Anti-Federalists that the government was not properly restrained—the promise was made to more explicitly guarantee individual rights in the nation's founding document. With this act, the Founders sought to specify the rights America owed its citizens. No more would the people be subject to an overreaching government. They were now citizens, and citizens required rights and protections to prevent subjugation.[4]

Citizenship in the new nation, however, was narrowly defined. Only a select few—the White, male, and property owning—actually enjoyed the full slate of negative freedoms enumerated in the Bill of Rights. Women, children, enslaved people, Native Americans, the poor: these groups would have to fight over centuries to secure the Bill of Rights' protections. And as they sought equal footing in the American polity, these groups continued to speak the language of negative freedom. Abraham Lincoln, for example, spoke the language of negative freedom in the Emancipation Proclamation: "all persons held as slaves . . . shall be then, thenceforward, and forever free; and the Executive Government of the United States . . . will recognize and maintain the freedom of such persons, and will do no act or acts to repress such persons, or any of them, in any efforts they may make for their actual freedom."[5] So too did countless suffragists, including Elizabeth Cady Stanton, who in her remarks at Seneca Falls argued that women must "protest against a form of government existing without the consent of the governed" and "declare our right to be free as man is free." For Stanton, women's freedom was freedom from the tyranny of government and men.[6]

While American women were mobilizing to democratize the vote, the US Supreme Court was making sure democracy didn't affect the economy. Beginning in 1905—when the Supreme Court struck down a state law that limited bakers' working hours, noting in its decision that such restrictions "interfered" with "the rights of individuals, both employers and employees"—and until 1937, the so-called Lochner era was defined by the Court's assault on economic regulations, including worker protections, tax policy, and antitrust enforcement.

The Court was relentless in its crusade to protect the laissez-faire doctrine of free markets, free contracts, and minimal state interference (except, of course, to create and protect markets and contracts). They would go so far as to strike down laws to limit child labor and, later, major New Deal legislation like the National Industrial Recovery Act.[7]

The American faith in classical liberalism and the free market essentially collapsed—though not forever—with the onset of the Great Depression. Although free-market liberalism had faced a number of challenges during the early Lochner era, most vehemently by the socialist presidential candidate Eugene Debs and Progressive Era reformers, the virtual disintegration of the economy before the public's eyes caused workers to realize, all too late, that they were free only in Marx's "double sense": free to sell their labor or free to starve.[8]

As the breadlines grew, so did the people's discontent with the limits of negative freedom. The light touch that had characterized the Hoover administration's early approach to the Depression was repudiated with the election of Franklin D. Roosevelt in 1932. On the campaign trail, Hoover had denounced FDR's proposed New Deal, likening it to a frontal assault on the American system. For Hoover, a significant departure from laissez-faire's unrestrained markets amounted to a "fascist" intervention, which posed a challenge to American freedom. For voters, the choice was clear. Hoover's hands-off approach had left them starving and homeless. It was time for something new.[9] On election day voters handed a decisive victory to Roosevelt, embracing *his* vision of freedom, one that didn't conflate free markets and free people. But old ideas die hard, and laissez-faire would in time return with a vengeance.

The Triumph of John Maynard Keynes

To understand how classical liberalism was reinvented as neoliberalism, it's essential to know what—or perhaps whom—neoliberalism was a reaction to. If the first 150 years of American political economy was dedicated to the ideas of John Locke and a narrow reading of

Adam Smith, then its orientation between 1933 and the early 1970s—the era of the New Deal, the Great Compression, and the golden age of capitalism—belonged to John Maynard Keynes.

Born in Cambridge, England, in 1883, Keynes ("Maynard" to his friends) studied mathematics at Cambridge but later devoted himself to economics, eventually revolutionizing the discipline, moving it away from the marginalist revolution and free-market ideology that had come to dominate it. Today college students learn that Keynes, in addition to creating the field of macroeconomics, developed an interventionist approach to the inevitable crises that capitalism produces. It is because of Keynes that we have, for example, deficit-financed stimulus packages to combat recessions and other government-led interventions that smooth out capitalism's jagged edges. Keynes understood the economy as unable to self-correct, as his classically liberal intellectual predecessors believed would be the case; often, Keynes argued, the government had to govern.

But Keynes's insight extends far beyond arguments for governments and pump priming; he was, in the words of his biographer Zach Carter, "the last of the Enlightenment intellectuals who pursued political theory, economics, and ethics as a unified design." A case in point is his 1924 lecture "The End of Laissez-Faire" (a simplification of the initial title, "Prolegomena to a New Socialism—The Origins and End of Laissez-Faire"). For Keynes, the laissez-faire system had largely arisen by mistake, leaving, as Carter writes, "the most important elements of social management without a manager." The laissez-faire order had gained traction by bringing together two irreconcilable ideas: strong individual private property rights and equality in the political system through democracy. In this system, government had no right to intervene in the economic realm beyond protecting markets and property rights: the economy resided in the private sphere. Any interference in this realm would impose on the natural order of things and, worse, trample on people's freedom. In short: Hands off the economy.

In Keynes's view, the marriage of inviolable property rights and democratic equality was rotten from the beginning. He rejected the notion that property rights were "natural"; rather, he argued, property rights were a creation of modern nation-states. For example, the property rights that tie the laptop I'm using to write this paragraph to me are rights that are created by the state. They're part of a set of rules that we, as members of this society, have agreed to abide by. The same goes for this book. You can share it with friends, but you can't freely distribute the book online to everyone; that would be illegal due to copyright law, which is in practice another form of property law. Rather than a natural outgrowth of private life, property rights were willed into existence by states. To be clear, Keynes was not arguing for the collective ownership of property; he believed individuals should be able to own and dispose of property—but with limits.

Along with his critique of property rights, Keynes rejected a key underlying assumption of laissez-faire economics—that people acting in their own interests leads to a harmonious and prosperous society. Rather, Keynes argued that self-interest, especially where it took the form of business investments, conflicted with the social good. This principle can be observed in matters of employment. Firms, and the capitalist class as a whole, seek to reduce costs (because reductions in costs are in their interests) by keeping some workers unemployed in order to maintain low wages and workers' discipline. After all, the threat of unemployment, coupled with people at the ready to replace current workers should they demand too much, is a powerful weapon to maintain class positions. Such unemployment, however, has micro and macro effects. At the level of the individual, the unemployed suffer poverty, a lack of meaning, and, frequently, the degradation of their physical and mental health. The economy as a whole suffers too: higher levels of unemployment suppress labor force growth, aggregate demand, and productivity growth. We are all poorer for it. In this case, as in many others—for example, investment decisions and, critically, the buildout of a green economy—the pursuit of self-interest, and the corresponding lack of coordination, is socially destructive.

Keynes's main contribution to the critique of laissez-faire, however, was his demonstration that markets simply can't do everything the classical liberal says they can. For example, Keynes demonstrated that markets are not self-correcting (i.e., resolve recessions and depressions on their own), nor do they bring about full employment or a reasonable distribution of resources, especially toward socially important ends. Coordination failures were too rampant and the wealthy were simply too powerful. Keynes believed that economic planning was essential to solve the coordination problems that ravaged capitalism, promoting both macroeconomic stability and social prosperity, a belief that culminated in his call for the "somewhat comprehensive socialization of investment" and the state's "taking an ever greater responsibility for directly organizing investment."[10]

While Keynes's magnum opus, *The General Theory of Employment, Interest, and Money*, would not be published until 1936, a few years into FDR's New Deal, his influence on America's political economy was immeasurable. In December 1933, less than a year into Roosevelt's presidency, Keynes, already a towering figure in international political economy, penned an open letter to Roosevelt in the *New York Times* praising the president's work to date on the "double task, recovery and reform—recovery from the slump, and the passage of those business and social reforms which are long overdue." But Keynes's letter also acknowledged that the American president, whom he admired greatly, had a lot of work still to do. To increase the chances of permanent recovery and reform, Keynes urged Roosevelt to direct all efforts toward more expansionary policies, including massive increases in "government expenditure which is financed by loans and is not merely a transfer through taxation," which would require that Roosevelt cast aside his interest in balanced budgets.[11]

Keynes met with Roosevelt at the White House in 1935, urging him forward with New Deal efforts to address both recovery and reform. Later, when FDR pulled back government spending, a decision that resulted in the Roosevelt recession of 1937–38, Keynes wrote to the president once again, this time privately, to recommend he double down on the policies from his first term that had worked so well: payments to the unemployed, deficit-financed investments in public works to support employment and aggregate demand, and the continuation of cheap and easy short-term money.[12] Keynes feared that if Roosevelt failed to deliver full employment via adequate expansionary measures, the entire New Deal would be at risk. Lucky for Keynes—and for the New Deal—Roosevelt's policy advisers, among them Harry Hopkins, Marriner Eccles, and Henry Wallace, increasingly adopted a Keynesian worldview.[13]

Keynes's foundational ideal was a "society which shall be ethically tolerable and economically not intolerable." To this end his work endeavored "to move out of the nineteenth-century laissez-faire state into an era of liberal socialism, by which I mean a system where we can act as an organized community for common purposes to promote social and economic justice, whilst respecting and protecting the individual—his freedom of choice, his faith, his mind and its expression, his enterprise and his property."[14] Keynes's vision was, more or less, the system toward which FDR and his administration were moving. But for all its demonstrated economic and social benefits, this system was not without its detractors. For these critics, "liberal socialism" was simply a way station on the road to a new form of feudalism—a revocation of liberal freedoms. Soon enough, these detractors would again have policy makers' ears.

Friedrich Hayek and the Critique of Keynesianism

The success of the New Deal in righting a capsized American economy was the great validation of Keynes's theories. But though laissez-faire liberalism was down, it was not out. Its catastrophic failures notwithstanding, it had retained a coterie of true believers, including the man who would become its most effective modern champion, Friedrich A. Hayek.

Born just before the turn of the century in Vienna and educated there in the 1910s and 1920s, Hayek was a devotee of the conservative Austrian school of economics, which sought to critique the social democratic policies that were ascendant in Europe and advocate for a return to liberalism. Like many intellectuals of the day, Hayek was deeply concerned with the rise of fascism. While many traced fascism's emergence to a failing capitalist system, one that could not provide full employment and necessities for the masses, Hayek argued that fascism was the result not of free markets but rather of *unfree* ones. That is, the blame for fascism lay at the feet of creeping socialist "tendencies." For Hayek, socialism was the antithesis of freedom.[15]

Teaching in London in the 1930s, Hayek sparred with economists sympathetic to socialist approaches, including Keynes himself. As the German bombs fell, Hayek and his London School of Economics colleagues were evacuated to Cambridge. With his fear of the demise of the liberal order intensifying, Hayek set aside ongoing projects to write the book that would make him famous: *The Road to Serfdom*.

The Road to Serfdom was animated by Hayek's distrust of Keynesian economic arrangements, especially those embodied in Roosevelt's New Deal and in the English economist William Beveridge's famous report of 1942 that advocated for a welfare state and laid the foundation for the British National Health Service. These "liberal socialist" approaches, Hayek argued, dangerously fused classical negative freedoms—freedoms from government overreach—with positive freedoms: rights to life-enriching things like education and a standard of living. For Hayek, such a synthesis was impossible. Governments did not exist to ameliorate their citizens' wants and needs; any attempt to institutionalize a freedom from want, he argued, would inevitably put them on "the High Road to Servitude."[16]

Hayek's book argued that positive freedoms required a stronger and more active state, one that would necessarily deemphasize its commitment to property rights in the pursuit of redistributive aims. For Hayek, this expansion of the state into the economic realm would lead ineluctably to disaster. If the state were to engage in directing the economy, whether through production or distribution, doing so would amount to a gross overreach of power—power that would be corrupted and poorly allocated by inefficient bureaucrats, to the larger detriment of the private economy. Even if this directing of the economy were done to achieve social progress and by democratic means, significant government action in the economy would "destroy personal freedom . . . completely."[17]

Since positive and negative rights could not coexist, as *The Road to Serfdom* argued, without damaging the fabric of societies, Hayek counseled that the preservation of negative freedom—freedom from the "arbitrary power of other men"—was the thing most essential to warding off fascism and totalitarianism. For Hayek, such arbitrary power included the power of elected officials, meaning that strong barriers were needed to protect markets from democratic reach. Although Hayek did concede that political freedom necessitated economic freedom, his definition of economic freedom—a definition drawn from classical liberals such as Locke, Hume, and Smith—amounted to little more than access to ever expanding markets.

The key to accessing those markets was what Hayek called the greatest "instrument of freedom ever invented by man": money.[18] This is because money confers *choice*. If, in the marketplace, one seller turns down our wishes, we can simply bring our money to the next (and the next, and the next) until we are satiated.

Of course, if choice in the market constitutes freedom, it follows that any constraint on choice also amounts to an infringement of freedom. Since Hayek believed "socialist" governmental welfare-state policies would curtail choice, he was obligated to condemn them, their salutary goals notwithstanding. As far as Hayek was concerned, states could opt for one of two paths: they could embrace the market order to the maximum extent and be free; or they could choose government intervention in the economy, a slippery slope that would terminate in Soviet Union–style totalitarianism. The fact that freedom in the marketplace amounted to a false choice for the poor—since the threats of unemployment, poverty, and starvation remained ever present—did not appear to factor into his reasoning.[19]

To the surprise of both Hayek and his editor, *The Road to Serfdom* became a best seller in Britain and in the United States. Although intended for a British audience, the book took on a new life in America, where it struck a chord with conservatives who opposed the New Deal but lacked a clear intellectual framework for articulating why to policy makers and the broader electorate. *Road* provided that. The *New York Times Book Review* not only placed it on their cover, but proclaimed it "one of the most important books of our generation."[20] The book electrified readers across the country, especially after a condensed version was published in *Reader's Digest*, an outlet whose nine million subscribers made it the most widely circulated magazine of its time. The book transformed Hayek into a conservative icon.[21]

What Hayek's fans—and later his acolytes—neglected in their fulsome praise of *Road to Serfdom* was Hayek's own heterodoxy of thought when it came to laissez-faire economics. (This oversight might be attributable to the *Reader's Digest* version of the text—the version most were familiar with—which omitted Hayek's misgivings.) Importantly, Hayek's intent in *Road* was to bolster European liberalism, not simply revive—or turbocharge—laissez-faire. For example, Hayek's view on health care was decidedly collectivist. He saw no reason "why the state should not assist . . . in providing for those common hazards of life . . . sickness and accident . . . where, in short, we deal with genuinely insurable risks—the case for the state's helping to organize a comprehensive system of social insurance is very strong." Hayek also saw a role for the state in fostering and maintaining competition, including the curtailment of monopolies in some instances (though Hayek never explained what such a program could look like). American conservatives, however, latched onto *The Road to Serfdom* for its free-market rhetoric and disdain for socialism while casting aside the author's friendliness to certain welfarist policies.

For careful readers of Hayek's text, questions remained: When and to what degree is state intervention justified, beyond structuring markets and protecting private property? Would the unfettered market facilitate freedom of choice? Or would true freedom of choice require greater government intervention than Hayek was willing to admit?[22]

It was these questions that concerned Keynes himself. In a personal letter to Hayek following the book's publication—the two were friends despite their intellectual and political disagreements—Keynes praised the work while offering an incisive critique of the flawed bargain Hayek had had to strike in order to make laissez-faire palatable

again, that of embracing an unspecified degree of government intervention to support the poor, prevent monopolies, and limit coercion.
"You admit here and there that it is a question of knowing where to
draw the line," Keynes wrote.

> You agree that the line has to be drawn somewhere, and that the logi-
> cal extreme is not possible. But you give us no guidance whatever as
> to where to draw it. . . . But as soon as you admit that the extreme is
> not possible, and that a line has to be drawn, you are, on your own
> argument, done for, since you are trying to persuade us that so soon
> as one moves an inch in the planned direction you are necessarily
> launched on the slippery path which will lead you in due course over
> the precipice.[23]

Keynes's critique would have been devastating to the logic of Hayek's
argument—and, *pari passu*, to similar exaltations of the market order.
But it mattered little to the Austrian's growing legion of admirers,
especially those at the forefront of a resurgent conservative movement in the United States.

Along with *The Road to Serfdom*, Hayek's legacy in American thought
was cemented by his founding of the Mont Pelerin Society (MPS).
Established in 1947 and named after its inaugural meeting in the
village of Mont Pelerin, Switzerland, MPS was designed to marshal
and coordinate the efforts of conservative intellectuals in their fight
against socialism and communism. No longer would these thinkers—
economists, philosophers, journalists, and politicians—be lonely voices
at their universities or places of work; now they would be part of what
Hayek termed "the neoliberal movement." Among the attendees at
the first meeting were a who's who of conservative thought, including
Hayek, Ludwig Von Mises, George Stigler, Frank Knight, Lionel Robbins, Wilhelm Röpke, and Milton Friedman.

In the statement of aims developed at the society's maiden gathering, the members declared that a "decline of belief in private property
and the competitive market" had resulted in the disappearance of

"the essential conditions of human dignity and freedom."[24] Without the market, they believed, coercive power simply could not be kept in check—no matter the reach and rights of the electorate—and freedom would continue to wane. Indeed, it was the existence and domination of markets that would diffuse any concentrations of power that may arise.

The members of MPS would work together over the years, as the historian Quinn Slobodian argues in his book *Globalists*, to encase markets and "inoculate capitalism against the threat of democracy."[25] And as their members became more prominent—four inaugural members (Hayek, Milton Friedman, George Stigler, and Maurice Allais) would win the Nobel Prize in economics—they were increasingly able to influence politics and policy. Such was their objective. For members of MPS, matters of political economy were not purely intellectual debates to be hashed out in ivory towers; rather, for all their disdain of Karl Marx, they did agree with him on one point: "The philosophers have only interpreted the world, in various ways; the point," Marx said of the world, "is to change it."[26]

Perhaps no MPS attendee took this principle more to heart than Milton Friedman. He would later describe that inaugural gathering as a revelation. In his autobiography, written with his wife and frequent coauthor, Rose, Friedman notes how the organization shaped his thinking and work, particularly in the realm of public policy. In fact, he writes, it was the first meeting of MPS that marked "the beginning of my active involvement in the political process."[27] He would never look back.

Milton Friedman and the Canonization of Neoliberalism

If Hayek is the father of neoliberalism, Friedman is its favorite son. Born in Brooklyn to Ukrainian Jewish immigrants, Friedman graduated from high school at sixteen and studied mathematics and economics at Rutgers University in New Jersey. Though intending to become an actuary, he received a fellowship to study economics at

the University of Chicago, where he learned under such towering figures as Jacob Viner, Frank Knight, and Henry Simons.

Although he excelled in graduate school, he struggled to find academic work after graduating. Roosevelt's New Deal would come to
his aid, however, as it had for countless Americans. The buildout of its
government programs had created a surge in employment for young
economists, and so Friedman packed his bags and headed to Washington. After starting off at the National Resources Planning Board—a
cornerstone of government planning—Friedman bounced around
through stints with the Treasury Department and government-
funded think tanks. But he would soon leave government work and
return to the academy. After leaving his first faculty position at the
University of Minnesota, where he shared workspace with George
Stigler, he landed in his long-term home: the University of Chicago.[28]

Over the course of his long career—he died in 2006, at the age of
ninety-four—Friedman would become one of the most influential
economists to have ever lived, advising prominent politicians from
Barry Goldwater to Ronald Reagan, as well as dictators such as Chile's
Augusto Pinochet, all the while fueling and championing the neoliberal revolution. Upon his death, the *Washington Post* ran the headline, "Friedman Debunked the Gospel of Keynes." Larry Summers,
former chief economist of the World Bank and top adviser in both
the Clinton and the Obama White House, announced, "We are all
Friedmanites now."[29]

In his early work, however, Friedman's position vis-à-vis the market resembles Hayek's—and many MPS members'—in its ambiva-
lence. In an essential early paper, "Neo-Liberalism and Its Prospects"
(1951), written at a time when the Great Depression still lingered in
many Americans' minds, the young Friedman acknowledges the failure of pure laissez-faire economics to secure the individual liberty
that is essential to a liberal order. He argues that laissez-faire doctrine
had taken its faith in markets and hatred of the state too far, thereby
triggering a reactionary embrace of socialism and state solutions
to economic problems. Put another way, promises of freedom ring

hollow to those in breadlines and shantytowns. According to Friedman, a new theory of liberalism would have to offer more than mere belief in the market; it would have to address the misery of the masses.

Friedman's proposal was a compromise system, one that embraced liberalism by restricting the state's power to coerce individuals and limit choice while recognizing the state indeed had a positive role to play in the economy. That role was to "police the system, establish conditions favorable to competition and prevent monopoly, provide a stable monetary framework," and, most interestingly, "relieve acute misery and distress."[30] In Friedman's view, capitalism had to be kept in check, and these were the necessary compromises to make liberalism palatable to the masses once again.

For all these concessions, however, the state nevertheless remained the center of oppression in Friedman's narratives. Markets and private property rights—which were both creations of the state, it bears repeating—needed to be strong in order to protect individuals from undue power wielded by the state or large corporations. Competition also had power to mitigate state or corporation coercion. Friedman was committed to the idea of competitive markets, which he believed would not only protect individuals from one another but also increase freedom. The more competitors, the more choices; the more choices, the more freedom.

Like Hayek in *The Road to Serfdom*, Friedman is vague on the details of state provisioning, noting only that the state should provide public works along with some humanitarian assistance to those in desperate need. What was paramount for Friedman was the protection of the market order, which in practice meant that any state-assistance initiative must involve minimum distortions to the market. Friedman believed the best way to realize maximum market participation was by "trying to achieve a minimum income for all," which amounted to a negative income tax (a variety of basic income, which I return to later). With this bare minimum in place, individuals could take to the market, and other types of assistance—subsidies, minimum wage, and various forms of price controls, that is, the armature of the New Deal—could be abolished.

It was a bold proposal, almost messianic in its praise of the market. But, like his forbear Hayek, Friedman styled himself a visionary. He had "a new faith to offer": the faith of neoliberalism.[31]

Between 1951, when Friedman won the John Bates Clarke Medal as the most accomplished young economist in the United States, and 1962, when Friedman's most influential book, *Capitalism and Freedom*, was published, the doctrines of the neoliberal faith would change considerably. Whereas both Hayek and Friedman initially sought to revitalize laissez-faire by including a role for the state—limiting monopolies and preserving competition; providing for the poor; financing and regulating public works projects; managing over-all fluctuations in the economy and the attendant waves of mass unemployment—they would later decide that laissez-faire was, in fact, unimprovable. Give the government an inch, and it would take a mile. By the 1960s, any neoliberal misgivings about the unfettered market had seemingly disappeared; for the neoliberals, the benefits of negative freedom, and the perils of state intervention, were too significant to ignore.

Capitalism and Freedom in America

The definitive statement of this new understanding, a sort of neo-liberal middle era, was Friedman's *Capitalism and Freedom*. Little remarked upon its publication, it would become one of the best-selling economics books of all time and the ne plus ultra distillation of canonical neoliberalism. The title said it all: capitalism gives rise to freedom, and without capitalism—the unbounded market—freedom is lost.

Friedman devotes a substantial portion of *Capitalism and Freedom* to a history of freedom and liberalism, including a rhetorical case for their earlier conventions. He observes that "the nineteenth-century liberal regarded an extension of freedom as the most effective way to promote welfare and equality; the twentieth-century liberal regards welfare and equality as either prerequisites of or alternatives to freedom." Freedom, to Friedman, is exclusively negative. The emerging focus in the United States on positive rights and social justice, luxuries bequeathed by the New Deal, were a dangerous development, one that imperiled not only his own preferred economic arrangements, but society itself. His antidote was a version of laissez-faire far more devout than that proposed by Hayek, a vision of the economy that has never existed in the United States—or, for that matter, any country on earth.

His program consisted of seven steps: (1) cut taxes anywhere and everywhere and suppress government spending; (2) promote stable monetary policy and reduce reliance on fiscal policy to balance the budget over a number of years; (3) promote private enterprise and restrain governmental intervention wherever possible by minimizing regulations and the direct provisioning of goods and services; (4) repeal policies associated with the war on poverty and achieve the objective of meeting minimum needs for Americans through philanthropy; (5) greatly reduce the federal bureaucracy by eliminating federal programs to assist state and local governments; (6) eliminate government "paternalism" by promoting free trade, free markets, and free choice; and (7) preserve free markets and negative freedom by means of a large and powerful military.

Friedman's faith in the private market was total, his view of publicly funded entities unrelenting critical. Public schools? Socialist. Libraries? Socialist. Fire departments? Socialist. Agencies like the Food and Drug Administration and the Environmental Protection Agency? Socialist. Friedman wanted them (and many more, including Medicare and Medicaid, OSHA, EEOC, Head Start, and others) gone. The New Deal he had once supported and worked on behalf of had grown too big and too powerful, and now it needed paring to preserve freedom.

A notable idiosyncrasy of Friedman's vision of freedom was its *narrowness*. The suppression of Black Americans' civil rights, for example—as clear-cut an infringement of (any kind of) freedom as you could ask for—receives nary a mention. Neither does the patent unfreedom of the countless impoverished people living in the richest country the earth had ever seen. For Friedman, unfreedom could only be caused by government overreach in the market. The New Deal and Great Society had been dangerous follies; welfare programs to help the poor imperiled freedom rather than delivered it. Big government was antithetical to freedom, and freeing the market would, in turn, free the people.

Although it would be some years before *Capitalism and Freedom* entered the zeitgeist, its ideas received an early airing in Barry Goldwater's 1964 presidential campaign, for which Friedman served as an economic adviser. In Goldwater, a conservative businessman and senator from Arizona, Friedman found the first political vessel for his radical vision. Writing in defense of the Goldwater view of economics in the *New York Times*, Friedman summarizes his own book, telling readers that Goldwater dreamed of the "freedom of the individual to pursue his own interest so long as he does not interfere with the freedom of others to do likewise . . . [and the] opportunity for the ordinary man to use his resources as effectively as possible to advance the well-being of himself and his family." "Government exists," Friedman continued, "to protect this freedom and to widen this opportunity."[32]

Friedman's economic program manifested in a simple agenda for the Goldwater campaign: enact a laissez-faire, market-centric economy coupled with a strong police and militarist state to support property rights and continued US imperialism. While the young Friedman had renounced nineteenth-century liberalism for its uncritical embrace of laissez-faire, the older Friedman reverted to an extreme flavor of the same principles. The New Deal had gone too far, Friedman and Goldwater held, in rewriting the rules of the economy and restructuring markets with multiple aims in mind—workers' rights, communities' rights, equality, freedom from want—rather than a singular focus on expanding market access. Democracy had turned on the liberal order, Friedman opined, so democracy had to be contained.

Goldwater would be defeated by an incumbent Lyndon Johnson in a landslide, winning just six states. Americans, it appeared, were not yet ready for Friedman's radical economic vision of the economy. But Friedman's reach into American politics was just beginning. In time, his ideas would gain a larger audience, especially after the 1980 publication of *Free to Choose*, Friedman's more popular portrayal of his vision, again cowritten with his wife, Rose. Here the Friedmans packaged Milton's ideas for the mass market, combining a best-selling book, an eighteen-month tour around the world, and a ten-part PBS series of the same title. The timing was impeccable; the book and TV series launched just before the beginning of the Republican primary that Ronald Reagan, whom Friedman also advised, would win on his way to the presidency. His election wouldn't be just a Reagan revolution but a Friedman revolution as well.

Free to Choose wasn't merely a simplified rehashing of the ideas in *Capitalism and Freedom*; rather, it marked Friedman's adoption of an even more radical notion of freedom. He was crystal clear in identifying his (and freedom's) antagonist: government. "Sooner or later—and perhaps sooner than many of us expect," he wrote, "an ever bigger government would destroy both the prosperity that we owe to the free market and the human freedom proclaimed so eloquently in the Declaration of Independence."[33]

To realize free markets and free people, Friedman preached the trifecta Reagan would later embrace: deregulation, cuts to taxes and spending, and labor movement suppression. These proposals would be familiar to readers of *Capitalism and Freedom*. But Friedman went further, railing against the government correction of market failures, something economists from across the political spectrum had largely embraced as an appropriate role for the state. Friedman claimed, without substantiation, that if the government worked to address market failures, it would only make matters worse. In Friedman's estimation, government was as incapable as a toddler, and any state action to address *any* market failure—even one with cataclysmic potential, such as environmental threats—was off-limits.

Determined to save the market from a dangerous state, Friedman recommended a bold course of action: constitutional amendments. In Friedman's view, market prices were a form of free speech, and he advocated for an amendment to outlaw wage and price controls: "Congress shall make no laws abridging the freedom of sellers of goods or labor to price their products or services." The effects of an amendment like this, as Friedman recognized and welcomed, would be various and sundry: No minimum wages. No maximum hours of work. Perhaps even no child labor laws. The poor would be free to sell their organs, or any other part of them, while the rich would be free to hire servants at starvation wages if those servants acquiesced to such terms. Other amendments Friedman proposed included a limit on the growth of government spending and the requirement of a balanced budget, developments that would have drastically curtailed the influence of Congress and the public over the economy while tying the legislature's hands to respond to capitalism's inevitable boom-bust cycles.

These ideas sound familiar because they are the ideas Ronald Reagan trumpeted in his 1980 presidential campaign, over his eight years in the White House, and in his July 3, 1987, call for an economic bill of rights. While his bill of rights never became law, Reagan nonetheless adopted his economic adviser's program wholesale over two terms in office.[34] Friedman was, after all, one of the six intellectual leaders who had fundamentally shaped Reagan's thoughts over time, a distinction shared with Fredrick Hayek and Ludwig Von Mises, both founding members of the Mont Pelerin Society. With the rise of Reagan, MPS's project to revive liberalism—inaugurated by Hayek, furthered by Friedman—had finally succeeded.[35]

What Neoliberals Wrought

Reagan won the presidential election of 1980 with 51 percent of the popular vote, a relative landslide over Jimmy Carter's 41 percent. (Independent candidate, John B. Anderson, took the remaining margin.) It was the first time in nearly fifty years, since FDR ousted Herbert Hoover, that a challenger unseated a sitting president. Carter's predecessor, Gerald Ford, in the year leading up to Reagan's victory, had declared with confidence that "a very conservative Republican can't win in a national election."[36] Ford would eat his words.

Why did America elect Reagan? Some argue that Carter had embodied the failure of American leadership globally, a failure that was on full display every evening during the news coverage of the Iranian hostage crisis in the midst of the election. Others point to the electorate's fear regarding the downfall of the American dream; the economy was faltering—both unemployment and inflation were relatively high at the time—and people were deeply concerned that their children wouldn't have the chance to experience the upward economic mobility that had been fairly widespread during the previous few decades. Some commentators also attribute Reagan's rise to his exemplar ability to work a crowd: the great communicator knew how to put his talents to use, rousing thousands as he spread his populist message. A component of this talent was Reagan's frequent and eloquent invocation of freedom, a freedom that would protect the people from, as the historian Kim Phillips-Fein has described the narrative, "the new aristocracy: the government bureaucrats steadily expanding the state."[37]

In office, Reagan followed Friedman and the neoliberals' advice to the letter. The first priority was tax cuts. While the top marginal tax rate had sat at 91 percent during (Republican) President Eisenhower's eight years in office, Reagan would, in time, slash it from 70 percent to 28 percent. It would be the biggest giveaway to the rich the country had ever seen. But Reagan didn't do this alone; he had the support of conservative Democrats in Congress, who were increasingly taking up the so-called market turn of the late twentieth century. These cuts, detailed in the previous chapter, delivered neither freedom nor growth. In fact, the era of neoliberalism has been marked by significantly slower economic growth than the Keynesian era that preceded it, as well as a severe constraining of workers' freedoms.[38]

Alongside his prized tax cuts, Reagan deregulated industry, gutted the Environmental Protection Agency, froze workers' salaries, and halted increases in the minimum wage—all under the guise of advancing freedom.

Although Reagan was the conservative lion Friedman had always sought, Friedman's ideas—cut taxes (especially for the rich), reduce government spending (especially entitlements), deregulate (to "free" markets—and those who dominate them), promote federalism (to limit the reach of centralized government), and maximize market choices (for market choices are coextensive with freedom)—would live on after Reagan left office.[39] Friedman's intellectual legacy can be seen in the presidencies of George H. W. Bush, who awarded Hayek the Presidential Medal of Freedom, and of his son George W. Bush, who awarded Friedman the same. It can be seen in the policies embraced by the New Democrats—"workfare," tax cuts, and deregulation—whose torchbearer, Bill Clinton, captured the White House in 1992. It can be seen in the radical Right Tea Party, whose "Contract with America" was Reagan's bill of rights all over again. It was even seen in the presidency of Donald Trump, whose only legislative success was a massive supply-side tax cut (which, like the neoliberal tax cuts that preceded it, failed to boost growth, though did deepen inequality).[40] Gone are the days of Republicans supporting large-scale redistributive taxation, as they had under Eisenhower. Gone too are the days of Republicans supporting universal public goods, as they did in 1971 when the Senate passed a childcare bill with substantial Republican support (only for Richard Nixon, surprisingly, to veto it). And gone are the days of Republicans supporting regulations in the name of the common good, such as Nixon's signing of the Clean Air Act and his establishment of the Environmental Protection Agency.[41]

Democrats, for their part, have facilitated the further cementing of Friedmanite policies by ceasing to champion policies that continue the legacy of the New Deal and Great Society. The natural outgrowths of FDR's policies—today's calls for universal health care, a federal minimum wage increase, or full employment—have received no sincere attempts at uptake from the liberal party. As Friedman's ideas infiltrated every nook and cranny of American politics, Democrats too have been tamed by neoliberalism.[42]

Friedman and Hayek agreed, as would most people, that political freedom requires economic freedom. Differences emerge in how one defines that economic freedom. For Friedman and Hayek, economic freedom amounts to no more than negative freedom: freedom from constraint. Everywhere and anywhere, replace the government with the market, and you maximize freedom. Problems emerge only from failures to optimize. The neoliberal titans claimed that their solution not only provided the maximum degree of freedom and choice for the rich, but for all members of society. Significant government redistribution, regulation, and planning would amount to an assault on the very freedom the Founders and their fellow patriots died for.

This program has failed miserably in practice. An economy and society modeled on delivering only negative freedom has resulted in far too many Americans ill clothed, ill housed, ill educated, and ill fed. It has forced a country long divided along racial lines to remain cloven in two, separate and unequal. And it even failed on its own terms, delivering far slower growth than was achieved during the Keynesian era.

But that's not all. Neoliberalism has failed to provide people with adequate negative freedom too, by ignoring what the philosopher Elizabeth Anderson calls "private government." By focusing exclusively on limiting traditional public government, Friedman and his ilk failed to account for the authority of where people spend a great deal of their waking hours: the workplace. In the workplace, people are regularly subject to what Anderson describes as "dictators of little communist governments," or the tyranny of the workplace in a market-dominated society. Private governments constrain not only what workers do on the job—think, for example, of workers subjected to sweatshop-like conditions, including lack of access to bathrooms— but also what they do off the job, policing their speech, who they support politically, their diets, even their sexual preferences. Workers, in short, are subject to regular coercion by employers, whose agency to coerce has been facilitated by neoliberalism. Work in the twenty-first century is an antagonist to freedom. To this, Friedman might argue that workers can leave; they always have an exit option. Anderson rejects this, noting workers' supposed freedom of exit from the workplace is akin to saying "Mussolini wasn't a dictator, because Italians could emigrate." The freedoms promised by the almighty market have not only failed to materialize; they have produced new dictators.[43]

But it isn't only the economics that neoliberalism has gotten wrong; it's the history. It is true that negative freedoms like those enshrined in the Bill of Rights were an integral part of the Founders' vision for the government. But positive freedoms—rights to physical and social well-being, to the material support for human self-actualization and dignity—was an essential facet of the Founders' understanding as well. Far from accepting the "natural rights" associated with negative freedom as handed down by the gods, Americans have long held, as FDR would proclaim from the podium while accepting the Democratic nomination for president in Chicago, "Economic laws are not made by nature. They are made by human beings."

3

America's Other Freedom

Royalists of the economic order . . . granted that the government
could protect the citizen in his right to vote, but they denied that the
government could do anything to protect the citizen in his right to
work and his right to live.
FRANKLIN DELANO ROOSEVELT

For freedom from want is the basic freedom from which all others
flow. This nation has learned that it must provide freedom for all if any
of us is to be free.
FREEDOM BUDGET, 1967

On January 11, 1944, four decades before Reagan stood in front of the
Jefferson Memorial and promised to amend the Constitution in the
name of freedom, a very different president made an almost identical promise.

The augurs were not in favor of a landmark speech. It was Roosevelt's eleventh State of the Union address, and, due to a spell of flu,
he was forced to deliver his remarks via radio from the White House.
There was no pageantry—no brass band and fluttering American
flags, no majestic backdrop or historical event to commemorate. Just
the president's Brahmin voice, perhaps a bit more nasal than usual
from his illness.

The humbleness of the performance notwithstanding, it was a
time of great optimism. The Allies had successfully turned the tide

in World War II, and the defeat of the Nazis was in sight. And the
war effort had stoked the economy too: 17 million new civilian jobs
had been created; production in industry had more or less doubled, as
had union membership; and wages in manufacturing had *more* than
doubled. The war still raged, but Roosevelt could finally take a breath
and begin to turn his attention—and the attention of the American
people—to the postwar order.

Paramount in that order, so said Roosevelt, was security: "not only
physical security . . . but economic security, social security, moral
security." The economic benefits bestowed by war production notwithstanding, the social minimum Roosevelt had fought for since
the New Deal had yet to be realized universally, and the president's
speech acknowledged the work to be done to address the country's
widespread poverty and sweeping inequality. This task was a moral
imperative but also a practical and political one. Roosevelt cautioned
Americans that "people who are hungry, people who are out of a job,
are the stuff of which dictatorships are made." (Germany, which had
been crushed by reparations payments under the Treaty of Versailles—
giving rise to the Third Reich—was the case in point.) To preempt tyranny and preserve freedom, Roosevelt believed, the American people
needed to be assured a baseline well-being. Because, he cautioned,
"necessitous men are not free men."[1]

To guarantee Americans' security and entrench true freedom—the
freedom to pursue happiness, one of Jefferson's hallowed inalienable rights—Roosevelt urged Congress to consider a "second Bill of
Rights," a set of policies "under which a new basis of security and
prosperity can be established for all." Roosevelt's sentiment was at
once magnanimous and politically canny. After asking citizens for
immense sacrifices to fight fascism abroad and fuel the war effort at
home, America owed its people a public contract greater than the negative liberties enshrined in the Constitution's first ten amendments. It
owed its people *positive* freedom—freedom from want, from destitution, from despair. FDR put forward a highly formed framework for
economic rights. It was not, however, new.

The Forgotten History of American Freedom: Economic Rights before Roosevelt

Although Roosevelt presented his economic bill of rights as an outgrowth of the war—a concession to the "economic truths" that poverty and desperation are the raw material of fascism—Americans as early as the country's founding recognized the necessity of economic provisioning. As Jefferson's phrasing in the Declaration of Independence made clear, American freedom has long comprised both negative and positive rights. The positive side of these rights has been extolled by figures as integral to the American story as Thomas Paine, Alexander Hamilton, Abraham Lincoln, Roosevelt, and Martin Luther King Jr.

ECONOMIC RIGHTS AS COMMON SENSE: THOMAS PAINE

In 1776, in the aftermath of the bloody confrontations at Lexington and Concord, an anonymously authored pamphlet appeared under the imprint of the Philadelphia publisher Robert Bell. Titled "Common Sense," the essay presented the case for American independence. Plainly written and unforgiving in its critiques of the British Crown, "Common Sense" would light a fire under the American people, selling hundreds of thousands of copies and quickly becoming "the most incendiary and popular pamphlet of the entire revolutionary era."[2] The work would convince weary colonists still committed to reconciliation with the British that "'tis time to part" with the Crown. And it would make its author, the English corset maker Thomas Paine, one of the most admired and influential thinkers of the revolutionary period.

In "Common Sense" and the *American Crisis* papers—pamphlets written during the Revolutionary War to maintain morale and remind Americans why they were fighting—Paine was indefatigable in his case for democracy and equality. Paine swore off inheritance rights and the supposed distinctions in natural ability between rich and poor, arguing people were "originally equal in order of creation." In the words of the historian Harvey J. Kaye, Paine endowed the "American experience with democratic impulses and aspirations," effectively radicalizing the colonial American public. Paine's time in America would find him becoming one of history's great proponents of liberty, equality, and democracy.[3]

Paine's subsequent writings would stretch far beyond the borders of the new nation and the subject of self-government. In *Rights of Man* (1791), a defense of the French Revolution, Paine articulated the first vision of a social insurance policy to end poverty and deliver to all citizens well-being as a personal right. Paine notes that "man did not enter into society to become worse than he was before, nor to have fewer rights than he had before, but to have those rights better secured." To secure those rights, Paine calls for government payments to every poor family, with additional funds going to families with children; old-age pensions to render the elderly's "condition comfortable"; funding for children's education as well as teaching supplies, including "paper and spelling books"; and additional state funds for people facing major life changes: newlyweds, those welcoming a new child into the world, and those saying goodbye to loved ones. Rounding out this vision of the well-being state, Paine calls for living wages for all and "employment at all times for the casual poor."[4] In a later work, *Agrarian Justice* (1797), Paine develops the powerful idea that political freedom and economic freedom were "mutually interdependent," for "economic freedom served to assure equality of opportunity *and* results."[5] In other words, political freedom requires freedom from want.

The means to economic freedom, Paine argued, was progressive taxation. In both *Rights of Man* and *Agrarian Justice*, Paine makes the case that democratic societies have a responsibility to their people to mitigate inequality by taxing the rich and creating a system of social insurance that provides all with a socially determined, and acceptable, minimum. Nobody should be allowed to fall through the cracks that permeate our lives. As Paine recognized, there is nothing natural about poverty ("It is wrong to say God made both *rich* and *poor*," he writes in *Agrarian Justice*).[6] Inequality was a creation of society's contingent organization.

To rid the landscape of poverty, Paine proposed that the government should pay all people in the polis a citizen's dividend—that is, a form of basic income. In *Agrarian Justice* he also proposed universal grants to the young and universal pensions to the elderly, setting the groundwork for what was to become Social Security. For Paine, this was not charity to address destitution; it was what democratic societies owed their citizens to ensure that the collective benefits of society were shared equitably and no one was left behind.

THE SAGE OF DEVELOPMENT: ALEXANDER HAMILTON

Although Paine is perhaps the most underappreciated and progressive American founder, Alexander Hamilton, the first Treasury secretary of the United States, is not far behind. Hamilton's writings included threads of what would today pass as progressivism, including his characterization of a strong centralized state as a "better guarantor of liberty" than the free market and an essential mechanism for keeping the promises of the Declaration of Independence.

By dint of his writings on the formation of a new nation and new financial system, Hamilton would create what the economist Christian Parenti and others have characterized as "the American School" of governance: a central planner aimed at promoting the public welfare. During America's earliest days, Hamilton mapped a role for government as a developmentalist state—one that plays a more active role in economic planning to support growth, development, and macroeconomic stability. For Hamilton, the general welfare clause of the Constitution mandated a robust state that would utilize "the means proper" to deliver the people freedom from want. In short, Hamilton sought a strong central state that would leverage economic planning to benefit the American people and state.

Hamilton's "means proper" (a phrase that should be famous in its own right) included targeted state subsidies, protective tariffs to allow industry to develop, limited export bans on select raw materials, product controls to ensure quality and legitimacy, public investments in essential infrastructure, the recruitment and training of labor, and more—all in the name of economic freedom for the new nation.

In a crowning achievement, the 1791 "Report on the Subject of Manufactures," Hamilton not only eviscerated the prevailing economic views of the time—views that centered on laissez-faire market fundamentalism—but also articulated how a truly free economy required a large active role for government in structuring, limiting, and creating markets from the ground up.[7] While Hamilton's compatriot Paine focused on what the state owed the individual, Hamilton focused on building a strong and free state from tools that would today pass as macroeconomics (though the term didn't exist in Hamilton's time). For Hamilton, who was seeking to build a nation out of the ruins of the Revolutionary War, one that could survive and thrive in a world with multiple feuding imperial powers, "the mission was, in short, development or death."[8]

Many of Hamilton's ideas would be sidelined in favor of small-government initiatives during the Jeffersonian Revolution of 1800. Jefferson, who was "opposed in death as in life" to Hamilton and his ideas, was a believer in a smallholder agrarian society and minimalist state, and he worked to reduce drastically the power and planning of the nascent centralized state. It's thanks to Jefferson and his epigones that the country exhibits, in Parenti's description, the "balkanization of the economy by states' rights and localism."[9]

While the American School suffered a major setback with the rise of Jefferson, it was not defeated. Hamilton had worked to build up the developmentalist state not only to support robust economic growth—growth he believed was essential for national survival—but also to harness that growth as a means to the ultimate end: improving the general welfare. Hamilton's conception of a more active central state in developing the "means proper" and securing the good life, including the right to subsistence, was a precursor to Roosevelt's New Deal and more detailed economic bill of rights. But earlier political leaders drew on Hamilton's ideas as well, chief among them Whigs and Radical Republicans, along with President Lincoln himself.

THE POLITICAL ECONOMY OF RADICAL REPUBLICANISM

After decades out of favor, the swearing in of Lincoln and the Thirty-Seventh Congress (1861–63) marked the revival of the American developmental state. Although the country descended into civil war just weeks after the change in government, the Thirty-Seventh Congress would ultimately be one of the most productive in history (due in no small part to wartime secession), passing three groundbreaking pieces of legislation that reshaped the American landscape and economy.

The first was the Homestead Act (1862), which granted 160-acre plots to each homesteader to improve the land (i.e., build a home and till the soil). This radical land redistribution program, which would ultimately transfer 246 million acres—roughly the size of California and Texas combined, or nearly 10 percent of all US lands today—to homesteaders at no cost (though there was a minor filing fee), was open to any adult citizen or immigrant in the process of becoming a citizen. The land would go to 1.5 million families; today roughly one in four adults are direct descendants of those who benefited from the land redistribution. Perhaps more than any other act of government in US history, the Homestead Act affirmed the idea that a fully free citizen was someone who held a share of the means of production—in this case, land—freeing them from depending on others for their subsistence.

The second landmark piece of legislation was the Pacific Railroad Act (1862), which supported westward expansion by providing over a hundred million acres of public lands to the railroad companies, along with subsidies and loans for rail development. These provisions laid the groundwork for a unified national market and an industrialized nation.

Finally, the Morrill Act (1862) helped create America's public higher education system, a system I benefited from, founded on the enlightened notion of public education. The act, also known as the Land-Grant College Act, provided thirty thousand acres of public land to each state for every congressional seat it held—land that could be sold off to raise revenue for the establishment of public colleges, most of which were free. Today, some 1.7 million students are enrolled at the more than one hundred colleges and universities founded by the land-grant program.[10]

While these acts marked the return of the developmentalist state, it was the Civil War and the emancipation of nearly four million enslaved people that provided an opening, if a narrow one, for a more democratic state to deliver on the long-delayed promises of the Declaration of Independence. The Union Army's victory transformed formerly enslaved people from being capital themselves into members of the capitalist economy with (ostensibly) the freedom to own capital themselves.[11] But, as Frederick Douglass noted in 1875, formerly enslaved people "were free without roofs to cover them, or bread to eat, or land to cultivate, and as a consequence died in such numbers as to awaken the hope of their enemies that they would soon disappear."[12] Ending the enslavement of Black people in America was of course a far cry from granting them meaningful freedom: the formerly enslaved still needed land to work or another sustainable livelihood to achieve enduring freedom.[13]

To that end, for a brief moment in the aftermath of the war, the United States worked to cement not only civil and political rights for the newly free but economic rights as well. Most famous among these efforts was General William T. Sherman's signing of Special Field Orders No. 15, which granted these formerly enslaved Americans forty acres (ten acres per family member) and a mule. According to work by William A. Darity and A. Kirsten Mullen, this program— had it been enacted in full—would have provided roughly 5.3 million acres to the previously enslaved; it would have created a "Black Belt" across the South and laid the foundation for true equality and economic security. There the newly freed Black Americans would be something closer to free, at least enjoying the political and economic freedom necessary to grant them their full right to participate in the American project. But redistributing land meant confiscating the property of the erstwhile slaveholding elite (who themselves, it bears mentioning, had confiscated the land in the first place). Such an act was resisted furiously.[14]

Meanwhile, Congress's so-called Radical Republicans, members of the House and Senate steadfastly opposed to slavery and critical of Lincoln's perceived slow-walking of reforms, were working toward a "radical reorganization of Southern Institutions, habits, and manners." As the Pennsylvania Republican congressman Thaddeus Stevens would proclaim in a speech before the US House of Representatives in 1865, "The whole fabric of southern society must be changed, and never can it be done if this opportunity is lost. Without this, this government can never be, as it never has been, a true republic." Stevens would go on to articulate the necessity of basic economic rights for the previously enslaved:

> We have turned, or are about to turn, loose four million slaves without a hut to shelter them or a cent in their pockets. The infernal laws of slavery have prevented them from acquiring an education, understanding the common laws of contract, or of managing the ordinary business of life. This Congress is bound to provide for them until they can take care of themselves. If we do not furnish them with homesteads, and hedge them around with protective laws; if we leave them to the legislation of their late masters, we had better have left them in bondage.[15]

After the passage of the Freedmen's Bureau Act of 1865, which enshrined Sherman's order into law, it appeared as though Stevens's vision of a republic reborn would soon be realized. But the assassination of Lincoln by John Wilkes Booth would put an end to the march toward racial integration. In the end, only 40,000 freed Black people settled 400,000 acres under Sherman's order. The promise of land—of freedom—was withheld for the vast majority of freed people. As W. E. B Du Bois would later write, Reconstruction was the moment when the slave "went free; stood a brief moment in the sun; then moved back again toward slavery."[16]

The door to civil, political, and economic freedom for Black Americans shut once and for all with the Compromise of 1877, which gave Republican Rutherford B. Hayes the presidency in exchange for the withdrawal of federal troops from the former Confederacy and a total relinquishment of the South to Democrats. Although Congress had passed the Thirteenth, Fourteenth, and Fifteenth Amendments—known as the Reconstruction amendments—abolishing slavery and delivering citizenship rights for the recently emancipated slaves, the federal government's abandonment of the South resulted in a vicious backsliding. Black Americans' return to unfreedom was ushered in by a series of policy assaults: the Supreme Court's decision in *Plessy v. Ferguson*, which found segregation constitutional, followed by the rise of Jim Crow, a brutal regime of segregation akin to, as Douglas A. Blackmon has described it, slavery by another name.[17]

FDR and the Revival of Economic Rights

FDR's 1944 State of the Union address was an extension of the American tradition of Paine, Hamilton, and Lincoln. It was also consistent with Roosevelt's views on American freedom prior to the outbreak of World War II and the attack on Pearl Harbor. Roosevelt fought for a more capacious notion of freedom beginning with his presidential campaign of 1932, when he and Herbert Hoover debated the proper role of the federal government in managing the economy. And it was through Roosevelt's dogged effort—and his commitment to economic rights—over the course of his three-plus terms that America saw the greatest expansion of economic well-being in its history.

HOOVER, FDR, AND THE BLUEPRINTS FOR A NEW DEAL

Like no other economic event in history, the Great Depression laid bare the devastating failures of the laissez-faire order. The hands-off approach to the downturn taken by the Hoover administration was catastrophic: unemployment afflicted one in four American workers, and a third of Americans lived, or tried to live, without basic necessities such as sufficient housing, clothing, and food. With his policies failing and the country in disarray, Hoover approached the election of 1932 as more than just a contest between two presidential candidates; rather, as Hoover noted in front of twenty thousand Republicans at Madison Square Garden, it was "a contest between two philosophies of government." Hoover's ticket represented free-market capitalism and the exclusive focus on negative freedom. On the other side was Roosevelt, with his proclamation that the economy exists to serve the people and the notion that Americans had it in their power to will and legislate a different economy into existence. According to Hoover, this "so-called new deal," whose reforms necessitated the expansion and centralization of government (and thus, by Hoover's lights, a trampling of individual liberties) would "destroy the very foundations of our American system." Hoover's faith in the market was unshakable. However, as the economist and member of Roosevelt's brain trust Rexford Tugwell said, "The jig is up. The cat is out of the bag. There is no invisible hand. There never was. If the depression has not taught us that, we are incapable of education."[18]

On the campaign trail, Roosevelt demonstrated his vision for the New Deal iteratively, outlining in pieces the actions he and his appointees would take to reinvent the American economy and revise the social contract. Two months after accepting his party's nomination in Chicago, Roosevelt delivered his famed Commonwealth Club Address, in which he spoke of a new "economic declaration of rights" that would fulfill, once and for all, the Founders' promise of life, liberty, and the pursuit of happiness. Roosevelt was a proud American. He championed the development of industry and the strength that the nation drew from its economic engine when it was running well. But he also understood that the titans of industry and finance held the power of life and death over the people—the Depression was the case in point—and that simply could not be tolerated. To resolve the economic crisis, Roosevelt argued, government needed to address the dearth of investment and everyday Americans' lack of purchasing power, as well as the faltering coordination between production and needs; redistribute wealth and income more equitably; and, above all, adapt "existing economic organizations to the service of the people."[19]

Such adaptation was the chief aim of the New Deal. The object was not merely to revive the economy of the Roaring Twenties, as Roosevelt made clear ("I am not for a return to that definition of liberty under which for many years a free people were gradually regimented into the service [of capital]").[20] Instead he sought to rebuild the country's economic and political order brick by brick to forge a new social contract. Roosevelt sought revolution. But, crucially, he sought a revolution that was grounded in American ideals of equality—of opportunity *and* outcome—and the radical project of democracy itself.

Rejecting the idea that economic circumstances were dictated by nature and best supported by some elusive free market, Roosevelt and his advisers began to imagine how to restructure the economic system from the ground up. Market capitalism was not delivering the goods, nor was it delivering a stable economy: the country had been ransacked by dozens of economic crises. And the market order limited the scope of the people's will, thereby constraining democracy itself. In fact, the only outcome laissez-faire capitalism *did* consistently deliver was havoc for the country and the people.[21]

Thus the New Dealers embraced an active role for government in creating and directing economic activity. After all, without government, there was no economy. The question, as for Hayek and Keynes, was how, and to what ends, the government should wield its economic power. Ultimately this was a question only answerable through the democratic process. And Roosevelt was one of the most ardent practitioners of small-*d* democracy to have occupied the White House.[22]

The administration's solution was to institute a floor in certain markets to ensure a social minimum (a minimum wage), as well as a ceiling that limited the accumulation of both money and power (a maximum wage) and an increase in democratic planning to direct investment toward socially determined ends. To Roosevelt the extreme inequality that had characterized the 1920s was a clear and present danger to the country, not only because it unnecessarily damned millions to economic misery, but also because it provided economic elites with the means for political capture, allowing them to distort the political and economic system to serve *their* ends rather than those indicated by the democratic process. The economic "floor" Roosevelt sought wasn't merely metaphorical: it would quite literally ensure everyone had a floor under their feet (and a roof over their heads). Roosevelt made clear that markets should not wield the power of life and death and thus fought to tame and restructure markets through a robust social insurance program, a program that amounts to the *well-being state*.[23] For Roosevelt and his advisers, markets were but a tool to achieve socially desired ends, not an end in themselves.

While today the New Deal is hallowed for building parts of the floor—Social Security, the minimum wage, unemployment insurance, the modern mortgage—Roosevelt showed equal investment in constructing a ceiling in the economy, one that would reduce inequality and eliminate economic and political capture by cutting economic aristocrats down to size. Roosevelt observed that "royalists of the economic order . . . granted that the government could protect the citizen in his right to vote, but they denied that the government could do anything to protect the citizen in his right to work and his right to live."[24] That was about to change.

THE NEW DEAL IN ACTION

Upon taking the Oval Office in March 1933, Roosevelt instituted a crisis government to save the country from collapse. During the administration's first hundred days, Roosevelt sent multiple pieces of legislation to Congress—some to save the capitalist system from itself, others to provide much-needed employment and relief to those trampled by capital's bust. Among these bills were

- the Emergency Banking Act, which stopped the run on the banks that threatened to make the already deep Depression even worse;
- the Federal Emergency Relief Act, which provided short-term employment to millions of people through public works and

education programs for adults and children and spent big to deliver much-needed food, blankets, and shelter;

- the Agricultural Adjustment Act, which instituted a quasi-planned economy in agriculture to help save farmers (who comprised one in five employed Americans at the time);
- the National Industrial Recovery Act (NIRA), which not only gave workers the right to unionize, but regulated and *planned* large segments of the US economy by, among other levers, setting wages and directing investment; and
- the Civilian Conservation Corps, which employed three million hungry youths to plant trees, build trails, occupy fire towers, and help manage the country's public lands.[25]

The first hundred days set a breakneck pace for change. The administration had inherited a fire raging through the house of America, and its members knew that to save democracy, they had to implement far-reaching reform, and fast.

While these early New Deal initiatives were focused mostly on relief and recovery, Roosevelt soon turned to more structural change. The combination of the Supreme Court's invalidation of the NIRA, Roosevelt's souring relationship with big business, and an increasingly militant labor movement—including two significant general strikes in 1934, one in San Francisco led by the longshoremen's union and the other in Minneapolis led by the Teamsters—led the president to embrace Senator Robert F. Wagner's proposed National Labor Relations Act, which he signed into law in 1935. The bill substantially strengthened the hand of workers by giving them clear rights to unionize and bargain and established the National Labor Relations Board. This marked the administration's pivot to an increasing focus on worker's rights. Moving forward, labor, thanks to their militant class struggle, would have a sizable role in shaping the New Deal.[26]

In short order, the New Dealers extinguished the myth of the free market and the idea that economic circumstances were the culmination of natural outcomes. They demonstrated that the fortunes amassed by the leaders of industry and finance were extracted through the exploitation of workers, aided and abetted by a laissez-faire order supported by the state. Upon signing the NIRA into law, Roosevelt proclaimed that "no business which depends for existence on paying less than living wages to its workers has any right to continue in this country." This meant far more than wages to support mere subsistence, a bit of bread and soup; the policy gave people a right to wages that would support a comfortable life of meaning and dignity. The administration fought not only to redistribute resources after production through progressive taxation—a powerful tool to be sure—but also to implement "predistribution": policies like the minimum wage and the right to unionize and engage in collective bargaining that could mitigate inequalities before they occurred.[27]

But for all the good the New Deal did, it didn't go far enough to completely recover from the Great Depression. New Dealers restored economic activity through massive infusions of cash, but they never embraced the deficit spending required to achieve full employment and thereby pull the country out of crisis once and for all. (Despite the New Deal's triumphs, unemployment remained stubbornly high between 1933 and 1940, hovering between 15 and 20 percent, thus leaving millions of workers sidelined.) In truth, it was only with the mobilization for war—the deployment of the "arsenal of democracy"— that the country was finally freed from the grips of the Depression.

A WAR FOR FREEDOM

December 7, 1941, was—in FDR's indelible words—"a date which will live in infamy." The surprise attack by the Japanese on Pearl Harbor devastated the US Pacific Fleet, sinking half of the navy battleships stationed at the base and damaging the other half, all the while killing and wounding thousands of Americans. After two years of isolationism imposed by Congress, the United States finally entered the conflict ensnaring Europe, declaring war on Japan the following day in response to the attacks. Four days after the attack, Hitler and Mussolini declared war on the United States, thereby integrating the nation fully in a war that now spanned four continents. The toll would be immense. By the war's end, more than 400,000 Americans were dead. Another 671,000 were wounded. Many more people on the home front would perish or be disabled by work-related injuries due to the breakneck war pace set in America's factories and fields. Worldwide, the figures were incomprehensible: an estimated 85 million souls would perish from the earth.[28]

Entering a war of such staggering scale, Roosevelt knew what victory would cost and the sacrifices that would need to be made. How could he galvanize Americans to pay such a high price? He made the war about freedom.

Just weeks after Pearl Harbor, FDR delivered the 1942 State of the Union. Just elected to a third term—the first and only time that would occur in American history (he would go on to begin a fourth term too)—the president told the nation that the freedom the American people hold dear, along with basic human decency, was at stake. The very future of America, not to mention liberal democracies around the world, was in peril. FDR sent a clear message to Americans and Allies alike: America was standing firm in the name of freedom.[29]

But what did freedom mean? To rally the American people, Roosevelt needed to paint a vivid, specific picture of the freedom he told them they were defending. It had been 150 years since Congress enacted the Bill of Rights in the name of freedom. Throughout American history, freedom had worn many cloaks. Were Americans fighting for negative freedom, the kind of freedom that protected people from an oppressive government and enabled them to participate in a market economy? Perhaps they were, given the rise and spread of fascism and Nazism, ideologies that had a centralized state at their core. But to characterize freedom this way, and only this way, would constitute a retreat from the expansion and redefinition Roosevelt had instituted through the New Deal. Roosevelt and his advisers had mobilized an alternative notion of American freedom, one whose historical bona fides were considerable if lesser known. Would FDR double down on *this* idea of freedom, one that balanced both positive and negative freedom? And would he do it despite the critiques that his expansion of the state and immense war powers were a kind of fascism themselves?

Roosevelt's famed four freedoms provided the answer. As with the economic crisis of the Depression, Roosevelt approached the war's crisis of constitutional democracy as cause for a new social contract—in this case, one that would deliver four fundamental freedoms everywhere in the world:

- freedom of speech—the right to speak one's mind, including dissenting from government's actions;
- freedom of religion—the right to worship in one's own way;
- freedom from want—the right to employment, to food, to shelter: in short, cradle-to-grave economic security; and finally
- freedom from fear—the right to peace through disarmament across the globe.

According to Roosevelt's narrative, these four freedoms were as essential to people as air and light, bread and water, and were as American as apple pie. Withhold these critical freedoms from man, "and he dies," Roosevelt said. "Deprive him of a part of them, and a part of him withers."[30]

The four freedoms were not a vision of a distant future but the foundation for the very world Roosevelt and the New Dealers sought to legislate. With this expansive vision of freedom, the president called the country to arms. Attaining these freedoms, both on the home front and abroad, would require total commitment from the American people. It would require a full mobilization of the "arsenal of democracy"—America's people, America's factories, America's natural resources, and America's will—in the name of freedom.[31]

AN ECONOMIC BILL OF RIGHTS

The economic growth triggered by the war mobilization conferred historic benefits on the economy, and the people in it. For one, unemployment was essentially eradicated, averaging just 1.7 percent from

1943 to 1945. The all-out mobilization led to a boom in GDP, which climbed almost 80 percent between 1939 and 1944. And civilian wages and salaries were 170 percent higher in 1944 than they had been just four years earlier. Nevertheless, despite the wartime unleashing of America's productive capacity, there was more work to be done to secure Roosevelt's four freedoms on the home front—a nod, a progressive economist might add, to the limits of economic growth in advancing public welfare.[32]

And that work began with the codification of economic rights in the Constitution. In his historic 1944 State of Union address, Roosevelt set forth eight economic rights, together couched as attempts to advance the nation and security for all:

- The right to a useful and remunerative job in the industry or shops or farms or mines of the nation;
- The right to earn enough to provide adequate food and clothing and recreation;
- The right of every farmer to raise and sell his products at a return which will give him and his family a decent living;
- The right of every businessman, large and small, to trade in an atmosphere of freedom from unfair competition and domination by monopolies at home or abroad;
- The right of every family to a decent home;
- The right to adequate medical care and the opportunity to achieve and enjoy good health;
- The right to adequate protection from the economic fears of old age, sickness, accident, and unemployment; and
- The right to a good education.[33]

Together, Roosevelt proclaimed, "these rights spell security," linking his new bill of rights to the four freedoms. Acutely aware of the impending struggles that would arise as millions of returning soldiers reintegrated into civilian life, Roosevelt sought to hold the nation together through a common cause: economic rights.[34]

Roosevelt's description of these reforms was not just an outreach to the country's neglected and underserved groups but to the those who enjoyed traditional social advantages too. Soldiers across the board were nervous about the postwar order. White soldiers wondered if their jobs, now filled by women and minorities previously excluded from those opportunities, would be waiting for them. Black soldiers, who fought in a still segregated and deeply racist military, worried about what a homecoming meant for them as well. Langston Hughes, channeling these fears, wrote:

The Presidents Four Freedoms
Appeal to me.
I would like to see those Freedoms
Come to be.

If you believe
In the Four Freedoms, too,
Then share 'em with me—
Don't keep em all for you . . .

Freedom's not just
To be won Over There.
It means Freedom at home too—
Now—right here.[35]

Writing in July 1943, John Steinbeck—who traveled to Europe as a war correspondent for the *New York Tribune*—noted that the soldiers knew that "the destruction of the enemy is not the end of this war." The soldiers had a bigger concern: "a fear of what is going to happen after the war." Steinbeck reported that soldiers' letters home were full of anxiety. These were men raised in the Great Depression. They had never known freedom from want and were not, as Steinbeck described them, "a naïve Army." Would economic security be waiting for them, or would the fight continue on the home front, this time against the rich and powerful, or invisible enemies like inflation, which would erode "the $50 a month" they subsisted on?[36]

Roosevelt couldn't have been more outwardly serious about delivering for the soldiers and solidifying these rights for all Americans. His actions during the war reflected a postwar vision for a more prosperous and just nation, a nation where everyone—and notably, Roosevelt's words spoke of *everyone* in America—benefited from the fruits of the country's collective labor and resources. An economic bill of rights would ensure that no longer would the bankers of Wall Street and the titans of industry live in extravagance while their workers, subject to interminable workdays and gruesome conditions, remained mired in poverty. No longer would some elusive free market hold the American people hostage. People were meant to be free, and *that* meant quality living standards for everyone, full employment for everyone, health care for everyone, and security for everyone, especially those—the young, the elderly, the sick—who were unfit to work. Markets would be leveraged to serve people, not the other way around.

While Roosevelt's economic bill of rights placed but one of his four freedoms, freedom from want, at center stage, he acknowledged that the four freedoms were "eternally linked" to one another. The failure of Reconstruction proved how deeply intertwined civil rights and economic rights were. Political freedom was meaningless when people were penniless, landless, and hungry, yes; but economic security without democracy could result in fascism, or worse. At the conclusion of his 1944 State of the Union address, Roosevelt committed to asking "the Congress to explore the means of implementing this Economic Bill of Rights—for it is definitely the responsibility of the Congress so to do."[37] Despite polling showing economic rights were widely popular among the American people—according to one poll, 73 percent of Americans supported the idea that the federal government should guarantee a job to anyone in need of work, and 85 percent supported national health care coverage—Roosevelt was fully cognizant that achieving these goals would be an uphill battle, as substantial power still resided in the hands of business and weary southerners.[38]

The culmination of his decade-long project to redefine American freedom, Roosevelt's economic bill of rights was his clearest statement yet on the basic positive rights owed to the American people. Through the fulfillment of these rights, rights that Roosevelt wanted solidified through legislation, society would be woven together as one. All would benefit from the richness of the land and the collective engine that was the American economy. By vanquishing economic insecurity, all people would be whole enough to participate fully in the democratic project of America.

The freedom from want encapsulated in Roosevelt's economic bill of rights was not to be. Roosevelt died in Warm Springs, Georgia, at his retreat known as the Little White House, just over a year after his public call for economic rights.

Roosevelt saved America from the brink of disaster, helped win the bloodiest conflict the world has ever known, and moved the nation a great deal closer to true freedom. Without Roosevelt, the country may have, in the words of longtime Roosevelt adviser, Rexford Tugwell, "succumbed to a dictatorship."[39] (Homegrown demagogues, including Father Charles Coughlin and Huey Long, were ever present antagonists.) But for all FDR's triumphs, it is important also to note his missteps, many of which had, and have had, grave consequences.

FDR's greatest failure was his sacrificing of civil rights on the altar of economic reforms.[40] During Roosevelt's twelve years in office, he never seriously challenged the rule of Jim Crow. The progressive potential of the New Deal was throttled by what the historian Ira Katznelson calls the "southern cage," a cage Roosevelt didn't dare rattle. By cutting a deal with southern segregationists to exclude Black people from many of the New Deal initiatives (in the name of passing New Deal initiatives for others), Roosevelt reinforced and deepened racial inequality. Because Dixiecrats wielded veto power over Roosevelt's agenda, he continually bowed to their demands. For example, Roosevelt refused repeatedly to support antilynching legislation despite the fact that, in the first year of his presidency alone, twenty-eight Black lives were taken by lynching. Katznelson describes the brutal violence Whites imposed on Blacks, violence Roosevelt did nothing stop:

> In November, one year after FDR's election, Lloyd Warner was burned alive before a cheering crowd of ten thousand in Princess Anne, Maryland, after the attempt to hang him had failed. David Gregory was lynched in Kountze, Texas, his body burned and his heart and genitals carved from his corpse. Cord Cheek of Columbia, Tennessee, was found hanging from a tree limb after a grand jury had refused to indict him for molesting an eleven-year-old white girl. Freddy Moore was killed in Assumption Parish, Louisiana, for the murder of a white girl (another man, who was white, later admitted to the killing).[41]

During the war, the contradiction of fighting for the four freedoms abroad while they were neglected at home, especially for Black Americans, did not go unnoticed. Those within the Black civil rights movement who supported the war were committed to the "Double V": victory abroad against fascism and the Nazis and victory at home against Jim Crow.

Freedoms were withheld from others too under FDR. Internment camps imprisoned 112,000 people of Japanese ancestry, 79,000 of whom were American citizens. And despite the genocide of European Jewry, Roosevelt failed to increase the quota of Jewish refugees allowed to enter the country. America's denial of access for human beings fleeing the horrors across the ocean was one of many stains on the administration's legacy.

In terms of securing the future of his economic project, one of Roosevelt's biggest missteps was his failure to support Vice President Henry Wallace's place on the ticket during the 1944 Democratic National Convention. Wallace, the son of a prominent Iowa farming family, first served the administration as a wildly successful secretary of agriculture. From that post, Wallace had led one of the New Deal's most ambitious attempts to democratize economic planning, joining small farmers and economists to coordinate the nation's agricultural and land-use policies. Proving to be one of most "luminous liberals" in the administration (in the words of the New Deal historian Alan Brinkley), Wallace joined Roosevelt on the Democratic ticket in 1940. While conservative Democratic officials resisted Wallace's nomination, Roosevelt forced the party to accept his progressive running mate during his bid for a third term by threatening to withdraw unless Wallace accompanied him on the ticket.[42]

Wallace came to office a staunch supporter of the New Deal and used his clout within the administration to champion progressive causes. A stalwart anti-imperialist and advocate of universal civil and economic rights, Wallace inflamed both Wall Street and Southern Dixiecrats with his resounding calls for equality. "Century of the Common Man," his best-known speech, delivered in 1942, spoke of World War II as a great battle between the free world—the world that guarded Roosevelt's four freedoms—and the slave world. The fight was over the very freedom for the common man. Wallace believed that "men and women cannot be really free until they have plenty to eat, and time and ability to read and think and talk things over." For democracy to work, people needed not only food and education, but free time to choose to engage actively in the democratic process itself.[43]

Unsurprisingly given this pedigree—and his vocal opposition to Jim Crow—Wallace was not greatly beloved by the conservative elements in his party. At the Democratic Party Convention in 1944, the Dixiecrats mounted an effort to oust him from the presidential ticket. Despite a Gallup poll that year that showed 65 percent of Democrats stood behind Wallace for vice president, the ailing Roosevelt declined to fight for his vice president. He weakly endorsed Wallace publicly but later met with party leaders to agree on a compromise replacement: Harry Truman. Roosevelt had, in the end, "bowed to reactionaries."[44]

While the first round of ballots at the convention went strongly for Wallace, party leaders corralled their troops and pushed them to switch to the compromise choice. Truman's nomination for vice president was secured on the second ballot. A coup had effectively taken place, and with Wallace went the progressive future America might have known.[45]

Civil Rights Are Economic Rights

Perhaps no American figure is as admired as Dr. Martin Luther King Jr. America celebrates a national holiday in his name to remember his teachings and legacy. Every American child learns about his long, nonviolent fight for civil rights, a battle that began with the Montgomery Bus Boycott in 1955. Most US cities have a park or street named in his honor. In 2011 Washington, DC, opened the Martin Luther King Jr. Memorial, located at the center of the triangle created by the Washington, Lincoln, and Roosevelt Memorials. But the King most know and celebrate is, at best, a partial one. He's lauded, rightly, for being a nonviolent champion of civil rights and one of the great orators and public consciences of our time. But this official King comes at the expense of the more political Kings: the progressive King, the socialist King, the King who fought and died for the cause of universal economic rights.

In August 1967, King delivered his final presidential address to the Southern Christian Leadership Conference (SCLC). King expressed his belief that it was time for the civil rights movement to embrace a new phase in the fight for freedom, one that required measures beyond those that had delivered the Voting Rights Act of 1965. Black Americans had won the right to vote, a tremendous victory; but, as King saw, the vote was insufficient to secure Black Americans' freedom. And not only Black Americans': King saw poor Whites, poor Hispanics—poor *people* of every race and creed—being denied the fundamental freedoms the Founders had promised them. He dreamt of the ultimate fulfillment of that foundational promise—a country where all lived in comfort and dignity. But a truly free America required more than reform; it required posing the "question of restructuring the whole of American society."[46]

In his speech to SCLC, King pivoted from talking about the long denial of civil rights to the long denial of economic rights: "There are forty million poor people here, and one day we must ask the question, 'Why are there forty million poor people in America?'" There was nothing natural, King argued, about so great a number of people living in economic straits. He characterized poverty in the United States not as the will of God but rather as the outcome of the economic system—"the capitalistic economy"—that policy makers had empowered to reign over the nation.[47] He likewise rejected the core tenet of capitalism, namely, that people's value can be reduced to their wealth or productivity on the job. Further, he recognized that a market-based economy not only condoned discrimination but also *necessitated* a substantial mass of poor people (what Marx had called the reserve army of unemployed).

To remedy these injustices, King called for a broader distribution of wealth to tame the market. But even if that were attained, greater economic equality wouldn't be enough. Rather, what was needed was fundamental structural reform. For King, Johnson's Great Society programs had been timid and piecemeal; the president's agenda had left too many people economically insecure, wasting what King called "the potential of the individual" and the nation. King called on his fellow civil rights leaders to help him build and harness the power to create the "social, political, and economic change" they sought. He argued that the issues of racism, discrimination, and oppression— issues that had been central to the civil rights movement from day one—were inseparable from the problem of economic inequality and insecurity. The evils were intertwined. Political reforms had been won, indeed, but meaningful political freedom necessitated economic freedom, and vice versa.[48]

King's career turn toward economic causes came after his contributions to two legislative triumphs: the passage of the 1964 Civil Rights Act and the 1965 Voting Rights Act. This was not, however, a pivot: the fight for economic rights had always been part and parcel of the demand for civil rights. For evidence, one need look no further than the man King called the "dean of Negro leaders": A. Philip Randolph.

Born in Crescent City, Florida, in 1889, Randolph was the founder of the Brotherhood of the Sleeping Car Porters (BSCP), one of the first trade unions led by Black workers. After twelve years of organizing, the union won recognition in 1935, becoming the first Black-led union to win a contract with a White employer and the first Black-led union to earn a charter with the American Federation of Labor. It would be two more years before the BSCP would secure the first collective bargaining agreement with the Pullman Company—the first time in US history that a union of Black workers would strike a bargaining agreement with a major US employer—providing sizable pay increases and significant reductions in work hours.

After leading the BSCP through its struggle for a fair contract, Randolph turned his attention to the defense industry, an employment sector flush with cash from war production but demonstrably resistant to hiring Black employees. To press the case for Black workers, he organized the 1941 March on Washington Movement, a campaign focused on improving job opportunities for Black Americans. Before the March on Washington could actually take place, however, President Roosevelt issued Executive Order 8802, which prohibited discrimination in defense firms under federal contract and created the Fair Employment Practice Committee to purge discrimination from federal agencies, unions, and all war-related work. Once these concessions were made, the march was called off—but only because Executive Order 8802 resulted in real material improvement in people's lives.

His belief that "social and political freedom must be rooted in economic freedom" was dear to Randolph, who with Bayard Rustin was an organizer of the 1963 March on Washington—the full title of which was the March on Washington *for Jobs and Freedom* (my emphasis).[49] The march brought a quarter of a million Americans to the nation's capital to demand jobs and freedom. It would prove to be a defining moment in the history of the civil rights movement and the nation, one that forced the country to confront the continued denial of freedom—defined by its leaders as comprising both political and economic rights—to large swaths of the population.[50]

During the event, King delivered his celebrated "I Have a Dream" speech. Cornel West, in his introduction to *The Radical King*, a collection of King's most left-leaning work, writes that King's dream was "neither a black face in the White House nor a black presence on Wall Street. Rather, the fulfillment of his dream was for all poor and working people to live lives of decency and dignity."[51] King and fellow civil rights leaders, Randolph and Rustin primary among them, articulated how the dominant economic order of the day couldn't bring this dream to fruition. The true full employment at living wages they were fighting for—the universal economic security they demanded—would require a democratic economic system that put individual and collective needs first and ended the subordination of people to markets once and for all. Having cracked the foundation of Jim Crow, the civil rights movement was increasingly pivoting toward the future, a future whose brightness depended on the country's recognition that "the central problem" was not just "one of civil rights but of economic rights."[52]

The civil rights movement's fight for economic rights would culminate in *A "Freedom Budget" for All Americans*. Published by the A. Philip Randolph Institute, led by Randolph and Rustin, the Freedom Budget represented "a moral commitment to the fundamental principles on which this nation was founded"—that is, the American tradition of positive rights. The budget was coordinated by Rustin and drafted mainly by the New Deal economists Leon Keyersling—who was assisted by civil rights strategists including Vivian Henderson and Tom Kahn— and Gerhard Colm, along with a number of AFL-CIO staff members. (King was also involved, providing a foreword.) Randolph unveiled the Freedom Budget at the White House in 1966, as honorary chair of the aptly named conference "To Fulfill These Rights."[53]

Comprising a list of seven demands, the Freedom Budget was meant to reorient the budget of the United States toward the provision of all people's basic needs: housing, employment, education, nutrition, medical care, and clean air and water. According to the budget's drafters, the federal government already had the real resources— Hamilton's "means proper"—necessary to rid the land of poverty; all that was needed was the political will.[54]

The budget also signaled civil rights leaders' move toward reforms with cross-racial appeal. In the foreword to the budget, King extolled the virtues of universal programs. True freedom, for King, could not be obtained solely through a program for Black America or White America; what was needed was a program to wash away the poverty and inequality that stained the nation for *all* America: "We shall eliminate slums for Negroes when we destroy ghettos and build new cities for *all*. We shall eliminate unemployment for Negroes when we demand full and fair employment for *all*. We shall produce an educated and skilled Negro mass when we achieve a twentieth century education system for *all*."[55]

Purposely echoing Roosevelt's economic bill of rights (in his conference speech, Randolph noted that "poverty is not only a private tragedy but, in a sense, a public crime") the Freedom Budget demanded that government allocate spending as follows:

1. To provide *full employment* for all who are willing and able to work, including those who need education or training to make them willing and able;
2. To assure *decent and adequate* wages to all who work;
3. To assure a *decent living standard* to those who cannot or should not work;
4. To *wipe out slum ghettos* and provide decent homes for all Americans;
5. To provide *decent medical care and adequate educational opportunities* to all Americans, at a cost they can afford;
6. To *purify our air and water* and develop our transportation and natural resources on a scale suitable to our growing needs; and
7. To unite sustained full employment with sustained *full production and high economic growth*.[56]

Implicit in the budget's points is a fact of modern life and economy: *scarcity is a policy choice*. Poverty is not inevitable; it does not stem from society having access to too few homes, too little food, or too few jobs; rather, poverty is a creation of the rules that govern the economy. It is state sanctioned, and so with *different* policy choices, it can be abolished.

The Freedom Budget brought together "rights, religious, and labor leaders" in a way not seen since the March on Washington a few years before. Its plan was for mass mobilization. Thousands of copies of the Freedom Budget were distributed to policy makers, religious organizations, labor and civil rights groups, and students across the country. Yet the plan failed to gain traction. The Vietnam War, which was raging at the time, divided the Left. Facing the mounting costs of the war, Johnson had already begun to tap the brakes on his Great Society. Further, King and others had come out as ardent opponents of the war effort, a divisive stance at the time. Perhaps it was just bad timing. Perhaps the country just wasn't ready for the Freedom Budget.[57]

Its failure to launch notwithstanding, the budget had given King new direction. He spent most of 1967 planning the Poor People's Campaign, which he envisioned as a multiracial march of a million poor people on the Capitol. Although the Freedom Budget hadn't gained the traction he hoped, he kept the faith that "the right to get the basic necessities of life" could be achieved.

The demands of the Poor People's Campaign hewed closely to those of the Freedom Budget. They included the "right to have three square meals a day[,] . . . [t]he right to have a decent house to live in[,] . . . [t]he right to be able to educate our children[, and] . . . [t]he right to get proper medical care." And King was committed to radical action to get Washington to listen. He, along with the Southern Christian Leadership Conference, was prepared to go to Washington and occupy the Capitol until their demands were met.[58]

The occupation wasn't to be. On April 4, 1968, mere weeks before the Poor People's March, King was fatally shot outside his hotel room in Memphis, Tennessee, where he had been fighting for the rights of striking sanitation workers. He was just thirty-nine years old. He would never occupy the Capitol in solidarity with his poor brothers and sisters; he would never break bread with the residents of Resurrection City on the National Mall; and he would never achieve his goal of ending poverty and securing economic rights for all by ending the long reign of the "free" market.

King's last written work, published posthumously, was the essay, "We Need an Economic Bill of Rights." Drafted in preparation for the Poor People's Campaign, King was at pains to make the movement's demands clear. Echoing Roosevelt's call for freedom from want, King demanded a job guarantee to eliminate unemployment once and for all; an income guarantee to provide economic security for those unable to work; public works projects, including the buildout of public housing and necessary investment in high-quality schools for all; and more. King was not merely calling for civil rights; King was not merely calling for an expanded welfare state; King was not merely calling for more food and medical care. King was demanding economic rights—freedom from want—for all. For economic rights, combined with civil rights, would deliver those "unalienable rights" on which America was founded.[59]

The loss of yet another tribune for economic rights wouldn't end the fight for them. Freedom from want was far too powerful an idea to succumb to the passing of Roosevelt, and it was not about to be consigned to the dustbin of history with the assassination of King.[60] The struggle for economic rights would continue to be championed by the likes of Huey P. Newton and Bobby Seale, who, in the Black Panther Party's Ten-Point Program—the party's platform—demanded "land, bread, housing, education, clothing, justice and peace." In short, they wanted a right to a job for those who could work, a guaranteed income for those who couldn't, and far greater community control over the means of production.[61]

Reviving Economic Rights

From 1944 to 1988, the right to employment was a cornerstone of the Democratic Party's policy platform. But the catastrophe of the Vietnam War and the fracturing of the Democratic coalition in the South forced Democrats to retreat from their New Deal principles. The Democratic Party's last stand for bold progressive change—at least until Bernie Sanders's historic 2016 presidential campaign—would go down in flames in 1972, with Senator George McGovern's electoral drubbing by Nixon. The party of the New Deal was broken.

Although Democrats had been in retreat from the New Deal for well over a decade, it wasn't until Senator Gary Hart, who was the front-runner for the 1988 Democratic presidential nomination before dropping out amid a sex scandal, that the final link was severed. Hart ran on breaking the party's tie to Roosevelt, arguing for regressive tax reform, worker training rather than employment assurance, and expanding the reach of the market, all the while leaning on a stump speech provocatively titled "The End of the New Deal." By then, Democrats stood neither for Roosevelt's four freedoms nor for an extension of the New Deal to manage capitalism and tame markets. As the previous chapter demonstrated, neoliberalism—the abiding faith in a market ordering of society—dominated political discourse and policy making in the 1980s and 1990s, counting not only Republicans but New Democrats as well among its believers. To these New Democrats, inequality was simply the price Americans had to pay for robust economic growth. Job loss was natural—indeed, a sign of a well-functioning, dynamic labor market—and would shake out in the aggregate (especially if the safety net was threadbare enough to incentivize people to search hard for jobs). As a result of the bipartisan belief in neoliberalism, the fight for economic rights would move outside Washington's halls of power. For the next twenty years, as the American economy seemed to be on a permanent upward trajectory, demands for economic rights were marginal in the public debate.[62]

They returned in earnest in 2008. As unemployment skyrocketed, markets crashed, and homes were foreclosed on by the millions, public faith in the power of the market was again shaken to the core. Even the former Federal Reserve chair, Alan Greenspan, one of the most ardent supporters of the free-market system, admitted during congressional testimony that he had "found a flaw" in the economic ideology he and fellow neoliberal proponents had been championing. He had made a "mistake" in allowing markets to run amok, though he couldn't say how deep the fault line went.

While policy makers fumbled trying to figure out what went wrong with capitalism and how to fix it, the Left began to organize. In fall 2011, activists gathered in New York's Zuccotti Park to launch Occupy Wall Street. The self-proclaimed "99%" occupied the downtown public space in protest of the Reagan Revolution, the New Democrats and their embrace of neoliberalism (including the rebranded version embodied in President Obama's "Yes We Can" message), and an economic structure that put profits before human beings. "We are the 99%," was their rallying cry, and they were demanding a new system, one that embedded the economy in society. This iteration of the resurgent Left framed the market as Roosevelt had: as means to deliver on democratically decided ends. They called to subordinate the economy to politics rather than letting concerns about short-term profit maximization and shareholder value keep people's political dreams and aspirations in check.

Within weeks, the Occupy movement spread across the nation and the globe. Hundreds of cities featured occupations, and dozens of countries saw citizens rebel against the repressive nature of the existing economic order.

Criticisms of Occupy emerged from the media and from liberal elites, who criticized the movement for lacking a clear demand or set of demands. Occupy protesters wanted change, but what did that change look like? Where was their ten-point plan? This wasn't a question that could be answered in a general assembly meeting—or even a dozen of them. It was *the* question. How should society be reorganized? How can the economy be structured to help people achieve dignified, secure, stable, and fulfilling lives?

These questions posed were not limited to, nor did they end with, the Occupy movement. While the occupation of Zuccotti Park would not last, dozens of social movements, from Black Lives Matter to Moral Mondays to the Fight for $15, arose from a revived Left. This new Left reinvigorated old conceptions of freedom, including the demand for economic rights, an end to structural racism, and justice and dignity for people of all colors, creeds, and sexual orientations.

Although today's intellectual successors to Occupy are many, they are identifiable in their fight for a more just and inclusive society that delivers universal economic security and abolishes poverty once and for all—in short, economic rights. Black Lives Matter fights not only for racial justice but also for a jobs program, the right to unionize, a basic income, environmental justice, and economic justice where communities have "collective ownership." The Black Youth Project demands a job guarantee, living wages, economic security for all despite employment status, and more. In their *Freedom Papers*, the Dream Defenders—a group focused on abolishing the police and ending incarceration—declares that "a proper home, clothes, food, healthcare, and work are rights."[63] The Poor People's Campaign, which has undergone a revival under the leadership of Reverend William Barber II, demands a federal program to deliver "full employment as a right," living wages, unions, housing for all, and more. And the Democratic Socialists of America have swelled their ranks while successfully running candidates, and winning public offices, from local elections to the US Congress. After decades on the fringes, the American Left has been reborn.

And its demands are once again getting the attention of policy makers. The insurgent 2016 presidential campaign of Senator Bernie Sanders brought the fight for economic rights back into the national spotlight. In two speeches, one in 2015 at Georgetown University and one in June 2019 at George Washington University, Sanders defined his vision of democratic socialism and the future of America. He told the crowds:

> Now, we must take the next step forward and guarantee every man, woman and child in our country basic economic rights—the right to quality health care, the right to as much education as one needs to succeed in our society, the right to a good job that pays a living wage, the right to affordable housing, the right to a secure retirement, and the right to live in a clean environment. We must recognize that in the 21st century, in the wealthiest country in the history of the world,

economic rights are human rights. That is what I mean by democratic socialism.[64]

Is Sanders's version of democratic socialism indeed socialism? No. Socialism entails democratic ownership of the means of production. But in establishing and mainstreaming a social democratic vision for economic rights, one rooted in American history, Sanders has forged a public path to thinking in such terms.

Sanders's intent in these two addresses was clear. Roosevelt had died before he was able to solidify economic rights into law, thus leaving "our job," as Sanders told supporters, "to complete what Roosevelt started." The senator went on to propose a Twenty-First-Century Economic Bill of Rights, one that included the right to a job at a living wage, the right to medical care, the right to an education, the right to housing, the right to retirement, and—vitally for a time of ongoing environmental calamities—the right to a clean and *stable* environment. In his speeches, Sanders embedded economic rights as the core of civil rights. Racism, sexism, discrimination, economic insecurity, runaway inequality, and endangered voting rights are not discrete issues: these are the results sown over decades and centuries of systematically denying freedom.

After speaking engagingly of an economic bill of rights in these campaign speeches, Sanders wouldn't champion the idea regularly on the campaign trail or the debate stage. He spoke instead of creating "an economy and government which works for all Americans, and not just the one percent." He spoke of a society rooted in "economic justice, social justice, racial justice and environmental justice." And he spoke about the individual issues, including the right to health care ("Health care is a right, not a privilege") and the right to housing, frequently. But he backed away from earlier calls for economic rights and justice or a comprehensive vision that tied the individual policies together. Instead Sanders spoke of European successes in building miraculous welfare states. To be sure, digging into America's past—especially in front of a crowd at a political rally—is complex and challenging. The country has a deeply racist, sexist, and xenophobic history. But Sanders had an unprecedented opportunity to assume the mantle of Roosevelt and King—and chose not to.

On April 8, 2020, Bernie Sanders ended his second—and likely final—bid for the presidency. Although he would not occupy the highest office in the land, his campaigns succeeded in reinvigorating and expanding the American Left, which for the first time in well over a generation has started to amass real power. From Representative Alexandria Ocasio-Cortez—herself a former volunteer organizer on Sanders's 2016 campaign—to Representatives Pramila Jayapal, Jamaal Bowman, Cori Bush, Mondaire Jones, Ilhan Omar, Ayanna Presley, and Rashida Tlaib, the US legislature after the Sanders campaigns looks far different from what it looked like before: a core of progressive policy makers is demanding economic change. Sanders and the "Squad" moved the discussion beyond marginal tweaks to the existing tax system and welfare state; their conversations are about the type of transformative change needed to avert climate disaster and end poverty, unemployment, and persistent economic insecurity in one of the richest nations ever to have existed.

Advocates of economic rights, from FDR to King to others today, have conceded, even promised, that delivering economic rights requires a significant restructuring of the economy. Big questions are at stake, and ensuring universal economic security is no mean feat. It isn't just about running the economy hotter through more economic growth, as many modern macroeconomists contend (though that is a necessary condition). Nor is the solution simply to adopt FDR's economic bill of rights. Rather, the rights Roosevelt enumerated must be updated to fit the challenges society faces in the twenty-first century. That means that some of the rights Roosevelt championed, like farmers' right to a fair income (a right that should most certainly be guaranteed) can be deemphasized,[65] while other rights, such as the right to a safe and clean environment, are more pressing. We must continue to ask how the government can best deliver freedom from want. This is the question I turn to now.

Part II

Economic Rights

4

The Right to Work

He hated unemployment because it was stupid.
JOAN ROBINSON ON JOHN MAYNARD KEYNES

On May 22, 1933—seventy-nine days into Roosevelt's "First Hundred Days" (a phrase Roosevelt himself coined)—Harry Hopkins was summoned to the nation's capital. An Iowa boy from modest means, Hopkins grew up working on the family farm and delivering the morning paper to help his parents make ends meet. After graduating from Grinnell College in 1912, where he majored in history and political science and absorbed the school's ideals of democracy and public service, he headed to New York to begin a career as a counselor in a social settlement house for young boys. Over the ensuing years, Hopkins became intimately familiar with the horrors brought on by urban poverty. The solution to these horrors, at least as far as Hopkins saw it, was simple: people needed economic security; in fact, they had a *right* to it.

The question, though, was how to provide it. Prior to the Great Depression and the social policies that it launched, the delivery of assistance to the poor fell to religious organizations and private philanthropy. The federal government, especially under Hoover, had little interest in aiding the needy. The economic realm, after all, was located squarely in the private sphere.[1]

Harry Hopkins thought differently and set out to change it. In his view, government existed to serve the people; and, as a social worker, he was committed to lending a helping hand to those in need. Though he was a modest man, he had a big dream—"that poverty in America is abolished."[2] To achieve this goal, though, he knew he would need some semblance of power. A social worker could meaningfully improve individuals' lives on a daily basis—as important a responsibility as one could find—but to effect the social changes that were necessary to end poverty once and for all, public office was essential.

In 1933 Hopkins got his shot. He was tapped to run the Federal Emergency Relief Administration, President Roosevelt's first major initiative to help the destitute during the dark days of the depression. With the nation in crisis and facing ballooning poverty, Roosevelt needed an adviser to shepherd struggling Americans toward jobs and assistance, fast. Hopkins, who had transitioned from social work to social policy administrator, including administrator of New York's Temporary Emergency Relief Administration during Roosevelt's time as governor, was the president's man.

Hopkins's first objective was to get money—and lots of it—out the door and into workers' hands. He remarked that "when a house is on fire, you don't call a conference, you put it out." The Great Depression was the biggest inferno anyone had ever seen, and the extinguisher would be public works. The idea was straightforward: the federal government would provide millions of jobs on public works projects at prevailing wages for those without work. No means testing—the process by which governments measure citizens' eligibility for social benefits—just fair work at fair wages.

On November 9, 1933, Roosevelt signed Executive Order 6420B to create the experimental Civil Works Administration. Within a week, Hopkins had a plan to present to the nation. Within a month, the program was launched. Within two months, the program was fully operational, directly employing four million Americans—nearly one in ten workers across the nation. Its rollout alone was an astonishing accomplishment.

The program of dispensing wages and jobs wherever they were needed lasted only four months. In that brief span, the CWA and its workers would leave a lasting mark on the nation. People employed through the CWA built or improved 40,000 schools, nearly 1,000 airports, 255,000 miles of road, 12 million feet of sewer pipe, and 3,700 playgrounds. But it wasn't all traditional construction work; CWA employed thousands of writers and artists to make public art for schools, libraries, orphanages, town squares, post offices, and many other places where citizens congregate. Hopkins also created a dedicated Civil Works Service to employ women as administrators and support staff in relief agencies (Hopkins called on his staff to "pay particular attention that women are employed whenever possible," though women's work was often kept separate from men's).[3]

The goal of the CWA wasn't only to provide meaningful employment at wages that would keep a roof over people's heads and food on the table; it was also to produce socially meaningful goods and services for the country. For instance, in addition to the physical and aesthetic improvements noted above, Hopkins procured over 250,000 surplus bales of cotton through the Agricultural Adjustment Act and put women to work transforming them into mattresses—mattresses that were then distributed for free to those without a bed. In Bay City, Michigan, after an underwear factory employing 250 people went bankrupt due to the precipitous decline in consumer spending, the CWA intervened. The plant was rented and reopened, and the 250 employees were put back to work making underwear. Two pairs for the winter would be sent out, free of charge, to every family in need throughout Michigan. Time and time again, the CWA put people to work to build critical infrastructure, provide arts and entertainment, and help people secure the basic needs for a modest quality of life in the midst of unprecedented crisis.[4]

But CWA jobs weren't just a means to stabilize families financially; they were meant to restore the dignity of American workers and make a positive impact in workers' communities. Reflecting on a trip around the nation to evaluate the CWA in action, Frank Walker, president of the National Emergency Council, reported seeing old friends from school digging ditches and laying sewer pipe. One of his old friends told him, "This is the first money I've had in my pocket in a year and a half." Walker noted that the men took a great deal of pride in their work. The job wasn't only about money, but the sense of fulfillment one gained contributing to the wealth of the nation. The CWA attempted to forestall the workers thinking they were "charity cases" by, whenever possible, employing people in jobs that closely resembled their previous work and experience and that paid them prevailing wages.

The CWA was wildly successful. Its time was cut short not by a belief that its work was done or its efficacy poor but based on the wishes of conservative Democrats in Congress. The floor in the labor market created by the CWA—that is, the ubiquity of work for those who needed it—had proven too threatening for the Dixiecrats in the South and their business-friendly northern allies, both of whom were reliant on cheap and plentiful labor. The fear that workers would become accustomed to well-paying, quality public employment was real. According to these critics, the creation of jobs directly by government to eliminate unemployment would permanently weaken the class position of employers, threatening the power they maintained over workers: power that kept wages low, padded profits, and ensured that the bosses always had the upper hand. Further, with fewer unemployed people, unions would be dealt a stronger hand, as strikebreakers would be harder to come by. Conservatives were dead set against government competing with private industry for jobs. (This was, it bears mentioning, neither what was happening nor the intent of the program; rather, private industry simply had shown that it was incapable of hiring the nearly one in four people who were unemployed.) Nevertheless, Roosevelt caved. Though deeply troubled by the decision, Hopkins obeyed orders and helped wind down the program.

While the CWA lasted, there had been, in essence, a public option in employment. It's a precedent worth recalling.

Made to Measure: Why Unemployment Persists

The CWA gave people a taste of the government's ability to manage some of the most inhumane aspects of market economies, especially unemployment. Given that the vast majority of people work in order to pay for life's essentials and amusements, denying them access to well-paying employment, along with a say in their workplace, amounts to a denial of the fundamental American rights to life, liberty, and the pursuit of happiness. Today, the right to work, which for Roosevelt and Hopkins meant the right to a useful and remunerative job and the right to earn enough for adequate food and clothing and recreation, is regularly withheld from far too many, resulting in despair, poverty, and, not uncommonly, death.

Involuntary unemployment—people out of work despite wanting and seeking a living-wage job—remains a constant in the US economy. In fact, unemployment and underemployment are central features of today's labor market; they persist even in moments of historically strong market conditions. For example, on the eve of the COVID-19 crisis in January 2020, when headline unemployment dipped to 3.5 percent—a generational low—5.8 million people (by conventional measures) were still without work. Using broader measures of unemployment—the U-6, for example, which includes part-time workers who would like full-time work and those who are "marginally attached" to the "labor force" (as the Labor Department narrowly defines it)—an additional 5.8 million people were unemployed or underemployed. That's over 10 million Americans involuntarily unemployed or underemployed.

On top of these numbers, there are millions more workers who have left the labor force entirely due to persisting unemployment. From 2000 to the eve of the COVID-19 crisis, the labor market participation rate—the percentage of the civilian noninstitutional population above the age of sixteen that is working or actively looking for work—fell from over 67 percent to 63.4 percent. This type of mass exit from the labor force, a substantial portion of which was concentrated among workers in their prime working years, is a key sign of persistently weak labor markets. With few quality jobs to be had, wages stagnated and many workers simply gave up job hunting. The result was a lost decade for workers following the Great Recession—a recession that saw unemployment skyrocket into the double digits, effectively eliminating opportunities for tens of millions.

There are just too few good jobs. An international comparison of labor markets underscores the point. The US employment-to-population ratio—another measure that helps economists gauge slack in the labor market—falls well behind many other Organization for Economic Cooperation and Development (OECD) countries. Why? A dearth of quality jobs that allow people to earn a good living while maintaining work-life balance. In fact, the employment rate in the United States lags behind countries like Germany, Sweden, and Norway by an average of 8 percentage points, which translates into more than 16 million fewer Americans working.[5] The gap in people's ability to participate in the labor market is especially pronounced for women, in no small part due to the absence of adequate care policies—childcare, parental leave, eldercare—in the United States. Since care work disproportionately falls on women, they're simply forced out of the labor force—denied the opportunity to work. The amount of wasted human potential, and the economic hardship caused by the scarcity of good jobs, is hard to comprehend.

Other labor market indicators tell a similar story: too many workers chasing too few jobs. For the past twenty years, the US Bureau of Labor Statistics (BLS) has been publishing data on a job-seekers ratio, which shows the number of unemployed people per job opening in the economy.[6] From 2001, when the BLS started publishing the job-seekers ratio, to 2020, there were on average 2.4 people looking for work per job opening—and this is a conservative estimate. Of course, this ratio also includes the millions of extremely low-wage jobs on offer, many without benefits.[7] Broad and persistent unemployment isn't a matter of people pulling themselves up by their bootstraps. There just aren't enough good-paying jobs to go around.

The real scandal of the US labor market is that, in economic terms, weak labor markets aren't an accident; they exist by design. As the Polish economist Michal Kalecki pointed out in his classic 1943 essay, "Political Aspects of Full Employment," maintaining some baseline unemployment keeps power in the hands of employers, because it reduces the fallback position of workers and limits the power of unions. By preserving a pool of unemployed workers, employers maintain the upper hand in the workplace. With sidelined workers at the ready, employers can feel confident in their ability to mistreat—and underpay—workers. The result is stagnant wages and precarity, especially for those at the low end of the labor market. And as Kalecki wrote, "It is true that profits would be higher under a regime of full employment. . . . But 'discipline in the factories' and 'political stability' are more appreciated than profits by business leaders."[8]

Employer power—the power to squeeze more work out of people, pay them lower wages, slash benefits, and treat them as if they are less than human—only grows during economic downturns. As unemployment climbs, workers' fallback positions evaporate. No longer can they so easily secure another job if things aren't working out in their current workplace. They're left with a Hobson's choice: either give employers what they want or get in the unemployment line (a line, it so happens, that's intentionally laden with booby traps and administrative pitfalls).[9]

An extreme form of deteriorating labor conditions was on display during the economic catastrophe associated with the COVID-19 pandemic, when tens of millions were thrown out of work, saw take-home pay slashed, or were put in danger without hazard pay. In one California poultry plant, unsafe working conditions led to a major COVID-19 outbreak, killing eight workers and infecting hundreds. When cities like Seattle passed hazard-pay mandates during the crisis—ensuring frontline workers were compensated somewhat for the extra risks they were taking—employers such as the grocery store chain Kroger (which was seeing record profits at the time) responded by closing stores and laying people off rather than cut modestly into its profit margin. The message from private industry was clear: profits over people.[10]

But it isn't just employers that create the imbalances of the US labor market; monetary policy too serves to entrench unemployment. The Federal Reserve, the central bank of the United States charged with maintaining price stability and maximum employment, maintains a curious notion of what full employment means. To the layperson, "full employment" connotes something like a 0 percent unemployment rate—a scenario in which everyone who wants a job has a job or in which there are more jobs available than workers. The Fed, as well as mainstream economists and some government agencies, has defined full employment as "an economy in which the unemployment rate equals the nonaccelerating inflation rate of unemployment (NAIRU) and output is at its potential." (Perhaps unsurprisingly, this is an idea popularized by Milton Friedman.) In plain language, for American policy makers, full employment is whatever level of employment happens to coincide with stable prices.

Underlying this use of the NAIRU is a quiet assumption—that inflation will accelerate if unemployment falls below the NAIRU. This assumption follows from the theory that an unemployment rate below the NAIRU could cause what economists call a wage-price spiral—an unstable economic situation in which prices increase to meet rising wages, resulting in a significant decrease in consumer purchasing power. In short, under the NAIRU-pegged definition of full employment, tight labor markets—which are essential to realizing people's right to work; securing strong wage gains for workers, especially low-income ones; and redistributing the economic pie from owners to workers—are unsustainable and make everyone in the economy worse off. It's a convenient thesis, if you're an employer.

Perhaps the NAIRU's biggest flaw, however, is that it's unobservable. Federal Reserve chair Jerome Powell has admitted as much. In a landmark 2018 speech, after acknowledging that unemployment in the economy tends to "fluctuate around values that are considered 'normal,' or 'natural,' or 'desired,'" Powell notes that these "values are not directly observed, nor can they be chosen by anyone."[11] Put another way, the NAIRU ties unemployment and inflation together in a crude formula, one that results in vague estimates of what level of unemployment corresponds with stable prices. (According to the Fed, this means a 2 percent inflation rate.)[12]

The upshot is that full employment has been defined according to a "percentage game"—historically the 5 to 6 percentage-point range using the standard measure of unemployment, the "U-3." Meanwhile, for decades the Fed has continued to tweak its measure of NAIRU to be roughly in line with its price target. It's this kind of circular reasoning—adjusting the unemployment rate that is considered "full employment" to meet an arbitrary price target—that allowed the Fed to pay attention to one of its mandates, price stability, at the expense of the other, maximum employment.[13]

The percentage game also allows policy makers to claim that the economy is at "full employment" while millions of people—Black and Brown people in particular—are forced into involuntary un- and underemployment or pushed from the labor force entirely. In some cases, officials go so far as to claim that the economy is operating *beyond* full employment, despite the fact that the right to work is still denied to millions. For example, as noted above, headline unemployment was 3.5 percent just before the COVID-19 crisis, which was *a full point* below the NAIRU. According to mainstream economic theory, this would be a situation in which workers could bid up wages—because there were too many jobs chasing too few workers—setting off an out-of-control price spiral. Real wage growth, however, was modest: year-over-year compensation growth in the fourth quarter of 2019 was a meager 2.7 percent, down from 3 percent a year before. And despite the low headline unemployment number, labor's share of income—the portion of the economic pie going to workers as opposed to owners—remained near historic lows, yet another sign of significant slack in the labor market. (Weak labor markets are not the only source of this income imbalance: the downfall of American unions has certainly played an important role as well.)[14] Moreover, inflation expectations—people's thoughts on what future inflation might be—remained below the Fed's inflation target. In sum, NAIRU didn't even satisfy its own definition.[15]

As demonstrated by Harry Hopkins's CWA, the American labor market need not be structured in a way that chronically underserves its people. Imagine, for a moment, if Americans had the right to a well-paying job as Roosevelt and Hopkins dreamed. Those participating in the workforce would never have to worry about poor economic conditions shrinking the demand for their labor. People would leave abusive or unremunerative jobs, knowing they always had a fallback. And tight labor markets would shift the balance of power from bosses to workers, allowing them to press for unionization, better wages, more generous benefits, and greater control over their time spent at work.[16] This economy may sound like the stuff of fantasy, but it's not.

Toward a Full Employment Economy

To ensure sustainability, an economy that provides remunerative and dignified work to anyone who wants it must feature three components:

1. a commitment from the federal government to run the economy at full capacity;
2. a permanent increase in public unionized employment at the local, state, and federal levels; and
3. a federal job guarantee.

RUNNING A FULL-CAPACITY ECONOMY

Economics textbooks tell us that the economy normally operates at "full capacity," meaning all economic resources—people, factories, land, and capital—are effectively deployed. The textbooks acknowledge that downturns happen but are only temporary. In fact, all the lost income, growth, and employment that occurs from a recession will quickly be clawed back. The economy will return to full capacity, including full employment (indicated by the NAIRU), in short order.

For the tens of millions who suffered during the prolonged Great Recession, the textbook story provided little comfort. In the aftermath of the 2008 crisis, the economy did not rebound quickly; in fact, it never rebounded at all. While unemployment finally declined to its pre-crisis levels—a decade later—the employment-to-population ratio has never recovered, resulting in an economy that is considerably smaller today than CBO economists estimated it would be.[17]

The weak decade following the Great Recession is not an outlier. Contrary to the textbooks, the story of the economy is that it consistently operates *below* capacity. The evidence is everywhere. The 2010s were characterized by low inflation, low interest rates, low business investment, slow growth in labor productivity, and slow growth in output. Combine these with the Federal Reserve's estimate of the economy's capacity utilization—which hovered at around 77 percent for the decade—and all indicators point to substantial excess slack.[18] The result is fewer jobs, lower wages, higher rates of poverty, and an economy that may be permanently smaller due to hysteresis (the theory that GDP today has an effect on GDP tomorrow).[19]

The answer to chronic slack in the economy is a commitment by policy makers to run the economy at true full capacity.[20] One part of the equation is a Congress willing to leverage fiscal policy (more on this just below); the other is a Federal Reserve finally ready to prioritize labor market outcomes—meaning high levels of employment and sustained rising wages—over policing inflation. This means keeping its foot on the economic pedal longer. In other words, the Fed shouldn't raise interest rates at the first sign of tightening labor markets, as they have historically done. Instead, it should let the economy run hot by maintaining a low interest rate environment and being slower to raise rates. This *may* mean higher levels of inflation, but that's okay: workers enjoying power in the workforce can navigate higher than usual inflation if it arises.

And that's precisely the direction the Fed headed during the recovery following the COVID-19 crisis.[21] This adjustment of the Fed's framework occurred under the leadership of Jerome Powell, a Trump appointee, who publicly committed to low interest rates until "labor market conditions have reached levels consistent with the committee's assessments of *maximum employment* and inflation has risen to 2 percent and is on track to moderately exceed 2 percent for some time."[22] The "and"s in the FOMC's statement were particularly noteworthy. What they signified was that the Fed wouldn't tap the brakes just because prices rose a bit; rather, they would wait to see both rising prices and "maximum employment" before doing so. And indeed the

Fed waited until March 2022 to raise rates, with headline unemployment sitting at 3.8 percent.[23]

For the Federal Reserve truly to realize its employment mandate, however, it will need to do more than maintain low interest rates. First, it must eliminate its use of the NAIRU and commit to an economy in which unemployment is kept *below* 3 percent. While it is now embarking on a new framework supporting "maximum employment," this has yet to be defined.[24]

Second, it must—as Janelle Jones, former chief economist at the Department of Labor, and Jared Bernstein, member of President Biden's Council of Economic Advisers, have argued—target not only the overall "unemployment rate, but the Black rate," which has been persistently *twice* as high as the White unemployment rate. The Federal Reserve should certainly target the Black unemployment rate, but it must also account for other groups that experience worse labor market outcomes than White people.[25]

Third, it needs to broaden how it thinks about labor market slack, taking into consideration that people not traditionally counted as "unemployed" would join the workforce if decent jobs were on offer.

Fourth and finally, it must be willing to treat price stability as a target rather than a hard ceiling, allowing inflation to float above 2 percent—and maybe well above 2 percent, as was seen in 2021-22—if that's what it takes to build and sustain tighter labor markets.

EXPANDED PUBLIC EMPLOYMENT

The Federal Reserve alone cannot bring about full employment. Nor can it manage prices across the economy seamlessly (prices are, after all, set primarily by private firms). As Keynes notes in *The General Theory*, "it seems unlikely" that monetary policy can deliver investment levels sufficient to deliver full employment; rather, "a somewhat comprehensive socialization of investment will prove the only means of securing an approximation to full employment."[26]

Keynes was right. For the economy to reach full employment, Congress will need to exercise the power of the purse to expand public

employment—to enact real fiscal policies prepared by elected officials, not technocratic ones by appointees like those at the Federal
Reserve. Think about more teachers to reduce class sizes; expanded
postal services; public service workers providing high-quality, fare-
free, and carbon-free public transit; and so much more.

Such an expansion would have vast benefits across the economy.
By offering stable employment less susceptible to the fluctuations
of the business cycle, expanded public employment backed by the
federal government would ensure high-quality services continue
wherever the economy is in the business cycle. It would also act as
a stabilizing force when downturns did occur. The federal government doesn't face the same pressures to tighten its belt as firms do
during economic downturns; thus public jobs could keep paychecks
flowing—and aggregate demand more stable—during recessions.
The result? Milder business cycles—and therefore less disruptive for
actual people.

Further, more public employment, coupled with union-friendly
reforms—such as the Protecting the Right to Organize (PRO) Act,
which has been stuck in Congress along with other bills proposed
by the Biden administration's Task Force on Worker Organizing and
Empowerment—could help revitalize America's struggling labor movement. While just one in fifteen American private sector workers are
unionized, a full one in three public sector workers are, and over half
are covered by collective bargaining agreements. Unions are crucial
if the jobs created to meet the needs of a full employment economy
are to be good jobs.[27]

An expansion of the public sector would also put the United States
on equal footing with other high-income countries. Despite its size, the
United States has a substantially smaller public sector than other rich
nations. Domestically, government employment as a proportion of total
employment is just 15 percent. In countries like France, public employment accounts for more than one in five workers. In the Nordic countries, nearly one in three workers are employed in the public sector.[28]

Properly staffing up permanent government services—schools,
post offices, social work agencies, public parks—and offering new

services, like government-run day care facilities, eldercare facilities, and summer camps, would prove invaluable. And it will build on meaningful lessons from US history. The WPA, a successor to the CWA and also led by Hopkins, put 8.5 million Americans to work creating or improving 39,000 schools, 8,000 new parks, 16,000 miles of water lines, 650,000 miles of roads, 4,000 utility plants, 950 airports, 84,000 public buildings (excluding schools), and more. The CCC, another landmark New Deal program, employed over 3 million hungry youths between 1933 and 1942, planting trees, building trails, occupying fire towers, and engaging in numerous other vital conservation tasks. Participants in the CCC saw immense benefit, receiving education, training, and work experience along with consistent pay, food, shelter, and medical care. On average, youths gained eleven pounds during their stint in the CCC.[29]

Roosevelt never meant for these programs to be temporary; in fact, he pushed, after initially caving to the interests of business, for direct employment programs to be a permanent feature of American life. Today the promise held by permanent public employment programs as a means to achieve full employment and improve the myriad public services the government already provides—and those it should—is undeniable.

Changes like these produce growing pains. Substantially increasing federal employment will likely not happen smoothly overnight. Government capacity has been gutted over the past few decades and cannot be fully reinvigorated on a dime. But that's partly the point: there's a need for a long-term, sustained increase in permanent government employment not only to reach full employment, but to fill existing gaps. An increase in public investment shouldn't be a temporary reactionary fix during times of crisis. It should be a permanent feature of the economy.

A FEDERAL JOB GUARANTEE

Running the economy near full capacity and permanently expanding public employment will go a long way toward delivering employment assurance. But to guard against involuntary unemployment, the economy needs one final piece: a federal job guarantee.

The idea is straightforward. The government establishes a permanent right to a job and enforces that right through the creation of a job-guarantee program that would provide direct public employment for those in need of work. The jobs would pay a living wage—at least $15 an hour—and include benefits such as health insurance (consistent with insurance received by other federal employees), paid vacation days, and paid family and sick leave.[30] Such a program would have a set of jobs ready to go for workers in need, guaranteeing that quality employment is available at the ready for all who want it.

Ambitious though it is, it's eminently feasible. In my earlier work with the economists William A. Darity Jr., Darrick Hamilton, and others, we established just how the program could be organized. The program would be administered by the Department of Labor, with the secretary of labor functioning as the primary supervisor. While the administration and funding would be conducted in a relatively top-down manner, the projects would be determined at the federal, state, and local levels. This would be similar, in many respects, to the structure of the Works Progress Administration.[31] The secretary of labor would provide employment grants to local and state governments, as well as Indian nations, to hire job guarantee workers. If local agencies do not take advantage of these opportunities to provide adequate jobs, then the Labor Department would be tasked with providing sufficient employment opportunities for local workers. This is necessary, especially given the recent refusal to expand Medicaid in some conservative states, a sign that some states may not work in good faith with a job-guarantee program. Finally, this work would be done in conjunction with the Treasury Department, which would be in charge of dispersing funds for the program.[32]

On a per-worker basis, I estimate the average cost of a full-time job in the program would be approximately $62,000, though workers may opt to work part-time if they desire. This calculation assumes an average wage of $17.50, though all workers will make at least $15.00. The wage ladder allows for individuals to be promoted during their

time as job-guarantee employees as well as for those with more experience to receive modestly higher wages. This will not, to be sure,
match the six-figure salaries received by some workers; thus some job-
guarantee workers can expect to receive a substantial pay cut should
they participate in the program (similarly, unemployment benefits are
capped for high-income workers). Benefits, including health care and
modest contributions to retirement funds, would also be provided
for all workers. In line with current spending on federal health care
benefits for public servants, this would cost an estimated $10,500 per
worker. However, once other economic rights are adopted, including universal health care, health care will no longer need to be provided through the program, thus lowering the sticker cost per worker.
In addition, workers will need supplies with which to do their jobs.
Drawing on historical cost estimates from previous direct employment programs, I estimate spending on supplies would amount to
$1 per $3 spent on wages, resulting in material costs of just over
$12,000 per full-time worker. Finally, payroll taxes must be paid,
amounting to roughly $2,800 per full-time job.

The benefits of such a program would be immense. In one fell
swoop, the United States would eliminate involuntary unemployment
and poverty wages and realize true full employment—meaning that
anyone who wants a job at a fair wage can get one. As the economist
Pavlina Tcherneva has noted, under a job guarantee, policy makers
would literally turn unemployment offices into employment offices.[33]
No more subsidizing poverty-level employment—the preferred
approach in Washington today—through programs like the Earned
Income Tax Credit (EITC). And no more blaming people without
jobs when, in truth, there are too few jobs by design. Instead, the government would provide quality employment directly in order to guarantee permanent full employment. No longer would people be subject
to the massive volatility that has always dominated capitalist economies. People would know that, no matter what, they could find a job
at a living wage and provide for themselves and their families.

In addition, the program would function as powerful countervail-
ing weight against employers' ability to treat workers as disposable.

To date, policy makers have structured the labor market to protect employers' near-complete domination over their workforces in the name of flexible labor markets, even allowing employers to dictate bathroom breaks (with the expected horrifying and dehumanizing results).[34] With a reliable and decent fallback position always available—that is, with a *real* floor in place in the labor market—employers would be forced to offer employment conditions at least as favorable as those offered by the government. (Of course, it was precisely this change in the balance of power between employers and employees that drove big business's fierce opposition to the CWA during the Great Depression.)

Although all Americans would benefit from the job guarantee, members of groups that face persistent discrimination in the labor market—women, people of color, people in the LGBTQ+ community, people with disabilities, previously incarcerated individuals, and others—would benefit disproportionately. This is only fitting: the concept of a federal job guarantee has deep roots in the American civil rights movement. Already in the ferment in 1963—"Civil Rights + Full Employment = Freedom" signs were a common sight at the March on Washington—full employment legislation became the focus of Coretta Scott King's and others' activism in the aftermath of Martin Luther King Jr.'s assassination.[35]

Not only would a job-guarantee program improve individual workers' lives; it would improve the well-being of communities. Akin to organizations like the CWA, the WPA, and the CCC, the job guarantee will employ workers in socially meaningful work that will enhance people's lives in ways big and small. The possibilities are endless. Walk outside your door, look around your community, and think about the types of work that could be done to improve your life, the lives of your loved ones, and the lives of your community members. This is the work a job guarantee can facilitate.

Many economists and other skeptics will balk at such a program. It'll be too expensive, they'll say (I treat the cost of this program and others in depth in chapter 10); the program will simply subsidize lazy workers—especially if people are *guaranteed* a job (meaning they can't be fired); and there's simply not enough meaningful work for job-guarantee workers to do.[36]

Implicit in these critiques is the assumption, embraced by most economists, that workers don't want to work very hard. Indeed, for most economists, it's the threat of unemployment—or, at the very least, a demotion—that keeps workers motivated on the job. Even Janet Yellen, a former Democratic appointee to the chairpersonship of the Federal Reserve and the Treasury secretary appointed under President Biden, argued forcefully that full employment would naturally result in workers shirking on the job. Without an adequate stick for employers to wield, the thinking goes, people just won't put in the work.[37]

It should be noted that workers aren't exclusively self-interested and lazy as so many economists, and their models, assume. Indeed, the evidence is clear that when labor markets are tight labor productivity—meaning how productive workers are in a given hour—tends to *increase*, not decrease. And in fact much research has shown that work effort is by no means tied to compensation—or the threat of a lost job—alone.[38] Behavioral economists, drawing on actual experiments and observations of real workers, have consistently documented that people work hard for many reasons: honor, prestige, dignity, and, not surprisingly, incentives—whether a promotion, a raise, or another form of social recognition that they are performing well.[39]

Will productivity challenges emerge with full employment? They probably will. As with the WPA, the existence of an oversight committee, a wage ladder to provide rewards and incentives for employees of the program, and disciplinary protocols to temporarily put workers on leave without pay if they fail to show up or do their job can all provide effective interventions.

Another common concern is what workers will actually *do*. One public employment program the government could inaugurate immediately, and which could absorb scores of job-guarantee workers, is a CCC reimagined for our rapidly warming world: a Civilian Climate Corps. The new CCC would employ workers to engage in meaningful climate mitigation and adaptation work, from forest management to coastal restoration, tree planting (especially in cities where canopy cover can help mitigate rising temperatures), and retrofitting buildings from coast to coast. To rectify the past injustices of the program, communities of color and environmental justice communities would be prioritized in terms of employment opportunities with and investments from the CCC.[40] To head off the crises that await a warming planet, there is no shortage of work to be done. And there are no shortage of workers, especially young people, to do the work. Although it was not a controlled experiment by any stretch of the imagination, I asked one of my classes in 2020 if they would work for a CCC right out of school. I was surprised when 80 percent of the hands went up immediately. Such enthusiasm has played out in the polls too, with likely voters ages eighteen to twenty-nine supporting the CCC by an overwhelming 50-point margin. Young people want to work. They want to contribute to averting the worst of the climate crisis. They want to leave this planet better off. A new CCC would give them the chance to do so.[41]

Another area where a job guarantee would prove pivotal is care, whether for children or the elderly. In many states, childcare exceeds the cost of college tuition, severely limiting parents' ability to work. Fifty-two percent of Latinas, 44 percent of Black women, and 34 percent of White women report that the unpaid care work they must perform negatively affects their ability to do paid work.[42] And a dearth of care stipends (which I discuss in detail below) means those parents can't afford to stay home either.

A job-guarantee program could lessen these obstacles to accessing remunerative work. For example, an expanded public workforce could finally make universal pre-K, which has been proven to increase workforce participation, a reality.[43] It could also employ more Americans directly in care work.[44]

Those employed under the job guarantee won't be the only ones to benefit from the program; workers in the private sector stand to benefit too. By facilitating competition between government and private employers, the job guarantee will improve labor's position throughout the entire economy, helping rebalance the power scales that, thanks to the neoliberal turn and Washington's revolving door, have tipped way too far in the direction of bosses. Private sector workers will be empowered to demand fair wages, a dignified work environment, unions, and quality fringe benefits.

And to ensure projects undertaken through the program are locally appropriate, community leaders, local and state government officials, labor organizations, local residents, and tribes will be encouraged to collaborate on developing employment proposals to be submitted through government agencies. To ensure such programs complement existing work rather than replace it (unless by design, of course), officials will take care that proposals do not displace any existing public employees doing similar work.[45]

A job guarantee is by no means the only labor market reform necessary to build a just and people-centered economy that empowers workers, but, coupled with the other two reforms mentioned above, it will go a long way. That said, complementary changes to the labor market are critical to achieving not only full employment but also an economy that provides quality and dignified work. Essential to this is the rebuilding of the American labor movement, which can be helped along with the passage of currently languishing legislation like the PRO Act, as well as increases in the minimum wage, sectoral bargaining—which sets minimum pay standards by specific occupation and sector—and other measures. Nevertheless, the full employment policies presented here would help realize a transformative change in the American economy. Together, they constitute a reasonable path to full employment.

Full Employment Returns to the Agenda

After a long hiatus, the idea of full employment, like many of the other economic rights outlined in this book, has returned to the national stage. During the 2020 presidential race, a federal job guarantee was championed by numerous Democratic presidential hopefuls, from progressives like Senators Bernie Sanders and Elizabeth Warren to more moderate candidates like Senators Cory Booker and Kirsten Gillibrand. In fact, Senator Booker introduced a pilot job-guarantee program to Congress.[46]

Democrats, including moderates, sought a job guarantee for good reason. Not only was it sound economics, but it was sound politics. A national poll of voters by Harris/HillTV found 70 percent of voters supported a federal jobs program, with 42 percent saying they "somewhat support" the program and an additional 36 percent saying they "strongly support" it. Opposition was weak, with just 5 percent "somewhat" opposed and a meager 6 percent "strongly opposed." One in ten were unsure about the policy.[47]

And that was *before* the crisis that was 2020 ravaged the nation. Recall that 2019 was a year with a fairly strong labor market; when the economy hit the skids in 2020, a job guarantee became even more popular. A national poll conducted by Gallup in the midst of the crisis—from October 21 to November 5, 2020—found that support for a job-guarantee program was off the charts. A whopping 93 percent of Americans favored a direct employment program run by the federal government that put people to work to "address national or community needs." Support by Democrats registered at an astounding 98 percent. But Republicans were not far behind: 87 percent supported the program.[48]

Again, massive majorities in both parties want the federal government to create a direct employment program. A job guarantee is as bipartisan as it gets.

A Federal Reserve willing to prioritize maximum employment and a Congress willing to expand the public sector and enact a job guarantee: these approaches together would make the right to work—not the slogan co-opted by conservative politicians and attached to regressive labor legislation but the positive right to remunerative employment—a reality. A job is a fundamental human right.[49] If people want work, they should be able to find meaningful jobs that pay a living wage with benefits and contributes to the well-being of society. The idea of a job guarantee is gaining momentum. It's feasible. And it would complete the work Harry Hopkins began in 1933, delivering the right to work once and for all.

5

The Right to Housing

Most immediately, there is a conflict between housing as lived, social space and housing as an instrument for profit making—a conflict between housing as home and as real estate.
DAVID J. MADDEN AND PETER MARCUSE, *IN DEFENSE OF HOUSING*

Homelessness is, among other things, "the loneliest feeling in the world." That's a description from Tiana Caldwell, who with her husband and two children lost their home in Kansas City in 2018 following Caldwell's diagnosis of cancer. Despite being struck by something sudden and painfully common among Americans—40 percent of US residents will have a cancer diagnosis during their lives—it was, accordingly to Caldwell, still "not exactly something you want to talk about. There's a lot of shame and guilt."[1]

Caldwell was a nurse and a community college instructor prior to her diagnosis. When the financial shock of medical expenses led to their eviction from the home they rented, their six months of ensuing homelessness affected their children far more than Caldwell and her husband. They hadn't accounted for "how much it would follow our kids everywhere they went." She summed up the effect on the children in one word: "devastating."

Caldwell describes efforts to escape the cycle of homelessness as impaired by the sheer paralysis of it: "You can't be productive on any level if you don't know where you're going to lay your head at night."

Shelter, especially in cold winter climates like Kansas City, preoccupies those who don't have it at the expense of virtually everything else. Without it, bare survival—to say nothing of human flourishing—becomes impossible.

Caldwell describes how homelessness changed her. What had previously been an occupational fondness for care work—and doing what she could to make people happy and comfortable in times of need—became a commitment later to organizing on behalf of other homeless families. Just as the Kansas City Public School District helped her family get back on their feet by assisting with food and housing—Caldwell and family ended up in a home owned by the district dedicated to helping families of homeless students—Caldwell in turn decided to start organizing. She knew that "someone else would go through this if I did nothing about it." She resolved to "make change or die trying."

Despite shelter being an absolute necessity for human health and flourishing, millions of Americans struggle, and all too often fail, to find a place to call home. Every night more than half a million Americans are homeless; each year some 4.2 million young people (ages thirteen to twenty-five) experience homelessness. People in families with children account for more than 30 percent of the homeless population. On a cold January night in 2020—the most recent homeless count—some 171,575 people in families were on the streets. Of those struggling with inconsistent housing, some 110,000 are chronically homeless, meaning they have been homeless for at least a year or have been homeless four or more times over the past three years, with a combined time without a home equal to a full year. And like all forms of economic insecurity, homelessness falls disproportionately on people of color, with Pacific Islanders nearly ten times more likely to be homeless than White people and Black people nearly five times more likely.[2]

The American housing crisis isn't just about homelessness, however, which has an array of causes; it's also about the *cost* of housing. As of this writing, 43 million households—roughly one in three households in America—rent.[3] While renting can provide long-term housing, it can do so only when it remains affordable for current tenants. However, *affordable* is not the word I would use to describe the rental experience of most tenants. Nearly half of renting households, disproportionately people of color, cannot afford their rent—and thus are "rent burdened" according to the guidelines set by the US government.[4] Among these renters, 11 million households, or 24 million people, have to turn over at least half of their income to the landlord every month. The proportion of households facing this severe rent burden has increased by more than 40 percent over the past twenty years.[5]

At the same time, builders and landlords have systematically underinvested in affordable housing, instead concentrating on domiciles that qualify as "luxury apartments," which earn a higher return on investment. In fact, affordable units have been disappearing from the landscape at an alarming rate, with low-cost units falling from 33 percent of rentals in 2012 to just 25 percent in 2017. This has put the housing affordability and insecurity crisis into overdrive.

For those families fortunate enough to own their homes, the story is a bit different. Not only does home ownership provide for secure housing; it has been shown to lead to wealth generation, greater neighborhood stability, higher levels of civic engagement, and improved educational outcomes for children.[6] However, despite the government's emphasis on promoting home ownership—from Clinton's "National Homeownership Strategy" to the mortgage interest deduction—home ownership in the United States has barely budged since the 1960s. (In fact, it hit a fifty-year low in 2016, while the number of renting households has steadily risen.)[7] And in comparison to other high-income countries—despite the national rhetoric touting it as a "home ownership society"—the United States isn't even close to a leader in the category. In 2015 the United States had a home ownership rate of 63.7 percent, whereas other high-income countries had an average rate just shy of 70 percent.[8] Indeed, the United States had a lower home ownership rate than some of the social democratic countries, including Finland (ahead by 9 percentage points) and Sweden (ahead by 7 percentage points).[9]

While housing insecurity in the United States has been on the rise for decades—the percentage of households that are rent burdened has doubled since the 1960s—it has actually been the norm for well over a century. In 1890, Jacob Riis, a photojournalist and one of the country's earliest documenters of economic and social inequity, published a groundbreaking book revealing the squalor and extreme poverty rampant in the tenements of New York's Lower East Side. He set out to show the widest swath of Americans precisely how "the other half lives." The photos, accompanied by Riis's detailed account of his subjects' parlous circumstances, shook the moral conscience of the nation. Yet despite Riis's exposition of the plight of the renting class, there would be no national housing policy for another forty years—until the Depression made its absence untenable.

The Birth of the American Housing Market

The Federal Home Loan Bank (FHLB) Act of 1932, signed by Herbert Hoover to both "meet the present emergency" and ease access to home ownership in general, marked a major restructuring—nay, the *creation*—of the modern housing market in the United States. Hoover stated it was "self-evident" that "every thrifty family has an inherent right to own a home."[10] The FHLB would create a secondary market for mortgages, which would improve liquidity and reduce risk for lenders. Modeled on the Federal Reserve System, which functioned to backstop the commercial banks, the FHLB helped backstop mortgage lenders, increasing, as a result, both access to and affordability of mortgages across the nation.[11]

However, it was with the New Deal that the modern American housing market truly came into being. Prior to the New Deal, the structure of housing finance—and thus the housing market—was precarious. Mortgages during the early twentieth century were typically granted for less than half the value of the property, thereby excluding large numbers of people who could not come up with a "down payment" equal to half a home's value. For those who *could* get a mortgage, loan terms tended to be a minuscule three to five years in length—compared to the stalwart thirty-year mortgage today—thus barely spreading out the cost of the property.

What's more, the loans were not fully amortized, which meant that the regular mortgage payments wouldn't cover the cost of the entire loan. These loans—so-called bullet mortgages—required a massive payment at the end of the mortgage period to satisfy the loan. Of course, most borrowers didn't have the cash to make the giant "bullet" payment when the loan term was up, so they would go back to the trough in search of a new mortgage to prevent foreclosure. It was essentially a game of musical chairs, with borrowers—that is, those without the financial or political resources to change the rules—doing all the scrambling.

The financial strain on borrowers wasn't just a problem for them; it created instability in the entire housing system and, in turn, the economy as a whole. When the Great Depression caused a massive credit crunch, followed by a foreclosure crisis, the effects rippled throughout the economy. It was then that regulators realized they had to stabilize the mortgage market if they were to starve a deepening economic crisis.

The upshot was the stable thirty-year mortgage Americans are familiar with today. This instrument, so integral to home ownership and wealth creation in the United States, wasn't a "natural" development wrought by market forces; rather, it was created out of whole cloth by the New Deal government and one its chief innovations, the Homeowner Loan Corporation (HOLC).[12]

Designed to keep mortgagees in their homes, the HOLC purchased defaulted mortgages and refinanced them into a new, stable structure: fixed-rate, long-term, and fully amortizing. In setting the new terms of the loans to improve stability, the government redistributed the bundle of risks to protect borrowers and steady the once-erratic mortgage market. Reflecting on the impact of the HOLC, the historian Arthur Schlesinger Jr. noted that "probably no single measure consolidated so much middle-class support for the New Deal."[13] The HOLC, along with other New Deal agencies like the Federal Housing Authority, the Veterans Administration (which provided mortgage insurance), and Fannie Mae (which provided liquidity in mortgage finance) allowed the US government to put its weight into the mortgage market. The result was the "American Mortgage," an option that effectively crowded out competing mortgage products that disadvantaged borrowers (in other words, neoliberals' worst nightmare). This unprecedented *public* option in consumer lending—there is no other way to characterize it—"transformed the shape of American homeownership and mortgages. It created the . . . standard American housing finance option."[14]

The Homes Guarantee

For millions of aspiring home owners in America, however, that public option isn't available today. Maybe they don't have the giant down payment required—a down payment that is often handed down, at least in part, from family members with wealth.[15] Or perhaps they can't qualify for a mortgage, because their income hasn't risen in years or their credit score took a hit when they were laid off or fell ill. So they continue as renters, for whom there's no public option at all.

To finally realize the human right to housing in the United States, a right invoked by American presidents from Roosevelt to Biden, the nation must build on the interventions government has already made in the housing market and provide a true public option for housing. The nation needs a homes guarantee.

THE ORIGINS OF THE HOMES GUARANTEE

In May 2019 I was invited by Tara Raghuveer, a housing advocate and organizer for People's Action—one of the largest grassroots organizations in the country—to help draft a comprehensive housing policy proposal. The previous summer, Tara, housing rights leaders (including Tiana Caldwell, who had worked with Tara and others to found Kansas City Tenants, a tenants' rights organization), public housing tenants, Section 8 voucher holders, and grassroots housing activists had gathered at a retreat to discuss their political and policy priorities moving forward. At first, the discussions nibbled around the edges.

The lead organizers pitched the group of fifty on various campaigns to center housing in the policy discourse. The grassroots attendees, however, pushed back. These were the public housing tenants and Section 8 participants, those who had suffered the trials and indignities of housing insecurity personally. They thought the ideas on the table were far too modest. The proposals weren't commensurate with the pain that the housing crisis forced on them, and the millions like them, on a daily basis. They were hungry for a concrete plan, grounded in research, that could end the housing crisis once and for all.

In collaboration with that original group of activists and stakeholders, the policy team drafted a policy brief that reimagines the American housing landscape. Rather than the piecemeal, incrementalist reforms put forward by analysts past and present, the brief outlines a specific and achievable suite of policies to guarantee quality housing to every American as a right. Among those policies are

- a massive buildout of green social housing;
- a substantial reinvestment push in America's existing public housing stock, including retrofits to decarbonize these structures;
- an expansion of tenants' rights through a Tenants Bill of Rights;
- rent control to ensure affordability and stability in the private housing market;
- reparations for centuries of racist housing policy; and
- the end of land and real estate speculation as society moves to decommodify housing.[16]

Enacted together, these measures would effectively end homelessness and housing insecurity in the United States. Full stop.

In what follows, I focus on the two aspects of the homes guarantee that will have the greatest effect on the most housing insecure: renters. First, the country should commit to a robust social housing program that will provide a high-quality public housing option to whoever wants it. Second, the government should institute universal rent control to stabilize the private rental sector and rebalance the power differential between renters and landlords.

SOCIAL HOUSING

To realize the right to housing, the United States must *guarantee* housing—by building on its earlier interventions in the housing market and committing to the creation of a social housing program. Under this program, rental accommodations, in structures ranging from high-rises to townhouses, would be provided to renters across the income spectrum in return for cost-based and/or income-based calculations of "fair" rent. These rental units would offer people a tangible alternative housing option to the private housing market (and the landlords that set prices in it). Vitally, a social housing program would aim to build enough units to match need, thereby drastically increasing the supply of affordable housing units. Unlike current public housing, whose design and manufacture shortcomings are legion, social housing will be built to the highest standards to ensure each domicile is safe, carbon-free, and socially beneficial. And in stark contrast to the private housing market, which puts profit before all else, social housing will help decommodify the housing market, turning housing from a nexus of profit into one of security and community.

A successful social housing program—one that guarantees a home to anyone who wants it—would require the construction of at least 12 million new units over the next decade (and even more thereafter). Like current public housing in the United States, these units will be permanently excluded from the private housing market, thus severing the link between the profit motive and people's access to secure and stable housing.[17]

Social housing constitutes a sea change in terms of current solutions to affordable housing shortages. Currently, most proposals for solving the housing crisis consist of tax credits and zoning adjustments for private industry (that is to say, bribes).[18] A social housing regime, on the contrary, repositions the government vis-à-vis the market. No longer must the government entice private industry to build affordable housing; rather, the government finances, builds, and, in some cases, owns the housing itself. This would be a stark reversal of the government's abdication of the responsibility to build affordable, high-quality housing.

In some ways, social housing is similar to existing public housing; in other ways, it differs tremendously. The housing is still publicly owned, for example—as are current public housing units—but it is no longer offered exclusively to the poor, an approach that has been shown to deepen economic and social segregation by isolating low-income households.[19] Rather, social housing is available to middle-class, as well as working-class, families and has the capacity to slow, and eventually stop, the tide of gentrification by allowing people to stay in their homes even, or rather especially, when public investments are made in their community. This stability can thereby create more rooted and vibrant neighborhoods economically, racially, and ethnically.

This neighborhood diversity is crucial. Currently, low-income rental options tend to be located far from employment opportunities and public amenities (parks, transit, etc.). When public investments do come into a neighborhood, say, a new transit station, many of the benefits tend to be captured by landlords by means of higher rents. Existing tenants, all too frequently, benefit neither economically nor socially from these public investments; instead, they are often replaced by tenants able to absorb the higher rents brought on by the new public amenities. The result is gentrification rather than the economic development of existing communities.

Social housing disrupts this dynamic. Comprising off-market rental accommodations, whose rents are based on a percentage of residents' income and building expenses, social housing is immune from pressures to increase rents based on local amenities and/or the cachet of a particular location (once land is acquired and social housing is built, that is; if land were to be acquired by government *after* an area experienced a substantial inflow of investment, it would increase land values and make the initial purchase of land for social housing more expensive). The goal would be to attract investment not as a way to charge higher rents but to serve the social good.

To some, this may sound like a utopic vision. I can hear the critics now: *Sure, social housing is a nice idea, but it's too expensive . . . another well-intentioned liberal policy that'll fall flat . . . logistically, it's impossible.* And yet it has been done, with success, elsewhere.

There's Vienna, Austria, for example. For ten years running, Vienna has been rated the most livable city in the world.[20] Why? One major reason is its extremely affordable, high-quality public housing, which is home to more than six in ten city residents.[21] On average, per square foot, residents of Vienna pay roughly a third of what renters pay in other sought-after European cities. And I'm not talking about dilapidated units in crumbling buildings. The social housing in Vienna comprises beautiful, desirable, and well-maintained dwellings located in sought-after areas of the city. Many of these buildings include amenities typically reserved for luxury housing in the United States: shops, community meeting rooms, rooftop pools and community green spaces, childcare centers, and more. It's an example of what the sociologist Daniel Aldana Cohen calls "temples of public luxury."[22]

Vienna isn't alone. Many cities across the globe are building well-appointed lodgings to house their residents, from Norwich in the United Kingdom, where an energy-efficient social housing complex won the country's prestigious Stirling Prize for architecture; to Bordeaux, France, where the city undertook an award-winning energy retrofit of existing social housing; to Finland, which has been dramatically reducing homelessness by simply giving people homes, and not just any homes, but social housing equipped with saunas, gyms, and communal kitchens.[23] It could happen here, in the United States, too. In a 2020 study Cohen and I conducted for Data for Progress and the Justice Collaborative, we found that 63 percent of likely voters supported federal investment in social housing, including a majority of Republicans and Independents.[24]

RENT CONTROL

Social housing will put a floor in the rental marketplace—and under millions of tenants' feet. It's a crucial public option, one that will satisfy people's basic need for shelter outside a profit-driven market unable and unwilling to meet that need. But not all renters will live in social housing (at least not yet). Even if the government builds the necessary 12 million social housing units, tens of millions of people will continue to rent from private landlords. And with vacancy rates near thirty-year lows and rent increasing faster than inflation in recent years, workers and those living on fixed incomes are vulnerable to being rent burdened—or worse.[25] While social housing will help anchor rents by offering an alternative to the private market, complementary housing policies are necessary to ensure the bumper rails are strong enough in the rental market to keep housing affordable. And no policy lever is as effective at controlling the cost of rent as rent control.

Rent control has been part of America's housing conversation since 1918, when rental prices boomed during World War I. It wasn't until World War II, however, that the nation enacted far-reaching rent-control policies. In 1941, Roosevelt directed the Office of Price Administration and Civilian Supply to "develop programs with the objective of stabilizing rents." A year later, when the United States formally entered the war, rent control was deployed to protect against "rent profiteering." These measures targeted areas where the defense industry—and thus the inflow of workers—was rapidly expanding. As the war wound down, however, these rent controls—which have become known as "first-generation" rent control, often placing a hard freeze on rental increases—largely went by the wayside.

The second wave of rent controls came in the 1970s. This generation of policy focused on taming the rise of rental prices as inflation ate into workers' living standards. Unlike first-generation controls, second-generation rent controls, adopted primarily at the city level, allowed rental prices to increase but only at a certain rate (often a given percentage per year, sometimes linked to inflation). During the neoliberal era, this approach to rent control was discarded, having been deemed an inefficient and counterproductive policy tool incompatible with a "free" market.[26,27]

These days rent control is making a comeback. In 2019, New York State passed a law allowing New York City, along with cities across the state, to strengthen rent control for the first time since the 1940s. The legislation solidified rent control as a permanent feature of the state's housing law while drastically limiting the ability to decontrol apartments. The same year, Oregon and California passed the nation's first statewide rent control laws (though limits on rental increases were weaker than many had hoped for). And, during the 2020 presidential primary, Senator Bernie Sanders made national rent control a key feature of his "Housing for All" campaign platform.[28]

In returning rent control to the policy conversation, politicians are simply responding to the electorate. Polling conducted in 2019 by Data for Progress found 58 percent of registered voters supported universal rent control, with just half as many voters opposed.[29]

Despite the renewed interest in rent control, however, most economists are dead set against it. In fact, Milton Friedman's first influential essay, written with fellow Chicago school economist George Stigler, was a takedown of rent control. The piece, titled "Roofs or Ceilings? The Current Housing Problem," argued that rent control limited construction of new housing, made housing more unequal, reduced people's mobility (which the authors viewed as exclusively bad), and restricted landlords' right to profit from their property to the max. Friedman and Stigler's central claim was that price controls— of which rent control and the minimum wage are the most common examples—distort the "free" market. In Friedman and Stigler's model, price controls artificially restrict supply and prevent the market from clearing. (Anyone who took Econ 101 will remember rent control's effect on a market with perfect competition. The price control constitutes an artificial floor, preventing the economy from reaching equilibrium—that magical value where the supply and demand lines intersect.) If rent controls are removed, according to Friedman and Stigler, the "free market" ensures that housing is "immediately available for rent—at all rent levels."[30]

Friedman and Stigler's analysis remains the conventional wisdom in economics today; the economist Gilbert Metcalf recently opined that "opposition to rent control is something like an oath of office for the profession."[31] A poll of economists at prominent universities conducted by the Initiative on Global Markets at the Chicago Booth School showed just how true this is, finding that 81 percent of economists oppose rent control and only 2 percent support it.

The individual responses were telling. Cecilia Rouse, Princeton economist and chair of the Council of Economic Advisers under President Biden, noted that while rent control is "well intended," it's ultimately misguided because it will "likely limit expansion in supply and improvements in quality" of the rental stock. Richard Schmalensee, an MIT economist, went further, writing that "unless al [sic] textbooks are wrong," the idea that rent control improves the affordability of housing "is wrong." And Richard Thaler, a Nobel laureate, when asked about rent control's improving housing affordability, scoffed, "Next question: Does the sun revolve around the earth."[32] If this weren't enough, Greg Mankiw, economist at Harvard and former chair of the Council of Economic Advisors to President George W. Bush, goes so far as to note in his best-selling undergraduate textbook that rent control is "the best way to destroy a city, other than bombing it."

Economists' criticism of rent control hinges on two arguments: (1) rent control restricts the supply of new housing; and (2) while rent control creates winners (tenants living in controlled apartments) and losers (landlords and would-be renters), the net result is a misallocation of housing and a deadweight loss for society as a whole.[33] But, as was the case with the minimum wage—which most economists opposed until new empirical research shifted the field—the criticism of rent control largely ignores how the policy has performed in the real world.

Let's take the economists' arguments in turn. Does rent control reduce housing supply? The evidence shows that it does not.[34] This is because rent control targets rent *increases* rather than the *absolute level* of rents. Under a rent-control regime, when a new apartment building is constructed, its units can be rented at landlord-set rates (what neoclassical economists call "'market rent"); only future *increases* in rent are limited.

Further, housing tends to be an inelastic good in that it doesn't respond much to changes in prices (or, indeed, price controls). If it did, high-cost cities like Los Angeles, San Francisco, New York, and Boston would see major housing booms (because developers would see an opportunity to turn a tidy profit). Yet these areas have seen relatively little in terms of new construction.[35] The result is that existing homes in many large cities cost much, much more than the costs of construction, an outgrowth of geographic constraints coupled with poor zoning regulations and NIMBYism.[36]

So no, housing starts—that is, increases in supply—aren't contingent on prices, or price controls, for that matter, in the way economists typically assume. In fact, empirical research finds that rent regulations have little to no effect on housing supply. (It also bears mentioning that the supply critique is a bit of a red herring: the goal of rent control is to stabilize rents and maintain the existing stock of affordable units, not to increase supply.)[37]

Does rent control result in a "misallocation" of housing and leave society worse off? Again, the answer is no. It does indeed result in winners and losers, however—just like the current structure of the housing market does—so it's necessary to describe in detail exactly how the winnings and losses are allocated. The fact is that, contrary to the opinion of most economists, there is indeed a positive economic case for rent regulation. Rent control can deliver a number of important benefits, including stabilizing rents, thereby alleviating rent burdens somewhat and reducing economic inequality; and protecting the rights of tenants to stay in their homes, especially as neighborhoods become more desirable, thereby improving neighborhood stability and diversity.

The literature shows that rent control indeed stabilizes rents. In study after study, from Massachusetts to California, researchers find that rent control improves affordability for tenants in controlled units, just as intended. In Cambridge, Massachusetts, one study found that—after accounting for the size and quality of the units—tenants in rent-control units paid about half what tenants in noncontrolled units paid. Another study, conducted in Los Angeles, found that tenants in controlled units paid 26 to 31 percent less in rent, with those living in two-bedroom units—most likely people with children—receiving an even larger break.[38] When rent control is repealed, studies find that rents often jump hundreds of dollars per month.[39]

What's more, rent control doesn't only affect the rents on controlled units. While Econ 101 tells us rents in noncontrolled units should go up, the empirical evidence points to the opposite: rents for noncontrolled units in areas where rent control is present stabilized too. In other words, rent control can anchor prices in an area, improving affordability for all.[40]

Further, rent control helps people stay in their homes, thereby improving neighborhood stability and combating gentrification. As noted above, when a geographic area begins to see rising productivity or improved amenities, rents tend to spike, forcing current tenants—the people who were supposed to benefit from the public investment in the first place—to seek housing elsewhere.

Besides the questions this all too common scenario raises about equity, there are economic costs. As rents rise, the working-class people who service the area are forced out, levying a cost on those households but also on local employers, who, as a result, are left with a smaller pool of local workers to hire from. Rent increases also frequently flatten the social and cultural dynamism that was the impetus for the improvements in the first place. Rent regulation, by allowing the area to retain its residents and character, helps reduce the conflict between the interests of the current residents and the economic imperatives of the city at large.

Many economists believe this key impetus for rent control—keeping tenants in their homes—is a negative. Landlords, according to the conventional wisdom, should be able to raise rents according to whatever the market would bear; such an action, after all, would be "efficient." But this approach fails to account for the serious possibility of homelessness and housing insecurity, driven by the false faith in the idea that the market will provide sufficient housing at all price points.

It's important to note, also, that the vast majority of rent increases aren't born of increased capital investment by the landlord. Rather, they are rents in the pure economic sense of the word. For most people, "rent" means the amount of money one pays to gain the right to live in a dwelling for, say, a given month. For economists, "rent" means the price above and beyond what would be paid under perfect market conditions (which, in point of fact, never exist). Thus, when landlords are able to increase rents, often because a neighborhood becomes more desirable rather than some capital investment the landlord made to improve the dwelling, they are simply reaping economic rents.

In the final analysis, are price controls indeed the most efficient means for securing renters' rights? Absolutely. Wherever there are pervasive economic rents and market power, some regulation of prices is an acceptable policy response. From the regulation of railroad rates in the late nineteenth century to the regulation of electricity rates through highly managed utilities to the regulation of interest rates through much of the twentieth and twenty-first centuries to the regulation (albeit insufficient) of health insurance today, limitations on prices are a well-established tool to govern markets for essential needs in which sellers enjoy proprietary information and/or market power. In each case, these regulatory cases help constrain the undue power of owners and improve the economic well-being of everyday people, from those who rode the railroad to those who buy electricity to those with preexisting conditions. Despite the cries from landlords, the rental market shouldn't be an exception.

Realizing housing as a right in the United States may sound like a bridge too far. But, like the overarching concept of economic rights, it too has a rich and complicated history in the United States. In the 1930s, there was a serious movement for a comprehensive housing agenda, then called "modern housing," which would have made "a publicly supported, broadly targeted, noncommercial housing sector the centerpiece of federal housing policy."[41] With the support of Senator Robert Wagner, one of the most active New Deal members of the Senate, housing legislation was introduced that would (1) assure direct federal involvement in creating social housing for people across the income spectrum, (2) democratize social housing by providing an active role for future residents in running their communities, and

(3) treat housing as a utility and integrate it into the nation's industrial policy to secure full employment.[42] In the United States it wasn't to be: Wagner was opposed by the real estate lobby and never garnered sufficient support for his vision.

More recently, however, other nations, including those less rich in resources, have effectively ended homelessness and housing insecurity.[43] It's possible here. The resources—the people, the building sites, the materials, and the regulatory reforms—are available, and the policies are popular. We can have nice things, but—like the public option in the mortgage market—we need to legislate to get them.

6

The Right to an Education

On most mornings, 51 million American kids roll out of bed, grab
their backpacks, and step onto a yellow school bus—no fare needed—
destined for one of the one hundred thousand public schools that dot
the nation. Upon walking into the school building, they aren't asked
to show proof of purchase. No receipt is given. They simply stroll in
ready to learn. It's a *public* school: the cost of attendance is $0.[1]

Public schools are what economists call a *public good*. In econ-
speak, public goods are both nonexcludable—meaning people are not
deprived of the good based on their ability to pay—and nonrivalrous—
meaning the use of the good by one person does not exclude others
from accessing it. In plain language, public goods are simply goods
that benefit us all—things like free education, public parks, and clean
water. These goods aren't rationed by the market; they aren't subject
to the forces of supply and demand. Rather, they're provided to all.

The American decision to make education a public good is rooted in the belief that education is a human right and a necessity for people to live productive and dignified lives. Furthermore, an educated populace is an essential component of a democracy. As Thomas Jefferson argued, public education is "necessary to prepare citizens to participate effectively and intelligently in our open political system [and] to preserve freedom and independence."[2] Effective political participation requires far more than basic literacy; citizens must be provided with the opportunity to think critically about the kind of society they want to live in—how best to build their "new Jerusalem," as Keynes put it.

Yet the right to an education is not enshrined in the US Constitution. Education wasn't top of mind for the drafters; they were simply trying to prolong the radical experiment of self-government. So the American right to an education devolved to the states. Massachusetts, home to the oldest functioning constitution in the world, also has the distinction of being the first state to guarantee education. It was a priority of its author: John Adams believed that education "ought to be the care of the public" and that it should be "maintained at the public expense."[3]

But while some states (New York and Pennsylvania, for example) recognized the right to an education as early as the eighteenth century, others delayed. In fact, by the turn of the nineteenth century, just one-fifth of states guaranteed public education (and nearly all of it limited to primary school). It was only after the Civil War and the efforts during Reconstruction to expand democracy and foster greater equality that free public education appeared in each state's constitution. The passage of the Fourteenth Amendment meant that no state would ever again be admitted to the Union without a constitutional commitment to people's right to an education, a right that would be realized through free public schooling systems.[4]

By the start of the twentieth century, America's youths—in particular, its White youths—had access to quality primary public schools. High school, however, remained a luxury for the wealthy rather than a right for masses. In 1910, just 14 percent of teenagers were enrolled in high school, and fewer than 10 percent of adults held a high school diploma. But with a nation, government, and economy growing ever larger and more complex, a primary school education alone was proving insufficient to meet the intellectual demands of the era.

Around the same time, progressive reformers were fighting to end child labor. In the early twentieth century, one in five kids between the ages of ten and fifteen regularly worked as laborers.[5] Progressives argued that the youth should be allowed to devote more time to education—that they belonged in schools, not factories. To accommodate this lengthened school window, an expansion of the public education system would be necessary.

Thus arose the high school movement. A grassroots social movement that largely took place at the local level from 1910 to 1940, the high school movement oversaw a massive expansion of secondary schooling in America. From 1910 to 1920, high school enrollment doubled, reaching 31 percent. By 1940, half of all youths ages fourteen to eighteen were enrolled in high school. This expansion of education was revolutionary. As the economists Claudia Goldin and Lawrence Katz write in their book, *Race between Education and Technology*, the public high school system was built in the early 1900s "to be a quintessential American institution: open, forgiving, gender-neutral, practical but academic, universal, and often egalitarian."[6]

No other country moved to guarantee public secondary school at such an early time in history. It was an impressive accomplishment. From major metropolitan areas like Boston to small rural towns in Iowa, local school districts across the nation taxed the general population (often through property taxes) to provide universal public high school. With the advent of the modern public high school, educational attainment skyrocketed: in 1935, more than 40 percent of Americans earned a high school degree, compared to just 9 percent in 1910. Moreover, the average years of educational attainment climbed steadily throughout the century, nearly doubling, from 7.7 years to 14.1. No longer was a high school education an elite privilege for the professional class; it was now an entitlement for all.

This expansion of public education, which established the United States as the global leader in learning, paid off in immeasurable ways.

On the economic front, the better-educated workforce contributed to booms in productivity and advances in technology—the electric washing machine, modern air-conditioning, the television, and much more—that prolonged and improved people's lives. In fact, America's high degree of educational attainment relative to its peers was one of the key factors in the nation's tremendous rise as a global economic superpower in the twentieth century.[7]

But the benefits of delivering high school as a public good reach far beyond the economic. For one, individuals and society as a whole are wealthier. But education also helps craft a society that is healthier, more cohesive, less violent, more egalitarian, and more politically engaged.[8] Many intellectuals, including the Nobel laureate Amartya Sen, argue that education is essential to enhancing people's freedom to do, and be, what they have reason to value. That is, if people are to be truly free—to choose what and whom they want to be—they require education.[9]

As miraculous as the top-line history of public education in the United States may be, it is also marked by the inequities and prejudices that characterize most aspects of American history. A high-quality public education was not truly free and open to all until well into the twentieth century; it would be reasonable to question whether it even exists today. Black children, especially those living under Jim Crow, were largely excluded. A study by the NAACP of Georgia public schools in the 1920s found that spending for White students was roughly eight times higher than spending for Black students.[10] Further, the dire poverty imposed on Black households forced many kids out of school and into the workforce.[11] Also, at the very least, structural racism in education contributed substantially to the yawning racial gap in high school graduation rates. In 1940, for example, 41.2 percent of White people ages twenty-five to twenty-nine had a high school diploma, compared to just 12.3 percent of Black young adults. This gap has since narrowed, due in no small part to the forced integration of schools by the Supreme Court, and today Black students graduate from high school at nearly the same rate as White students (92.3% vs. 95.6%).

The same cannot be said for college, however. While 40.1 percent of Whites hold a bachelor's degree, only 26.1 percent of Blacks do.[12]

The expansion of America's right to education, that guaranteeing access to free public high school, marked a profound leap forward in this history. Realizing that a primary school education was no longer sufficient in the early twentieth century, the government, nudged along by the grassroots groups that together composed the high school movement, stepped in and expanded the public system to create an active and engaged citizenry ready to meet a rapidly changing world. High school, like primary school before it, was understood as a public good, one that would not only benefit individuals, but society as a whole. As a result, high school went from a privilege for the wealthy to an entitlement for all.

In a similar fashion today, with the advent of digital technologies and the demands of a global economy, a high school education has become insufficient for many to do, and be, what they hope to be. Economists and politicians alike, not to mention parents and youths, recognize this. A poll by Gallup found that 96 percent of Americans thought it was important for people to have a degree or credential beyond high school.[13] It has become accepted truth that a college degree is a prerequisite for economic security (though other economic rights discussed in this book aim to change that).

In short, a college education has become central to achieving the American dream. Some portions of the nation have recognized this and responded by creating free public college (more on that below). But for the most part college is not free. It is not treated as a public good or entitlement. Instead, policy makers have designed a system of "college on credit," a system that places a college degree out of reach for far too many and entrenches the class divide that already dictates so much of the American experience. As a result, we're left with a world where college is increasingly necessary but also increasingly unaffordable. Let's look at each of these—college's necessity and its expense—in turn.

The need for a college degree is most often made on economic grounds. Economists argue that today's economy—and certainly the economy of the future—requires workers to have a college degree. Georgetown University's Center on Education and the Workforce estimates that by 2027, 70 percent of jobs in the United States will require workers to have education beyond the high school level. For comparison's sake, in 2010, the Bureau of Labor Statistics estimated that only 31 percent of jobs required postsecondary education.[14]

Those who fail to get the credentials will pay the price. Already high school graduates are subject to unemployment rates nearly twice as high as those who have obtained the express pass to economic security—that is, a bachelor's degree. A quick snapshot of the labor market amid the recent economic recovery is illustrative. In July 2021, bachelor's degree holders had an average unemployment rate of 4 percent. High school graduates, by contrast, had an unemployment rate of a staggering 8.3 percent. But that's not all. The earnings gap is immense. In the first quarter of 2021, those with just a high school degree took home a measly $792 a week (median), far less than the $1,426 median weekly earnings of those with a bachelor's degree. For those who have the opportunity to go on to earn a master's degree, a professional degree, or a doctorate, the threat of unemployment only goes down; and pay keeps going up.[15]

But those who are seeking a degree also pay. Why? Because policy makers abandoned free college—college as a public good—in favor of college on credit.[16]

By now most people have seen the headlines lambasting the growing student loan crisis. Headlines like "Americans Are Drowning in Student-Loan Debt" and "I've Spent $60,000 to Pay Back Student Loans and Owe More than Before I Began" have become commonplace.[17] And with reason: student loan debt has been growing like an invasive species. In 2021, the Federal Reserve reported that student loan debt sat at $1.73 trillion, up from $250 billion in 2003. For context, this amounts to over 9 percent of national income—a massive burden on the shoulders of America's young people. Not only does debt at this level warp people's lives; it also suppresses economic growth and dynamism as borrowers send increasingly larger checks to debt servicers. And the number could have been even *higher*. On March 13, 2020, President Biden paused federal student loan payments and reduced the interest rate to 0 percent until August 31, 2022, saving borrowers tens of millions of dollars in interest and allowing them to keep as much money in their pockets as possible during the pandemic.[18]

Thinking about these numbers at the national level can be dizzying and somewhat abstract; when you break them down at the borrower level, their negative impacts become plain. A study by the National Center for Education Statistics found that among people who graduated with a bachelor's degree during the 2015–16 academic year and took out at least one loan, the average debt load was $32,300. For those with an associate's degree, average debt levels upon graduation sat at $20,000.[19] These amounts may seem modest compared to the headlines touting six-figure loan balances, balances that in fact saddle one in fourteen borrowers (among those with a postgraduate degree and student loans, the proportion with six-figure debt is even higher: 23%).[20] But while the six-figure debt burdens tend to grab headlines, it's often people with more modest debt burdens, especially low-income people who did not end up graduating and who do not reap the financial benefits of a degree, who are particularly crushed by student debt.[21]

Of course, not everyone graduates with debt. Wealthy students are largely able to avoid taking out student loans. But low- and middle-income students are shackled by student debt for decades of their adult lives. In fact, a larger and larger share of students are taking on larger and larger loans. The Pew Research Center found that the share of students borrowing increased by half from 1993 to 2012, amounting to 69 percent, and that the average loan amount grew threefold from 1993 to 2020. Furthermore, these loans stay with people longer, burdening an increasingly large share of people into their forties and fifties. That is because, as debt burdens grow and are inflicted upon a larger share of students, an increasing proportion can't pay them back, especially as wages stagnate. The economist Marshall Steinbaum has found that more than half of students with education loans now owe *more* than they initially borrowed. The loan balance is heading in the wrong direction, leaving America's young people—and increasingly America's middle-aged—in crisis.[22]

This debt mountain didn't arise overnight; rather, it's the result of a gradual shifting of the economic tectonic plates, pushing debt further and further into the stratosphere. On one side is the cost of college. The average $105,050 price tag for a bachelor's degree at a public institution is well beyond the reach of most middle-class families, though this pales in comparison to the average cost of a private nonprofit school, which is $47,541 *per year*.[23] Of course, the supposedly "elite" private schools charge even more. According to CBS News, the University of Chicago tops the list for America's most expensive colleges, with a staggering price tag of $81,521 per year.[24]

These costs have been growing far faster than the overall price level in the economy. From 1985 to 2015, college costs rose an astronomical 500 percent, while the overall consumer price index rose just 115 percent. In other words, a college degree is much more expensive today relative to other goods than it was for the Boomer generation (though the increases in tuition rates have slowed since the onset of the COVID-19 crisis). As Greg Schoofs, who teaches at the University of California, Berkeley, pointed out, Boomers could have reasonably paid for college by working a minimum-wage job over the summer. They would even have a bit of cash left over to help with room and board. (I know this is true, because it's precisely what my father did: a low-income, first-generation student at Berkeley in 1974–78, he shined shoes to get by.) But times have changed. Today a minimum-wage worker would need to labor full-time for 32.4 weeks a year just to meet tuition and fees at a public four-year university. If they want to live on campus and cover all their expenses for the academic year—tuition, fees, room, and board—they would need to work 68 hours a week, 52 weeks a year. That leaves precisely zero time to attend class, do homework, or kick back with friends.[25]

The Right to College

The nation needs a new high school movement but this time for college. It's time to recognize that college is a public good, one that should be available to all regardless of family income and financial resources and for the same cost as public primary and secondary school: $0.

Americans agree. According to a 2021 poll by the Pew Research Center, 63 percent of Americans thought tuition at public colleges and universities should be free for *all* American students. Support is highest among women (68%), Black and Hispanic adults (86% and 82%, respectively), and young adults eighteen to twenty-nine (73%). Interestingly, free college has the strongest support among those who have yet to benefit from college—those who have only acquired a high school degree or less (69%). Perhaps they wonder what could have been had they been given a real opportunity to get a college education.[26]

College for all is a kitchen table issue. It resonates. This is in part because going to college is one of the most momentous decisions people make in their lives and in part because the idea is a straightforward solution to a major problem: how to successfully overcome the financial hurdles to a degree.

The kicker in the conversation about free college is that at a national level it is so *affordable*. Yes, a right to public college does mean socialized costs—that is, higher taxes, about which I have more to say later—but all indicators point to this approach being *cheaper* than current public and private expenditures on higher education. No more ridiculously expensive private schools. No more predatory for-profit schools. And no more profit seeking by the financial industry—and the government—when it comes to student loans.

The neoliberal view on college is that it's an individual investment. If the student is the one to benefit from the degree, the thinking goes, the student should be the one to foot the bill. The Foundation for

Economic Education, a self-described "conservative libertarian eco-nomic think tank"—which, in fact, published Friedman's pamphlet against rent control in the 1960s—argues that "there's no reason to subsidize some people's preferences at the expense of others." Spe-cifically, these conservatives argue that the benefit of college "accrues specifically and *only* to the person holding the degree."[27] In other words, they do not see any society-wide benefits from expanding people's right to an education.

The shortcomings of this line of thinking are numerous. Simply put, higher education is not just an individual investment. Sure, individu-als reap financial benefits from acquiring more education—workers with a postsecondary education do indeed earn substantially more over their working careers, despite entering the workforce later—as well as nonpecuniary benefits. More educated workers live longer, report enjoying work more, and tend to be happier with their lives. But the benefits of having a more educated population are not lim-ited to the individual.[28] Indeed, more education comes with a whole swath of what economists call "positive externalities"—that is, social benefits. This is because education is a public good.

Let's begin with the economic benefits. More educated societies are associated with higher levels of economic growth; limit people's ability to get an education, and you also limit your country as a whole. A widely cited report by OECD confirms this, finding that inequal-ity and a lack of investment in—and access to—education substan-tially limited economic growth in the United States from 1990 to 2010.[29] Other studies find that increasing the number of universities in a country, and access to them, leads to higher rates of economic growth.[30] Overall failure to provide sufficient access to education acts as a dropped anchor, slowing the economy *in toto* (which includes, of course, those lucky enough to get a college degree in the first place).[31]

But this line of thinking is overly narrow. Education is not just prep-aration for work or a means to boosting GDP; it is also necessary for the creation of good citizens and the good society. A 2006 paper has found education is a driving force in supporting democratic life. It fos-ters democracy not through indoctrination or material self-interest but through the cultivation of collaboration and interaction, both of which facilitate participation.[32]

The American people do in fact see these benefits and reject the conservative line of thinking. Their stance doesn't arise solely from self-interest (i.e. hoping for a free ride for themselves and their loved ones); rather, they reject conservatives' arguments on philosophical grounds. It turns out that, as a survey from Columbia University's Teachers College has shown, Americans already "believe in higher education as a public good." The survey, conducted in 2018, found that the "perceived impact on society [of a greater proportion of college graduates] is just as big as the believed benefits for college graduates." Survey participants recognized the direct benefits of a college education that accrue to an individual, indeed. But they also observed the wider societal benefits—the public benefits—of higher education, benefits far too often overlooked in the framing of college as "an investment." The broader benefits participants cited included major scientific advances that benefited people at large rather than simply the inventor(s); the general encouragement of national well-being, both economically and socially; and civic participation. In short, people understand that higher education enriches society, not just the individual. Americans have come around to free college. It's the policy makers who are lagging behind.[33]

After decades on the fringes, college for all exploded into mainstream political discourse during the 2016 presidential primary. Among his suite of policies to strengthen the well-being state, Bernie Sanders gave pride of place to expanded higher education. To realize his other priorities—mitigating inequality, arresting climate change, and ending the influence of money in politics—he argued that education was essential. His solution to the education deficit in America was simple: free college. As he would famously repeat time and time again on the campaign trail, he was committed to the idea that "college should be a right, not a privilege."

Free college represented a break with the incremental reforms—free community college, means-tested programs, repayments based on future income—that had dominated liberal circles for decades. College for all was the resounding egalitarian alternative to the increasingly unequal, supposedly "meritocratic," individualistic society we live in today.

Of course, the details matter. Sure, one can fit "College for all" on a bumper sticker, but what does it really mean? And how would it work? These are precisely the debates policy makers and the American people should be having now. But before turning to these questions, I want to highlight two points often left out of the conversation:

1. College used to be free in the United States.
2. Some states and cities—and not just blue strongholds—have already begun to implement free college.

That is to say, free college is not a new idea. And it is not one that exclusively draws on the experience and policies of other countries that have implemented it, among them Germany, Finland, France, and Sweden. Rather, the idea used to be the law of the land here in the United States. In fact, President Lyndon B. Johnson went so far as to dub education America's "fifth freedom," adding it to Roosevelt's four.[34]

During Johnson's presidency, a number of public universities were already free; some institutions had been free since their founding as federal land-grant schools in the 1860s. The 1960s were the apex for free public higher education in America, especially in places like New York and Florida. Indeed, the University of Florida didn't charge tuition until 1969. While many students in other regions had to pay modest tuition and fees for college at the time, millions benefited from the GI Bill, which was essentially free college for veterans. (White veterans, that is: Black veterans received limited assistance and far too few available slots at predominantly Black institutions.)

But no state went so far as California. The 1960 Donahoe Act, commonly known as the Master Plan, guaranteed a tuition-free spot at one of the University of California's campuses for those who graduated in the top eighth of their high school class. Students graduating in the top third of their class were guaranteed a tuition-free seat at one of the state universities. But one needn't have graduated at the top of the class to qualify for a free education in California; anyone with a high school degree or a GED could attend one of the state's community colleges.

Recalling this history is precisely what some cities and states across America have begun to do. Bills related to free college have been introduced in over half the states across the nation in recent years. And some state and city governments have already begun to act, including Tennessee.[35]

Tennessee, which has voted for the Republican candidate during the previous six presidential elections by substantial margins, has been offering two years of tuition-free community college or technical school to all high school graduates, regardless of income, since 2014. And the program has been a smashing success. In its first year, administrators anticipated 8,000 students would apply for free college. A whopping 33,258 completed applications in that first year, and nearly 15,000 would eventually enroll in the free college program. Bill Haslam, a Republican who served as the state's governor from 2011 to 2019 and was an active proponent of the plan, believed the program would better Tennessee and its people. Haslam explained that the *simplicity* of the program was a feature, not a bug. "We wanted it to be an easy thing to sell and describe," the governor said. "If I say, 'Well, it's free unless your income's above this level,' or 'it's free unless you make a 2.5 GPA.' . . . Free was an easy discussion so we could say, 'if you walk across the high school stage, then you could go to college free.' And that was a conversation we wanted people to have around their dinner tables."[36]

Some states are acting to put America's youths on solid footing, but they can't do it alone. There must be a *national* right to a college education. All public four-year colleges and universities, as well as public community colleges and trade schools, must be made free for all.

This right would require the federal government to step in with tens of billions of dollars a year in funding, delivered either to states, which administer public higher education, or directly to schools that agree to participate in debt-free college. In exchange for federal funds, which could be provided through a 2–1 federal-to-state match program (others have proposed a dollar-for-dollar program), schools would have to eliminate tuition and fees. Although the program would primarily be geared to public schools, private institutions serving minority populations and tribal colleges would also be able to participate, as they have played a crucial role in educating people of color in stereotype-safe environments, despite having severely constrained financial resources.[37]

As many scholars have pointed out, tuition-free college is insufficient to provide people with an actionable right to a debt-free education; for that, assistance with non-tuition- and fee-related expenses, ranging from books to room and board, is required. One idea for supplying these extra funds is to double Pell grants (to $12,990) and allow students to use this money to pay for living and non-tuition-related expenses. But that solution is based on an isolated view of free college rather than one that embeds it in a broader economic bill of rights. If people are guaranteed a right to basic economic security through housing, health care, and universal services—broadband, banking, transit, and more—along with a basic income (conceived of as a negative income tax), then students should have all their needs met.

Of course there are further details to be fleshed out. And it remains an open question if all states will even opt into such a program. But these are precisely the conversations families and policy makers should be having.

Yet not everyone wants to have them. In fact, it's not only conservatives who resist the idea of free college; many prominent liberals do too. In 2016, Hillary Clinton blasted college for all, saying, "Now, I'm a little different from those who say free college for everybody." She went on, "I am not in favor of making college free for Donald Trump's kids."[38] Similar lines were repeated by Pete Buttigieg, who argued that college for all is regressive and that making school "free even for the kids of millionaires" would "turn off half the country."[39] Critics' arguments tend to look like this:

- *The proposal isn't well targeted.* This is central to the way New Democrats think about policies: "Free College for All would waste tax dollars on students who have no debt or whose debt is manageable," argues Joe English in *Politico*.[40] According to this line of thinking, anyone who can pay their own bills should.
- *College for all is regressive.* A headline in the *Atlantic* against free college even called it a "regressive scandal." The subtitle of the article connects the second argument with the first, noting that "college graduates benefit from their education for decades. They should bear part of the costs."[41] No free rides here.
- *It's too expensive.* As one right-wing commentator argued, it would be "scandalous" for him to have gone to school for free when there is homelessness and people are working multiple jobs just to get by.[42]

Each of these arguments is wrong. First, should college be means-tested? Absolutely not. In fact, the children of the rich deserve to go to college just as much as the children of the poor. That's the whole point. Think about it: Should libraries be limited to the poor? After all, the rich can simply buy their own books. Of course, if society decided to do this, it would mean the end of libraries as we know them. As Wilbur Cohen, a prominent architect of social legislation during the New Deal and Great Society quipped, "Programs for the poor make for poor programs."[43] Including all people in government programs yields robust, high-quality, and entrenched programs. Public schools, Medicare, Social Security—all benefit from their universal nature. And for people worried that too many benefits might flow to wealthy families, well, there's an easy solution: progressive income and wealth taxation.

A recent study at the University of Michigan on free college is particularly revealing when it comes to the benefits of simple universal programs. The researchers conducted an experiment wherein they promised low-income students—who already qualified for tuition-free college through the existing means-tested program—"free college."

Essentially, the authors were trying to understand if a simple universal approach, and the straightforward messaging that accompanies it, would boost applications and enrollment (the program was not actually universal, but the students didn't know that). The results were astounding: 58 percent of students who received the "free college" message applied, more than twice the rate of the control group (26%). Enrollment also shot up, with 27 percent of the treatment group enrolling in school, compared to just 12 percent of the control group. While this may sound surprising, it shouldn't be. The participation rate in means-tested programs—from food stamps to the earned income tax credit—is known to be problematically low. In other words, people often fail to fully take up the benefits available to them when the benefits are means tested. But this is not so for universal programs like Medicare (or, in this case, free college). Further, the number one reason people give both for not attending college and for dropping out of college is the cost.[44] People get "free college," and it seems to get them too.[45]

But will putting an end to means testing be regressive, as critics at centrist think tanks like Third Way have argued?[46] No. It turns out this same argument was made against public high school during the high school movement of the early twentieth century. It was false then, and it is false now. Critics at the time pointed out (rightly) that primarily wealthy students attended high school; they then argued that paying for free high school out of public funds would simply subsidize the rich. But these critics neglected a crucial fact: times change. The reason students from wealthier families disproportionately attended high school—and today attend and graduate from college—is that they have the means to do so. Provide education as a right, giving all people the means to earn a degree, and this will no longer be the case. Remember, there are far more low- and middle-income potential students than wealthy ones. The wealthy are the few; thus the benefits will primarily flow to the many.[47]

In research that I and my colleagues conducted, we found that providing universal tuition-free higher education would benefit historically educationally disenfranchised groups the most. Black and

Latinx students are less likely to attend college largely because of financial constraints. After all, family wealth for Black and Latinx households amounts to pennies on the dollar compared to White households, thus constraining their ability to attend school in the first place. When Black and Latinx students do attend, they are less likely to leave school with a degree in hand. And those who graduate tend to spend a longer time obtaining the degree and are much more likely to graduate with student loans weighing them down. Black students who graduate with a bachelor's degree, for instance, carry over 20 percent more debt on average than White students who also take out loans.

Making college free would help mitigate many of these inequalities. We estimate that among those students currently enrolled free public higher education could add a million additional Black and Latinx graduates, return public education to its former status as a public good, and extend higher education to those who have largely been excluded to date. And that does not account for all the new students who would enroll in college in the first place, as the Michigan and Tennessee examples suggest.

To be sure, making college free is by no means a silver bullet to address the widespread inequality and racial discrimination that permeates the education system, the economy, and our entire society. For instance, it wouldn't address the substantial barriers students of color face in America's K–12 schooling system, a system that implements racialized tracking and hoards resources for well-to-do neighborhoods. But it's a start.[48]

However, despite the evidence regarding the distributional impacts of free college, it is not clear that questions about distribution are the right ones. The economist J. W. Mason provides a nice analogy with the service provided by fire departments and firefighters. Fire protection in the United States is free (though this wasn't always the case, and cities burned because of it). Yet it benefits the rich more than the poor. The rich have larger, more expensive, and often more fire-prone houses. The poor, on the other hand, often don't own homes. They tend to live in apartment buildings, and when they do own homes, they certainly tend to be worth much less monetarily than mansions situated in, say, the tinderbox hills of Los Angeles. Thus fire protection is, it seems, regressive. Does that mean we should abolish fire departments? Or means test them? Of course not.[49]

Finally, there's the "it's too expensive" claim that financing free college will have "very negative economic growth implications" and will bring about the "worst of all possible worlds."[50] Strong words! I address these arguments in greater detail in chapter 10, but they're worth touching on now.

From a purely economic standpoint, people need to recognize that the current system is already very costly. It's expensive on two fronts, in that a college degree in the current system is already astronomically expensive, and college costs have been far outpacing inflation in recent decades, leaving students more and more unable to pay.

While there are a multitude of reasons for these rising costs, two of the driving forces are the availability of loans and rising administrative overhead. Deep cuts to state funding for higher education, especially after the 2008 financial crisis, hamstrung schools, which closed the gap by hiking tuition. This alone accounts for more than three-quarters of the increase in tuition, with much of the rest stemming from administrative bloat.[51] What's more, socializing the costs through a right to public college can help put downward pressure on overall education costs, bringing education inflation back in line with the overall economy.

Besides tuition hikes in response to budget cuts, college is expensive today because of who doesn't go and who doesn't graduate. In the 1970s, the United States ranked first globally in college attainment. Today, among people twenty-five to thirty-four, the United States ranks just 14th.[52] The lack of degree holders, coupled with the student debt that weighs down those who have attended at least some school, acts as a strong headwind for the economy, leaving everyone poorer in the end.[53]

So will providing a universal right to a college degree cost money? Yes. And if student debt cancellation is included in the program, it will cost even more (at least initially: formerly indebted people's ability to purchase more goods and services will likely offset a substantial portion of the cost of discharging their debt). But that doesn't mean that college shouldn't be included among the public goods—parks, libraries, K–12 education, fire protection, and more—financed by general tax revenues and provided free to each and every person regardless of supposed "need." College shouldn't be a debt-riddled risk or a privilege of the wealthy. It should be a universal right.

The Right to Early Childhood Education

Like free college, the right to early childhood education is not a new idea. The fight for universal pre-K and childcare has been waged for decades, and, as recently as 1971, such a program was within the country's grasp. That year Congress passed the bipartisan Comprehensive Child Development Act, which would have established nationally funded comprehensive childcare centers to educate, feed, and care for the young. President Richard Nixon vetoed it. So, instead of federally subsidized universal day care, which would have provided working families with necessary financial relief, enabled caregivers—disproportionately young women—the *actual choice* of entering the workforce, and children the benefits that come with early education, benefits that pay off well into adulthood, we got our current system, a system that is fraught, expensive, and mediocre at best.

Today day care exceeds the cost of a public college education in the majority of states. A full-time minimum-wage worker would have to devote two-thirds of their annual income just to day care to cover the bill, leaving not nearly enough for food, rent, and other necessities. Those in the nation's capital, in particular, suffer from the financial burden of childcare, paying an average of $22,631 a year per child. For most families, covering the expenses of a second child is simply out of the question. Despite extensive research highlighting the social and personal gains obtained from investing in early childhood programs, the government has continuously failed to act.[54]

Expanding the public education system to cover preschool for three- and four-year-olds is precisely what is needed. I can't treat universal pre-K fully here, but it's vitally important for downstream outcomes and must be part of any expansion of public education. Such a move would provide a more level playing field for children and parents alike while helping the United States catch up with the rest of the world. Among OECD nations, the United States ranks among the worst in preschool enrollment and in expenditures on early childhood education. And the welcomeness of such an expansion has already been proven in places like Washington, DC, New York City, and Oklahoma. In fact, Oklahoma has had free universal pre-K since 1998, and it's wildly popular.[55]

Building the program would be straightforward. The federal government would fully fund universal pre-K by providing block grants to states and local school districts. The public school districts, as was done in Oklahoma, would simply expand public educational offerings for three- and four-year-olds. If some local governments fail to deliver, the federal government could step in and set up local preschools, thus short-circuiting the concerns arising from states' refusing free money to benefit the public (the country's experience with Medicaid expansion comes to mind). The benefits of such a program would be immense—for children, parents, and society alike. Importantly, such services would free caregivers to make the choice of keeping their little ones at home or sending them to school, for free, at an early age. And the economics of it? Those add up rather nicely. A study by the Washington Center for Equitable Growth, an economics think tank, found universal kindergarten would yield $8.90 in benefits for every dollar put toward it. Of course, the goal isn't to earn a high "return on investment"; it's to expand children's right to an education and socialize the costs of children, who are, after all, public goods too. But the massive economic benefits certainly don't hurt.[56]

The right to an education is a cornerstone of the American project. Of late, however, the country has neglected that right. With the rise of Reagan and the neoliberal revolution, the nation moved toward the privatization of education, providing coupons and loans to purchase an education in the private marketplace. Who needs rights when you have loans? Unfortunately, the results have been disastrous. It is time to learn these hard lessons and redirect efforts to expanding the right to an education—by making early childhood and higher education free for all. Benjamin Franklin said it best: "Nothing can more effectually contribute to the Cultivation and Improvement of a Country, the Wisdom, Riches, and Strength, Virtue and Piety, the Welfare and Happiness of a People, than a proper Education of youth."[57]

7

The Right to Health Care

The enjoyment of the highest attainable standards of health is one
of the fundamental rights of every human being.
CONSTITUTION OF THE WORLD HEALTH ORGANIZATION, 1945

In February 1933, with the United States in full-blown crisis—an economy in shambles, one in four workers unemployed, breadlines and shantytowns popping up by the day—President-elect Franklin Roosevelt was sequestered in his New York City townhouse working to finalize his cabinet. He had promised the American people a new deal, and now he had to find the people to help him fulfill that promise.

No cabinet position would be as important as secretary of the Department of Labor. Roosevelt's choice for the position would need to address not only the catastrophe at hand but also the myriad entrenched injustices of American labor: rampant child labor, excessive work hours that ground workers to a pulp, the complete lack of worker-safety protocols, and the nation's threadbare safety net. As with his selection of Harry Hopkins to oversee the Civil Works Administration, Roosevelt selected a social worker and labor activist he had known when he was governor of New York to head the department. Under the guise of a social invitation on a nippy day in February, Frances Perkins arrived at Roosevelt's residence on East Sixty-Fifth Street.

Although the president-elect hadn't said as much, Perkins knew she was being offered the job of Labor secretary. It was an unprecedented honor: she would be the first woman appointed to a presidential cabinet. Perkins hoped that the significance of her nomination would not end there, however. She sought to make far-reaching changes in the way America—and Americans—worked, and she would only accept the position if she were empowered to do so.

Before the meeting, she jotted down a list of demands on a piece of paper: a forty-hour workweek to reduce workers' burden; a minimum wage to ensure workers could afford a decent life; worker's compensation to aid workers when they were injured; unemployment insurance; a ban on child labor; Social Security; a robust public employment service; and universal health insurance. She presented the list to Roosevelt as a precondition of accepting his offer.

The day after meeting with Perkins at his home, Roosevelt acceded to her demands. And Perkins, after visiting her husband in a sanatorium (he struggled with mental illness and was institutionalized for most of his adult life), telephoned Roosevelt to accept. Their partnership, it is no exaggeration to say, would change the course of the nation's history.

Once Roosevelt's administration was in place, Perkins worked her way through her list. Early on, she was instrumental in advocating for and guiding many of the nation's public works programs, which got money out the door and people back to work during the Depression's darkest days. But it wasn't until 1934, when the president asked Perkins to head the Committee on Economic Security, that she was presented with her first major legislative opportunity. Her work with the committee would result in one of the most significant pieces of legislation the country has ever seen: the Social Security Act of 1935. The act contained sweeping provisions, among them the creation of old-age pensions (Social Security), unemployment insurance, workers' compensation, and financial assistance for the disabled. It laid the foundation for the modern American "well-being" state: a safety net that would catch people when, through no fault of their own, they fell.

However, for all its breadth, the Social Security Act had left a key recommendation of Perkins's committee on the cutting room floor: health insurance.[1] The committee had cautioned the president that "a national program of economic security would be inadequate unless it made adequate provisions against insecurity arising out of illness," writing that "tens of millions of families live in dread of sickness" and that the "burden of medical debts" threatened people's lives and families' economic security. The committee's report also noted that the United States stood apart from nearly every other industrial nation by failing to provide health insurance for its people. The failure to institute universal health insurance would be a glaring omission in the administration's efforts to create a comprehensive well-being state.[2]

Of course, a universal public health insurance program was never instituted in the United States. The opposition, including members of the American Medical Association and business leaders, was fierce. Faced with the possibility that universal health insurance would "doom the whole bill," Roosevelt demurred. Despite being a part of the progressive agenda since Franklin Roosevelt's cousin, Teddy Roosevelt, included "sick insurance" in his 1912 presidential platform, health insurance for all would have to wait.[3]

It would be nearly a decade before Roosevelt would spotlight universal health care again, this time in two of the most famed pillars of his economic bill of rights: "the right to adequate protection from the economic fears of old age, sickness, accident, and unemployment" and "the right to adequate medical care and the opportunity to achieve and enjoy good health."[4] Alas, Roosevelt would not survive to fight for these rights.

Perkins would serve the president, and the nation, as secretary of labor until 1945, the longest tenure for that office in history. Reflecting on her time at the helm in summer 1945, she summoned the list of demands she had presented to Roosevelt on that February afternoon in 1933: "The program is almost accomplished. Everything except health insurance."[5]

The goal of universal health insurance remains elusive almost a century later. Presidents on both sides of the political aisle—Truman, Johnson, Nixon, Clinton, and Obama—have tried and failed.[6] Some, however, have succeeded more than others. President Johnson, for instance, was able to get Medicare—which currently provides government-sponsored health insurance coverage to some 63 million Americans—across the finish line.[7] To do it, though, he had to abandon Medicare's original object: to cover *all* Americans, not just the elderly. As Robert Ball, a key architect of the Social Security system, wrote, reflecting on Medicare's thirtieth anniversary, "All of us who developed Medicare and fought for it . . . had been advocates of universal national health insurance. We all saw insurance for the elderly as a fallback position." Indeed, Johnson, who faced vehement opposition to publicly funded health insurance from businesses, economists, and doctors, backed off Medicare for all. He decided it was a good political maneuver to limit coverage to the elderly, who found it nearly impossible to acquire private health insurance at the time. Advocates of universal health care agreed to go along with the compromise, expecting, as Ball put it, "Medicare to be a first step towards universal national health insurance, perhaps with 'Kiddicare' as another step."[8] And so we have Medicare as we know it today: government health insurance—for some.

Although some modest expansions of the covered population occurred after Medicare's passage—including in 1972, when Nixon extended Medicare's coverage to vulnerable populations such as the disabled and those with end-stage renal disease—it wasn't until some fifty years later, when President Barack Obama signed the Patient Protection and Affordable Care Act (ACA, or "Obamacare") into law, that a major expansion of coverage would occur. The ACA, which amounted to a grand compromise between the Democrats and corporate health care interests, would, over time, expand coverage to some 20 million Americans, improve access to contraceptives, end some harmful practices by insurance companies, and modestly curb inflation in the health care sector. Despite these gains, today over 33 million Americans remain without health care coverage, and another 41 million are underinsured (i.e., their insurance is of such poor quality that they are unable to reasonably afford medical treatment).[9] Thus, a right to health care, which the political scientist Theodore

Marmor has defined as universal and "equal access to equivalent medical services," remains unrealized.[10]

The costs of neglecting this right are astronomical, both financially and in terms of human lives. The money the United States spends on health care is literally off the charts and has been for decades. According to the US government's Centers for Medicare and Medicaid Services (CMS), which publishes data on health care costs every year, the United States is expected to spend $4.502 trillion on health care in 2022. This amounts to 18.2 percent of GDP—nearly one in five dollars produced by the US economy. And health care costs are expected to rise much faster than overall inflation over the next decade, resulting in health care gobbling up a bigger and bigger share of the economic pie.[11]

Context is helpful here. How does US health care spending compare to other nations? The US spends more on health care than any other country in the world: twice the OECD average in terms of share of GDP and 50 percent more per capita than Switzerland, the next highest spender on the list.[12] The US system also features far greater waste and inefficiency. Employers, who provide insurance for roughly half of America, spend about $50 billion a year—4 percent of employer-provided health insurance costs—on consultants and brokers who help them pick out and negotiate health coverage for workers.[13] The United States requires far more staff to process medical bills compared to other nations,[14] and a 2011 study estimated that the average American doctor spends $82,975 annually simply dealing with insurance companies. Just over the border in Ontario, Canada, doctors in the universal health care system spend just a quarter of that.[15]

These outrageous levels of spending and rampant inefficiencies—problems flowing directly from a market-based health care "nonsystem" and policy makers' failure to regulate that nonsystem properly—aren't just issues for employers and insurance carriers; they hamper—and all too often destroy—the finances of individuals as well.[16] Take those who get coverage through their jobs, for example. From 2006 to 2016, this half of the population saw their deductibles increase a staggering 300 percent. Average deductibles today are about $2,000 for individual plans and nearly $3,500 for family plans—far higher than the emergency funds many Americans have on hand. However, these deductibles are a pittance compared to those on the health insurance marketplaces. Families who bought into more modestly priced silver plans in the ACA marketplace now face a staggering $8,439 deductible on average.[17]

The results of cost sharing at these levels are as you would expect. One in five people are currently burdened by medical debt—a leading cause of individual bankruptcy in the United States[18]—and health troubles often entail a loss of income, making paying off that debt even more difficult.[19] This despite Americans seeing the doctor *less* than their peers in other wealthy countries. In fact, one in four Americans reported to the Federal Reserve that they had *avoided* obtaining medical care because of their inability to foot the bill.[20]

Well, one might say, *having the best health care in the world costs money*. It does, but that's not what US health care is. Among high-income nations, US performance in key metrics puts the nation near the bottom in health care quality and accessibility. Nearly one in four Americans are uninsured or underinsured. In terms of life expectancy, the United States ranks 28th of 36 countries, coming in well below the OECD average. (It is currently sandwiched between the Czech Republic and Estonia, countries that are more than $20,000 behind the United States in terms of GDP per capita.) The United States also ranks terribly in terms of infant and maternal mortality: 5.7 children perish per 1,000 live births, roughly three times more children than perish in nations such as Japan, Norway, Finland, and Sweden.[21] And in Switzerland, the country that spends the most on health care after the United States, on average, a person can expect to live 4.3 years longer than an American.[22]

Of course, life expectancy in the United States isn't low for everyone. The rich have a life expectancy among the longest in the world thanks to their access to high-quality medical treatment. It's the *access*—that is, having insurance—that's key. For instance, research by the economist Gerald Friedman finds that the life expectancy gap between the United States and other OECD countries is the widest right before people reach the eligibility age for Medicare. If people make it to age sixty-five, when public health insurance kicks in and the portion of Americans who are uninsured drops off a cliff, the life expectancy gap narrows considerably. Friedman reports that those who make it into their ninth decade of life in the United States can expect to live as long as their neighbors in Canada.

Nothing has laid bare the inequities of US health care like the COVID-19 pandemic. Tens of millions lost health insurance precisely when they needed it most: in the midst of a global health crisis. Those living without insurance, or in states that failed to expand Medicaid, were more likely to get sick and die during the pandemic.[23] A study published in the *Journal of the American Medical Association* found that if all Americans had died at the rate of college-educated White people, 71 percent fewer people of color would have lost their lives, and overall half of Americans who perished would still be alive today.[24]

Unsurprisingly, looking beyond the pandemic, the people who are losing precious years of life and experiencing fewer healthy years, all while being crushed by medical debt, are primarily low-income people and people of color.[25] Some of the most shocking disparities are clear when we look at infant and maternal mortality—the pregnancy- or childbirth-related death of a baby or its mother. Infant mortality rates for Black children are 2.3 times higher than for White children, a gap that is wider than it was in 1850, just a few years after chattel slavery was officially ended. Over the course of a year, that gap adds up to 4,000 Black baby deaths.[26]

At present, the system's injustices seem entrenched and unresolvable. But there is another way. In fact, right now, the United States could deliver on the near-century-old promise of the right to healthcare, covering every single person from coast to coast, all while *saving* money.

Health Care for All

What is Medicare for all? And, more important, how would the right to health care work in the United States?

For one, "Medicare for all," which aims to legislate the right to health care into existence, is a bit of a catchphrase. It means different things to different people. There are numerous bills and ideas floating around that go by this name, each with its own packaging for delivering health care through public and private means. The questions are many: Should private insurance be eliminated? How will the program be financed? Can people keep their existing doctors? What about copays and deductibles?

From an economics perspective, to truly realize the right to health care, any reform must include the following:

- universal coverage (i.e., nobody left uninsured or uncovered);
- the elimination of financial barriers to care (i.e., no copayments or deductibles);
- comprehensive coverage (including services currently uncovered or partially covered, like dental and vision); and
- no inferior "tiers" of coverage or access for particular groups.[27]

Achieving these provisions will require nothing short of the complete decommodification of health care and the implementation of a universal system—whether one calls it Medicare for all, single payer, or something else—wherein the federal government is the sole provider of health insurance in the United States. (For ease of reference, I'm using "Medicare for all" as the name for a single-payer model of universal health insurance.)

First and foremost, a single-payer system means no more market competition between insurance providers—because, in a single-payer system, private health insurers will be eliminated. Instead, the government will simply cover everybody, thereby ending in one fell swoop the very idea of "uninsured."

To end financial barriers to care, a universal health care program will put an end to the recent tides of rising deductibles and copays by eliminating them entirely. That's because, with the implementation of Medicare for all, health care becomes a *public good*. Think about it: Children aren't charged to walk into public classrooms in the mornings or spend time at the local library; nor do we receive a bill when we call the fire department in an emergency. These goods are free and open to the public, period. A right to health care would put it in a similar category, where the amount of money in one's bank account will have precisely zero connection to one's access to care. The only way to achieve this is to ensure health care is completely free at a point of service.

What about vision? Dental? Hearing? Last I checked, my eyes and teeth are connected to my body. So why is it that people should need a separate plan to cover those body parts?

And what about our mental well-being? Depression, for example, ranks as one of the leading causes of disability worldwide, according to the World Health Organization; further, the World Economic Forum notes that this has major ramifications for economies around the globe.[28] Yet studies show that the lack of access to mental health care due to limited insurance constitutes a major impediment to treating depression in the United States, especially in comparison to countries like Canada.[29]

The right to health care means covering people from head to toe and caring for both body and mind. After all, the point of a universal health care program is not to provide the bare bones through "skinny" coverage but rather to provide care intended to be a "reasonable maximum" for society. This logic is in stark contrast to the means-tested programs aimed at providing some minimum semblance of coverage, which only wards off the absolute worst health outcomes. Instead, universal health care will deliver effective, high-quality care through comprehensive coverage.

The final aspect of true universal care is the elimination of tiered coverage. Unequal coverage, whether secured through financial means or political favors, is fundamentally in conflict with the idea of equal coverage for all. The rich shouldn't be able to jump the line, and the treatment of White people should not come first or be of superior quality. This means that the current inequalities in the system—such as the fact that minority and unemployed patients wait 25 percent longer, on average, to see a health care professional—will need to be remedied.[30] As one Canadian scholar, reflecting on the country's ban on private health care providers offering treatment covered under the public system, put it: "Canadians don't mind waiting in lines, as long as the rich Canadian and the poor Canadian have to wait about the same amount of time."[31] Government-sponsored health insurance would level the playing field and make sure all enjoy the right to health care equally.

A plan meeting these benchmarks would mark a wholesale departure from the approaches taken by recent presidents to delivering universal coverage, all of whom tried (at least rhetorically) to achieve universal coverage by building on the existing hodgepodge health care system. Such a plan would provide what is sometimes thought of as "generous" coverage—more generous, in fact, than some of America's peer nations. Canada, for example, does not offer universal vision and dental care, but that's the point. Ensuring that all people have access to quality care, the type of care enjoyed today by America's well-to-do, requires generous coverage delivered through complete decommodification. This would deliver on Medicare's original intent and Roosevelt's promise of "adequate medical care and the opportunity to achieve and enjoy good health" and finally bring the United States in line with—perhaps even position it as a leader among—other high-income countries.

The benefits of a right to health care would be tremendous. Delivered in a Medicare for all–type program, this right would save tens of thousands of lives a year. In fact, research conducted by Yale University's Center for Infectious Disease Modeling and Analysis and published in the medical journal *The Lancet* found that a program of this type would save *68,000 lives a year* in the United States. That's the population of a small American city saved every year into perpetuity.[32]

Nevertheless, there are some common concerns regarding the right to health care in the United States. Can America afford such a lavish program? Wouldn't it bankrupt the country (or, at the very least, eat up an ever larger share of the nation's output, leaving fewer resources for necessities like housing and education)? And where do we find the trillions needed to fund it?

The answers are, yes, no, and wrong question.

In terms of affordability, the economic case for Medicare for all is irrefutable. In 2020, the CBO, the official scorekeeper that estimates the effects of legislation on the federal budget, released a deep analysis of universal health care in the United States, providing estimates for five different single-payer options. The findings were clear and concise. Replacing the current health care nonsystem with universal coverage through a single-payer system would provide *insurance for all while substantially reducing national health care spending*, resulting in more and better coverage for less money.[33]

How could this be? Well, a single-payer system would obviate many of the inefficiencies that currently wreak havoc on health care in America. The two primary drivers of healthcare costs in the United States are prices for medicines and services—which are far out of line with those of other high-income countries—and administrative costs associated with billing and patient enrollment. Many services, from the delivery of a new addition to the family to an inpatient appendectomy, cost two or three times more in the United States than many peer nations, while prices for lifesaving drugs like insulin, used by many of the 30 million people living in the United States with diabetes, are *eight times* higher than in Canada.[34] And administrative costs are off the charts too, with the United States spending roughly three times more than Canada, amounting to over 2 percent of GDP simply wasted.[35]

A single-payer system, the CBO estimates, would bring health care costs in the United States down drastically, cutting hundreds of billions in wasteful spending from these two areas. By reducing excessive prices currently paid for medical services and prescription drugs, along with massive savings from reducing painfully inefficient administrative processes, the CBO estimates that a single-payer system would result in a 5 percent reduction in national health care expenditures on an annual basis while providing quality coverage for the 33 million Americans still uninsured Americans and the 41 million underinsured. And while providing long-term supports and services to all, supports that are often not covered by skinny coverage plans.[36] In short, Medicare for all means *more coverage and services for less money.*

As for how we pay for it, it's important to note first that not every policy in the federal budget is linked to specific revenue streams (is there a specific "military" tax?) and rightly so, because this way of proceeding assumes that the current budget position is "ideal" (i.e., that a new program is revenue-neutral so as not to tamper with present budget allocations). Nevertheless, proponents of Medicare for all have offered a variety of pathways to finance such a program, including some that bend over backward to assure that middle-class tax rates won't go up.

But this type of promise misses the mark. What is important is not people's tax bills but rather their discretionary income—that is, what they have left after taxes and necessities like housing and health care. People already pay "taxes" for health insurance today; we just call them premiums, deductibles, copays, and so on. These, of course, will disappear in a single-payer system. Workers with employer-sponsored health insurance also pay a "tax" through lower wages. Once employers no longer have to insure their workers, those outlays can be rerouted to salaries. (Or, alternatively, the government could raise employer-side payroll taxes to capture those savings and ensure workers don't get the short end of the stick.)

In the end, might taxes increase a bit? Yes, and I want to be honest about that. But will those people have more discretionary income in their pockets at the end of the day—more money to spend on whatever gives them joy—because they no longer face staggering health insurance and medical bills, as well as the means to lead longer, healthier, and more stable lives? Absolutely.[37]

Another common concern is whether under Medicare for all people can keep their current doctors. The answer is yes. Given that public insurance will be universal and private insurance eliminated, the vast majority of doctors will accept Medicare (as they already do). Indeed, Medicare for all will do little to nothing to change health care provisioning for those already covered; rather, it will focus on changing who is covered and how it is financed.[38]

It's also worth noting that a onetime transition—to guaranteed health care for life—pales in comparison to what most workers contend with under the status quo. According to the BLS, people change jobs roughly a *dozen times* during their lives, meaning, since most people receive their health insurance through their employer, that the average worker is dealing with changing insurance carriers and provider networks frequently. More direct measures looking at consistency in health care coverage are even more shocking. A study of people in Michigan done by researchers at the University of Michigan in 2014 found that one in four people with employer-sponsored plans had to change insurance providers over just a twelve-month period. With these numbers in mind, a onetime change doesn't sound so bad.[39]

Fears about wait times are also unfounded. For example, Australia and the United Kingdom, two counties with universal systems, have shorter wait times than are experienced in the United States. In fact, the United States does pretty poorly in general regarding wait times compared to international peers with universal coverage.[40] And this critique implies that US health care isn't *already* rationed. But, of course, it is: at the moment, health care is reserved for those who have a good job, are older than sixty-five, or have the means to pay the high costs.

Others argue that Medicare for all goes too far. They claim that the same benefits could be achieved by simply creating a public option—a health insurance plan offered by the government to compete with private insurance—that would be included among current health insurance offerings. Proponents of the public option tout it as far less disruptive (for them a feature, not a bug) and a reform that would offer "more choice, not less."[41] President Biden, for instance, proposed a public option coupled with more robust subsidies for those buying health care on the exchanges.

But there are severe limitations to this approach. According to Biden's own estimates, a public option coupled with more generous subsidies would still leave 3 percent of Americans uninsured. Matt

Bruenig, founding director of the People's Policy Institute, finds that that gap in coverage would result in 125,000 preventable deaths over a ten-year period. And this analysis doesn't even account for the underinsured.

Other forms of the public option fare even worse in terms of expanding coverage, with the CBO estimating in 2013 that a public option added to the Affordable Care Act "would have minimal effects . . . on the number of people who would be uninsured."[42] While Bruenig finds that Biden's proposed public option might save some money compared to the existing system, the CBO estimates that it would still cost well over $100 billion a year *more* than a Medicare for all–type program.[43]

In short, a public option is not a viable pathway to realizing universal coverage and eliminating the financial barriers to health care. It prescribes the wrong medicine—competition—for the dysfunctional health care landscape. When it comes to the health care market, what is needed is not a floor provided by a public option, or a ceiling through more regulation, but a demolition. The only option that will cover everyone—thereby delivering on the right to health care—while driving down costs is Medicare for all.

Guaranteeing people the right to health care is good economics, but, as Frances Perkins knew, it's also the humane and right thing to do. People will be healthier. They'll be able to enjoy more—and better—years of life. The evidence shows that Medicare for all would cover everyone while reducing health care expenditures. It would drastically reduce the waste in the health care system resulting from private insurance and save tens of thousands of lives a year. The long-standing question in the United States is whether the public's interests can be placed ahead of private ones.

8

The Right to a Basic Income and Banking

Foremost was the idea that poverty is preventable, that poverty is destructive, wasteful, demoralizing, and that poverty is morally unacceptable.
FRANCES PERKINS

I am now convinced that the simplest approach will prove the most effective—the solution to poverty is to abolish it directly by a now widely discussed measure: the guaranteed income.
MARTIN LUTHER KING JR.

The twofold terror of the COVID-19 pandemic was that it threatened people's health *and* livelihoods. Illnesses were both acute and prolonged; months of school were missed, along with time with elderly relatives and working days; more than one million deaths occurred followed by goodbyes at a distance. The economic toll was similarly unprecedented: 22 million jobs obliterated in the blink of an eye. (In 1933, at the height of the Great Depression, only 15.5 million were unemployed, though it represented a larger percentage of the population.)

Given this frightening crash of the labor market, poverty should have ballooned as well, as it always does during economic downturns. Only this time, it didn't. In fact, *the poverty rate was cut nearly in half*, dropping to the lowest level on record. In the midst of the largest economic contraction since the Great Depression, a full 20 million people were lifted temporarily out of poverty.[1] How did it happen? The government gave people money.

Starting with the CARES Act, signed into law on March 27, 2020, the federal government shoveled cash out the door and into people's hands, and fast. Between March 2020 and March 2021, the government authorized three separate "economic impact payments"—that is, stimulus checks. Each adult qualified for up to $3,200 in total; families received an additional payment of up to $2,500 per child. This kind of money produces extraordinary effects. The average low- to middle-income family with two kids received $11,400 in cash from the combined stimulus payments, an amount that boosted the incomes of millions of families *above* pre-pandemic levels.[2] It was enough cash to cover the rent or mortgage for a few months, or keep food on the table for the better part of a year.

Adding up all the money from these payments to the American people leaves us with a big number—$850 billion, or nearly 4 percent of GDP—but it was money that was put to the best use: saving families. In fact, estimates from the US Census Bureau put the number of Americans lifted out of poverty by the emergency checks alone at 11.7 million people—more than half the total number raised above the poverty line during the pandemic.[3]

How were the others lifted out of poverty in the midst of an economic crisis? The government provided far more support than deposits in bank accounts. For example, unemployment insurance benefits, which are particularly meager in conservative states, were temporarily supplemented by a $600 per week federal "enhancement." The rules concerning who was eligible for unemployment benefits were also expanded, and the number of weeks people could receive those benefits was increased as well, from twenty-six weeks for most unemployed workers to thirty-nine weeks. The more robust unemployment assistance—coupled with the stimulus checks and other programs—kept an additional 6.7 million out of poverty.[4]

Then there was the temporary increase in the maximum benefit people could receive from the Supplemental Nutrition Assistance Program (SNAP), commonly referred to as "food stamps." Food is one of the largest line items in low-income families' budgets, and

SNAP helped keep people fed, lifting another 7.9 million struggling people out of poverty during the crisis.[5]

In addition to these changes, the government made sweeping alterations to yet another pillar of the well-being state: the child tax credit (CTC). Before the crisis, the government offered a modest tax credit for families with children ($2,000 maximum per child), but it was only partially refundable; that is, the millions of families without earned income or who didn't owe federal income taxes received just a portion (if any) of the benefit. Further, the benefit came during tax season, forcing cash-strapped families to wait for the disbursement—or get it in advance from predatory lenders—as the bills continued to arrive.

The Biden administration, working with Congress, made the tax credit fully refundable while expanding it: up to $3,600 for children under the age of six and $3,000 for children six to seventeen. The administration also changed the way the credit was disbursed. Rather than remit the funds to eligible families in one lump sum at tax time, the money was sent in monthly amounts over the course of the year.

The effects were astounding. For instance, before the change, 23.7 percent of Black children were in poverty. With these adjustments, Black child poverty is projected to fall to 11.3 percent. With the stroke of a pen, effectively, 1.5 million fewer Black children will live in poverty. Let that sink in: a small tweak to the tax code, and child poverty—which affects one in six kids nationally, predominantly children of color—tumbled dramatically.[6] (Unfortunately, it didn't last. Congress allowed the expanded child tax credit to expire, and as a result nearly 4 million children were thrust back into poverty.)[7]

These examples point to a vital but too often overlooked fact that underscores the arguments in this book: *poverty is a policy choice*. As evidenced by the precipitous drop in poverty as a result of government initiatives, the poverty rate isn't some unpredictable and uncontrollable phenomenon. It's whatever the government wants it to be. Send people enough cash, provide them with benefits like SNAP and the child tax credit, and poverty shrinks. To end poverty in the United States, policy makers need only *choose* to eliminate poverty—no pandemic necessary.

One of the central ideas of the New Deal, long faded from America's collective memory, is what Roosevelt called cradle-to-grave security. According to this notion, in a decent society poverty is nonexistent; everyone, always, is taken care of. It was for this purpose that Roosevelt imagined the Social Security Act. In the early discussions that led to its drafting, Roosevelt told Frances Perkins that he saw "no reason why every child from the day he is born, shouldn't be a member of the social security system." Children should come into the world knowing that old-age benefits will be there. They should also know that if they become unemployed, they get a benefit. If they become ill, they get a benefit. If they're widowed, they get benefits. And if disability should render them unable to engage in paid work, they get benefits sufficient to lead a dignified life.[8]

This vision culminated in the Social Security Act passed by Congress and signed into law in 1935. As I discussed in the previous chapter, this law laid the foundation for the modern American well-being state: a basic income for the elderly (i.e., Social Security), unemployment insurance, workers' compensation, and direct financial aid for the disabled and widows. It also established Aid to Dependent Children (ADC), later renamed Aid to Families with Dependent Children (AFDC), which would eventually become known as "welfare."

With the rise of the so-called New Democrats in the 1980s and 1990s, Roosevelt's vision of cradle-to-grave security came under attack from both sides of the aisle. The coup de grâce came in 1996, when President Bill Clinton gutted AFDC, delivering on his longtime promise to "end welfare as we know it."[9] "Welfare reform," the legal scholar Dorothy E. Roberts has observed, "eliminated the federal guarantee of a basic income support for all families."[10]

As a result, many of the nation's poor have had to go without cash assistance. The outcomes are, unsurprisingly, devastating. As Kathryn J. Edin and H. Luke Shaefer document in their book, *$2.00 a Day: Living on Almost Nothing in America*, the end of direct cash assistance for the poor has *doubled* extreme poverty; that is, twice as many families have had to make do on $2 a day or less for each person in their family. Without cash in their pockets, families—and solo mothers in particular—are pushed into true desperation to afford basic necessities. Edin and Shaefer tell stories of some selling plasma and others resorting to selling sex; still others simply go without many of life's essentials: housing, medical care, heat, or air-conditioning. The end of welfare, which was coupled with reforms intended to push people into the paid labor force, has simply widened the gaps in the social safety net (if that's even the right term for it). It is true that the poor get SNAP benefits, but SNAP doesn't pay the rent or warm the house during a bitter winter.[11]

To be sure, there are benefits for some poor families. The largest poverty reduction program in the United States remains Social Security, which provides cash directly to the elderly, keeping tens of millions of seniors from falling into destitution. But the second largest poverty reduction program, the Earned Income Tax Credit—which refunds taxes to supplement the earnings of workers receiving poverty wages—features a massive flaw: it provides zero benefits to those without work. Ever since the war on welfare in the 1980s and 1990s, which aimed to rid the nation of "welfare queens"—a racist and sexist slur with no basis in reality—people who cannot (or who are without) work are deemed "undeserving" and largely deprived of support, despite the fact that (1) there's never enough wage work to go around and (2) some people—people caring for sick or disabled loved ones, for example—are doing unremunerated labor at home. The fact that care work, which is work in every sense of the word, doesn't occur in the almighty market doesn't mean that its workers should be ineligible for support.

Of course, the economic rights discussed thus far would put up guardrails here, ensuring that people can get many of life's basic needs (housing, health care, an education) regardless of their income or wealth; they are an essential way to reduce the importance of the market in securing a decent standard of living and realizing one's potential and dreams. Nevertheless, the fact remains that we exist in a market economy wherein people need cash to purchase goods and services. Some kind of income, then, is also an economic right. Yet today that right is far from being realized.

To illustrate the problem, let's look at who the poor are. The single largest group of people in poverty in the United States is children. People under the age of eighteen account for roughly one in three of those forced to live in extreme scarcity, mostly because so many families are pushed into poverty immediately upon having to provide for their children. In 2018, nearly 12 million children were in poverty, and another 9 million children lived just above the poverty line.

The second biggest group, accounting for over 15 percent of all people in poverty, comprises those living with a disability. Measured in the absence of modest government assistance, half of disabled people live in poverty; once transfers are accounted for, the poverty rate is cut in half, but still one in four disabled people live below the meager poverty line. Even after accounting for benefits, the disabled are two and a half times more likely to live in poverty than those without a disability.[12]

Closely tied for third place are seniors (those over the age of sixty-five) and caregivers (those taking care of loved ones, whether a young child or a sick parent or spouse). Then there are those working full-time (10% of the poor), students (7%), and the unemployed (6%). To be sure, the gender and racial dimensions of poverty are ever present as well, with women and people of color much more likely to be in poverty. This is particularly true for single mothers, one in four of whom live in poverty with their child or children.[13]

What is to be done? There is no question that the rights discussed thus far will go a long way toward assuring economic security; for instance, the right to housing will eliminate homelessness and housing insecurity, two of the biggest concerns for people in or near poverty; and the job guarantee will eradicate unemployment and poverty wages while setting a real floor in the labor market. But not everyone works in the paid labor market—children, full-time caregivers, the severely disabled, the elderly—and yet everyone needs an income.

The answer is the same one policy makers hit upon during the pandemic: give people money. To recognize and respect at-home care work, support those who are excluded from the marketplace because of a disability, and ensure the elderly are able to live out their years with dignity, the United States must deliver on the right to "adequate protection from economic fears." It must provide its people with a basic income.

The Right to a Basic Income

Simply put, giving people cash is good. Cash means warm (or cool) apartments, stocked refrigerators, a charged-up car, bills paid on time. It means purchasing power, the kind one needs to afford health-ful food, a current cellphone, or even a night at the movies.

Giving people cash outright is an old idea, one that dates at least to Thomas Paine, who advocated for a basic income in his 1797 trea-tise *Agrarian Justice*.[14] A basic income, as Paine and others have envi-sioned it, simply acknowledges that everyone should be entitled to a minimum amount of cash on an annual basis as a matter of right. It is what is owed to each and every citizen as part of the social contract.

Fifty years ago, Congress agreed. On April 16, 1970, the US House of Representatives passed a basic income plan with bipartisan sup-port, including backing from the Republican-controlled White House. The following morning, the *New York Times* reported on the front page that the passage of the bill had just "established for the first time the principle that the government should guarantee every family a mini-mum annual income."[15]

The legislation had its origins in a report commissioned by Nixon and issued the year before. *Poverty amid Plenty: The American Paradox* explained that poverty was "not some personal failure" but a feature of the current structure of American capitalism. The problem was that the poor, especially those without work, didn't have a way to claim life's necessary resources. The report's authors suggested to Nixon that it was possible to rid the nation of poverty and "assure basic economic security for all Americans." Although broad reforms were needed, the key recommendation was straightforward: "make cash payments to all members of the population with income needs."[16]

Nixon, over the opposition of his more conservative advisers, embraced the idea. In fact, during his first year in office, he proposed a negative income tax (NIT) that would have provided the equivalent of roughly $11,000 today for a family of four. The plan stipulated that as recipients increased their income, the NIT would be taxed away at a 50 percent rate (the "phase-out" rate) until the family earned roughly $22,000; then the basic income would cease. The plan was not intended to replace existing programs for those in need, like food stamps, but rather to top them off.

The idea would pass muster in the House—twice, in fact—but meet opposition in the Senate. Conservative senators were concerned the payments were too generous (despite being below the poverty line and stingier than levels of support provided by some northern states at the time). Further, some conservatives complained the legislation didn't pay enough attention to work requirements. Nixon, for his part, replied, "I don't give a damn about work requirements." Nevertheless, he added a provision to appease conservatives: unemployed recipients would have to register with the Department of Labor, though the requirement wasn't expected to have any teeth.[17]

There was also opposition on the Left, for the opposite reason. Many viewed the reform as too stingy. Numerous progressive lawmakers decided to hold out under the impression that a better deal, consisting of a more generous basic income, would soon be on the table. Progressive groups such as the National Welfare Rights Organization were pushing for annual payments to Americans that were *three and a half times* the size of Nixon's Family Assistance Plan. Alas, they would never get it. The bill died in the Senate.[18]

But that was the 1970s. What would a basic income look like now? Although there are dozens of flavors—some originating on the Left, others on the Right—any effective basic income program must answer the following questions:

1. What is the right basic income amount?
2. Who qualifies for the basic income?
3. Is the basic income phased out? If so, how?

4. Should the basic income *replace* other aspects of the well-being state or *complement* them?

5. How should the basic income be paid, and how often?

Let's examine each of these in turn.

The Right Amount. Proposals are all over the map in terms of the level of the basic income, ranging from as little as $200 or so a month to over $2,000 a month, but many are in the ballpark of the amount proposed by 2020 Democratic presidential candidate, Andrew Yang: $1,000 a month.[19] With an official poverty line of $12,880 for a single person, however, this amount would still leave those without another source of income in poverty.

Although there are many issues with official definitions of poverty, in this instance I believe the official poverty line is a reasonable guide, especially, as I discuss below, when combined with the other economic rights. With the full slate of economic rights in place, a basic income set at $12,880 annually—or $1,073 a month—would indeed eradicate poverty.

The Eligible. In general, to minimize the possibility of someone falling through the safety net, broad coverage is preferable to narrow coverage. Further, universal coverage builds strong political support (just look at Social Security and Medicare, politics' proverbial "third rails"). Most proposals apply payments only to American citizens over the age of eighteen. This is a problem. Leaving those younger than eighteen out of the equation means that child poverty and poverty among families, especially those with young children, would remain features of the American landscape. It's also a problem since it leaves many who are living in the United States but who do not yet have citizenship out of the picture. And rather than support caregivers and recognize children as public goods and parenting as a public service—as the economist Nancy Folbre long has—this flavor of basic income would actually penalize families with children by failing to account for the added financial burden they place on a household.[20]

In short, to satisfy the aims of a basic income, a "child allowance" must be included. However, since children are part of a family unit and generally require less income than an individual adult, a smaller benefit should suffice. And the program could replace the child tax credit, among whose laundry list of problems are insufficient amounts, obstacles to access, and the intentional exclusion of some of the poorest of the poor.[21]

Allowances to help parents raise kids have already been tried, and they work. For example, most European countries provide parents with cash support. Nations like Luxembourg, Austria, Ireland, Sweden, and Germany give parents thousands of dollars a year to help meet their families' financial needs (hence the far lower rates of child poverty in Europe compared to the United States).[22] Mainstream economists too are in favor of such an allowance. In fact, when they've crunched the numbers, they've consistently found direct cash assistance to families with children pays off with dividends.[23] A 2021 study by the Center on Poverty and Social Policy at Columbia University, for example, estimated that a fairly robust child allowance would pay for itself *eight times over* while, most important, drastically slashing poverty and improving children's lives now and well into the future.[24]

In terms of the amount of the child allowance, some have suggested $378 a month, which would amount to just over $4,500 annually. This sum represents the difference between the one-person and two-person poverty line. I agree. Combined with the adult basic income, this amount would give a single-parent household with one child up to $17,420 a year—enough to eradicate all poverty.[25] When this benefit is combined with other economic rights—from universal free pre-K and health care to social housing that limits rent to a third of people's income—one can begin to see how all families could lead good lives.

The Phase-Out. All basic incomes, whatever their particular provisions, are phased out to a degree given the progressive income tax code (notwithstanding the loopholes and legal legerdemain that allow some of the richest households to pay less than the poor). As economists correctly contend, taxes and transfers should not be conceptualized in isolation but rather as two sides of the same coin. That's why I believe an NIT is the best means of providing a basic income, for it solves two problems in one: it guarantees an income for all people while simultaneously addressing the arbitrary fact that the tax code only applies to those with positive incomes. Why, after all, should the progressivity of the tax code stop at zero rather than reach into negative territory by paying out a basic income to those who need it?

I propose that the basic income for adults should begin to phase out at $15,000 for one-person households and $20,000 for two-person households. The child allowance would not be subject to phasing out, as children should be treated as public goods and therefore entitled to support regardless of family income. The phase-out rate for the adult benefit would be set at 50 percent, meaning benefits are reduced by $1 for every $2 in earnings above the threshold. For example, a single parent with one child and no earnings would receive the full $17,420 per year. If that parent decided to engage in paid employment—say, for a public program through the job guarantee while their little one spent those hours at free public day care—every $2 the parent made over $20,000 (the threshold for a two-person household) would result in a $1 reduction in their basic income. The child allowance would stay the same.[26]

The Relation to Other Programs. Taken for granted in the above example is the parent's access to a range of social programs, in addition to receiving a basic income. Simply put, cash alone—at least in the modest amounts made possible by an NIT—cannot do the job of providing universal economic security. While many economists and politicians, ranging from Milton Friedman to Andrew Yang, have proposed a basic income as an "efficient" replacement for other well-being programs—housing assistance, health care benefits—studies show that most people would actually be *worse off*. A recent report by the OECD confirmed that a basic income that replaced the existing social welfare state would indeed exacerbate poverty.[27] Take the example of housing. A single person receiving the basic income couldn't afford an apartment anywhere in the country (those with dependents would be even worse off). Or what about health care? According to the Kaiser Family Foundation, the average health care premium for a single person in the United States in 2021 was $7,739 (and a whopping $22,221 for the average family).[28] With a basic income set at the poverty line, a single adult without paid work would be left with $5,410 to meet all other needs: housing, transportation, food, electricity, clothing, and so on. It can't be done.

Thus a basic income must be but one economic right among many. A guaranteed income, delivered in combination with the other economic rights proposed in this book, would drastically improve the freedom and well-being of Americans. People would have actual choices: Do I want to stay home with my young children or go into the paid labor market? Will I stay in this toxic relationship or leave, knowing I'll always have a home, a job, and an income? Do I take a year off my current job to pursue my dream of being an artist or small farmer? Together, a basic income and the other economic rights will expand people's freedom, giving them far more control over their day-to-day lives while simultaneously taming "the market," which all too often *decides* those lives.

The Timing. How often should benefits be distributed? Payday tends to occur every two weeks in the United States, but many government benefits, such as the EITC and CTC, are administered when people file taxes—that is, just once a year, and after the fact. For folks living paycheck to paycheck, most of whom cannot wait an entire year for essential cash, this is a travesty; they can't go to the store and say, "I'll pay you when my tax credit comes in." Some might be able to put essential expenses on a credit card, but paying the interest on their balances, which tend to be around 15 to 18 percent these days for people with high credit scores, would be financially ruinous and wasteful.

There is a simple solution to this dilemma: make payments directly to people on a monthly basis. This is exactly what Social Security does, after all, and with great success. In 2021, the government rolled out a monthly payment scheme as part of Democrats' temporary improvement and expansion of the child tax credit. The intuition was that people need to pay bills today, so they should get the benefits sooner rather than later.

There were snags, however. The government had a difficult time getting stimulus money to all Americans during the pandemic, and it faced similar hurdles getting the monthly child tax credits out the door and into the hands of the poorest households, especially those who do not regularly file income taxes. Estimates show that monthly benefits failed to reach millions (in fact, the majority) of children living in nonfiling households—which, again, tend to be the poorest of the poor.[29] The reason? People who file their taxes electronically often provide the IRS with bank account information, which the IRS then uses to rapidly deposit funds in everyday people's bank accounts. But for those without bank accounts or who do not file taxes—tens of millions of households—the government ran into an infrastructure problem: How to get the money to people, fast?

The Right to Banking and Financial Services

The answer to the infrastructure problem described above lies in a further economic right: the right to banking and financial services. Being poor is expensive. Poor people are hit with fines and fees at nearly every turn—for cashing a check, for having too low a balance in their bank accounts, for falling behind on utility bills when cash is tight, for submitting applications for apartments or college—all afterthoughts for affluent households, yet a major barrier for those living paycheck to paycheck. These financial penalties just keep piling up, weighing low- and middle-income households down day in and day out, while the well-to-do enjoy favorable treatment by the financial powers that be.[30] To use myself as an example, last year alone I racked up over $1,000 in free money from credit card points while paying $0 in interest or fees.[31] (Money accrued from points isn't exactly free, though, as it drives the higher prices that disproportionately punish the poor.) I also had access to free banking services: I paid $0 for ATM withdrawals, $0 for my checking and savings accounts, and $0 for the financial transactions essential to paying all my bills. I was even able to convince my bank to forgive the $15 fee for a cashier's check I needed.[32]

This is a far cry from the experience of many low- and middle-income people. Private Main Street banks exclude millions from basic access to everyday financial needs: cashing a paycheck, paying a bill, receiving a stimulus payment or a tax credit from the government, or storing money in a safe and secure place without being pummeled by fees. This is not a problem that affects just the few; a survey by the Federal Deposit Insurance Corporation found that one in five American households are either unbanked (meaning they do not have a bank account) or underbanked (meaning they rely regularly on high-cost alternative financial services, such as payday lenders, to meet their basic needs).[33] And like most failures in the economy, the broken financial system doesn't affect all groups equally. Black and Brown households are excluded from basic banking services at double the rate of White households, with roughly half of Black households and two in five Hispanic households deprived of Main Street banking. Even after controlling for education, income, and home ownership, stark disparities in access to necessary financial services remain, with Black households 2.5 times more likely to be financially excluded than White households. In part, this disparity is fueled by a lack of access to brick-and-mortar banks. Bank branches have been rapidly shuttering their doors in low-income communities and communities of color.[34]

The challenges of getting stimulus payments to some of the nation's neediest families threw these disparities into stark relief. A report published by the Brookings Institution found that the unequal banking infrastructure of the United States resulted in delayed payments and excess fees for millions in need, exacerbating inequality and causing painful delays in the midst of a crisis. For example, only 45 percent of direct payments from the CARES Act were distributed in the first wave of payments, meaning more than half of Americans—disproportionately those in economic distress—had to wait for their money. In fact, four months after the first wave of payments, one in ten Americans were still waiting to get their checks.

But, of course, bills don't wait. Increasingly desperate people turned to payday lenders—whose average annual interest rate is an unconscionable *400 percent*—while standing by for their economic assistance. And once the payments were finally sent, scores of people had to pay exorbitant fees—an estimated total of $66 million, in fact—to check cashers actually to access their stimulus money. In the least regulated states, a family of five might have paid as much as $195 to cash their government stimulus checks, taking away necessary resources during a time of dire need.[35]

It need not be this way. A crucial, yet forgotten, lesson from the New Deal era is that a public option for basic banking services can secure universal access to banking as public infrastructure *and* empower regulators to curtail abuses in the financial system. Its rationale is the same as the other public options discussed in this book. A public option can set a floor in a given market, preventing a race to the bottom and the exclusion of certain groups from basic needs; at the same time, it can compete directly in markets, forcing private options to be just as good or better than those offered by the government. Institutions like the Consumer Financial Protection Bureau (CFPB) have worked tirelessly to improve financial inclusion, but they can only do so much; what is needed is a public option for banking and financial services, one that acknowledges banking as public infrastructure and exists not to maximize short-term profits but rather to serve the people.

America has done it before. From 1911 to 1966, people were able to open interest-bearing bank accounts, make deposits and withdrawals, cash checks, and secure loans through than their local post offices. The impetus was financial inclusion—to serve immigrants (information was provided in twenty-four languages), rural people, and low-income households—and financial security. In fact, the postal bank for a time served as an alternative to federal deposit insurance. By 1934, writes the law professor Mehrsa Baradaran, "postal banking had $1.2 billion in assets—about 10 percent of the entire commercial banking system." Deposits would peak in 1947: $3.4 billion in assets from 4 million users.[36]

However, as a result of ongoing pressure from the financial lobby, the public banking system was weaker than intended and never achieved all it could have. By the 1960s, interest on secured deposits had been capped at 2.5 percent—well below the average rate paid to depositors at a private bank. By 1967, the public bank was no longer able to compete due to these legislative handcuffs, and Congress voted to eliminate it.

Much has changed since then, but the approach still functions. Recent work by Baradaran, along with joint research I've published with Thomas Herndon, shows that a revival of the postal bank would have a profound effect on the banking landscape.[37] Post offices already exist all over the country, in low-income and rural areas as well as wealthy and densely populated ones. (There are 31,000 brick-and-mortar US Postal Service locations—over six times the number of branches of Wells Fargo, the bank with the most branches in the United States.) Alongside an app featuring many of the same services as private banks—mobile deposit, automatic bill pay—a postal bank could achieve the goal of universal access to financial services.

To guarantee that access is indeed universal, every person could be assigned a postal account at birth or upon moving to the United States. Whatever a person's banking preferences, the account would be available, free of charge, into perpetuity. This way the government could get money to people directly whenever needed, whether a basic income payment, a child allowance, or an economic stimulus payment during some future crisis.

But it isn't just about access; it's about the services themselves. As Herndon and I propose, "plain vanilla" consumer loans, ranging from small-dollar loans to auto loans and mortgages, should also be provided by the public bank. Subprime mortgages, which unscrupulous lenders pushed on creditworthy Latinx and Black borrowers, as well as the outrageous lending practices in the payday and auto loan industries, show just how much a truly inclusive financial option is needed. Competition from the postal bank will force private and predatory finance to shape up—or risk obsolescence.

Together, a basic income and a right to banking and financial services guarantee that poverty amid plenty is remedied once and for all. But, like the other rights in this book, cash alone is not a silver bullet. True economic security can't be provided by any one right alone. Rather, when the power of economic rights are combined, they create a tightly woven well-being state that offers economic freedom to all—regardless of their birth, their luck in the marketplace, or an accident or mishap that may befall them.

The Right to a Healthy Environment

They have come to understand that as soon as they admit that climate
change is real, they will lose the central ideological battle of our time—
whether we need to plan and manage our societies to reflect our goals
and values, or whether that task can be left to the magic of the market.
NAOMI KLEIN

The climate is a common good, belonging to all and meant for all.
POPE FRANCIS

In the environmental history of the United States, the American public's obliviousness to environmental problems has been a reliable
constant. Some of this can be reasonably attributed to how industries
hide their environmental harms from public view; the rest is likely a
reflection of how the United States, as a rich country, insulates the
most powerful swaths of its population from the effects of environmental harm.

America's dissonance on environmental issues became less sustainable in the 1960s—in part because the incidence of dramatic environmental events left no choice but to acknowledge them.

At the fortieth annual Macy's Thanksgiving Day Parade in 1966,
the assembly of crowds, marching bands, and dance troupes along
Manhattan's Fifth Avenue were treated to performances by Dusty
Springfield and Nina Simone (who, getting into the spirit of things, was
adorned in a "Queen of the Butterflies" costume); the debut of the
Smokey Bear balloon; and new floats featuring dinosaurs, confectionary

treats, and Grand Prix race cars. Leading the procession was a brand-new seventy-five-foot Superman balloon.

But there was also a more unwelcome participant in the festivities that day: the sudden onset of what New York press dubbed "Killer smog." On November 23, the day before the parade, a toxic cloud composed of sulfur dioxide and carbon monoxide had descended on the city. It would hover for three days, until a cold front blew it off. At the time, most New Yorkers were seemingly unaffected; some reported various minor respiratory symptoms and mild eye irritation but nothing more. Decreased visibility was the topmost concern. Nobody suspected that New Yorkers—about two hundred, later analyses would show—were dying from it.[1]

The environment is humanity's greatest collective resource, but long before the 1960s, America was trashing it. Pollution and environmental degradation were everywhere: in the air, the water, the earth. Pulmonary emphysema, caused by air pollution and smoking, was the fastest-growing cause of death for New Yorkers.[2] The Cuyahoga River, which runs through the heart of Cleveland, was so contaminated with sewage, spent oil, and industrial waste that it caught fire—more than a dozen times.[3] Streets were "made hideous by litter," and families on road trips could, according to a famed passage by the economist John Kenneth Galbraith describing the environmental dissonance exhibited by most Americans, "picnic on exquisitely packaged food from a portable icebox by a polluted stream and go on to spend the night at a park which is a menace to public health" because it is chock full of "decaying refuse."[4]

Killer smog and flammable rivers weren't the only sensational environmental events. In 1969, a government-sanctioned, cost-cutting measure taken by Union Oil led to a devastating oil spill near the coast of Santa Barbara, California. On the morning of the spill, a panicked observer called in to the local newspaper, stating that "the ocean is boiling." With no regulations and no contingency plans in place, the catastrophe would only intensify. All told, more than three million gallons of oil would spill into the ocean, killing upwards of nine thousand birds and coating dozens of miles of beautiful coastline in oil sludge.[5] Galdwin Hill, the *New York Times*'s first environmental correspondent, called the disaster the "ecological 'shot heard round the world.'"[6]

While the 1970s may be known as the "environmental decade," it was, in fact, the crises of the 1960s that drove Americans to action. Tales of environmental despoliation, and the harm it was causing American citizens, began to find purchase in people's imaginations. Rachel Carson's *Silent Spring* is a case in point. Serialized in the *New Yorker*, Carson's reporting explained in plain language how pesticides poisoned everything they touched: the land, the air, the water—and, eventually, the food supply. The dangers of these inventions, intentionally concealed by some of the country's most powerful corporations (including DuPont, a major manufacturer of the lethal pesticide DDT) were wreaking havoc on the earth.[7] Technological advances indeed helped give rise to unparalleled growth after World War II, but some of these advances caused significant harms. As a result, both the environment and people's health suffered.

Increasingly frequent disasters, coupled with popular accounts of industrial malfeasance vis-à-vis the environment, contributed to an explosion of interest in groups like the Sierra Club and laid the groundwork for a decade of action. In short order, the ranks of the Sierra Club would go from hundreds to hundreds of thousands. And from the late 1950s to the late 1960s, media coverage of environmental issues would increase some 300 percent. The nation was watching.[8]

By 1970, *Time* was dubbing the environment its "Issue of the Year,"[9] and Richard Nixon—no environmentalist, to be sure—was using his State of the Union address to urge the nation to "begin to make reparations for the damage we have done to our air, to our land, and to our water." He would go on to argue, "Clean air, clean water, open spaces—these should once again be the birthright of every American. If we act now, they can be."[10]

That same year, on the first Earth Day, some 20 million Americans took to the streets. Senator Edmund Muskie (D-ME), the leading environmentalist in Congress at the time, was the keynote speaker at the Earth Day gathering in Philadelphia. Talking to the enormous crowd, Muskie argued that "man's environment includes more than natural resources. It includes the shape of the communities in which he lives: his home, his school, his place of work." He further contended that cleaning up the environment could not be done in isolation, for "the only society that has a chance" is "a society that will not tolerate slums for some and decent homes for others, rats for some and playgrounds for others, clean air for some and filth for others."[11] There must, according to Muskie, be a clean environment for all or a clean environment for none.

In response to mounting public pressure, Congress and the White House took swift action on the environmental front. In 1970, Nixon created the Environmental Protection Agency to "make a coordinated attack on the pollutants which debase the air we breathe, the water we drink, and the land that grows our food."[12] The National Environmental Policy Act would be signed into law, marking the start of a national environmental policy framework and imposing the requirement that all federal agencies assess the environmental effects of proposed major federal actions. But policy makers weren't done. Later that year, they introduced the Clean Air Act; in 1972, they passed the Federal Water and Pollution Control Act (known as the Clean Water Act). With these two pieces of legislation, clean water and clean air became something Americans no longer needed to purchase. They were not luxury goods; they were rights.[13]

The environmental decade brought about myriad positive environmental (and, in turn, health) developments. American rivers no longer combust, and one can actually swim in the Charles River in Boston—as I did growing up—which was once so filthy it inspired the rock song "Dirty Water" by the Standells. Air quality too has drastically improved. People across Los Angeles—an infamously smoggy city—can now spot the San Gabriel Mountains from downtown on most days, and children no longer need to stay indoors during frequent smog alerts (except, of course, when wildfires, turbocharged by climate change, engulf the state).

Not all Americans, however, have equal access to clean air and water. The have-nots of the United States—poor communities, especially communities of color—face environmental harms at astonishing rates. Between 2014, when the city switched the water supply from Detroit's system to the Flint River, and 2019, the residents of Flint, Michigan, a predominantly Black city and home to the nation's second highest poverty rate (also, incidentally, the birthplace of General Motors), were exposed to drinking water with lead levels so high that according to the EPA's guidelines it was classified as "toxic waste." As textbook an example of environmental racism and racialized capitalism as one could find, this dreadful and unnecessary development occurred due to cost-cutting measures—otherwise known as austerity—and horrendous instances of criminal negligence and lack of accountability by local officials. While the full health effects are still playing out, as of this writing twelve people died and eighty people became seriously ill.[14]

For all its improvements, we know that the air is still deadly too. A 2021 study by researchers at Harvard University and in the United Kingdom confirmed that air pollution generated from the combustion of fossil fuels alone—what are referred to as co-pollutants—remains a leading cause of death in the United States, responsible for over 350,000 American deaths annually. That's a death every two minutes.

Globally, the numbers are even more staggering. Air pollution from burning fossil fuels is responsible for over eight million premature deaths a year—mostly among, as you might expect, those without the economic and political power to fight back.[15]

Yet, incredibly, the dangers of air pollution go beyond these millions of unnecessary deaths. For the burning of fossil carbon isn't just a driver of environmental injustice: it's a threat to humanity itself.

The great problem of the twenty-first century is climate breakdown. It is a problem that is increasingly here and now. According to the United Nations Intergovernmental Panel on Climate Change (IPCC), the global community must slash emissions in half by 2030 and reach carbon neutrality by 2050 simply to have a *chance* at avoiding the most catastrophic consequences of a warming world. Wealthy nations, especially those like the United States that have already produced far more than their fair share of emissions, must act even faster. In short, carbon pollution must be abolished. That means every corner of the economy must be decarbonized. Power must be generated exclusively from clean and renewable sources; transportation—the leading emitter of greenhouse gas (GHG) emissions in the United States—must transition to mass transit and be fully electrified; nearly all buildings—homes, schools, office spaces, restaurants, you name it—need to be retrofitted to improve efficiency and stripped of any fossil fuel systems (no more oil or gas heating); and agricultural practices must become far more sustainable. The problem, which is immense, can feel overwhelming. But in a sense it's fairly straightforward: to have a healthy environment, the burning of fossil fuel must come to an end.

Economists have spilled plenty of ink weighing in on the issue. However, mainstream economists have taken (and continue to take) an unfortunate—and incorrect—line: rapid climate action would send the economy into a tailspin, increasing unemployment and reducing living standards across the nation. In their fantasy, markets are efficient, government not so; thus public intervention, whether through regulation or investment, would only gum up the works. Even when they acknowledge that *some* government intervention might be necessary—because pollution is a "negative externality," meaning companies and people don't pay for their pollution and so can't respond to price incentives—they focus on a single (market-based) solution: the almighty carbon tax. The goal is to get the price "right" in the market; once a modest price signal, the carbon tax, is in place, businesses, consumers, and governments will figure out the best—that is, the most efficient—ways to reduce emissions themselves (or accept the price on pollution). Home owners will turn down the heat a bit in the winter, or workers will ride their bikes to work rather than drive. If the tax is big enough, and gas prices go up enough, people might even buy fewer—or electric—Suburbans and Ford F-150s. The point is that market nudges let people figure it out for themselves.

A group of eminent economists from both political parties, including Nobel laureates and former Federal Reserve chairs, recently endorsed this approach to climate change. They argue that markets, rather than regulation or public spending, are the *ideal* tool for spurring the energy transition; in fact, markets are so efficient, they say, that those pesky environmental protections can be rolled back. What they don't disclose to the public is that their "optimal" worldview would lead to a planet with average temperatures that are 3.5°C (6.3°F) above preindustrial levels by 2100, with even more warming thereafter. The environmental repercussions of a planet allowed to warm by this much are hard to summarize, but a neat formulation is "hell on earth." Nevertheless, the Yale economist William Nordhaus recently won a Nobel Prize for pioneering this approach.[16]

Solutions to the climate crisis that rely exclusively on markets—that assume economic growth alone will save humanity from a burning world—lead to a fundamental misunderstanding of the challenges at hand. For one, market solutions are at once too broad and too narrow. They're too broad because they mold climate policy into a generic claim on economic output rather than a specific set of interventions needed to retool the economy to preserve our one and only planet. And they're too narrow because they focus on one policy tool—a carbon price in the form of a tax or tradable permit often given away for free to polluters—rather than look at the full range of policy tools available. Following the neoliberal line of thinking discussed earlier, market solutions assume that public investments are wasteful and regulatory efforts bound to be inefficient; Milton Friedman even went so far as to condemn all environmental regulation and suggest the EPA should be eliminated, noting it probably increased environmental damage by virtue of all the paper it used to print its regulations.[17]

In addition to being too broad and too narrow, market fundamentalism makes the energy transition appear too easy *and* too hard. Because mainstream economists treat a stable climate as just one economic good among others—rather than as the fundamental condition of our very existence—the problem becomes an easy one of incentives and signals. In this framing, even the worst outcome from climate change will cost humanity no more than a few years' worth of economic growth—the only measure most economists seem to care about—with the worst estimates putting the tally at about 10 percent of GDP by the century's end.[18] (Who bears these costs, both in the United States and across the globe, is an afterthought, as the models employed by economists like Nordhaus completely ignore distributional concerns.)

But these approaches also make the problem too hard—and in fact inaccurate—because they suggest that every step toward decarbonization must come at the expense of some other human need. Want to reduce emissions? All well and good, but you get fewer public schools or a less effective health care system. Scarcity and austerity, in other words, undergird mainstream analysts' thinking, which then gives the public the idea that addressing climate change means shortchanging other essentials. The trade-offs, so they say, are all too real and all too firm.

The upshot of this account is that society can't afford to address the climate crisis. It would cost too many jobs and lead to too many inefficiencies (which, it's worth pointing out again, assumes that we currently live in the most efficient world possible; a mere glance at the unemployment rolls or ranks of homeless gives the lie to this notion). Addressing climate change in a substantive and comprehensive way would disrupt the economy too much—so we should skip it. What the economy and people's everyday lives look like when the world heats by 3°, 4°, or 5°C is simply omitted.[19]

The arguments that posit climate action as too onerous, coupled with the bipartisan faith in neoliberal austerity politics over the last few decades, have cost us precious time.[20] The world has already warmed by 1.1°C; and the land—where humans, of course, *live*—has already warmed by 1.5°C (2.7°F). (Land warms about twice as fast as the planet overall; the ocean warms considerably more slowly.)[21] Average temperatures are on track to blow past the Paris Climate Accords limit of 1.5 to 2ºC (2.7–3.6ºF) above preindustrial levels, and if we persist with "business as usual," the world will have warmed by roughly 3ºC (5.4ºF) by the year 2100 (though an even greater increase is a distinct possibility). As noted above, this would be disastrous: entire cities—for example, Shanghai, home to over 25 million people—would be submerged; heat waves in Africa would increase fivefold, rendering significant portions of the continent uninhabitable; and armed conflicts would intensify substantially across the globe, adding even more death and destruction. There is no safe place in a 3ºC hotter world.

We're already experiencing the opening salvos of climate catastrophe, from intensifying heat waves, as experienced in the Pacific Northwest in 2021, and massive wildfires, such as California's Camp, Dixie, and August Complex fires, just to name a few, to more extreme storms like 2017's Hurricane Irma, which caused over $130 billion in damage when it made landfall in the Northeast, and 2018's Hurricane Harvey, which killed sixty-eight people, the deadliest storm in a decade. These events will only worsen—taking more lives, laying waste to more homes and businesses, and turbocharging the ongoing sixth extinction—as the climate continues to warm. It truly is a matter of now or never.

Changing the Conversation

Some have recognized the urgency. In November 2018, a group of roughly two hundred youth climate activists occupied the office of Democratic Leader Nancy Pelosi. Democrats had just regained control of the House in the midterm elections, and the activists—members of a relatively unknown group called the Sunrise Movement—wanted Democrats to use their new majority to fight climate change. The protesters had a wonky demand: the creation of a "Select Committee on the Green New Deal," which would be tasked with devising a climate plan that delivered on decarbonization, jobs, and justice. The kids were demanding that adults take climate change seriously.

Democratic leadership scoffed—and refused. But the idea of a "Green New Deal" had struck a chord. Three months later, Representative Alexandria Ocasio-Cortez (D-NY), a newly elected democratic socialist who had protested at Standing Rock, and Senator Ed Markey (D-MA), a longtime climate advocate, introduced a Green New Deal resolution to Congress.[22] It called for a program of deep decarbonization to meet the IPCC's timeline of 1.5°C of warming by reaching net-zero by 2050 (a target the United States had already agreed to try to achieve in the Paris Accord).[23] And it linked the climate crisis to broader environmental problems, including a lack of clean air and clean water. At its core—and despite the hysterical coverage of it in the media—the Green New Deal resolution simply called for the Democrats to establish a comprehensive plan to meet the moment, which at the time they still lacked.

But it was the call for economic rights in the resolution—a job guarantee; health care for all; housing for all; economic security for all; clean air, clean water, and healthy food for all—that set the Green New Deal, and those fighting for it, apart. Not only did it foreground climate and inequality as the two great challenges of our time, but it took for granted their inextricable link: policy makers cannot address environmental concerns without addressing economic insecurity, and, by the same token, they can't remedy economic insecurity in a dying world.

In the environmental policy arena, this was a sea change. Before the introduction of the Green New Deal, climate policy discussion largely happened in a vacuum (if at all). It was, at least according to the conventional wisdom in Washington, DC, distinct from social policy and belonged squarely to the wonk crowd and elite environmentalists.[24] To be sure, there were environmental justice groups that had long argued that economic and environmental security were inseparable; for example, the Jemez Principles of 1996—a platform for democratic organizing developed by a diverse coalition of environmental and economic justice groups at a key gathering in Jemez, New Mexico—envisioned a world where "all people have an equitable share of the health and the work of this world."[25] But environmental justice movements had largely been sidelined by the big green groups, whose preferred course of action was to lobby political elites. Typifying this approach, a 2019 *Washington Post* editorial argued that activists and policy makers really shouldn't "muddle [fighting climate change] with other social policy, such as creating a federal job guarantee."

This is precisely wrong. Properly caring for the earth and ensuring that every American enjoys the right to a healthy environment will require a major, decades-long restructuring of the economy, so economic rights—to employment, stable housing, health insurance—are paramount. Coal miners—all forty-two thousand of them across the nation—will need to be transitioned to other industries and, in some cases, assisted to retire early.[26] States dependent on fossil fuel revenue will have to search elsewhere as extraction and royalties come to an end. People will need to adjust their eating habits, consuming less meat from cows and other ruminants that spew methane into the atmosphere and require ever larger tracks of land. (No, hamburgers don't need to be banned, but Americans will have to eat fewer of them.) And new green jobs in the solar and wind industries—which are already two of the fastest-growing sectors in America—will either be well-paying union jobs that protect workers and give them a say in their work environment or not.[27]

Policy makers may choose to ignore these distributional questions, in which case the transition—if it happens at all—will be immensely painful and deepen inequality along existing fault lines. Or policy makers can meet them head-on, treating the energy transition as an *opportunity* to create a more equitable economy, and planet, for all.

What Green New Deal advocates recognized was that environmental concerns are inseparable from the nation's broader social and economic issues.[28] A healthy and stable environment cannot be achieved without massive social transformation, transformation that can only take place by recognizing and delivering economic rights. Ensure that diverse communities—from fossil fuel workers to environmental justice communities to those just trying to keep the heat on in winter—have good jobs, quality housing, and clean and safe schools, and they'll jump on board.[29] Which, this late in the day, is precisely what we need.

A Healthy Environment for All

As with the Green New Deal, environmental and social policy must be discussed in concert. But, really, each is the necessary condition of the other. Without a habitable planet, discussion of economic rights—the right to a job or health insurance—becomes absurd. And so the right to a healthy environment is, in fact, the most important right of all: it's the ground from which all other rights—civil, political, and economic—spring.[30]

First things first. To ensure the right to a healthy environment, we must change how we *conceptualize* the environment. Heretofore, the environment has been treated as an open-access resource, one that firms (as well as individuals and governments) have been free to pillage and pollute.[31] No longer. The right to a healthy environment necessitates treating the earth, and its natural resources, as a collective resource—a commons—to which all have a birthright and which must be protected for the public health and good. This means that the air, rather than being freely available for industry's greenhouse gases and other pollutants, will be regulated to ensure public health, whether by dint of a carbon tax or cap system or top-down regulation (see below).[32] The same goes for water and land: firms will be charged for or barred from polluting key waterways and poisoning the soil.

Second, the country will need to embark on a course of rapid decarbonization. Inspired by Ocasio-Cortez's and Markey's initial Green New Deal resolution, legislators have already introduced a number of promising proposals to this end, including but not limited to a Green New Deal for Public Schools and a Green New Deal for Public Housing. However, the exact suite of policies is still being debated. Like the original New Deal, there won't to be a single bill that contemporaries—or historians, for that matter—call the "Green New Deal." The New Deal as we know it today took many years, coalition politics, and comprised dozens of pieces of legislation, and the Green New Deal will likely follow the same path, taking many years and multiple bites at the apple.

Those bites should fall into three broad categories, which I refer to as the "three legs" of the climate policy stool: green investment, smart regulations, and carbon pricing. The Green New Deal is most often associated with the first leg—investment (i.e., the carrot)—while economists have long favored the third—carbon pricing (i.e., market signals). However, to achieve rapid decarbonization and ensure that emissions targets are hit, policy makers will have to engage the second leg—the "stick" of regulation—as well.[33]

Green New Deal advocates have it right: to realize decarbonization goals and build the green economy of the twenty-first century, green investments must lead the way. Of course, these investments are tied to the economic rights already discussed in the book, namely, the job guarantee, which will create a substantial workforce to assist in delivering a healthy environment for all, and the homes guarantee, which can help lead the way to constructing energy-efficient carbon-free structures. The study of past transitions and major economic mobilizations is revelatory. During World War II, entire industries were retooled for the war effort, and public spending as a share of GDP ballooned from 10 percent to over 44 percent in four short years. These interventions highlight the necessity of both direct *public* investment and the government's direction of *private* investment, whether through green lending (i.e., credit policy), tax incentives, procurement policy, or, most likely, some combination of these and other levers.[34] Estimates range, but most agree that decarbonization will require 3 to 5% of GDP a year, sustained over at least a ten-year period. This amounts to roughly $1 trillion a year in green investment, investments that will go toward creating new electric vehicle and transit plants; hiring millions to retrofit buildings; increasing green research and development; deploying existing technologies, such as wind, solar, and storage at a substantially faster rate; and much more.

These investments are crucial if the transition is to happen in a way that improves living standards equally (rather than forcing climate austerity on the have-nots). By virtue of project labor agreements—a form of collective bargaining that sets the wages and benefits of all workers employed on a given project—and other protections for workers, the investments will ensure that the millions of jobs created throughout the transition are good union jobs. And the public investments will help keep the benefits *with* the public rather than their being leached away by corporations and their shareholders.[35]

Increased public investment will also fill the gaps left by private industry. Research and development (R&D) is a case in point. Today, the private sector drastically underinvests in basic R&D; the public sector, through programs such as the Advanced Research Projects Agency (ARPA), makes up the difference. With an influx of investment, ARPA's energy group, ARPA-E, can build on the advances it has already made in clean energy, advances that have proved instrumental in drastic cost reductions for solar photovoltaic and electric vehicles.[36]

Public investment will also play a sizable role in *scaling* these new sustainable methods of energy production, storage, and use, especially the less proven technologies designed to address the last 10 to 15 percent of emissions that are hard to abate.[37] The example of solar is illuminating. Here researchers have documented how public investment was responsible for the majority of a historic price decline. In fact, prices tumbled 99 percent in the industry over the past forty years, making solar energy the cheapest electricity in history.[38]

But public investment is just the first leg of the stool; the transition will also require environmental regulations. Regulations have already played a substantial role in cleaning up the environment, from the introduction of catalytic converters and car fuel efficiency standards (which reduced GHG emissions more than any other policy during the past few decades) to the monitoring of the amount of lead and other toxins in drinking water to the recent bans on some hydrofluorocarbons (the most powerful GHGs in existence). On the climate front, the government will need to impose new regulations to guarantee certain goals are met. For example, the government needs to update its building standards to promote energy-efficient carbon-neutral structures. But other, more controversial regulations are needed, for example, a complete halt on new permits for fossil fuel extraction. That means no new fracking, no new offshore drilling, and certainly no more mountaintop removal in coal country.

Keeping fossil fuels in the ground is absolutely essential to limiting runaway warming. According to a major report on mitigating global warming by the fossil fuel–friendly International Energy Agency—an organization founded by Henry Kissinger to counter OPEC—there can be "no new oil and gas fields approved for development in our pathway, and no new coal mines or mine extensions." Other regulations, such as bans on the sale of gas- and diesel-powered cars, will have to be enacted too. California has already prohibited the sale of new gasoline-powered cars past 2035. And many other regulations, ranging from a clean electricity standard—which would dictate that utilities must derive a certain percentage of their energy from clean and/or renewable sources—to eliminating fossil fuel appliances in buildings to drastic improvements in zoning regulations and building codes, will need to be considered.[39]

Finally, there's the third leg: carbon pricing. Believe it or not, there already is a carbon price in the United States—only it's *negative*. That is, rather than charge firms for poisoning our air, land, and water, the government *spends* tens of billions a year directly subsidizing fossil fuel companies (broader definitions of subsidies put that number far higher: the International Monetary Fund estimates the United States spends $660 billion annually to secure cheap fossil fuels, just $100 billion shy of what the nation spends on K–12 public education).[40] An easy starting place is to stop paying polluters to destroy the environment and public health.[41]

But that's only the first step. The second is to implement an *equitable* carbon pricing scheme. This will entail a second measure: a carbon cap.

Allow me to explain. The goal of a carbon price, in this case created through a tax, is to reduce emissions. It does this, the theory goes, by changing incentives. Carbon-intensive goods and services become more expensive—because the companies providing them have to pay the tax—relative to low-carbon ones, so consumers gravitate toward the cheaper (cleaner) products. As demand declines for carbon-intensive products, so too do carbon emissions.

The problem, though, is twofold. First, economists don't know how much emissions will be reduced by a given tax on carbon. Would $40 a ton be enough? $60? Analysts simply don't know, which means it would be hard to meet emission reduction goals. Second, carbon taxes are highly regressive, meaning they disproportionately burden low- and middle-income households since these groups spend a higher percentage of their income on carbon-intensive goods and services even though they have a far smaller carbon footprint than wealthy households.

The solution is a carbon cap, which would limit the amount of emissions allowed in a given year. The government would auction permits, which firms would need to buy in order to pollute. Like a carbon tax, this would result in more expensive goods and services that are carbon-intensive. Every year the government would offer up fewer and fewer permits, ratcheting the amount of pollution down to zero. Estimates suggest that to reach net-zero emissions in 2050, the United States would have to reduce emissions by roughly 8 percent per year. To hit this target, the government could issue 8 percent fewer permits on an annual basis.

And the money? The government would give it back to taxpayers, just like Alaska gives money from *its* natural resources back to those living in the state (through a program inaugurated by a Republican governor called the Alaska Permanent Fund). The redistribution of revenue in this manner, known as a "carbon dividend," ensures that most people end up with more money in their pockets at the end of the day than they would absent the program. In other words, the vast majority of Americans would not need to pay anything to help address climate change. The dividend is a crucial aspect of the policy that puts equity front and center and thereby avoids deepening inequality as so many previous carbon pricing plans have. Think of a cap-and-dividend plan as an insurance policy for the planet: policy makers can, and must, push full steam ahead with investments, with the cap-and-dividend in place as a backstop.[42]

As drastic as these changes may seem, they are feasible *and* economically sound. A recent report published by experts at the University of California, Berkeley's Center for Environmental Public Policy found that not only is achieving 90 percent clean energy by 2035 possible, but it would actually *reduce* electricity bills, ensure a more dependable energy grid, create more jobs than the status quo, and bring about immense environmental benefits in terms of drastically lower GHG emissions and co-pollutants responsible for dirty air.[43]

Other researchers have arrived at similar conclusions. Study after study demonstrates that rapidly decarbonizing the economy—especially the energy sector—by deploying clean and renewable technology at a breakneck pace is not only doable but also good policy. A study by Rewire America, for example, led by the MacArthur "Genius Grant" recipient Saul Griffith, found that if the United States slashed emissions by 70 to 80 percent by 2035, it would create 15 to 20 million jobs over the next decade, all while saving consumers money. The trick? Electrify everything, and decarbonize electricity by deploying renewable energy plus energy storage.[44] (The best mantra for what is needed is, "deploy, deploy, deploy.") Of course, decarbonizing that last 10 to 15 percent will be harder, but it's achievable.[45]

Green investments, smart climate regulations, and carbon pricing can set the United States on the right path. But it won't be easy. For one thing, fossil fuel companies are heavily invested in the extraction and burning of fossil carbon; as atmospheric carbon declines, so too will their profits. Indeed, averting a heating planet will require fossil fuel companies to forgo $10 trillion in wealth by "stranding" fossil fuel reserves in the ground—not something they'll do out of the goodness of their hearts. Reflecting on the political economy of the situation, Chris Hayes notes that "the last time in American history that some powerful set of interests relinquished its claim on $10 trillion of wealth was in 1865—and then only after four years and more than 600,000 lives lost in the bloodiest, most horrific war we've ever fought."[46]

However, the economic case for rapid mobilization against climate change is incontrovertible. Keynes taught us that society need

not choose between a robust response to crisis and meeting people's material needs; America's collective capabilities are not fixed,
and a fundamental economic and societal transformation cannot
be thought of in terms of a fixed stock of resources. In tackling climate change, policy makers should not start from the idea that the
economy is operating at capacity—meaning labor, factories, money,
and other factors of production are currently being utilized to their
fullest—because, contrary to orthodox theory, it isn't. This means
there are ample resources that a major public investment program
could put to good use.

And it is just such a public program that the climate challenge
requires. Under a public investment–led program, a rapid move to a
carbon-neutral economy would not imply a fall in living standards
for working Americans. On the contrary. In an economy that has
been dominated by persistent demand constraints, supply chain
bottlenecks, volatile energy prices, and weak labor markets, public
spending on decarbonization will raise wages and living standards
for the masses while promoting full employment, public health, and
economic stability.

In short, the right to a healthy environment is achievable, fiscally
responsible—and necessary. As the bumper stickers in Amherst say,
there is no Planet B. Society cannot survive, let alone flourish, without
a habitable earth; there is no security—no achieving the good life we
all deserve—in a dirty and burning world.

But, as the 2018 Green New Deal proposal demonstrated, economic
rights and planetary stability go hand in hand. Universal health care
and a job guarantee ease the employment transitions millions will
have to undergo as the economy is restructured. Increased labor power
can help set new labor standards—such as the four-day workweek—
that will further reduce emissions.[47] New social housing will be green,
and new transit will be carbon-free.

This reimagined country—one without poverty, homelessness,
unemployment, the rationing of health care, and, most important,
the prospect of extinction—may sound like a utopic fantasy. I can hear

the bipartisan "fiscally responsible" crowd now: *Our national debt is already over $20 trillion—equal to our entire GDP—without these massive expenditures. How can we possibly afford what you're advocating?*

But we can afford it, practically and economically. What follows is an overview of how.

Part III

A Budget for the People

10

How Do We Pay for It?

> Let us not submit to the vile doctrine of the nineteenth century that
> every enterprise must justify itself in pounds, shillings and pence of
> cash income. . . . Why should we not add in every substantial city the
> dignity of an ancient university or a European capital[,] . . . an ample
> theater, a concert hall, a dance hall, a gallery, cafes, and so forth.
> Assuredly we can afford this and so much more. Anything we can
> actually do, we can afford.
> **JOHN MAYNARD KEYNES**

The programs entailed in an economic bill of rights will be many
things, but one thing they won't be is small. Legislation for causes
like a federal job guarantee, Medicare for all, free college and pre-K,
abundant and high-quality social housing, a rapid transition to
a carbon-free economy, the provision of clean air and water for
everyone—these initiatives and others will require large and permanent increases in the US government's annual budget, increases that
will inevitably drive skeptical, hostile, or just plain nervous politicians
to ask how we can afford it. (It is interesting to note that the affordability question never comes up with certain exigencies—economic crisis,
war, tax cuts—but inevitably arises with others, e.g., social welfare.)

Whereas most people who ask how it will be paid for are thinking
of it in one way—Where will the dollars come from?—there's another
way to understand it: as a question about the real resources—teachers,
wind technicians, electric vehicle factories, solar panels, medica-
tions, raw materials, and more—necessary to make universal economic rights a reality. Although I contend with both valences in what

follows, the latter meaning is the far more pressing one. The financing? That's the easy part.

Financing an Economic Bill of Rights

Simply put, and based on voluminous economics literature, the question of whether the US government can find the cash to provide economic rights to its citizens isn't a serious one. This is because, contrary to popular belief, there isn't some finite sum of dollars out there that the government needs either to tax or reallocate to fund its operations; the US economy is not a checking account that risks being overdrawn. At any given time, the US government can raise capital through the issuance of new government debt (e.g., US Treasury securities) and selling it. The country's sovereignty over its money, coupled with its position as the issuer of the global reserve currency, makes it so. That is, at any given time, the US government can create its own funding.[1]

But, the fiscal hawks will squawk, *what about the deficit?* The deficit—and debt—will indeed increase; in fact, it will likely increase quite a bit, as every dollar of new borrowing on an annual basis will add a dollar to the annual deficit. This might give the average American—and especially the average conservative—heartburn. But, economically speaking, the absolute value of the debt isn't important; what matters is the *ratio* of debt to GDP, along with the interest rate on government debt. And by these measures all signs indicate that the national debt has in fact tended to be *too small* and that increasing it would yield major economic benefits if that money is spent on pressing social priorities—priorities that the economic bill of rights puts front and center.

Where do these common misperceptions come from? In part, the country's finances have been held in thrall to the intellectual heirs of Milton Friedman, to whom deficit spending—and the future tax increases it ostensibly entails—is anathema.[2] The Friedman rationale goes like this: because every dollar the government spends (or borrows) must eventually be matched by a dollar in taxes, high deficits risk crushing the economy by forcing businesses and taxpayers to redirect their precious money to Uncle Sam rather than savings and investment. In this story, the result of too much government spending is rising interest rates (as investors demand greater returns to hold government debt), declining investment in the private sector, fewer jobs, and an overall contraction of the economy.[3] To counteract these effects, deficit hawks call for austerity (the slashing of government spending, especially spending on social and public goods like Social Security), just as they did, for example, in 2010; if things get bad enough, a government default may ensue, and perhaps another Great Depression, breadlines and all.

Unfortunately, it isn't only Republicans who have internalized this account. Although Democrats are rightly skeptical of parts of the Friedmanian view—for example, lowering taxes on corporations and the wealthy "trickles down" to the rest of the economy—they *do* tend to subscribe to the notion that all government spending must be "paid for" (i.e., funded without increasing the deficit). It's why President Obama and congressional Democrats tied themselves in knots trying to make sure Obama's signature Affordable Care Act was "revenue-neutral" over its first ten years. It's why Speaker Nancy Pelosi, over strong opposition from progressive members of the Democratic caucus, helped pass the "PAYGO" rule, a statute that requires Congress to offset new spending proposals with commensurate tax increases or cuts in other spending areas.[4] And it's why President Biden—who supported a balanced budget amendment as a senator—pitched his Build Back Better bill as economically "responsible," promising that "we pay for everything we spend."[5]

The problem, though, is that this bipartisan allergy to increasing the national debt is grounded neither in empirical facts nor in sound economic theory. The horror story of deficit spending, which has dictated so much of American fiscal policy over the past fifty years, is dead wrong.

To begin, the odds of a US government bankruptcy—that is, the government's literally running out of dollars to pay its debts—are near nil. The federal government, in conjunction with the Federal Reserve, can literally create all the money it needs to meet its debt obligations. In fact, the odds would be nil if not for congressional Republicans' continuous threats to vote against raising the debt limit (which would force the government into default) for purely political, that is, *not economic*, reasons.

Second, it isn't obvious that linking policy proposals to specific revenue sources ("pay-fors") is necessarily a good idea. Money, by its nature, is fungible: it moves around and circulates. Any potential side effects associated with higher government spending—excessive debt, an overheating economy—are functions of the budget position as a whole rather than the spending or revenue of any specific proposal. The economy is a huge ecosystem, in which changes in one part affect every other part, so it's not at all clear that any one proposal, say, a job guarantee, needs to be financed via, say, a direct job guarantee tax. (Neither would the tax revenue and policy costs exactly balance.) Linking programs to specific revenue streams may create barriers to reallocating funds in response to shifting priorities or economic conditions. If proof is needed that this is a bad idea, just consider the one in five Americans who are unable to access housing assistance despite qualifying for it under current law because of systematic underfunding of this specific budget line item, driven by supposed budgetary concerns.

But there's an even bigger issue with the notion of a pay-for. Because its intent is to maintain the budgetary status quo, it implicitly assumes that the current fiscal balance—that is, the difference between government expenditures and the revenues it collects in taxes and gets from assets—is ideal. This is in fact almost never the case. Indeed, when the economy has room to run, because people are un- or underemployed and resources are idle, a larger deficit would actually be a feature of public spending; similarly, if the economy is running too hot, additional taxes, perhaps levied on the wealthy, would help contain demand and bring economic growth back to a safe speed.

While not often discussed this way, the budgetary balance is one of the government's most powerful tools for managing the economy. When Congress decides to run a large deficit, the government is putting more money into the economy than it is taking out. This is akin to pushing on the economic accelerator. As spending in the economy creates new jobs, the people working those jobs are able to afford more stuff—groceries, the rent, a new gym membership. Further, government spending can increase the productivity of the economy in the first place, thus allowing people and businesses to operate more efficiently in the first place. Following what economists call the multiplier effect—which measures the effect a change in government spending has on the overall economy, an effect that is often larger than 1—the result of deficit-financed public investment tends to be overall *economic expansion*.

A recent example of the power of government spending is the federal stimulus in response to COVID-19 (which the Congress passed without asking how they would pay for it—and rightly so). But how much the economy expands in response to deficit spending depends on a number of factors, ranging from labor market conditions to what the money is spent on. Both spending when the economy is in the dumps—meaning there's more excess capacity than normal—and spending on building new infrastructure, for instance, deliver a big bang for each buck, whereas shoveling money into the hands of the wealthy through corporate or top-marginal-rate tax cuts does essentially nothing to bolster the economy (though it does bolster inequality).[6]

On the flip side, the government can decide to run a surplus, as it did briefly during the Clinton years. In this case, the government is tapping the economic brakes—taking more money out of the economy than it's putting in—which tends to decelerate economic activity and slow if not halt or even reverse growth. This means fewer jobs, slow or stagnant wage growth, and a general increase in inequality. While the Clinton years were not accompanied by abnormally excessive levels of unemployment, they did set the economy on the path to the housing crash of 2008.

Less public debt—counterintuitive though it may sound—can indeed be costly. Without sufficient levels of safe government debt on offer, which provides savers an interest-bearing place to put their cash, the result can be macroeconomic instability. In fact, there's evidence to suggest a larger issuance of public debt could have helped mitigate the 2008 financial crisis. Why? Because US Treasury bonds are a vital safe asset for the global economy given the dollar's role as the global reserve currency, and in the years leading up to the crash there just weren't enough to go around. This pushed investors to seek out alternative "safe" assets, like those on offer in the mortgage-backed security market, with disastrous results.[7]

The final fallacy of the conventional deficit story is that public spending is inherently less efficient—less conducive to economic growth—than private investment.[8] While many models of the economy simply assume this is true, the reality tells a very different story, one where public investment is just as—or often *more*—productive than private investment (though there are measures other than productivity, for example, lives improved and saved or education, that policy makers and the public should care deeply about). The truth is that public investment *complements* private investment; they go hand in hand. Without bridges, water and sewer pipes, research and development; investments in housing, energy, education, health care, and the like, the economy would simply be dead in the water.[9]

And there's another key piece of the puzzle here. Debt is particularly beneficial when interest rates are low. In 2018, the former International Monetary Fund chief economist, Olivier Blanchard, made waves by arguing that in a world with persistently low interest rates, and in particular when the interest rate is below the growth rate of the economy—the case now and likely for the foreseeable future—"public borrowing may have no fiscal cost." Even a controversial figure like Larry Summers (in a piece subtitled "Washington Should End Its Debt Obsession") has argued that public spending shouldn't be feared.[10] And the best part about low interest rates? The Federal Reserve—America's "central planner"[11]—can simply keep them there.

Up to this point, I have been concentrating on fiscal policy, the stuff of budgets and taxes; but monetary policy, the remit of the Federal

Reserve, will play a large and important role in financing economic rights as well.

The US central banker is tasked with a dual mandate: delivering maximum employment and ensuring price stability. As we've seen, though, the Federal Reserve has heretofore prioritized price stability—which it aims to maintain largely through adjustments to the short-term federal funds rate—at the expense of maximum employment.[12] And, obviously, the Federal Reserve's existence has not solved the problem of financial crises and recessions.[13]

To promote an economic bill of rights and ensure it can be paid for in terms of both dollars—which is where the Federal Reserve will have the greatest impact—and the real resource capacity of the economy, the Federal Reserve needs to support running a hotter economy, one that receives more direction via targeted credit policy and one in which the government carries a higher debt load than it has traditionally. This means a Federal Reserve that keeps interest rates, both short and long term, low (which helps ensure the growth in deficit financing remains on a smooth and sustainable path), credit flowing (especially in areas of the economy deemed critical, like the green transition),[14] and occasionally engaging in quantitative easing (the purchase of longer-term assets, including government treasuries and mortgage debt, which serves to accelerate the economy and manage long-term interest rates and those that affect strategic economic sectors).[15]

Most important, though, the Federal Reserve needs to do more to increase support for public borrowing. One key means is to work more closely with the Treasury Department to better coordinate bond purchases and interest rates to ensure government debt remains sustainable as economic rights—and the universal economic security they entail become the financial priority of the United States. Any number of actions might be taken to facilitate this coordination, which is necessary to ease any financing constraint the government may face (e.g., a shortage of demand for government treasuries at certain points on the yield curve). A simple step is for government bonds to be issued directly to the Federal Reserve, which can finance the purchase of government debt through the creation of new money, as was done extensively in the past two economic crises.[16]

Given the nugatory risks and immense benefits of deficit spending—especially if the Federal Reserve cooperates—there is no reason not to increase the public debt to deliver economic rights. Of course, those obsessed with the national debt clock prominently on display across from One Bryant Park in Manhattan will balk.[17] But the evidence is there: the debt can grow substantially *and* sustainably in ways that benefit current and future generations alike. This is because when interest rates on government debt are below the rate of economic growth for the economy, any increase in government debt will lead to a government debt ratio—the ratio of debt to GDP, which is a measure of the debt in relation to the economy overall—that stabilizes. And indeed, although the debt-to-GDP ratio is fairly high by historical standards, the costs of servicing that debt remains fairly low when one looks at the historical record, thanks to persistently low interest rates on government debt.

At the moment, for all the public and political agitation over the deficit, the present US debt-to-GDP ratio, a far better measure of the debt than the absolute level, is not an outlier. Indeed, there are numerous European nations with debt-to-GDP ratios similar to that of the United States. For a true outlier in terms of the debt-to-GDP ratio, one can look across the Pacific to Japan, which has a debt-to-GDP ratio over 250 percent (and which still borrows at very low rates).

The case for growing the debt is especially strong when public spending is directed toward socially important needs rather than handouts to the rich. For example, in the aftermath of World War II, the federal government borrowed more than it took in—a lot more. The debt-to-GDP ratio peaked in 1946, just after the war, at 120 percent, yet the size of the debt relative to the economy rapidly *fell*. This was because a good deal of the borrowed cash was used for socially beneficial investments, things like new forms of production, education, and health care, all of which contributed to a booming economy. In a nutshell, the numerator—public debt—didn't really fall, but the denominator—the size of the economy—ballooned, and in turn the relative size of the debt precipitously declined.

When deficit spending *is* used for handouts to the rich, on the other hand, growth is lethargic. For example, empirical studies of the effects of the Tax Cuts and Jobs Act of 2017—the massive supply-side tax cut signed by President Trump—find that the cuts did not spur investment and economic growth; instead, they simply added fuel to the raging inequality fire by giving the rich more money.[18]

Programs designed to deliver economic rights, on the flip side, are *investments* and should be treated as such. Expanded education, infrastructure, housing, renewable energy, and more will not only increase demand in the short run but also increase the long-term potential of the economy. In other words, the expenditures will pay for themselves.

Real Resources: The Constraints That Matter

As I have tried to demonstrate, the fearmongering over spending, debt, and national bankruptcy has resulted in a misunderstanding of the limits of the federal government in financing its initiatives. The United States can always find the necessary dollars to fund its priorities; it's a matter of public and political will. While this was considered blasphemy during the heyday of neoliberalism (and still is in many quarters), the resurgence of Keynesian thought in response to the 2008 financial crisis—along with the growing influence of economists like Stephanie Kelton, the previous chief economist to Senate Democrats on the Budget Committee and the leading proponent of modern monetary theory (MMT)—has fundamentally changed the conversation.[19]

However, the question of constraints—of limits and trade-offs in regard to *actual resources*—is a real one. Do we have enough nurses, medicines, hospital beds, and MRI machines to make sure every

American can get decent health care once they are insured? Is there enough wood and concrete and steel—all of which need to be carbon-neutral—to build a comfortable home for every American and a good school for every child? Are there sufficient amounts of silicon, precious metals, and other material inputs to build an advanced national electricity grid, as well as batteries, solar panels, and wind turbines to power it? Is there enough food and land to keep every person in the country—and the world, for that matter—well fed? And if there aren't, how can government policy bring more resources on board, improve the efficiency of current resources, and redirect the economy to repurpose currently deployed resources to more important uses?

To the majority of these questions, the answer is yes. The nation already commands a great deal of the real resources to meet many of its most pressing needs, from affordable housing to childcare to free public higher education. But the availability of real resources plays a crucial role in setting the speed limit of the economy. After all, supply isn't unlimited—we live on a finite planet, after all—so it's necessary to break down where real resource constraints ("supply constraints") might become an issue—and how the country can overcome them.

ECONOMIC HEADROOM

When it comes to concerns about supply constraints, the first and most important point is that the economy is almost always operating below potential. At any given moment, there are likely to be idle resources: unused factories and land, workers who are un- or underemployed, and other means of production sitting on the sideline growing rusty. When these conditions prevail, deficit-financed public investment to spur demand and utilize excess capacity is just what the doctor ordered.

The story of the past few decades has been one in which there is plenty of room to run in the American economy. Before the pandemic—despite the CBO's pronouncement that the economy had returned to its full potential, a finding based on the CBO's own continual downgrading of what the economy's potential really was[20]—staff at the Federal Reserve Bank of San Francisco estimated that the nation's economy was actually *12 percentage points smaller* than it should have been. The main culprit? A lack of aggregate demand—econ-speak for insufficient spending—largely due to prolonged high levels of unemployment and flatlined wages, both of which could have been mitigated by more robust public spending to put un- and underutilized resources to work.[21]

Another token of an underperforming economy is persistent slack in the labor market. The unemployment rate is one measure, but I already covered the pitfalls of this notoriously narrow indicator in chapter 4. A better way to determine labor market slack is the labor force participation rate, which measures the percentage of adults actually working for pay at a given time. Before the 2020 recession it peaked at 63.4 percent, nearly 4 percentage points—or about 10 million workers—below its peak in 2000. Some may point to demographic shifts—that is, workers aging out of the workforce without commensurate replacements—but even if we look at prime-age workers (those twenty-five to fifty-four), rates of labor force participation were still depressed. During the economic recovery at the start of 2022, for example, prime-age labor force participation was 82 percent, 2.6 percentage points below its peak in 1999 and substantially below other nations such as Germany (85.2%), Portugal (86.3%), and Switzerland (86.6%).[22]

Failing to address slack in the labor market not only hurts individuals; it can also leave the entire economy worse off, a phenomenon known as *hysteresis*.[23] Akin to a case of frostbite, hysteresis is when a prolonged cold economy causes lasting damage, slowing investment, business formation, and productivity growth.[24]

There's no good reason, or data, for that matter, to believe that the market will "naturally" reverse a hysteretic economy—and certainly not by means that benefit society and provide all with their economic rights. Fortunately, the economy can be brought back on track by increasing the national debt as economic rights are deployed. Again, given the economic conditions the country has faced over the past few decades, additional public spending and a permanently more active public sector are *features*, not bugs, of economic rights.

EASING SUPPLY CONSTRAINTS

As the economy nears actual full potential—characterized by true full employment and strong growth—real resource problems are likely to arise. The answer here is macroeconomic management policies aimed to better coordinate economic activity, ranging from supply-side public investment and industrial policy to ease the supply constraints to price controls that help limit owners of capital from taking advantage of people when supply constraints are present to the reallocation of spending priorities in the federal budget to move resources from one use to another deemed more important given resource constraints.

Supply-Side Public Investment

When demand outstrips supply—whether economy-wide or for a few specific goods and services—inflation, meaning a rise in the price level, can occur. This is what happened in 2021–22. Demand for specific goods like new vehicles remained high while supply drastically slowed, resulting in a shortage of cars and a corresponding increase in prices. (Indeed, used and new car prices were a major component of the rise in inflation observed during the recovery.)[25]

Describing inflation this way makes clear the phenomenon is two-sided. Demand may be too high (at least for specific goods), but supply may be too low. Government policy can affect *both*, but under neoliberalism, policy makers have limited themselves to the demand side of the equation—which they seek to reduce by raising interest rates with the intent of suppressing wages and employment (thus making people too poor to buy more stuff, therefore reducing demand). This is even the position of liberal economists like Paul Krugman, who advocated pushing *up* the unemployment rate in spring 2022 in the pages of the *New York Times*.[26] The neoliberal position is that it isn't the government's responsibility to increase supply directly when the economy is heating up; rather, government should work to rein in demand by, put bluntly, limiting people's ability to work and buy the things they need.

Earlier I covered what damage a reduction in demand does to jobs and wages. But it does second-order damage to supply, that is, the availability of real resources, as well. For one thing, investment— which is what increases the supply of goods and services—is itself driven by demand (contra mainstream economic theory, which argues exclusively that supply creates demand). But a market in which consumers don't have money to spend—perhaps due to low wages or a lack of jobs—isn't a market that new players will enter. Nor is it a market in which existing companies will expand their capacity. This phenomenon contributed greatly to the lack of sufficient supply in critical areas like housing, a sector that experienced chronic and historic underinvestment following the 2008 crisis, resulting in a shortage of millions of homes (i.e., inadequate supply).

Once again, the economy needs a better way forward, one that dispenses with the neoliberal emphasis on austerity and regulates supply as a tool to manage the economy. This need came into stark relief during the supply chain woes of 2021–22, but the issue was present before then, in supply shortages in childcare, health care, affordable housing, and other vital areas of the economy.

Some of the ideas I have explored for implementing an economic bill of rights would also give policy makers a chance to influence supply. Building fresh reserves of public housing and opening new public colleges and universities, for example, do double duty: in the direct public services they provide *and* supply-side investment (which creates more stuff and helps manage prices). In fact, not only would these policies increase the supply of housing and education specifically, but they would also make workers more productive *in general*, boosting the supply-side effect even further.

A federal job guarantee, meanwhile, would operate as a kind of open-ended platform for identifying opportunities for local and community investment, a means to increasing the availability of goods and services. And the massive buildout of public transit would provide people with real alternatives to continued reliance on private car infrastructure, making them less vulnerable to swings in energy or car prices.

Price Controls

This intervention is relatively straightforward: the government should establish and enforce regulations on what prices private companies can charge. Price controls are a vital tool for keeping inflation down and inequality in check when supply constraints are present. In fact, price controls were a key feature of the strongest economy ever recorded—the booming economy during World War II—and a tool deemed very important by previous administrations, including the Nixon administration. These controls were managed in such a way that guaranteed profits but also fairness; that is, when demand began to outstrip supply, firms didn't have the power to gouge consumers and engage in profiteering. (A great deal of modern mainstream economic wisdom, one comes to realize, requires memory-holing the policies used during World War II.)[27]

As I discussed earlier, rent control is the quintessential example of a price control. But price controls currently exist in other areas of the economy too, from public utilities—which have the power to set rates on necessities like electricity, water, and sewage—to Medicare and Medicaid, which often set prices via their reimbursement rates for specific medical goods and services. The government should utilize price controls once again, especially in particularly volatile and opaque sectors like housing, cars, energy, and health care (at least until it is decommodified). In fact, had the government deployed price controls in these key areas during the 2021–22 recovery, those struggling to pay rent, or afford a necessary new car, might not have been left high and dry. To be sure, price controls should not be expected to increase supply; that's now what they are designed to do. Instead, they manage prices and provide precious *time* as supply chain bottlenecks are broken and new resources are brought online (or efficiency is improved). Further, they can play an important role in limiting the degree to which firms and landlords benefit when there are supply constraints, thereby ensuring that the risks associated with a lack of supply are not born exclusively by consumers.

There are several types of price controls, including upper bounds beyond which prices may not rise, limited price increases based on a certain percentage of the previous year's price or some measure of overall inflation (the preferred option in most cases), and prices established by the government. Public options (as discussed previously) can also be used to manage prices. For example, by creating nonmarket social housing, the government sets a floor in the marketplace, effectively competing with the private sector from below. Such activity can serve as a price anchor: if the private sector tries to raise prices too much, people will simply shift over to the public sector. In other words, people will have more options, which will function as a safety valve for prices.[28]

Reallocating the Budget

When real resource constraints start to bite, a reassessment of current budget priorities—and the reallocation of spending away from less valuable, or even destructive, areas of the economy—may become necessary. Military spending is a case in point. The United States spends 16 percent of the federal budget (nearly $700 billion annually) on the military and so-called defense—about *twice* the current expenditures dedicated to the piecemeal safety net.[29] Tens of billions more go toward subsidizing the extraction of fossil fuels—subsidies that enrich fossil fuel corporations and contribute to global warming and deadly air pollution. And the government could save over $450 billion if Congress quit kowtowing to the pharmaceutical industry and allowed Medicare to negotiate drug prices.[30]

While it's true that spending on areas like defense need not be reduced to finance an economic bill of rights—because the economy is often operating below potential regardless, and taxes on the rich will create even more space in the economy—it's also true that redirecting resources away from certain activities, including through tax policy (more on this below), can free up the necessary real resources to do *more*.[31] A shift in spending priorities—to housing, education, and medical care from defense and dirty energy—can move the country further along the path to building a just economy.

It would also mark a sea change in American society. Strange as it may sound, a nation's budget reflects its vision of itself, its *national* priorities. Would we rather utilize public resources to wage war or house people? To enrich corporations or provide high-quality education for all? To extract every last drop of oil or preserve our one and only planet? These are precisely the questions the drafters of the Freedom Budget sought to elevate, and it's high time these debates were had today.

On Taxes

Deficit spending and industrial policy will play a prominent role in bringing the economic bill of rights to fruition. But given the scale of the economic transformation required, other changes to the federal budget and the country's allocation of real resources, including but not limited to new taxes, will be desirable.[32]

New and higher taxes will doubtless set Republicans' heads spinning—and worry plenty of everyday Americans too. But it's important to recognize that the vast majority of Americans will be better off (i.e., realize a net gain) from what, for most people, will be a modest tax increase. No one likes to see their taxes go up. But if after a tax hike you're left with *more* disposable income, far greater economic security, and more life options than you had before—because your wages went up, your health care or college education became free, and your apartment became a lot more affordable—that's clearly a win. And that's precisely what will happen with an economic bill of rights.

To put things in perspective, it's worth recalling that Americans pay far less in taxes than most citizens of high-income countries (the United States ranks second to last in terms of taxation, one place above Ireland, a notorious tax haven).[33] The total tax burden in the United States, accounting for taxation at the local, state, and federal levels, was 24.5 percent of GDP in 2019. That's 12 percentage points below most European nations and a full 20 percentage points below nations with particularly strong well-being states like Norway, Sweden, France, and Denmark. Even by US standards, taxes are shockingly low right now. Before the 2017 tax cuts, a middle-income family of four was paying 59 percent less in income taxes than they would have paid in 1955; after the cuts, they were paying even less. And in a perverse inversion of the way things ought to be, the rich have seen their taxes cut by two-thirds relative to what they paid in 1950. In fact, the wealthiest Americans send a smaller portion of their income to Uncle Sam than any other income group in America.[34]

Yet despite these low levels of taxation, many Americans still quail at the mere mention of a tax increase. In part, this is because of how taxes are covered in the media. American reporters believe they are being responsible public advocates when they grill a politician on the amount of a tax increase, but they regularly neglect to inform their readers what they stand to *gain* from that increase.[35] Another part is the long war by conservatives to fuel distrust in government, an effort epitomized by Reagan's infamous quip, "The nine most terrifying words in the English language are: I'm from the government and I'm here to help."[36]

One way to change this narrative is for Americans to see government working overtly on their behalf. That families will no longer need to struggle to afford pre-K, that young adults will no longer be saddled with enormous levels of student debt, that people will be housed and their rent substantially more affordable, that everyone will get the health care they need without thinking twice about the balance in their bank accounts—these benefits will demonstrate clearly that the American government is Americans' government, that *it* works for *them*.

So as programs are inaugurated to establish economic rights and policy makers seek to finance and resource them, taxes will indeed be an essential tool. Some of these tax increases will be broad-based— perhaps a payroll tax hike or modest increases to income taxes for low- and middle-income Americans—whereas others will be targeted to particular income levels and activities.

For example, most of the tax increases associated with the transition to an economic bill of rights will come in the form of "Pigouvian" taxes—taxes on social harms. Traditional examples include taxes on polluting industries or on goods with negative impacts on public health, such as alcohol and tobacco. But other Pigouvian taxes, ranging from a financial transaction tax (which taxes speculation-driven financial trading) to the corporate income tax (which can help promote healthier competition by taxing firms with outsized market power) to progressive taxation on high incomes and wealth, should be enacted too. Together, these Pigouvian taxes do double duty: they free up space in the economy, allowing for an even greater degree of resources to be allocated to delivering economic rights, all the while discouraging socially harmful activities and often reducing inequality.[37]

In fact, one of the most important ways to realize economic rights in America is to implement a real progressive income tax. A progressive tax code curbs the power of the rich and corporations and establishes imposts on socially destructive activities. Ostensibly that's what we already have, but America's "progressive" income tax is a mere shadow of what it could and should be. For example, as it stands as of this writing, the income tax has just seven brackets, with the highest bracket (income above $523,601 for a single filer or $628,301 for those who are married, filing jointly) taxed at a rate of 37 percent. This means that those receiving, say, $630,000 in income and those receiving $100+ million (a common enough figure for America's CEOs) pay the same rate—a travesty if there ever was one.

But it's actually worse than that. Remember, most of the wealthiest Americans don't take their "pay" as ordinary W-2 income; rather, they receive (untaxed) stock options, which they can then cash in at the 15 to 20% capital gains rate—roughly the same rate that applies to low-income families living paycheck to paycheck. And this doesn't even account for the wealthy's extensive use of offshore tax havens.[38]

It wasn't always like this. During World War II and the two decades that followed, there were roughly thirty tax brackets, and for a lot of that time, including when Eisenhower occupied the White House, the tax rate on the highest bracket was over 90 percent.[39] Those sorts of numbers will send many voters and politicians into apoplexy, and plenty of economists would argue they would crush the economy. But the historical record contradicts that claim. The midcentury period saw the biggest boom in jobs and incomes of the entire twentieth century. (After being asked how high he would raise taxes, Bernie Sanders once quipped, "I'm not that much of a socialist compared to Eisenhower.")[40]

Latter-day politicians have contemplated a return to a midcentury-style tax code. In a 2019 *60 Minutes* interview, Representative Ocasio-Cortez floated the idea of a massive increase in the income tax, with a top marginal bracket number of 70 percent.[41] Many scoffed at her proposal, and the antitax icon Grover Norquist went so far as to compare the idea to slavery. (Of course, Norquist claimed that the 70 percent rate would apply to one's *entire* income, revealing that he either doesn't know or, more likely, was intentionally misrepresenting how marginal taxes work.)

Other Republicans, like Representative Steve Scalise of Louisiana, didn't go quite as far as Norquist, but they nevertheless framed high marginal taxes as a rebarbative measure designed to fund "leftist fantasy programs."[42] However, high taxes on the rich are popular, with polling indicating that a majority of voters from both sides of the aisle are ready to raise taxes on the rich.[43]

They're backed by well-established economics research. Taxes in the range floated by Ocasio-Cortez have been shown to be "optimal" in work by MIT's Peter Diamond and Berkeley's Emmanuel Saez, economists whose groundbreaking 2012 paper argued that a 73 percent top marginal tax bracket in the United States would be economically sound. (Research led by the economist Thomas Piketty, published just a few years later, made an even bolder case: top tax rates should rise to 83%.) Moreover, by adding tax brackets, policy makers will better be able to ensure differentiation among economic classes, taxing those who get a larger income at substantially higher rates than those in the middle.[44]

If the goal is to truly tame the market, however, and put ceilings as well as floors in place, a return to Roosevelt's proposal of a maximum income—that is, a top marginal tax rate of 100 percent—might be in order. In Roosevelt's view, "No American citizen ought to have a net income of . . . more than $25,000 a year" (just over $400,000 as of 2022).[45] Today the appropriate maximum income level should be the subject of vigorous debate—maybe it's $400,000 (about six times the median income of a US household); maybe $625,000 (about twenty times the annual salary of a worker making $15 an hour); maybe $1 million. But one thing is certain: a hard cap on income will result in a far healthier democracy and create plenty of space in the US economy for universal economic rights.[46]

To create a tax regime commensurate with economic rights, income tax reform is essential. There are many gross inequities in the tax code that need reform, from the suppressed rates on dividends, capital gains, and corporate revenue to the present lack of a tax penalty for pollution and a lack of land taxes.

Among these promising avenues for reform, the idea of a wealth tax—that is, a tax on assets rather than income—stands out. Of course, most American families already pay a wealth tax in the form of property taxes on their home, which is their most important asset and the basket in which the vast majority of the average person's wealth resides. But this isn't the type of wealth tax I'm talking about. A true wealth tax—akin to those proposed by Senators Elizabeth Warren and Bernie Sanders during the 2020 Democratic presidential primary— would assess a tax on an individual's net wealth, what they own minus what they owe, on an annual basis. Senator Warren's plan called for a 3 percent tax, which, according to estimates, would have raised around $210 billion per year (equal to 1 percent of GDP). The wealth tax proposed by Sanders reached 8 percent at its topmost bracket and would have raised more: $335 billion per year (1.6 percent of GDP).

However, even Sanders's proposal is below what the economists Saez and Zucman find to be the "revenue-maximizing" rate (i.e., the rate that maximizes the amount of money the government receives). They recommend 10 percent for wealth above $1 billion.[47]

The revenues the government stands to realize from a wealth tax are indeed eye-popping, but revenue is only one goal of these taxes; another is reducing the power of the wealthy to distort and degrade the political system by flooding politics with their wealth and influence. With this in mind, even more progressive wealth taxation, including hard limits on the accumulation of fortunes, may be in order. This would take a degree of international cooperation, a precedent for which was on display in 2021, when the G7 finance ministers announced an agreement on a global minimum corporate tax rate. However, a hard cap of this kind may not be necessary. With progressive income and wealth taxes and bulletproof corporate income taxes, the government will not only offset a substantial part of the increased public spending necessary for economic rights but also foster greater economic equality, a key component of stable democracies.

It should come as no surprise that present-day advocates of economic rights aren't the first to face the skepticism of the "fiscally responsible." When Roosevelt won his first presidential election, he was accused of radical fiscal irresponsibility by Hoover, who believed that the ongoing crisis was only being inflamed by Roosevelt's promises to prioritize spending rather than set his sights on balancing the budget. And, as he relates in *How Much Does Finance Matter?*, Keynes's plans to rebuild London after World War II were rebuffed by an eminent architect who asked, in a fashion all too familiar, "Where's the money to come from?"

> "The money?" I said. "But surely, Sir John, you don't build houses with money? Do you mean that there won't be enough bricks and mortar and steel and cement?"
>
> "Oh no," he replied, "of course there will be plenty of all that."

"Do you mean," I went on, "that there won't be enough labour? For what will the builders be doing if they are not building houses?"

"Oh no, that's all right," he agreed.

"Then there is only one conclusion. You must be meaning, Sir John, that there won't be enough architects." But there I was trespassing on the boundaries of politeness. So I hurried to add: "Well, if there are bricks and mortar and steel and concrete and labour and architects, why not assemble all this good material into houses?"

But he was, I fear, quite unconvinced. "What I want to know," he repeated, "is where the money is coming from."[48]

Keynes was undeterred by this kind of resistance. Because he knew—as we ought to know—that when it comes to building a just economy, "anything we can actually do, we can afford."

Conclusion

One way to understand the history of the United States is as a slow movement toward realizing the ideals of its Founders. The nation was intended to be one where all were created equal and entitled to life, liberty, and the pursuit of happiness—a high bar the country has historically not met. As scores of human beings—women, slaves, the landless poor, the peoples who had inhabited the Americas for generations before Europeans arrived—were excluded from those lofty affordances from the start, America's room for improvement has always been on display.

In time and through struggle, the political rights enumerated in the Constitution and the Bill of Rights were expanded to most Americans. The women's suffrage movement won women the vote in 1920 when the Nineteenth Amendment was ratified. The Civil Rights Act of 1964 and the Voting Rights Act of 1965 delivered the long-ignored political and civil rights of Black Americans.[1] But economic rights, which preoccupied members of the founding generation and was a cornerstone of the New Deal and the civil rights movement, have yet to be realized.

This is intentional. The United States is the most prosperous nation ever to have existed, yet the country sits by and watches as fellow Americans go without, enduring senseless pain, suffering, and, far too often, death. Once one recognizes that scarcity is no longer *the* barrier, it becomes clear that poverty and economic insecurity are neither natural nor necessary and have not been for some time. Nevertheless, as I have detailed in these pages, America's political leaders continuously *choose* to consign tens of millions to chronic want—of shelter, food, clean water, a quality education.

The excuse is that we can't afford it. This claim is supported by the majority of economists, who believe there's an insurmountable trade-off between supporting economic growth and creating a more just and equitable society through redistributive measures. Redistribution, this same story goes, will foster a society of takers and eventually leave everyone worse off.

For other economists, like Hayek and Friedman, the issue was less affordability than the slippery slope toward socialism—or, as Hayek called it, serfdom. Give the government an inch, they said, and it would take a mile. Their solution was to leave distribution up to the market, which they believed was an information processor more powerful than any person or government. And they equated freedom with supposedly "free" markets, washing away any semblance of positive rights. A freer society, so they said, was one with less taxation, fewer regulations, and a sidelined labor movement (which they likened to the mob). Democracy may have a place in politics; but when it comes to economics, the almighty dollar reigns.

As this book has endeavored to show, these ideas are not scientific truths but rather the axioms of a particular approach to political economy: neoliberalism. According to neoliberalism, capitalism is the only reasonable organization of society, and embracing it in its *extreme* form is not only patriotic, but essential to maintaining liberty and democracy. Economic rights be damned; superior are work requirements (despite a consistent lack of jobs) and underfunded and often poorly administered voucher programs (which have given rise to a coupon state, where direct public provisioning was replaced with subsidies—such as food stamps—for the poor).[2] Served with a side of rugged individualism, which admonished the desperate to pull themselves up by their bootstraps, this approach has left millions isolated and economically helpless.

And so we are where we are today: living in a country where economic insecurity remains commonplace for the poor and the middle class alike and the extremely wealthy continue to amass ever larger fortunes. Today's billionaires hold power reminiscent of yesteryear's feudal lords (which is, funnily enough, exactly what Hayek said *wouldn't* happen). The nation has become richer, but how has that benefited the unemployed young parent who is the family's sole breadwinner? What about those struggling to pay their rent knowing it will be years before they'll actually get the housing voucher they qualify for—or a job that pays enough to actually cover the bills? How about the diabetic living on Skid Row, terrified of what is to come without the insulin they simply can't afford?

The current economic system's inability to answer, and more important to solve, pressing questions like these is fueling a creative ferment in American politics and policy. People are realizing that the current organization of society, including today's distribution of goods, services, and jobs, is not the only way the puzzle pieces of life can be arranged. Nor is it the most "efficient"—economists' favorite criterion—not by a long shot. Alternatives are indeed possible and urgently needed. And many of them are desirable.

This is what the policies detailed in the preceding pages offer: concrete alternatives that would provide all with universal security by guaranteeing economic rights. While the idea of an economic bill of rights has yet to feature in the national debate, many of its pieces are floating about and gaining steam. The electorate is demanding a right to health care, a right that people in nearly all other high-income countries already have. (And no, serfdom has not followed.) People are coalescing around the idea that the right to an education should be expanded beyond K–12 to include pre-K and college, both of which are increasingly unaffordable yet increasingly necessary. Americans agree that if people are willing and able to work, they should be able to—and for a fair wage. And Americans—though especially the young people—are demanding a healthy environment as the planet burns before our eyes. An economic bill of rights brings these ideas together, foregrounding their connections, interrelations, and mutual dependencies.

In this book, I have outlined seven economic rights that can serve as the foundation for a richer form of freedom in America, one that partakes of positive liberty as well as negative. Leveling the playing field by ensuring that all who are able to work have a quality job will rid the nation of ruinous and wasteful unemployment. Providing everyone with a high-quality education will provide each and every person with greater agency to determine the type of life they want to lead, and the type of person they want to be. And ensuring a basic income for everyone in the United States, paired with the other rights outlined here, will finally accomplish the long-standing goal of achieving universal economic security against life's inevitable ups and downs. In short, the economic bill of rights yields an economy that is ethically tolerable and not economically intolerable.

Implicit in my account is that there is no silver bullet—no single policy—to address economic insecurity. I've described how easy it is for someone to fall from the tightrope that is "getting by" in America; if there's only one strand in the net below—say, a basic income—people will still be wobbling along the tightrope, terrified of falling into the abyss. Landlords, bosses, and health insurance firms will still have the power to push people into economic ruin. The policy prescription that is the economic bill of rights instead creates a tightly woven net—the *well-being state*—through which nobody can fall.

I hasten to add that these seven rights are not the only economic rights that should be recognized and protected. Rather, I view them as a foundation as Americans democratically decide what additional economic rights to guarantee. The particular economic rights discussed in this book are worth highlighting, first, for the crucial role they would play in fostering a well-being state that treats people as human beings and, second, for their unique history in America's struggle to provide people with more freedom. These rights have been on American minds for centuries—and will continue to be.

There are many economic rights to which I wish I could have given more attention. The right to unionize, for example, should be a top priority, and the passage of the Protect the Right to Organize (PRO) Act—which as of this writing is languishing in Congress—would go a great way toward achieving it.

Other rights, such as the right to basic services, should be on the table too. In chapter 8, I talked about the right to some services (banking, for example), but one can imagine the value of universal access to additional services: broadband; basic utilities, including some base amount of energy and water for free; public transportation; and more. And while the scope of this book has been broad, it has perhaps not been broad enough. I have limited my discussion of economic rights to the United States. Far more work is needed to reimagine the global economy in ways that reduce the leverage of global economic superpowers and instead promote international cooperation to supply everyone on the planet with a decent and dignified life.

Even when limited to the United States, the realization of positive rights won't be easy. Although neoliberalism's obituary has been written many times over, first after the 2008 Great Financial Crisis and again following the economic plunge that stemmed from the pandemic, it is not dead yet. It is true that the sizable (thought insufficient) government response in 2008, and the improved government response in 2020–21, put many chinks in neoliberalism's armor. But the US economy is still distorted by the neoliberal program: Corporate profits are still breaking records while the share of the economic pie going to workers persists near historic lows. Taxes, especially on the rich and corporations, remain rock bottom. "Full employment" still means millions in the unemployment line. And when the government *does* dip its toes into industrial policy, it continues to socialize risk and privatize profit. (Just look at the companies that reaped insane profits from the government-financed COVID-19 vaccine program.)[3]

Attempting to end the neoliberal program will be met with resistance. The rich and powerful have grown comfortable with their ability to always find workers willing to do their bidding; they're accustomed to the fact that their wealth shields them from the suffering of others. The beneficiaries of the status quo won't relinquish their privilege without a fight. So, much like the victories won during the New Deal and the civil rights movement, economic rights will require mass movements and mass struggle.

Politically, these are indeed dire times. Fascism is again sprouting in America after decades of dormancy. The planet is careening toward disaster as planet-warming emissions continue to be locked in for decades to come. The civil and political rights people already enjoy are under attack, and the courts seem more interested in stripping rights than strengthening them. White supremacy continues to grow, and the political Right, having learned from Mitt Romney's infamous quip that 47 percent of Americans were simply takers, has changed its tone, lambasting hedge funds and praising the little man. (This new-found populism is, of course, purely rhetorical: President Trump, for example, promised voters that he would improve health care coverage and protect programs like Social Security during his campaign, yet once in office he worked tirelessly to destroy the Affordable Care Act and defund Social Security.) The Right has also shown that it's willing to flirt with extremism, embracing not only neo-Nazis and threats of physical violence against their colleagues, but pumping their fists in support of mobs during the January 6, 2021, coup attempt at the Capitol.

At the same time, though, despite the challenges, this is the most promising political moment since the Civil Rights era. The time has have never seemed so ripe for major changes to the way the economy, and America's society, is organized. Despite the well-founded accounts of US dysfunction and polarization, I believe that economic rights are within reach.

Progress is already under way. A self-proclaimed democratic socialist from Vermont nearly won the Democratic presidential primary—and clearly dominated the youth vote—in both the 2016 and 2020 presidential election cycles. Democratic socialists, running on various pieces of the economic bill of rights, continue to be elected to national office. And while President Biden doesn't support these causes, there were many candidates on the Democratic presidential debate stage who advocated for the abolishment of private health insurance, who supported a jobs guarantee, and who stood behind expanding people's right to an education.

Change is percolating outside the Beltway as well. The largest protest movement in American history arose in the midst of the pandemic in response to police brutality, turning a spotlight on the Movement for Black Lives, whose platform includes an array of economic rights. Young people in the Sunrise Movement and other groups didn't just put the idea of a Green New Deal on the map; they made it central to the conversation about America's path forward and forced politicians to take the climate crisis seriously. Workers—from teachers in West Virginia and Arizona to John Deere workers in Missouri to Amazon warehouse workers on Staten Island—took to the streets in a wave of strikes and union organizing drives to demand better wages, good benefits, and humane working conditions. And groups like the Democratic Socialists of America have seen their ranks and influence swell as young people embrace ideas like Medicare for all, a job guarantee, free college, and housing for all.[4]

The resurgence of progressivism in the United States is promising. But progressives do not have the power—at least not yet—to win an economic bill of rights. To see poverty eradicated, progressives will have to continue pressing their case—via mass movements and grassroots organizing, over the dinner table and in the public sphere. I hope this book provides a starting point for some of those conversations. If America is to address the most urgent issues that face it—grotesque levels of inequality; a climate crisis threatening planetary stability; the continued economic suppression of communities of color that denies tens of millions of people justice, wellness, and freedom; declining faith in liberal democracy and rising fascism—an economic bill of rights is essential.

That's because, while an economic bill of rights is indeed about material security—making sure all are able to put food on the table and a roof over their heads—it's also about advancing a new social contract, one that truly honors people's inalienable rights to life, liberty, and the pursuit of happiness. It's about rooting out the deep power imbalances that warp America's economy and society. It's about building a sustainable economy and world that works for current and future generations alike. It's about freedom.

Acknowledgments

There are so many people in my life that helped make this book a reality. I first pondered writing it while sitting in the Black Sheep Deli in Amherst, Massachusetts, in 2015. I was finishing my dissertation at the University of Massachusetts Amherst, where I was privileged to study not just economics, but political economy. It was over pastries with one of my longtime mentors, Jerry Friedman, that the idea took root. We were discussing Roosevelt's 1944 State of the Union address, in which he proposed his famed economic bill of rights, in the context of the 2016 Democratic presidential primary. At the time, economists were out in full force. They were explaining to the nation precisely why proposals like a $15 minimum wage, universal health care, and free public higher education, however well intended, were *bad ideas*. Neoliberalism, after all, was the conventional wisdom. And bold ideas to build an actual well-being state, many of which were grounded in Roosevelt's New Deal, were simply brushed aside.

By dint of my training as a political economist, I knew this conventional economic wisdom was wrong and wanted to set the record straight. But I didn't just want to write about economics; rather, I wanted to better understand how these ideas had played out throughout American history. Jerry, an economic historian, encouraged me to study the history of economic rights, from the Founders through the New Deal and the civil rights movement. So I did.

It was over the next two years, during my time as a postdoc at Duke University's Cook Center on Social Equity, where I worked under the supervision of William "Sandy" Darity Jr., that the idea for this book really started to come together. Working closely with Sandy and fellow economist Darrick Hamilton, I devoted my research to many of the ideas that have become chapters in this book. It was during that time that Sandy, Darrick, and I wrote an article for the *American Prospect* on the idea of an economic bill of rights for the twenty-first century. I am thankful to Sandy and Darrick for the mentorship and support they provided me during this formative period of my career.

When I took my first tenure-track job as an assistant professor of economics at New College of Florida, I had reservations about writing this book. Economics is no longer a book field. But my colleagues—especially Rick Coe—gave me the needed support and encouragement to pursue this project to its fullest. I am thankful for that freedom and openness. I am also grateful to my students and research assistants at New College, including the hard work of Anaïs Goubert, Olivia Lowrey, Kaylie McCarthy, Rory Renzy, and Connor Rupp.

The manuscript came together in earnest while I was a 2021–22 fellow at the Berggruen Institute and the University of Southern California's Center on Science, Technology, and Public Life. I cherished my time at Berggruen, and I benefited greatly from the insights of my colleagues in the Rethinking Capitalism working group there, including Devika Dutt, Yakov Feygin, Nils Gilman, Martijn Konings, Leila Lorenzo, and Michael McCarthy. I am grateful to them for the opportunity to workshop many pieces of the book, and to the staff of the institute who helped make the year a productive one.

My thinking on positive freedom and economic rights was shaped by conversations, debates, and collaborations with many friends throughout my intellectual journey. Special thanks are due to Nellie Abernathy, Alan Aja, Jared Bernstein, Johanna Bozuwa, Matt Bruenig, Brian Callaci, Raúl Carrillo, Mijin Cha, Daniel Aldana Cohen, Billy Fleming, Anders Fremstad, Ilaria Giglioli, Michael Gorup, Rohan Grey, Thomas Herndon, Adam Hersh, Janelle Jones, Stephanie Kelton, Den Lewis, Rakeen Mabud, J. W. Mason, Alan Minskey, Lindsay Owens, Anne E. Price, Tara Raghuveer, Collin Reese, Thea Riofrancos, David Rosnick, Sean Sellers, Drew Serres, Mark Silverman, Ben Spielberg,

Jeff Spross, Mark Stelzner, Nathan Tankus, Daniele Tavani, Pavlina Tcherneva, Todd Tucker, Anastasia Wilson, and Khai Zaw. Many of them read chapters and provided feedback throughout the process, and to them I am forever grateful.

Arguments in the book were honed during various research presentations, including at Connecticut College; California State University, San Bernardino; the Equity Research Institute at the University of Southern California; the Russell Sage Foundation; the University of North Carolina, Greensboro; the Stanford Biofutures Seminar series; the University of Massachusetts Amherst; and the University of Missouri Kansas City. Many thanks to the organizers of these talks.

None of this would have been possible without the nurturing teachers and mentors I have had over the years, including Michael Ash, Jim Boyce, Jim Crotty, Nancy Folbre, Harvey J. Kaye, Steven Resnick, and John Stifler.

I am indebted to my friend Zach Carter, who encouraged me to take the book proposal out of the drawer and get back to work; and to Jia Lynn Yang, for introducing me to my agent, Lauren Sharp. Lauren has been supportive every step of the way, and her professional expertise navigating the publishing waters was invaluable.

The first time I spoke with Chad Zimmerman, my editor at the University of Chicago Press, I knew it was a match. Chad believed in the book and brought a level of excitement and support to the project that kept me invigorated during the writing and editing process. Chad was always patient with me, offering friendly encouragement and expert advice at each and every step. For that, I am deeply grateful.

I owe a great deal of thanks to my dear friend Jed Phillip Cohen, who worked tirelessly with me to make this book what it is today. Jed spent countless hours discussing the arguments, ideas, and prose presented here, providing critical feedback and helping me find my voice as a writer. The book wouldn't be what it is without him.

Finally, I would like to thank my family. My mother, Maria, was always there to talk, no matter what. My three dogs remained loyal companions when I struggled to put words on the page. And most important, I want to thank my loving partner, Chelsea. For the better part of a decade she has been my companion in this journey we call life. She has relentlessly and lovingly encouraged me to grow both personally and professionally over the years. It is hiking through the woods by her side that makes me feel at home and gives me everything I need.

Notes

Introduction

1. "Statement on the Visit to the USA, by Professor Philip Alston, United Nations Special Rapporteur on Extreme Poverty and Human Rights," December 2017, United Nations, https://www.ohchr.org/en/taxonomy/term/1265?page=19.
2. "Statement on the Visit to the USA."
3. The distinction between negative freedom ("freedom from") and positive freedom ("freedom to") was first drawn by Isaiah Berlin in his influential lecture "Two Concepts of Liberty." Berlin used the terms *freedom* and *liberty* interchangeably, as I do throughout the book.
4. Isaiah Berlin, *Liberty: Incorporating Four Essays on Liberty* (Oxford: Oxford University Press, 2002).
5. "No Place to Go: An Audit of the Public Toilet Crisis in Skid Row," A Special Project of the Los Angeles Central Providers Collaborative, Skid Row Community Residents and Partners, June 2017, https://lafla.org/wp-content/uploads/2017/08/No-Place-To-Go-final.pdf.
6. Berlin, *Liberty: Incorporating Four Essays on Liberty*, 171.
7. Positive freedom is closely associated with the work of philosopher and economist Amartya Sen, who argues for a capability approach to freedom, one where human welfare is focused on the actual ability of a person, through tangible options available to them, to realize one's human potential as one sees fit. The idea also builds on the work of T. H. Green, a leading intellectual of what came to be known as "social" liberalism. For Green, "the mere removal of compulsion, the mere enabling a man to do as he likes, is in itself no contribution to true freedom." Instead, that freedom rests in the "positive power or capacity of doing or enjoying something worth doing or enjoying." Thus a state that actively legislates to deliver freedom—education, health, quality employment, housing—Green argued, is like a powerful friend who enables individuals to pursue something better than what they have. Thus free markets and a minimal state cannot deliver freedom, for freedom to actually determine one's life requires a democratic state that embeds the economy in society. A market economy is not an end in itself but rather the means for socially determined ends. T. H. Green, *Liberal Legislation and Freedom of*

Contract (1881), reprinted in David Miller, ed., *The Liberty Reader* (London: Routledge, 2006).

Chapter One

1. "USA," World Inequality Database, https://wid.world/country/usa/.
2. "Out of Reach 2020," National Low Income Housing Coalition, accessed October 28, 2021, https://reports.nlihc.org/sites/default/files/oor/oor_2020.pdf.
3. "America's Rental Housing 2017," Joint Center for Housing Studies of Harvard University, https://www.jchs.harvard.edu/sites/default/files/media/imp/harvard_jchs_americas_rental_housing_2017_0.pdf.
4. "Homelessness in America: Overview of Data and Causes," National Law Center on Homelessness and Poverty. https://homelesslaw.org/wp-content/uploads/2018/10/Homeless_Stats_Fact_Sheet.pdf.
5. Lily Katz and Tim Ellis, "Rental Market Tracker: Rents Rise 14% in December—Biggest Jump in over Two Years," Redfin, January 21, 2022, https://www.redfin.com/news/redfin-rental-report-december-2021/.
6. Daniel Aldana Cohen and Mark Paul, "The Case for Social Housing," Data for Progress and the Justice Collaborative Institute, November 2, 2020, https://theappeal.org/the-lab/report/the-case-for-social-housing/.
7. "National Estimates: Eviction in America," Eviction Lab of Princeton University, https://evictionlab.org/national-estimates/.
8. Matthew Desmond and Carl Gershenson, "Who Gets Evicted? Assessing Individual, Neighborhood, and Network Factors," *Social Science Research* 62 (2017): 362–77.
9. Michael Sainato, "Billionaires Add $1tn to Net Worth during Pandemic as Their Workers Struggle," *The Guardian*, January 15, 2021.
10. Rupert Neate, "Billionaires' Wealth Rises to $10.2 Trillion amid Covid Crisis," *The Guardian*, October 6, 2021; Abha Bhattarai and Hannah Denham, "Stealing to Survive: More Americans Are Shoplifting Food as Aid Runs Out during the Pandemic," *Washington Post*, December 10, 2020.
11. Mitchell Hartman, "FICO Scores Rose to Record High in 2019," *Marketplace*, January 13, 2020, https://www.marketplace.org/2020/01/13/fico-scores-rose-to-record-high-in-2019/.
12. Kristin Schwab, "Fidelity Investments Says Average Retirement Account Balance at Record High," *Marketplace*, February 17, 2020, https://www.marketplace.org/2020/02/17/fidelity-investments-average-retirement-account-growing/.
13. Mitchell Harman, "Housing Starts Down for the Month, Up for the Year," *Marketplace*, February 19, 2020, https://www.marketplace.org/2020/02/19/housing-starts-down-for-the-month-up-for-the-year/.
14. Jessica Semega, Melissa Kollar, John Creamer, and Abinash Mohanty, "Income and Poverty in the United States: 2018," United States Census Bureau, September 2019, https://www.census.gov/library/publications/2019/demo/p60-266.html.
15. "Financial Accounts of the United States—Z.1," Board of Governors of the Federal Reserve System, https://www.federalreserve.gov/releases/z1/20200611/html/b101h.htm.
16. "Table B-3. Average Hourly and Weekly Earnings of All Employees on Private Nonfarm Payrolls by Industry Sector, Seasonally Adjusted," US Bureau of Labor Statistics, accessed October 27, 2021, https://www.bls.gov/news.release/empsit.t19.htm.

17. "Characteristics of New Housing," United States Census Bureau, https://www
     .census.gov/construction/chars/highlights.html#:~:text=Of%20the%20371
     %2C000%20multifamily%20units,16%2C000%20had%20shared%20laundry
     %20facilities; Witold Rybczynski, "Living Smaller," *Atlantic*, February 1991.

18. "Economic Report of the President—February 2020," White House, https://www
     .whitehouse.gov/wp-content/uploads/2021/07/2020-ERP.pdf.

19. Lawrence Mishel and Julia Wolfe, "CEO Compensation Has Growth 940% since
     1978," Economic Policy Institute, August 14, 2019; "Home Health Aides and Per-
     sonal Care Aids," US Bureau of Labor Statistics, https://www.bls.gov/oes/current
     /oes311120.htm; "Occupational Employment and Wages, May 2018—Preschool
     Teachers," US Bureau of Labor Statistics, https://www.bls.gov/ooh/education
     -training-and-library/preschool-teachers.htm; "Occupational Employment and
     Wages, May 2018—35-3021 Combined Food Preparation and Serving Workers,
     Including Fast Food," US Bureau of Labor Statistics, https://www.bls.gov/news
     .release/archives/ocwage_03292019.pdf.

20. Anne Case and Angus Deaton, *Deaths of Despair and the Future of Capitalism*
     (Princeton, NJ: Princeton University Press, 2020), 5–6, 32–33.

21. Raj Chetty, Michael Stepner, Sarah Abraham, Shelby Lin, Benhamin Scuderi,
     Nicholar Turner, Augstin Bergeron, and David Cutler, "The Association between
     Income and Life Expectancy in the United States, 2001–2014," *Journal of the Amer-
     ican Medical Association* 315, no. 16 (2016): 1750–66; Paola Zaninotto, George David
     Batty, Sari Stenholm, Ichiro Kawachi, Martin Hyde, Marcel Goldberg, Hugo West-
     erlund, Jussi Vahtera, and Jenny Head, "Socioeconomic Inequalities in Disability-
     Free Life Expectancy in Older People from England and the United States: A
     Cross-national Population-Based Study," *Journal of Gerontology A Biol Sci Med
     Sci* 75, no. 5 (2020): 906–13.

22. Jung Choi et al., "Millennial Homeownership: Why Is It So Low, and How Can
     We Increase It?," Urban Institute, July 2018, https://www.urban.org/sites/default
     /files/publication/98729/millennial_homeownership_0.pdf.

23. Keeanga-Yamahtta Taylor, *Race for Profit: How Banks and the Real Estate Industry
     Undermined Black Homeownership* (Chapel Hill: University of North Carolina
     Press, 2019); Richard Rothstein, *The Color of Law* (New York: Liverright, 2017);
     Michela Zonta, "Racial Disparities in Home Appreciation," Center for American
     Progress, July 15, 2019, https://www.americanprogress.org/article/racial-disparities
     -home-appreciation/.

24. Malia Wollan, "At the San Antonio Food Bank, the Cars Kept Coming," *New York
     Times*, May 26, 2020; Lauren Bauer, "The COVID-19 Crisis Has Already Left Too
     Many Children Hungry in America," Brookings Institution, May 6, 2020, https://
     www.brookings.edu/blog/up-front/2020/05/06/the-covid-19-crisis-has-already
     -left-too-many-children-hungry-in-america/; Diane Schanzenbach and Abigail
     Pitts, "Food Insecurity Triples for Families with Children during COVID-19 Pan-
     demic," Northwestern Institute for Policy Research, May 13, 2020, https://www
     .ipr.northwestern.edu/news/2020/food-insecurity-triples-for-families-during
     -covid.html.

25. Mary McCarthy, *The Collected Essays*, vol. 2: *Mary McCarthy's Theatre Chronicles,
     1937–1962 and On the Contrary* (New York: ORIM, 2018).

26. "Unemployment Rate—Civilian Labor Force 14 Years & Over," US Bureau of
     Labor Statistics, https://www.bls.gov/opub/mlr/1948/article/pdf/labor-force
     -employment-and-unemployment-1929-39-estimating-methods.pdf.

27. "Inaugural Address—January 20, 1937," Franklin D. Roosevelt Presidential Library and Museum, http://www.fdrlibrary.marist.edu/_resources/images/msf/msf 01059.

28. As the historian Eric Rauchway highlights, the New Deal could have gone further, especially in its embrace of Keynesian theories regarding deficit spending to assist the economy in making a fuller and more timely recovery. See Eric Rauchway, "Learning from the New Deal Mistakes," *American Prospect*, December 20, 2008, https://prospect.org/article/learning-new-deal-s-mistakes/.

29. Claudia Goldin and Robert A. Margo, "The Great Compression: Wage Structure in the United States at Mid-Century," *Quarterly Journal of Economics* 107, no. 2 (February 1992): 1–34. For a nice discussion of the Great Compression and the way in which lifting all boats can actually occur in the economy, see Jim Tankersley, *The Riches of This Land: The Untold, True Story of America's Middle Class* (New York: Public Affairs, 2020).

30. "President John F. Kennedy's Inaugural Address (1961)," National Archives, https://www.archives.gov/milestone-documents/president-john-f-kennedys-inaugural-address.

31. Michael Harrington, *The Other America* (New York: Macmillan, 1962), 88.

32. Harrington, 162, 2.

33. "USA," World Inequality Database, accessed October 27, 2021, https://wid.world/country/usa/.

34. Bryon G. Lander, "Group Theory and Individuals: The Origin of Poverty as a Political Issue in 1964," *Western Political Quarterly* 24, no. 3 (1971): 514–26.

35. Maurice Isserman, *The Other American: The Life of Michael Harrington* (New York: Public Affairs, 2001); Julian E. Zelizer, *The Fierce Urgency of Now: Lyndon Jonson, Congress, and the Battle for the Great Society* (London: Penguin Books, 2015), chaps. 1 and 8; "Annual Message to the Congress on the State of the Union, January 8, 1964," the American Presidency Project, UC Santa Barbara, https://www.presidency.ucsb.edu/documents/annual-message-the-congress-the-state-the-union-25.

36. Douglas A. Blackmon, *Slavery by Another Name: The Re-Enslavement of Black Americans from the Civil War to World War II* (New York: Anchor Books, 2008), 643.

37. W. E. B. Du Bois, "Black North," *New York Times Magazine*, November 17, 1901.

38. "Remarks at the University of Michigan, May 22, 1964," UVA Miller Center, https://millercenter.org/the-presidency/presidential-speeches/may-22-1964-remarks-university-michigan.

39. Mohamed Younis, "Most Americans See American Dream as Achievable," Gallup, July 17, 2019. https://news.gallup.com/poll/260741/americans-american-dream-achievable.aspx.

40. Raj Chetty, David Grusky, Maximilian Hell, Nathaniel Hendren, Robert Manduca, and Jimmy Narang, "The Fading American Dream: Trends in Absolute Income Mobility since 1940," *Science* 356, no. 6336 (2017): 398–406.

41. "The Global Social Mobility Report 2020: Equality, Opportunity and a New Economic Imperative," World Economic Forum, January 2020, https://www3.weforum.org/docs/Global_Social_Mobility_Report.pdf.

42. Vicki Shabo, "Letting Emergency Paid Leave Lapse Is Unconscionable Choice as 'Dark Winter' Looms—Congressional Leaders Must Act," *New America*, December 15, 2020; Elise Gould, "Lack of Paid Sick Days and Large Numbers of Uninsured Increase Risks of Spreading the Coronavirus," Economic Policy Institute,

February 28, 2020, https://www.epi.org/blog/lack-of-paid-sick-days-and-large
-numbers-of-uninsured-increase-risks-of-spreading-the-coronavirus/.

43. "Report on the Economic Well-Being of U.S. Households in 2018—May 2019,"
Board of Governors of the Federal Reserve System, May 2019, https://www.federal
reserve.gov/publications/files/2018-report-economic-well-being-us-households
-201905.pdf.

44. For a detailed historical overview of inequality, see Walter Scheidel, *The Great
Leveler: Violence and the History of Inequality from the Stone Age to the Twenty-First
Century* (Princeton, NJ: Princeton University Press, 2017); Peter H. Lindert and
Jeffrey G. Williamson, "American Incomes before and after the Revolution," *Jour-
nal of Economic History* 73, no. 3 (2013): 725–65.

45. Joseph E. Stiglitz, "The American Economy Is Rigged: And What We Can Do about
It," *Scientific American*, November 1, 2018; Dean Baker, *Rigged: How Globalization
and the Rules of the Modern Economy Were Structured to Make the Rich Richer* (Washington, DC: Center for Economic and Policy Research, 2016).

46. Shawn Donnan, Ann Choi, Hannah Levitt, and Christopher Cannon, "Wells Fargo
Rejected Half Its Black Applicants in Mortgage Refinancing Boom," *Bloomberg*,
March 10, 2022, https://www.bloomberg.com/graphics/2022-wells-fargo-black
-home-loan-refinancing/.

47. Darrick Hamilton, William Darity, Jr., Anne E. Price, Vishnu Sridharan, an Rebecca
Tippett, "Umbrellas Don't Make It Rain: Why Studying and Working Hard Isn't
Enough for Black Americans," *New York: The New School* 779 (2015): 780–81; William Darity Jr., Darrick Hamilton, Mark Paul, Alan Aja, Anne Price, Antonio Moore,
and Caterina Chiopris, "What We Get Wrong about Closing the Racial Wealth
Gap," Samuel DuBois Cook Center on Social Equity, April 2018, https://social
equity.duke.edu/wp-content/uploads/2020/01/what-we-get-wrong.pdf; Darrick
Hamilton and William A. Darity Jr., "The Political Economy of Education, Financial Literacy, and the Racial Wealth Gap," *Federal Reserve Bank of St. Louis Review*,
1st Qtr, 99, no. 1 (2017): 59–76.

48. William A. Darity and Patrick L. Mason, "Evidence on Discrimination in Employment: Codes of Color, Codes of Gender," *Journal of Economic Perspective* 12, no. 2
(1998): 63–90.

49. "Remarks at Pueblo, Colorado, 17 August 1962," John F. Kennedy Presidential
Library and Museum, https://www.jfklibrary.org/asset-viewer/archives/JFKPOF
/039/JFKPOF-039-038.

50. Seiichiro Mozumi, "The Kennedy-Johnson Tax Cut of 1964, the Defeat of Keynes,
and Compressive Tax Reform in the United States," *Journal of Policy History* 30,
no. 1 (2018): 25–61.

51. Kim Phillips-Fein, *Invisible Hands: The Businessmen's Crusade against the New Deal*
(New York: Norton, 2010), 291–92; "The State of the Union Address Delivered
before a Joint Session of the Congress," American Presidency Project, https://
www.jimmycarterlibrary.gov/assets/documents/speeches/su78jec.phtml; Paul
Stephen Dempsey, "Flying Blind: The Failure of Airline Deregulation" (Economic
Policy Institute, Washington, DC, 1990).

52. "Inaugural Address—January 20,1981," Reagan Foundation, https://www.reagan
library.gov/reagans/reagan-administration/reagan-presidency.

53. Bryan Craig, "Reagan vs. Air Traffic Controllers," Miller Center, August 3, 1981,
https://millercenter.org/reagan-vs-air-traffic-controllers.

54. "Patco Decertification Vote Is Switched from 2–1 to 3–0," *New York Times*, November 5, 1981.

55. "Share of Labour Compensation in GDP at Current National Prices for United States," Federal Reserve Bank of St. Louis, https://fred.stlouisfed.org/series/LAB SHPUSA156NRUG.

56. Mike Konczal, Katy Milani, and Ariel Evans, "The Empirical Failures of Neoliberalism," Roosevelt Institute, January 15, 2020, https://rooseveltinstitute.org/wp -content/uploads/2020/07/RI_The-Empirical-Failures-of-Neoliberalism_brief -202001.pdf.

57. Thomas Piketty, Emmanuel Saez, and Gabriel Zucman, "Distributional National Accounts Methods and Estimates," *Quarterly Journal of Economics* 133, no. 2 (2018): 553–609.

58. "Warren Buffett, Secretary Debbie Bosanek Discuss Tax Rate Inequality in Interview," *ABC News*, January 26, 2012.

59. "Income Inequality, USA, 1913–2021," World Inequality Database, https://wid .world/country/usa/.

60. Juliana Menasce Horowitz, Ruth Igielnik, and Rakesh Kochnar, "Most Americans Say There Is Too Much Economic Inequality in the U.S., but Fewer than Half Call It a Top Priority," Pew Research Center, January 9, 2020, https://www.pewresearch .org/social-trends/2020/01/09/most-americans-say-there-is-too-much-economic -inequality-in-the-u-s-but-fewer-than-half-call-it-a-top-priority/.

61. Michael I. Norton and Dan Ariely, "Building a Better America—One Wealth Quintile at a Time," *Perspectives of Psychological Science* 6, no. 1 (2011): 9–12.

62. Emmanuel Saez and Gabriel Zucman, "Wealth Inequality in the United States since 1913: Evidence from Capitalized Income Tax Data," *Quarterly Journal of Economics* 131, no. 2 (2016): 519–76.

63. Ana Hernandez Kent and Lowell R. Ricketts, "Gender Wealth Gap: Families Headed by Women Have Lower Wealth," Federal Reserve Bank of St. Louis, 2021, https:// www.stlouisfed.org/publications/in-the-balance/2021/gender-wealth-gap-families -women-lower-wealth; Khaing Zaw, Jhumpa Bhattacharya, Anne Price, Darrick Hamilton, and William Darity Jr., "Women, Race and Wealth," Samuel DuBois Cook Center on Social Equity, January 2017, https://www.insightcced.org/wp-content /uploads/2017/01/January2017_ResearchBriefSeries_WomenRaceWealth-Volume1 -Pages-1.pdf.

64. Heather Long, Andrew Van Dam, Alyssa Fowers, and Leslie Shapiro, "The Covid-19 Recession Is the Most Unequal in Modern U.S. History," *Washington Post*, September 30, 2020.

65. Tim F. Lio and Fernando De Maio, "Association of Social and Economic Inequality with Coronavirus Disease 2019 Incidence and Mortality across US Counties," *JAMA Network Open* 4, no. 1 (January 2021): 1–10.

66. Julia Pyper, "UN Chief Guterres: The Status Quo on Climate Policy 'Is a Suicide,'" Greentech Media, June 7, 2019, https://www.greentechmedia.com/articles/read /un-chief-guterres-the-status-quo-is-a-suicide.

67. Eun-Soon Im, Jeremy S. Pal, and Elfatih A. B. Eltahir, "Deadly Heat Waves Projected in the Densely Populated Agricultural Regions of South Asia," *Science Advances* 3, no. 8 (April 2017), https://www.science.org/doi/full/10.1126/sciadv .1603322.

68. Dino Grandoni, "The Energy 202: California's Fires Are Putting a Huge Amount of Carbon Dioxide into the Air," *Washington Post*, September 17, 2020, https://

www.washingtonpost.com/politics/2020/09/17/energy-202-california-fires-are
-putting-huge-amount-carbon-dioxide-into-air/.

69.   "Secretary of Defense Speech—Conference of Defense Ministers of the Americas,"
US Dept. of Defense, https://www.defense.gov/News/Speeches/Speech/Article
/605617/; R. Jisung Park, Joshua Goodman, Michael Hurqitz, and Jonathan Smith,
"Heat and Learning," *American Economic Journal: Economic Policy* 12, no. 2 (2020):
306–39; Solomon Hsiang, Robert Kopp, Amir Jina, James Rising, Michael Delgado,
Shashank Mohan, D.J. Rasmussen, Robert Muir-Wood, Paul Wilson, Michael Oppen-
heimer, Kate Larsen, and Trvor Houser, "Estimating Economic Damage from Cli-
mate Change in the United States," *Science* 356, no. 6345 (2017): 1362–69; Marshall
Burke, Solomon M. Hsiang, and Edward Miguel, "Global Non-Linear Effect of
Temperature on Economic Production," *Nature* 527, no. 7577 (2015): 235–39.

70.   James K. Boyce, "Inequality as a Cause of Environmental Degradation," *Ecologi-
cal Economics* 11, no. 3 (1994): 169–78; James K. Boyce, Andrew R. Klemer, Paul H.
Templet, and Cleve E. Willis, "Power Distribution, the Environment, and Public
Health: A State-Level Analysis," *Ecological Economics* 29, no. 1 (1999): 127–40.

71.   Bill McKibben, Twitter Post, November 3, 2020, 5:38 p.m.

72.   Robert Dahl, *Democracy and Its Critics* (New Haven, CT: Yale University Press,
1989).

73.   Harold R. Bowen, *Report of the National Commission on Technology, Automation,
and Economic Progress* (Washington, DC: US Government Printing Office, 1966),
vol. 1.

Chapter Two

1.   "Remarks Announcing America's Economic Bill of Rights—July 2, 1987," Ronald
Reagan Presidential Library and Museum, https://www.reaganlibrary.gov/archives
/speech/remarks-announcing-americas-economic-bill-rights. The quotations in
the preceding paragraphs are drawn from this source.

2.   "America's Economic Bill of Rights—July 3, 1987," Ronald Reagan Presidential
Library and Museum, https://www.reaganlibrary.gov/archives/speech/americas
-economic-bill-rights.

3.   More recent analyses of negative freedom, its difference from positive freedom
as originally outlined by Berlin, along with discussions of freedom as nondomina-
tion can be found in the works of Alex Gourevitch, William Clare Roberts, and
Corey Robin.

4.   Eric Foner, *The Story of American Freedom* (New York: Norton), 21–38.

5.   Abraham Lincoln, "Emancipation Proclamation," January 1, 1863, https://consti
tutioncenter.org/media/files/ep_miniposter.pdf.

6.   Address by Elizabeth Cady Stanton on Woman's Rights, September 1848, https://
susanb.org/wp-content/uploads/2018/12/Elizabeth-Cady-Stanton-Sept.-1848
.pdf.

7.   For a more in-depth critique of the Lochner era and the rise of legal realism, see
Jedediah Britton-Purdy, David Singh Grewal, Amy Kapczynski, and K. Sabeel Rah-
man, "Building a Law-and-Political-Economy Framework: Beyond the Twentieth-
Century Synthesis," *Yale Law Journal* 129 (2019): 1784–1832. It should also be noted
that revisionist work has highlighted the fact that the Lochner era was not as straightforward as has often been portrayed. See Howard Gillman, *The Constitution Besieged*
(Durham, NC: Duke University Press, 1993).

8.   Karl Marx, "Chapter Six: The Buying and Selling of Labour-Power," in *Capital, Volume One* (repr., New York: Penguin Classics); Eric Rauchway, *Winter War: Hoover, Roosevelt, and The First Clash Over the New Deal* (New York: Basic Books, 2018), 13, 41–42.

9.   While Roosevelt was offering something entirely new at the federal level, it should be noted that his ideas built off the existence of a small, though important, welfare state at the local and state levels. For more, see Emily Zackin, *Looking for Rights in All the Wrong Places: Why State Constitutions Contain America's Positive Rights* (Princeton, NJ: Princeton University Press, 2013).

10. John Maynard Keynes, *The General Theory*, in *The Collected Writings of John Maynard Keynes*, vol. 7, ed. Elizabeth Johnson, Donald Moggridge, and Austin Robinson (New York: Cambridge University Press for the Royal Economic Society), 378.

11. John Maynard Keynes, "From Keynes to Roosevelt: Our Recovery Plan Assayed," *New York Times*, December 31, 1933; "A President's Evolving Approach to Fiscal Policy in Times of Crisis," Franklin D. Roosevelt Presidential Library, https://www.fdrlibrary.org/budget.

12. John Maynard Keynes, "Letter of February 1 to Franklin Delano Roosevelt" (1938), in *Collected Works*, vol. 21: *Activities 1931–1939* (London: Macmillan).

13. For a nice overview of Keynes's influence on Roosevelt and his cabinet, which, it should be said, was not complete, as disagreements in the cabinet over economic policy occurred, see Eric Rauchway, *The Money Makers: How Roosevelt and Keynes Ende the Depression, Defeated Fascism, and Secured a Prosperous Peace* (New York: Basic Books, 2015).

14. Joseph A. Schumpeter, "John Maynard Keynes: 1883–1946," *American Economic Review* 36, no. 4 (1946): 495–518; John Maynard Keynes, "Democracy and Efficiency," *New Statesman and Nation*, January 28, 1939, in *Collected Works*, vol. 11, 500.

15. Fred Block, "Introduction to *The Great Transformation* by Karl Polanyi" (Boston: Beacon Press: 2001); "A 'Mighty Endeavor': D-Day," Franklin D. Roosevelt Presidential Library and Museum; Bruce Caldwell, "The Road to Serfdom after 75 Years," *Journal of Economic Literature* 58, no. 3 (2020): 720–48; Philip Mirowski and Dieter Plehwe, eds., *The Road from Mont Pelerin: The Making of the Neoliberal Thought Collective* (Cambridge, MA: Harvard University Press, 2015).

16. F. A. Hayek, *The Road to Serfdom* (London: Routledge Classic, [1944] 2006), vii–viii, 25–27.

17. Hayek, 73–74.

18. Hayek, 94–104.

19. Hayek, 17–19, 25–27, 93–104.

20. Henry Hazlitt, "An Economist's View of 'Planning,'" *New York Times*, September 24, 1944.

21. In 2010, nearly twenty years after Hayek's death, *The Road to Serfdom* would see a resurgence, vaulting to Amazon's number one spot after Fox anchor and Tea Party icon Glenn Beck featured it on his show. He claimed the book delivered a Mike Tyson–style "right hook to socialism." Beck informed his audience that the book inspired decades of conservative thinkers and politicians, including President Reagan, and could serve as a vital text for the surge of a more radical right. "The Road to Serfdom," *Glenn Beck Program*, June 9, 2010.

22. Bruce Caldwell, "*The Road to Serfdom* after 75 Years," CHOPE Working Paper, No. 2019-13; Hayek, *The Road to Serfdom*, 125. It is worth noting that conservatives did not uniformly embrace Hayek's book. Some, such as Ayn Rand, thought the

book was "pure poison." Jennifer Schuessler, "Hayek: The Back Story," *New York Times*, July 9, 2010.

23. Zach D. Carter, *The Price of Peace: Money, Democracy, and the Life of John Maynard Keynes* (New York: Random House, 2020), 561.

24. F. A. Hayek, "A Rebirth of Liberalism," *The Freeman*, July 28, 1952, 731; "Statement of Aims," Mont Pelerin Society, https://www.montpelerin.org/statement-of-aims/. There have been many excellent books written on the history of the Mont Pelerin Society and the rise of neoliberalism. Angus Burgin's *The Great Persuasion*; *The Road from Mont Pelerin: The Making of the Neoliberal Thought Collective*, edited by Philip Mirowski and Dieter Plehwe; and Slobodian's *Globalists*, are all essential reads. Slobodian argues that rather than start the history of neoliberalism with the rise of the Mont Pelerin Society, we should instead look to the 1920s; Karl Marx, "Theses on Feuerbach," https://www.marxists.org/archive/marx/works/1845/theses/theses.htm#:~:text=I,activity%2C%20practice%2C%20not%20subjectively; Quinn Slobodian, *Globalists: The End of Empire and the Birth of Neoliberalism* (Cambridge, MA: Harvard University Press, 2018), 271.

25. Slobodian, *Globalists*, 1–6.

26. Marx, "Theses on Feuerbach"; Slobodian, *Globalists*, 271.

27. Milton Friedman and Rose D. Friedman, *Two Lucky People* (Chicago: University of Chicago Press, 1998), 158–59.

28. Binyamin Appelbaum, *The Economists' Hour: False Prophets, Free Markets, and the Fracture of Society* (Boston: Little, Brown, 2019).

29. Steve Pearlstein, "Friedman Debunked the Gospel of Keynes," *Washington Post*, November 17, 2006; Lawrence H. Summers, "The Great Liberator," *New York Times*, November 19, 2006.

30. Milton Friedman, "Neo-Liberalism and Its Prospects," *Farman*, February 17, 1951, https://miltonfriedman.hoover.org/internal/media/dispatcher/214957/full.

31. Friedman and Friedman, *Two Lucky People*, 28.

32. Milton Friedman, "The Goldwater View of Economics," *New York Times*, October 11, 1964.

33. Milton Friedman and Rose Friedman, *Free to Choose: A Personal Statement* (New York: Harcourt Brace Jovanovich, 1980), 6.

34. Although Friedman wouldn't follow Reagan to the White House, preferring to remain an outsider who could freely speak his mind, he would serve on Reagan's Economic Policy Advisory Board and was known as the "guru" of the Reagan administration.

35. Lanny Ebenstein, *Milton Friedman: A Biography* (London: Palgrave Macmillan, 2007), 205–8.

36. Adam Clymer, "Ford Declares Reagan Can't Win; Invited G.O.P. to Ask Him to Run," *New York Times*, March 2, 1980.

37. Kim Phillips-Fein, *Invisible Hands: The Businessmen's Crusade against the New Deal* (New York: Norton, 2009); Rick Perlstein, *Reaganland: America's Right Turn 1976–1980* (New York: Simon and Schuster, 2020).

38. Konczal, Milani, and Evans, "The Empirical Failures of Neoliberalism."

39. Friedman was, it should be noted, disappointed to a degree in Reagan's work during his tenure in the White House. Reagan never managed to cut government down to size the way Friedman had hoped, largely due to an expansion in military spending.

40. Emanuel Kopp, Daniel Leigh, Susanna Mursula, and Suchanan Tambunlertchai, "U.S. Investment since the Tax Cuts and Jobs Act of 2017," International Monetary

Fund Working Paper, 2019, https://www.imf.org/en/Publications/WP/Issues/2019 /05/31/U-S-46942.

41. For a nice account of how economics, namely, microeconomics, effectively influenced public policy, see Elizabeth Popp Berman, *Thinking Like an Economist: How Efficiency Replaced Equality in U.S. Public Policy* (Princeton, NJ: Princeton University Press, 2022).

42. Mark Paul, "A Job for Everyone," *U.S. News*, October 7, 2016.

43. Elizabeth Andersson, *Private Government: How Employers Rule Our Lives (and Why We Don't Talk about It)* (Princeton, NJ: Princeton University Press, 2017).

Chapter Three

1. Franklin D. Roosevelt, "State of the Union Message to Congress," January 11, 1944, https://www.fdrlibrary.org/address-text.

2. Gordon S. Wood, *The American Revolution: A History* (New York: Modern Library, 2002), 55; Thomas Paine, *Rights of Man, Common Sense, and Other Political Writings* (Oxford: Oxford University Press, 2008).

3. Harvey J. Kaye, *Thomas Paine and the Promise of America* (New York: Hill and Wang, 2005), 4-5, 76, 86-87; Thomas Paine, *Rights of Man, Common Sense, and Other Political Writings*, 11.

4. Paine, *Rights of Man, Common Sense, and Other Political Writings*, 119, 300.

5. Paine, 409-30.

6. Paine, 414.

7. Christian Parenti, *Radical Hamilton: Economic Lessons from a Misunderstood Founder* (London: Verso Books, 2020); Alexander Hamilton, "The Report on the Subject of Manufactures," National Archives, https://founders.archives.gov/documents /Hamilton/01-10-02-0001-0007.

8. Today we can see Hamilton's fingerprints on what's left of the developmentalist state in the United States. As Michael Lind, cofounder of the think tank New America, explains, "What is good about the American economy is largely the result of the Hamiltonian developmental tradition, and what is bad about it is largely the result of the Jeffersonian producerist school." America has reaped a great many benefits from the Hamiltonian tradition, ranging from the internet (which was developed by the US government) to the national rail, highway, and aviation systems to the continental market, which helped America become an economic powerhouse and triumph over the Axis powers during World War II. The cause of social justice too has benefited from developmentalism. For example, Lind attributes civil rights and minimum wage laws, advances that banished the conditions of slavery and serfdom once dominant in the American landscape, to Hamiltonian political economy. Michael Lind, *A Land of Promise: An Economic History of the United States* (New York: HarperCollins, 2012), 15.

9. Parenti, *Radical Hamilton*, 5; George Tucker, *The Life of Thomas Jefferson* (Philadelphia: Carey, Lea, & Blanchard, 1873), 503. Though Jefferson's story is far more complex than the common telling. He was an ardent supporter of small government, but he also wrote, "We hold these truths to be self-evident, that all men are created equal, that they are endowed by their Creator with certain unalienable Rights, that among these are Life, Liberty and the Pursuit of Happiness." These were radical words, with implications still playing out today. Setting himself apart from Locke, Jefferson chose to substitute "Pursuit of Happiness" for Locke's "Property." In his agrarian vision of the world, Jefferson argued that it was crucial that individuals—

excluding enslaved persons, which he owned many of—were able to develop their own potential and realize goals that the individuals themselves deemed necessary for the good life. This required property independence, according to Jefferson, for an ownership society was a precondition of freedom. But the radical side of Jefferson has been sterilized; today he is conveniently championed by the modern Republican Party for his views on private property and small government. But Jefferson was never the free-marketeer that twenty-first-century conservatives dream of. Jefferson was always more complicated, arguing that without near-universal property ownership, the individual would lack economic resources, and therefore lack freedom. Here Jefferson believed that America, endowed with abundant land up for forcible seizure, promised a great easing of the conflict between personal and property rights that haunted Europe. No more would the people be forced into wage labor, which amounted to a loss of freedom and gave rise to dependence. Instead, Jefferson's vision of freedom as widespread property ownership for White men would be seared into the American psyche, while his universal vision of freedom as the right to "life, liberty, and the pursuit of happiness," coupled with the claim that "all men are created equal" would be relegated to the back burner.

10.   Congressional Research Service, "The U.S. Land-Grant University System: An Overview," April 29, 2019, https://sgp.fas.org/crs/misc/R45897.pdf. For all the progressive motivations, however, these acts were based in settler colonialism. The land being given away was not idle: it was Indigenous land forcibly taken through mass extermination. Further, the provisions were not equitably applied. For example, even after the 1866 Civil Rights Act clarified that Black Americans were indeed citizens, the Homestead Act largely excluded women and Black people in practice, with only a few thousand Black homesteaders moving west, accounting for less than one percent of beneficiaries. Nick Estes, *Our History Is the Future* (London: Verso Books, 2019); Keri Leigh Merrit, "Land and the Roots of African-American Poverty," *Aeon*, March 11, 2016, https://aeon.co/ideas//land-and-the-roots-of-african-american-poverty.

11.   James Madison to Lafayette, November 25, 1820, Founders Online Archive, https://founders.archives.gov; Mehrsa Baradaran, *The Color of Money: Black Banks and the Racial Wealth Gap* (Cambridge, MA: Harvard University Press, 2017), 15.

12.   Frederick Douglass, "Celebrating the Past, Anticipating the Future," April 14, 1875, in *The Frederick Douglass Papers. Series One: Speeches, Debates, and Interviews*, vol. 4: *1864–80*, ed. John W. Blassingame and John R. McKivigan (New Haven, CT: Yale University Press, 1991), 413.

13.   Baradaran, *The Color of Money*, 30.

14.   William A. Darity and A. Kirsten Mullen, *From Here to Equality: Reparations for Black Americans in the Twenty-First Century* (Chapel Hill: University of North Carolina Press, 2020), 203–4.

15.   Darity and Mullen, chap. 8.

16.   W. E. B. Du Bois, *Black Reconstruction in America* (Oxford: Oxford University Press, 2007), 24.

17.   Blackmon, *Slavery by Another Name*.

18.   Herbert Hoover, "Campaign Speech in Madison Square Garden," October 21, 1932, https://millercenter.org/the-presidency/presidential-speeches/october-21-1932-campaign-speech-madison-square-garden; Tugwell, "Design for Government," quoted in Ira Katznelson, *Fear Itself: The New Deal and the Origins of Our Time* (New York: Liveright, 2013), 232.

19. Franklin D. Roosevelt, Commonwealth Club Address, September 23, 1932, https://
     www.presidency.ucsb.edu/documents/campaign-address-progressive-government
     -the-commonwealth-club-san-francisco-california.

20. Roosevelt.

21. Federal Reserve Bank of St. Louis, "NBER based Recession Indicators for the
     United States from the Period following the Peak through the Trough [USREC],"
     retrieved from FRED, Federal Reserve Bank of St. Louis; https://fred.stlouisfed
     .org/series/USREC, April 26, 2022; Franklin D. Roosevelt, "On Moving Forward
     to Greater Freedom and Greater Security," Radio Address of the President, Sep-
     tember 30, 1934, http://docs.fdrlibrary.marist.edu/093034.html.

22. Though it is important to mention that Roosevelt would arrogate immense power
     to himself as president to enact the social and economic changes he sought.

23. I've borrowed this term from the Finish author Anu Partanen.

24. Roosevelt, Commonwealth Club Address.

25. Katznelson, *Fear Itself*, 92–125; "Essay: The Federal Emergency Relief Administra-
     tion," Washington State University, https://content.lib.washington.edu/feraweb
     /essay.html; Carolyn Dimitri, Anne Effland, and Neilson Conklin, "The 20th Cen-
     tury Transformation of U.S. Agriculture and Farm Policy," Economic Research
     Service, US Department of Agriculture, https://www.ers.usda.gov/webdocs/publi
     cations/44197/13566_eib3_1_.pdf.

26. For a thoughtful labor-centric history of the New Deal, see Liz Cohen, *Making a
     New Deal: Industrial Workers in Chicago, 1919–1939* (New York: Cambridge Univer-
     sity Press, 1990).

27. Franklin D. Roosevelt, "Statement on the National Industrial Recovery Act,"
     June 16, 1933, http://docs.fdrlibrary.marist.edu/odnirast.html.

28. "Research Starters: US Military by the Numbers," National World War II Museum,
     https://www.nationalww2museum.org/students-teachers/student-resources
     /research-starters/research-starters-us-military-numbers; "Research Starters:
     Worldwide Deaths in World War II," National World War II Museum, https://www
     .nationalww2museum.org/students-teachers/student-resources/research-starters
     /research-starters-worldwide-deaths-world-war.

29. Franklin D. Roosevelt, "State of the Union Address," January 6, 1942, https://www
     .presidency.ucsb.edu/documents/state-the-union-address-1.

30. Franklin D. Roosevelt, "Annual Message to Congress, Four Freedoms Speech,"
     January 6, 1941, https://www.ourdocuments.gov/print_friendly.php?flash=false
     &page=transcript&doc=70&title=Transcript+of+President+Franklin+Roosevelts
     +Annual+Message+%28Four+Freedoms%29+to+Congress+%281941%29.

31. Harvey J. Kaye, *The Fight for the Four Freedoms: What Made FDR and the Greatest
     Generation Truly Great* (New York: Simon and Schuster, 2015), 72–76.

32. Alan Brinkley, *The End of Reform: New Deal Liberalism in Recession and War* (New
     York: Vintage Books, 1995), 102–6; https://data.bls.gov/timeseries/LFU21000100
     &series_id=LFU22000100&from_year=1929&to_year=1939&periods_option
     =specific_periods&periods=Annual+Data; https://data.bls.gov/timeseries/LNU
     04023554&series_id=LNU04000000&series_id=LNU03023554&series_id
     =LNU03000000&years_option=all_years&periods_option=specific_periods
     &periods=Annual+Data.

33. Franklin D. Roosevelt, "State of the Union Message to Congress," January 11, 1944.
     https://www.fdrlibrary.org/address-text.

34. Kaye, *The Fight for the Four Freedoms*. Other scholars have criticized Roosevelt's turn to economic rights. Samuel Moyn has argued that these rights were "about freedom, not equality," pointing to what he believes to be a deep tension between sufficiency and equality. Moyn notes that Roosevelt made a grave mistake by embracing the human rights rhetoric in his proposed economic bill of rights and believes this marked a shift away from some of the New Deal's earlier institutional reforms. I do not share Moyn's view. Samuel Moyn, *Not Enough: Human Rights in an Unequal World* (Cambridge, MA: Harvard University Press, 2018).

35. Langston Hughes, "How About It, Dixie" (October 1942), in *The Collected Poems of Langston Hughes*, ed. Arnold Rampersad (New York: Alfred A. Knopf, 1994), 291.

36. John Steinbeck, *Once There Was a War* (New York: Bantam Books, 1960), 68-70.

37. Roosevelt, "State of the Union Message to Congress," January 11, 1944.

38. Kaye, *The Fight for the Four Freedoms*, 125.

39. Rexford G. Tugwell, *The Democratic Roosevelt* (New York: Doubleday, 1957).

40. It is indeed unlikely that Roosevelt would have had the power to pass his New Deal agenda accompanied by civil rights legislation; indeed, the Faustian bargain he struck with southern segregationists was a troubling and deeply imperfect one.

41. Katznelson, *Fear Itself*, 3-29, 140-41, 156-95.

42. Jess Gilbert, *Planning Democracy: Agrarian Intellectuals and the Intended New Deal* (New Haven, CT: Yale University Press, 2015), chaps. 5, 6; Brinkley, *The End of Reform*, 149; John Nichols, *The Fight for the Soul of the Democratic Party: The Enduring Legacy of Henry Wallace's Anti-Fascist, Anti-Racist Politics* (London: Verso, 2020), chap. 1.

43. Henry Wallace, "Century of the Common Man," May 8, 1942. https://digital.library .cornell.edu/catalog/ss:19043116.

44. Brinkley, *The End of Reform*, 153.

45. Jeff Greenfield, "The Year the Veepstakes Really Mattered," *Politico Magazine*, July 10, 2016.

46. Martin Luther King Jr. "Where Do We Go from Here?," in *The Radical King*, ed. Cornel West (Boston: Beacon Press, 2015), 251.

47. Ibid.

48. West, *The Radical King*, 226.

49. Martin Luther King Jr. to A. Philip Randolph, April 8, 1958, Martin Luther King Jr. Research and Education Institute, https://kinginstitute.stanford.edu/king-papers /documents/philip-randolph-6; Bayard Rustin, *Time on Two Crosses: The Collected Writings of Bayard Rustin*, ed. Devon W. Carbado and Donald Weise (Hoboken, NJ: Cleis Press, 2015), 14-25.

50. For a discussion of the transformation of American politics regarding race and civil rights, see Eric Schickler, *Racial Realignment: The Transformation of American Liberalism, 1932-1965* (Princeton, NJ: Princeton University Press, 2016).

51. West, *The Radical King*, 8-9.

52. Rustin, *Time on Two Crosses*, 370-78.

53. Paul Le Blanc and Michael D. Yates, *A Freedom Budget for All Americans: Recapturing the Promise of the Civil Rights Movement in the Struggle for Economic Justice Today* (New York: Monthly Review Press, 2013), 91-93.

54. Rustin, *Time on Two Crosses*, 376; A. Philip Randolph and Bayard Rustin, *A "Freedom Budget" for All Americans* (New York: A. Philip Randolph Institute, 1967), https://www.prrac.org/pdf/FreedomBudget.pdf.

55. Randolph and Rustin, *A "Freedom Budget" for All Americans*; emphasis in original.

56. Randolph and Rustin; emphasis in original.

57. Thomas A. Johnson, "Rights, Religious and Labor Leaders Ask $185 Billion U.S. 'Freedom Budget,'" *New York Times*, October 27, 1966, https://timesmachine.ny times.com/timesmachine/1966/10/27/89650819.html?pageNumber=20.

58. Martin Luther King Jr., "Martin Luther King Jr.'s Call for a Poor People's Campaign," *The Atlantic*, March 20, 1968, https://www.theatlantic.com/magazine/archive /2018/02/martin-luther-king-jr-poor-peoples-campaign/552539/.

59. King too had his shortcomings. Chief among them were his conservative views on the nuclear family and gender norms, along with his overreliance reliance on ensuring that people "act right." For more, see Tommie Shelby and Brandon M. Terry, eds., *To Shape a New World: Essays on the Political Philosophy of Marin Luther King, Jr.* (Cambridge, MA: Harvard University Press, 2018).

60. Martin Luther King Jr., "We Need an Economic Bill of Rights," *The Guardian*, April 4, 2018, https://www.theguardian.com/commentisfree/2018/apr/04/martin -luther-king-jr--economic-bill-of-rights.

61. Joshua Bloom and Waldo E. Martin Jr., *Black against Empire: The History and Politics of the Black Panther Party* (Berkeley: University of California Press, 2012).

62. Ted Gittinger and Allen Fisher, "LBJ Champions the Civil Rights Act of 1964, Part 2," *Prologue Magazine* 36 no. 2 (Summer 2004), https://www.archives.gov /publications/prologue/2004/summer/civil-rights-act-2.html#:~:text=He%20 said%2C%20%22I%20think%20we,my%20life%2C%20and%20yours.%22 &text=Ted%20Gittinger%20conducted%20oral%20history,archivist%20at%20 the%20Lyndon%20B; David Shribman, "A Closer Look at the Hart Generation," *New York Times Magazine*, May 27, 1984, https://www.nytimes.com/1984/05/27 /magazine/a-closer-look-at-the-hart-generation.html.

63. Dream Defenders, https://dreamdefenders.org/freedom-papers/freedom-from -poverty/.

64. Transcript of Speech by Bernie Sanders, https://www.vox.com/2019/6/12/1866 3217/bernie-sanders-democratic-socialism-speech-transcript.

65. In 1944, farmers comprised one-fourth of the population. Today farmers make up less than 1 percent of the population.

Chapter Four

1. At the time state governments played a more prominent role in shaping social policy than the federal government. See William J. Novak, *The People's Welfare: Law and Regulation in Nineteenth-Century America* (Chapel Hill: University of North Carolina Press, 2013).

2. June Hopkins, *Harry Hopkins: Sudden Hero, Brash Reformer* (London: Palgrave MacMillan, 1991) 31.

3. "Public Works of Art Project (PWAP) (1933)," Living New Deal, accessed November 5, 2021, https://livingnewdeal.org/glossary/public-works-art-project-pwap -1933-2/.

4. Robert Sherwood, *Roosevelt and Hopkins: An Intimate History* (New York: Harper & Brothers, 1948).

5. "Employment Rate," OECD Data, OECD.org, 2021, https://data.oecd.org/emp /employment-rate.htm.

6.   William Beveridge in his 1944 report proclaims full employment meant "having always more vacant jobs than unemployed men." William Beveridge, *Full Employment in a Free Society* (London: Allen & Unwin, 1944), 18.

7.   Author analysis of Bureau of Labor Statistics Job Openings and Labor Turnover Survey and Current Population Survey. The number of seekers per job is likely higher given the narrow definition used for formal unemployment in the United States. (For instance, one must have actively searched for a job in the previous four weeks and must not have worked even one paid hour.) Further, the job openings numbers include poverty-level employment, thus inflating the denominator. "Job Openings and Labor Turnover Survey," US Bureau of Labor Statistics, US Department of Labor, August 2021, https://www.bls.gov/jlt/; "Labor Force Statistics from the Current Population Survey," US Bureau of Labor Statistics, US Department of Labor, October 2021, https://www.bls.gov/cps/.

8.   Michael Kalecki, "Political Aspects of Full Employment," *Political Quarterly* 14, no. 4 (1943): 322–31, https://doi.org/10.1111/j.1467-923X.1943.tb01016.x.

9.   The failures of the unemployment system were front and center during the COVID-19 crisis, especially in southern states such as Florida where unemployed individuals often waited weeks, and in some cases months, for assistance. Many unemployed workers found it simply impossible to get benefits, despite qualifying, and many more were terminated from the unemployment insurance (UI) system despite qualifying to stay in the program. In many localities the UI system has suffered from chronic disinvestment and in some cases administrations that intentionally weakened the system. Patricia Mazzei and Sabrina Tavernise, "Florida Is a Terrible State to Be an 'Unemployed Person,'" *New York Times*, April 24, 2020, https://www.nytimes.com/2020/04/23/us/florida-coronavirus-unemployment.html; "Statement of the Problem: Why Unemployment Insurance Reform Is Needed," Economic Policy Institute, https://www.epi.org/publication/statement-of-the-problem-why-unemployment-insurance-reform-is-needed/.

10. Eli Rosenberg, "Kroger to Close More Stores Instead of Giving Workers Hazard Pay," *Washington Post*, February 17, 2021, https://www.washingtonpost.com/business/2021/02/17/kroger-qfc-closing-hazard-pay/; David Li, "Coronavirus Kills 8, Infects over 350 at California Poultry Plant Now Told to Shut Down," NBC News, August 28, 2020, https://www.nbcnews.com/news/us-news/coronavirus-kills-8-infects-over-350-california-poultry-plant-now-n1238677.

11. Jerome Powell, "Monetary Policy in a Changing Economy," Board of Governors of the Federal Reserve System, August 24, 2018, https://www.federalreserve.gov/newsevents/speech/powell20180824a.htm.

12. For an in-depth critique of the NAIRU, see James Galbraith, "Time to Ditch the NAIRU," *Journal of Economic Perspectives* 11, no. 1 (1997): 93–108, doi: 10.1257/jep.11.1.93.

13. The CBO, for its part, takes the Federal Reserve's flawed reasoning a step further, estimating a natural rate of unemployment for different groups of workers based on key demographics. For instance, the CBO estimates that the natural rate of unemployment for White workers is 4.4%. For Black workers, according to the CBO, it is a whopping 10%—more than twice the rate of White workers. (For Latinx workers, the natural rate is 6%). In other words, a full-employment economy is one in which one in ten Black workers looking for a job can't find one.

14. At its peak in 1954, the unionization rate was 35%. In 2021, it was 10.3%.

15. William H. Beveridge, *Full Employment in a Free Society* (London: Allen & Unwin: 1944). Malcolm P. Baker, Daniel Bergstresser, George Serafeim, and Jeffrey Wurgler, "Financing the Response to Climate Change: The Pricing and Ownership of U.S. Green Bonds," *SSRN* (2018): 1–45, https://papers.ssrn.com/sol3/papers.cfm ?abstract_id=3275327; "Labor Force Participation Rate," FRED, Economic Research Federal Reserve Bank of St. Louis, https://fred.stlouisfed.org/series/CIVPART; "Wage Growth Tracker," Federal Reserve Bank of Atlanta, https://www.atlanta fed.org/chcs/wage-growth-tracker; "Share of Labour Compensation in GDP at Current National Prices for United States," FRED, Economic Research Federal Reserve Bank of St. Louis, https://fred.stlouisfed.org/series/LABSHPUSA156 NRUG; Henry S. Farber, Daniel Herbst, Ilyana Kuziemko, and Suresh Naidu, "Unions and Inequality over the Twentieth Century: New Evidence from Survey Data," *Quarterly Journal of Economics* 136, no. 3 (2021): 1325–85.

16. It's hard to overstate the devastation and despair imposed on people as a result of running the economy too cold. If, in contrast, the economy had been run closer to full employment, the economist Adam Hersh and I estimate that millions more jobs would have been created, and fast. But this wouldn't only benefit those who were left in the economic dust. It would have made the entire economy better off; in other words, running the economy at full speed would have been the rising tide that actually lifted all boats. We calculate the average American adult would have had an additional $32,317 in income from 2010 to 2019—enough to pay down burdensome student loans for the average borrower or to make a sizable down payment for a home. Adam Hersh and Mark Paul, "How Much Emergency Relief Will It Take to Revive the U.S. Economy?," Groundwork Collaborative, December 8, 2020, https://groundworkcollaborative.org/wp-content/uploads/2020 /12/GWC2065-How-Much-Emergency-Relief-Will-it-Take-to-Revive-the-US -Economy.pdf.

    Research by the economists Jared Bernstein and Keith Bentele finds that workers in the bottom fifth of the earnings distribution receive annual earnings 6.1% higher in tight labor markets compared to slack ones. Jared Bernstein and Keith Bentele, "The Increasing Benefits and Diminished Costs of Running a High-Pressure Labor Market," Center on Budget and Policy Priorities, May 15, 2019, https://www.cbpp.org/research/full-employment/the-increasing-benefits-and -diminished-costs-of-running-a-high-pressure.

17. "Unemployment Rate," FRED, Economic Research Federal Reserve Bank of St. Louis, https://fred.stlouisfed.org/series/UNRATE; "Unemployment-Population Ratio," FRED, Economic Research Federal Reserve Bank of St. Louis, https://fred .stlouisfed.org/series/EMRATIO; J. W. Mason, "What Recovery? The Case for Continued Expansionary Policy at the Fed," Roosevelt Institute, July 25, 2017, https://rooseveltinstitute.org/publications/what-recovery-expansionary-policy -federal-reserve/.

18. "Capacity Utilization: Total Index," FRED, Economic Research Federal Reserve Bank of St. Louis, https://fred.stlouisfed.org/series/TCU.

19. Lawrence Ball, "Monetary Policy for a High-Pressure Economy," Policy Futures, Center on Budget and Policy Priorities, March 30, 2015, https://www.cbpp.org /research/full-employment/monetary-policy-for-a-high-pressure-economy.

20. In truth, there is no agreed on definition of "full capacity."

21. While it's true that a rapid recovery and a hotter economy may—and recently has—meant higher levels of inflation, it's not exactly clear that raising rates faster, and

thereby reducing employment, would necessarily alleviate specific inflation phenomena, as was observed in 2021 and the first half of 2022. In fact, most inflation during the recent recovery stemmed from just three goods: vehicles, energy prices, and food. Housing also likely contributed substantially to inflation, though data are delayed. Importantly, an increase in the interest rate from the Federal Reserve should not be expected to slow inflation in these areas, as the price increases are stemming from particular geopolitical challenges that will not be solved with less investment; rather, they require alternative tools to manage price changes.

22. "Federal Reserve Issues FOMC Statement," Board of Governors of the Federal Reserve System, September 16, 2020, www.federalreserve.gov/newsevents/press releases/monetary20200916a.htm; emphasis added.

23. Why did Powell take this line? In part, the Fed's change in direction is undoubtedly due to analysts' move away from neoliberal thought, but grassroots movements such as the Fed Up campaign at the Center for Popular Democracy played an invaluable role in forcing the Fed to take full employment more seriously.

24. This was a key provision of the original Humphrey-Hawkins Act (1976), which I discuss further below. For more on the Fed's new framework, see Alex Williams and Skanda Amarnath, "Beyond the Phillips Curve: A Dynamic Approach to Communicating Assessments of 'Maximum Employment,'" Employ America, 2021, https://www.employamerica.org/researchreports/beyond-the-phillips-curve-a -dynamic-approach-to-communicating-assessments-of-maximum-employment/.

25. For more on new employment targets for the Fed, see J. W. Mason, Mike Konczal, and Lauren Melodia, "Reimagining Full Employment: 28 Million More Jobs and a More Equal Economy," Roosevelt Institute, 2021, https://rooseveltinstitute.org /wp-content/uploads/2021/07/RI_FullEmployment_Brief_202107.pdf.

26. John Maynard Keynes, "Chapter 24. Concluding Notes on the Social Philosophy towards which the General Theory might Lead," Marxists Internet Archive, https://www.marxists.org/reference/subject/economics/keynes/general-theory /ch24.htm.

27. White House Task Force on Worker Organizing and Empowerment: Report to the President, 2022, https://www.whitehouse.gov/wp-content/uploads/2022/02 /White-House-Task-Force-on-Worker-Organizing-and-Empowerment-Report.pdf.

28. "Employment in General Government," *Government at a Glance 2017*, OECD iLibrary, 2021, https://www.oecd-ilibrary.org/sites/gov_glance-2017-24-en/index .html?itemId=/content/component/gov_glance-2017-24-en.

29. To be sure, the CCC has a complicated and at times troubling legacy; the program largely excluded women and segregated work camps (Eleanor Roosevelt and Frances Perkins, secretary of labor, frustrated by the CCC's exclusion of women, created "SheSheShe" camps for unemployed women; however, only 8,500 young women were able to participate). Discrimination like this needs to be eradicated, and lessons—good and bad—must be taken from such historical examples.

30. Such benefits are vital for all jobs and better delivered through legislation that makes these benefits apply universally to all people; however, they should be part of a job guarantee until such legislation is passed.

31. The secretary of labor, along with state labor agencies, would also be tasked with ensuring that job guarantee employees do not replace existing public employment. It should be noted, however, that there have historically been challenges along these lines, where subsidized public jobs at the state and local levels replaced rather than supplemented existing public jobs.

32. For more details, see Mark Paul, William Darity Jr., Darrick Hamilton, and Khaing
     Zaw, "A Path to Ending Poverty by Way of Ending Unemployment," *Russell Sage
     Foundation Journal of the Social Sciences* 4, no. 3 (2018): 44–63, https://socialequity
     .duke.edu/wp-content/uploads/2019/10/A-Path-to-Ending-Poverty.pdf; Mark
     Paul, William Darity Jr., and Darrick Hamilton, "The Federal Job Guarantee—
     A Policy to Achieve Permanent Full Employment," Center on Budget and Policy
     Priorities, Policy Futures, March 9, 2018, https://www.cbpp.org/research/full
     -employment/the-federal-job-guarantee-a-policy-to-achieve-permanent-full
     -employment#_ftn1.

33. Pavlina R. Tcherneva, *The Case for A Job Guarantee* (Cambridge: Polity, 2020).

34. "No Relief: Denial of Bathroom Breaks in the Poultry Industry," Oxfam America,
     2016, https://s3.amazonaws.com/oxfam-us/www/static/media/files/No_Relief
     _Embargo.pdf.

35. And, believe it or not, she was successful. The Full Employment and Balanced
     Growth Act—more commonly known as the Humphrey-Hawkins Act—was signed
     into law in 1978. In its original form, the bill required the president and the Federal
     Reserve to work together to keep the economy at full employment (in essence,
     economic planning) and fill in the gaps of the private sector through direct public
     employment—that is, a job guarantee. But in the legislative fight to get the bill
     passed, key elements, like the "right" to employment and the creation of a "Job
     Guarantee Office," were stripped away, and the provisions that *did* survive have
     never been enforced.

36. Others, such as the persistent job guarantee critics Matt Bruenig and Guy Stand-
     ing, argue instead that a basic income should be adopted, which would reduce the
     economy's reliance on work. In this book, I present both a basic income and a job
     guarantee as basic rights. Importantly, I do not see a need to pit the two policies
     against one another, and in fact I argue they would provide people with more choices
     if they were allowed to coexist.

37. Janet Yellen, "Efficiency Wage Models of Unemployment," *American Economic
     Review* 74, no. 2 (1985): 200–205. For an in-depth review of critiques associated with
     the job guarantee, see Paul, Darity, and Hamilton, "The Federal Job Guarantee—
     A Policy to Achieve Permanent Full Employment."

38. Paula England, Michelle Budig, and Nancy Folbre, "Wages of Virtue: The Relative
     Pay of Care Work," *Social Problems* 49, no. 4 (2002): 455–73.

39. Samuel Bowles, *The New Economics of Inequality and Redistribution* (New York:
     Cambridge University Press, 2012).

40. My congressional testimony on the need for a new CCC can be found here: Mark
     Paul, "Testimony before the Bicameral Task Force on Climate Change: Hearing on
     'The Civilian Climate Corps,'" June 23, 2021, https://www.markey.senate.gov/imo
     /media/doc/mark_paul_testimony.pdf.

41. This program also enjoys tremendous public support. A poll from January 2021
     found 93% of likely voters support the government creating jobs directly to address
     national and community needs, including 87% of Republicans. When asked spe-
     cifically about the CCC, polls find that 65 to 85% of likely voters support a new
     CCC, including a majority of Republicans. Support like this is hard to come by in
     the era of polarization, especially on environmental issues. Data for Progress and
     the Justice Collaborative Institute, "Voters Support Reviving the Federal Civilian
     Conservation Corps Jobs Program," The Appeal, September 11, 2020, https://the
     appeal.org/the-lab/polling-memos/voters-support-reviving-the-federal-civilian

-conservation-corps-jobs-program/; Anthony Leiserowitz, Edward Maibach, Seth Rosenthal, and John Kotcher, "Politics & Global Warming, December 2020," Yale University and George Mason University, 2021, Yale Program on Climate Change Communication, https://www.climatechangecommunication.org/wp-content /uploads/2021/01/politics-global-warming-december-2020b.pdf.

42. Rakeen Mabud, Amity Paye, Maya Pinto, and Sanjay Pinto, "Foundations for a Just and Inclusive Recovery: Economic Security, Health and Safety, and Agency and Voice in the COVID-19 Era," Color of Change, National Employment Law Project, Time's Up Foundation, and IRL Worker Institute, February 3, 2021, https://www.nelp .org/wp-content/uploads/Foundations-for-Just-Inclusive-Recovery-Report.pdf.

43. When Washington, DC, launched a universal pre-K program, it increased the labor force participation of mothers by roughly 10 percentage points—a huge result.

44. Even the *New York Times* has advocated for direct public employment of care workers. During the COVID-19 crisis, the editorial board suggested, "The government could train America's newly unemployed to sanitize hospital equipment or to deliver food to the elderly and the immune-compromised. Child care for hospital workers on the front lines is desperately needed. Through a new public works program, corps of people could implement infection control in nursing homes and other high-risk facilities—or teach workers of all kinds how to best protect themselves. There could even be a network of individuals tasked with making phone calls to combat loneliness for people in nursing homes and prisons while they're unable to receive visitors." "Stop Saying That Everything Is Under Control. It Isn't." New York Times, March 17, 2020, https://www.nytimes.com/2020/03/17/opinion/war -crononavirus-trump-production.html.

45. Many lessons have been learned since the Comprehensive Employment and Training Act of 1973 whereby some public employment programs were used to replace existing public employees. The job guarantee program will avoid such pitfalls. Steven Attewell, *People Must Live by Work: Direct Job Creation in America from FDR to Reagan* (Philadelphia: University of Pennsylvania Press, 2018).

46. "Sen. Booker, Reps. Watson Coleman and Omar Introduce Bicameral Bill to Create Federal Jobs Guarantee Program," Cory Booker, September 12, 2019, https://www .booker.senate.gov/news/press/sen-booker-reps-watson-coleman-and-omar -introduce-bicameral-bill-to-create-federal-jobs-guarantee-program; Ayanna Pressley, "Federal Job Guarantee Resolution," https://pressley.house.gov/sites /pressley.house.gov/files/Pressley%20Federal%20Job%20Guarantee%20Reso lution%20Summary.pdf.

47. "Majority of Voters Support a Federal Jobs Guarantee," *The Hill*, October 30, 2019, https://thehill.com/hilltv/468236-majority-of-voters-support-a-federal-jobs -guarantee-program.

48. "Back to Work: Listening to Americans," Gallup, 2021, https://www.gallup.com /analytics/329573/back-to-work-listening-to-americans.aspx.

49. And not only according to Roosevelt. Article 23 of the United Nations Universal Declaration of Human Rights recognizes that "everyone has the right to work . . . and to protection against unemployment."

Chapter Five

1. Tiana Caldwell, in discussion with author, May 2021. Quotations from Caldwell that follow are from this discussion.

2.   "State of Homelessness: 2021 Edition," National Alliance to End Homelessness, https://endhomelessness.org/homelessness-in-america/homelessness-statistics/state-of-homelessness-2021/.

3.   Author calculation based on census data. "Characteristics for Occupied Housing Units," US Census Bureau, https://data.census.gov/cedsci/table?q=homeowner ship&tid=ACSST1Y2018.S2502&vintage=2018.

4.   "The State of the Nation's Housing," Joint Center for Housing Studies at Harvard University, 2019, https://www.jchs.harvard.edu/sites/default/files/Harvard_JCHS _State_of_the_Nations_Housing_2019.pdf.

5.   Author's calculation, Panel Study of Income Dynamics.

6.   William Rohe and Mark Lindblad, "Reexamining the Social Benefits of Home-ownership after the Housing Crisis," Joint Center for Housing Studies at Harvard University, August 2013, https://www.jchs.harvard.edu/sites/default/files/media /imp/hbtl-04.pdf.

7.   "Homeownership Rate in the United States," FRED, https://fred.stlouisfed.org /series/RHORUSQ156N.

8.   Laurie S. Goodman and Christopher Mayer, "Homeownership and the American Dream," *Journal of Economic Perspectives* 32, no. 1 (2018): 31–58, https://pubs.aea web.org/doi/pdfplus/10.1257/jep.32.1.31.

9.   Goodman and Mayer.

10. Herbert Hoover, "Statement about Signing the Federal Home Loan Bank Act," July 22, 1932, online by Gerhard Peters and John T. Woolley, American Presidency Project, https://www.presidency.ucsb.edu/node/207247; Rothstein, *The Color of Law*.

11. Adam J. Levitin and Susan M. Wachter, "The Public Option in Housing Finance," *UC Davis Law Review* 46, no. 4 (2013): 1111–1655, https://papers.ssrn.com/sol3 /papers.cfm?abstract_id=1966550.

12. The HOLC, in combination with the Federal Housing Administration, set a floor in the home-owning marketplace.

13. Arthur M. Schlesinger Jr., *The Age of Roosevelt*, vol. 2: *The Coming of the New Deal, 1933–1935* (New York: Houghton Mifflin, 2003), 586.

14. Gail Radford, *Modern Housing for America: Policy Struggles in the New Deal Era* (Chicago: University of Chicago Press, 1996) 179.

15. Jung Hyun Choi and Janneke Ratcliffe, "Down Payment Assistance Focused on First-Generation Buyers Could Help Millions Access the Benefits of Homeowner-ship," *Urban Wire: Housing and Housing Finance* (blog), April 7, 2021, https://www .urban.org/urban-wire/down-payment-assistance-focused-first-generation-buyers -could-help-millions-access-benefits-homeownership.

16. For detailed discussion of each of these, see People's Action, "A National Homes Guarantee," September 5, 2019, https://homesguarantee.com/wp-content/uploads /Homes-Guarantee-_-Briefing-Book.pdf.

17. For more on this, see People's Action, "A National Homes Guarantee," September 5, 2019, https://homesguarantee.com/wp-content/uploads/Homes-Guarantee -_-Briefing-Book.pdf; Peter Gowen and Ryan Cooper, "Social Housing in the United States," People's Policy Project, 2018, https://www.peoplespolicyproject.org/wp -content/uploads/2018/04/SocialHousing.pdf; Paul Williams, "Public Housing for All," *Noema Magazine*, August 26, 2021, https://www.noemamag.com/public -housing-for-all/.

18. Justin Peterson, "LIHTC Program Now Funds About 90% of U.S. Affordable Housing Projects," Reis, March 2017, https://www.reis.com/cre-news-and-resources/bisnow -lihtc-program- now-funds-about-90-percent-of-us-affordable- housing-projects.

19. Public housing was created as housing of last resort. The Byrd amendment ensured public housing would be constructed on the cheap. In the decades that followed it was systematically defunded, resulting in dilapidated public housing in dire need of repair. The concentration of poverty was also by design since public housing was only available to people struggling the most and was located far from quality employment opportunities. As a result, it amplified economic segregation and locked people further into a poverty trap.

20. Cathy Adams, "Vienna Ranked Best City in the World to Live in for 10th Year Running," *Independent*, March 13, 2019, https://www.independent.co.uk/travel/news -and-advice/vienna-best-city-live-quality-life-ranking-mercer-australia-europe -a8820396.html.

21. Adam Forrest, "Vienna's Affordable Housing Paradise," *Huffpost*, July 19, 2018, https://www.huffpost.com/entry/vienna-affordable-housing-paradise_n_5b4e0b 12e4b0b15aba88c7b0.

22. Wolfgang Förster and William Menking, *The Vienna Model 2: Housing for the City of the 21st Century* (Berlin: Jovis, 2018); Daniel Aldana Cohen, "A Green New Deal for Housing," *Jacobin*, February 8, 2019, https://jacobinmag.com/2019/02/green -new-deal-housing-ocasio-cortez-climate.

23. Alex Grey, "Here's How Finland Solved Its Homelessness Problem," World Economic Forum, February 13, 2018, https://www.weforum.org/agenda/2018/02 /how-finland-solved-homelessness/.

24. Oliver Wainwright, "I've Seen the Future and It's Norwich: The Energy-Saving, Social Housing Revolution," *The Guardian*, July 16, 2019, https://www.theguardian .com/artanddesign/2019/jul/16/norwich-goldsmith-street-social-housing-green -design; Daniel Aldana Cohen and Mark Paul, "The Case for Social Housing," The Lab, The Appeal, November 2, 2020, https://theappeal.org/the-lab/report/the -case-for-social-housing/.

25. "Rental Vacancy Rate in the United States," FRED, https://fred.stlouisfed.org /series/RRVRUSQ156N.

26. John W. Wills, "Short History of Rent Control Laws," *Cornell Law Review* 36, no. 1 (1950): 54–94, https://scholarship.law.cornell.edu/clr/vol36/iss1/3/; Daniel K. Fetter, "The Home Front: Rent Control and the Rapid Wartime Increase in Home Ownership," National Bureau of Economic Research, Working Paper no. 19604 (October 2013), doi: 10.3386/w19604.

27. Rent control remained throughout this period in some cities, though it came under a new wave of attack in the 1990s when areas such as Boston and surrounding communities saw their rent control repealed by a statewide ballot initiative.

28. "Issues: Housing for All," Bernie, Friends of Bernie Sanders, https://berniesanders .com/issues/housing-all/.

29. Daniel Aldana Cohen, Julian Brave NoiseCat, and Sean McElwee, "Americans Want to Live in a Just Society," Data for Progress, September 25, 2019, https://www .dataforprogress.org/blog/2019/9/25/americans-want-to-live-in-a-just-society.

30. Milton Friedman and George Stigler, "Roofs or Ceilings? The Current Housing Problem," *Foundation for Economic Education, Inc.* 1, no. 2 (1946): 7–22, https://fee .org/resources/roofs-or-ceilings-the-current-housing-problem/.

31. Gabriel Metcalf, "Sand Castles before the Tide? Affordable Housing in Expensive Cities," *Journal of Economic Perspectives* 32, no. 1 (2018): 59–80, doi:10.1257/jep.32.1.59.

32. "Rent Control," Chicago Booth: The Initiative on Global Markets, IGM Forum, 2021, https://www.igmchicago.org/surveys/rent-control/.

33. Milton Friedman and F. A. Hayek, *Rent Control: Myths and Realities*, ed. Walter Block and Edgar Olsen (Vancouver: Fraser Institute, 1981); Edward L. Glaeser and Erzo F. P. Luttmer, "The Misallocation of Housing under Rent Control," *American Economic Review* 93, no. 4 (2003):1027–46, doi: 10.1257/000282803769206188; Rebecca Diamond, Tim McQuade, and Franklin Qian, "The Effects of Rent Control Expansion on Tenants, Landlords, and Inequality: Evidence from San Francisco," *American Economic Review* 109, no. 9 (2019): 3365–94, doi: 10.1257/aer.20181289.

34. See, e.g., Joshua Ambrosius, John I. Gilderbloom, William J. Steele, Wesley L. Maeres, and Dennis Keating, "Forty Years of Rent Control: Reexamining New Jersey's Moderate Local Policies after the Great Recession," *Cities* 49 (2015): 121–33, https://doi.org/10.1016/j.cities.2015.08.001; John Gilderbloom and Lin Ye, "Thirty Years of Rent Control: A Survey of New Jersey Cities," *Journal of Urban Affairs* 29, no. 2 (2007): 207–20, https://doi.org/10.1111/j.1467-9906.2007.00334.x. The latter actually found that rent control led to an increase in supply, but this was apparently due to the fact that landlords subdivided existing units. There are few papers that find specific types of rent control reduce supply. An example is a study by Diamond, McQuade, and Qian that found a slight decrease in the supply of rental units; however, this was largely from units being converted to condos and could be avoided by closing loopholes in the regulation. Rebecca Diamond, Tim McQuade, and Franklin Qian, "The Effects of Rent Control Expansion on Tenants, Landlords, and Inequality: Evidence from San Francisco," *American Economic Review* 109, no. 9 (2019): 3365–94, doi:10.1257/aer.20181289.

35. In New York City (before the pandemic), for instance, despite rapidly rising rents, the housing stock was growing at less than half a percent per year, which is not nearly fast enough to keep up with demand. E. Gaumer, "Selected Initial Findings of the 2017 New York City Housing and Vacancy Survey," New York City Department of Housing Preservation and Development, 2018, https://www1.nyc.gov/assets/hpd/downloads/pdfs/about/2017-hvs-initial-findings.pdf.

36. In high-cost cities the value of the land may account for 80% or more of the cost of a home. This value was not created by the landowner; rather it reflects the presence of high-valued activities in the region. This means that when an area becomes more desirable, landowners receive a windfall gain while longtime tenants may be priced out—even though, in many cases, they helped increase the value of the neighborhood in the first place. Because these gains are not the result of any investment by landlords, taking them away will not discourage investment in housing.

37. Increasing supply, which is an important policy objective, must be achieved through complementary reforms to the housing landscape. For more, see Jackelyn Hwang, Iris Zhang, Jae Sik Jeon, Karen Chapple, Julia Greenberg, and Vasudha Kumar, "Who Benefits from Tenant Protections?," Research Brief, March 2022, https://www.urbandisplacement.org/wp-content/uploads/2022/03/IGS_2_Tenant-Protections_Brief_03.01.22.pdf.

38. A small number of studies argue that rent control does not limit rental increases, though these increases are likely due to the weak nature of rent controls in the study area. See Ambrosius et al., "Forty Years of Rent Control."

39. For an excellent review of the rent control literature, see Manuel Pastor, Vanessa Carter, and Maya Abood, "Rent Matters: What Are the Impacts of Rent Stabilization Measures?," USC Dornsife Program for Environmental and Regional Equity, 2018, https://dornsife.usc.edu/assets/sites/242/docs/Rent_Matters_PERE_Report_Final_02.pdf.

40. David P. Sims, "Out of Control: What Can We Learn from the End of Massachusetts Rent Control?," *Journal of Urban Economics* 61, no. 1 (2007): 129–51, https://doi.org/10.1016/j.jue.2006.06.004; David H. Autor, Christopher J. Palmer, and Parag A. Pathak, "Housing Market Spillovers: Evidence from the End of Rent Control in Cambridge Massachusetts," National Bureau of Economic Research, Working Paper no. 18125 (June 2012), doi: 10.3386/w18125; Allan D. Heskin, Ned Levine, and Mark Garrett, "The Effects of Vacancy Control," *Journal of the American Planning Association* 66, no. 2 (2000):162–76, doi: 10.1080/01944360008976096; Edward Glaeser, "Does Rent Control Reduce Segregation?," *Swedish Economic Policy Review* 10 (2003): 179–202, https://citeseerx.ist.psu.edu/viewdoc/download?doi=10.1.1.570.2113&rep=rep1&type=pdf.

41. Gail Radford, *Modern Housing for America: Policy Struggles in the New Deal Era* (Chicago: University of Chicago Press, 1996), 179.

42. While the Wagner bill finally passed in 1937 as the Housing Act, the teeth were gone. This evisceration of the housing bill was the first major victory for the conservative coalition in the Senate.

43. For a nice review, see Peter Gowen and Ryan Cooper, "A Plan to Solve the Housing Crisis through Social Housing," People's Policy Project, 2018, https://www.peoplespolicyproject.org/project/a-plan-to-solve-the-housing-crisis-through-social-housing/. In the United States, Utah made great strides with its Housing First approach to homelessness, though funding has been insufficient in recent years to maintain progress.

Chapter Six

1. National Center for Education Statistics (NCES), US Department of Education, "Enrollment and Percentage Distribution of Enrollment in Public Elementary and Secondary Schools, by Race/Ethnicity and Level of Education: Fall 1999 through Fall 2029," last modified September 2020, https://nces.ed.gov/programs/digest/d20/tables/dt20_203.60.asp; National Center for Education Statistics (NCES), US Department of Education, "Educational Institutions," last modified 2021, https://nces.ed.gov/fastfacts/display.asp?id=84.

2. Wisconsin v. Yoder, 406 U.S. 205, 221 (1971) (summarizing Jefferson).

3. John Adams, *The Works of John Adams*, vol 6: *Defence of the Constitutions*, ed. Charles Francis Adams (Boston: Little, Brown, 1851), 168.

4. Derek W. Black, *School House Burning: Public Education and the Assault on American Democracy* (New York: Public Affairs, 2020).

5. Michael Schuman, "History of Child Labor in the United States—Part 1: Little Children Working," *Monthly Labor Review*, US Bureau of Labor Statistics, January 2017, https://www.bls.gov/opub/mlr/2017/article/history-of-child-labor-in-the-united-states-part-1.htm.

6. Claudia Goldin and Lawrence F. Katz, *The Race between Education and Technology* (Cambridge, MA: Belknap Press of Harvard University Press, 2008); National

Center for Education Statistics (NCES), US Department of Education, Office of Educational Research and Improvement, "120 Years of American Education: A Statistical Portrait," accessed October 30, 2021, https://nces.ed.gov/pubs93/934 42.pdf.

7. J. Bradford Delong, Claudia Goldin, and Lawrence F. Katz, "Sustaining US Economic Growth," in *Agenda for the Nation* (Washington, DC: Brookings Institution, 2003), 17–60, https://scholar.harvard.edu/goldin/publications/sustaining-us -economic-growth.

8. Enrico Moretti, "Human Capital Externalities in Cities," *Handbook of Regional and Urban Economics* 4 (2004): 2243–91.

9. Amartya Sen, *Development as Freedom* (New York: Knopf, 1999).

10. Dick Startz, "The Achievement Gap in Education: Racial Segregation versus Segregation by Poverty," *Brown Center Chalkboard* (blog), Brookings Institution, January 20, 2020, https://www.brookings.edu/blog/brown-center-chalkboard/2020 /01/20/the-achievement-gap-in-education-racial-segregation-versus-segregation -by-poverty/.

11. Some commentators have even argued that the deeply racist history of public education helped stymie efforts to make university education free in America. Marshall Steinbaum, "Class & Inequality: A Brown v. Board for Higher Ed.," *Boston Review*, September 1, 2017, https://bostonreview.net/education-opportunity/marshall -steinbaum-brown-v-board-higher-ed.

12. National Center for Education Statistics (NCES), US Department of Education, "Percentage of Persons 25 to 29 Years Old with Selected Levels of Educational Attainment, by Race/Ethnicity and Sex: Selected Years, 1920 through 2017," accessed October 30, 2021, https://nces.ed.gov/programs/digest/d17/tables/dt17_104.20 .asp; US Census Bureau, US Department of Commerce, *U.S. Census Bureau Releases New Educational Attainment Data*, March 30, 2020, Release no. CB20-TPS.09, https://www.census.gov/newsroom/press-releases/2020/educational-attainment .html.

13. "Postsecondary Education Aspirations and Barriers: The 2014 Gallup-Lumina Foundation Study of the American Public's Opinion on Higher Education," April 16, 2015, Gallup, Inc., Lumina Foundation, https://www.luminafoundation.org/wp -content/uploads/2017/08/postsecondary-education-aspirations-and-barriers.pdf.

14. Goldie Blumenstyk, "By 2020, They Said, 2 Out of 3 Jobs Would Need More than a High-School Diploma. Were They Right?," *Chronicle for Higher Education*, January 22, 2020, https://www.chronicle.com/newsletter/the-edge/2020-01-22; Anthony Carnavale, Nicole Smith, and Jeff Strohl, "Recovery: Projections of Jobs and Education Requirements through 2020" (Center on Education and the Workforce, Georgetown Public Policy Institute, June 2013), https://1gyhoq479ufd3yna29x7 ubjn-wpengine.netdna-ssl.com/wp-content/uploads/2014/11/Recovery2020 .FR_.Web_.pdf.

15. Author calculation of data from the BLS.

16. Mark Paul and Anastasia Wilson, "Profiting Off Debt: Federal Student Loans Facilitate a Pernicious Profit Motive in Higher Education," *Jacobin Magazine*, September 29, 2016, https://jacobinmag.com/2016/09/student-debt-loans-government -sanders-clinton-college.

17. Molly Webster, "I've Spent $60,000 to Pay Back Student Loans and Owe More than Before I Began," *New York Times*, March 18, 2021, https://www.nytimes.com /2021/03/18/opinion/student-loans-cares-act.html; Katrina vanden Heuvel,

"Americans Are Drowning in Student-Loan Debt. The U.S. Should Forgive All of It," *Washington Post*, June 9, 2018, https://www.washingtonpost.com/opinions/amer icans-are-drowning-in-student-loan-debt-the-us-should-forgive-all-of-it/2018 /06/19/82565218-7314-11e8-9780-b1dd6a09b549_story.html.

18. Board of Governors, The Federal Reserve System, *Consumer Credit*, August 2021, G. 19, Washington DC, https://www.federalreserve.gov/releases/g19/current/g19 .pdf; Brad Hershbein and Kevin M. Hollenbeck, eds., *Student Loans and the Dynamics of Debt* (Kalamazoo, MI: W. E. Upjohn Institute for Employment Research, 2015), https://research.upjohn.org/cgi/viewcontent.cgi?article=1249&context=up_press; Scott Fullwiler, Stephanie Kelton, Catherine Ruetschlin, and Marshall Steinbaum, "The Macroeconomic Effects of Student Debt Cancellation," Levy Economics Institute, February 2018, https://nces.ed.gov/programs/coe/indicator/cub. A good deal of my thinking regarding debt stems from the work of David Graeber, whose book, *Debt: The First 5000 Years*, influenced me a great deal.

19. National Center for Education Statistics (NCES), US Department of Education, "Loans for Undergraduate Students," last modified May 2021, https://nces.ed.gov /programs/coe/indicator/cub.

20. Richard Fry, "Cumulative Student Debt among Recent College Graduates," Pew Research Center, October 7, 2014, https://www.pewresearch.org/social-trends /2014/10/07/cumulative-student-debt-among-recent-college-graduates/.

21. Janet L. Yellen, "Perspectives on Inequality and Opportunity from the Survey of Consumer Finances" (speech, Boston, MA, October 17, 2014), Board of Governors of the Federal Reserve System, https://www.federalreserve.gov/newsevents /speech/yellen20141017a.htm.

22. Fry, "Cumulative Student Debt among Recent College Graduates"; Marshall Steinbaum, "The Student Debt Crisis Is a Crisis of Non-repayment," Jain Family Institute, November 18, 2020, https://www.phenomenalworld.org/analysis/crisis-of-non -repayment.

23. Average annual room, board, tuition, and food amounts to $20,598; however, it takes an average of 5.1 years for students to complete a bachelor's degree. National Center for Education Statistics (NCES), US Department of Education, "Average Undergraduate Tuition and Fees and Room and Board Rates Charged for Full-Time Students in Degree-Granting Postsecondary Institutions, by Level and Control of Institution: Selected Years, 1963–64 through 2018–19," https://nces.ed.gov /programs/digest/d19/tables/dt19_330.10.asp; Doug Shapiro, Afet Dunbar, Phoebe Khasiala Wakhungu, Xin Yuan, Angel Nathan, and Youngsik Hwank, "Time to Degree—2016," National Student Clearinghouse Research Center, September 18, 2016, https://nscresearchcenter.org/signaturereport11/.

24. Jessica Learish, "The 50 Most Expensive Colleges in America, Ranked," *CBS News*, last updated May 4, 2021, https://www.cbsnews.com/pictures/the-50-most -expensive-colleges-in-america/2/.

25. Greg Schoofs, "These Charts Show How Much College A Minimum Wage Job Paid For, Then and Now," *BuzzFeed News*, September 4, 2014, https://www.buzzfeed news.com/article/gregschoofs/how-much-college-did-your-summer-job-pay-for.

26. "Broad Support for Tuition-Free College among Women, Young People, Black and Hispanic Adults," Pew Research Center, August 11, 2021, https://www.pew research.org/fact-tank/2021/08/11/democrats-overwhelmingly-favor-free-college -tuition-while-republicans-are-divided-by-age-education/ft_2021-08-11_free college_01/.

27. Anthony Davies and James Harrigan, "The High Cost of Free College," Foundation for Economic Education, May 17, 2019, https://fee.org/articles/the-high-cost -of-free-college/; emphasis added.

28. https://www.pnas.org/content/118/11/e2024777118; Philip Oreopoulos and Kjell Salvanes, "Priceless: The Nonpecuniary Benefits of Schooling," *Journal of Economic Perspectives* 25, no. 1 (Winter 2011): 159–84, https://pubs.aeaweb.org/doi /pdfplus/10.1257/jep.25.1.159.

29. Federic Cingano, "Trends in Income Inequality and Its Impact on Economic Growth," Organisation for Economic Cooperation and Development, December 9, 2014, https://www.oecd-ilibrary.org/social-issues-migration-health/trends -in-income-inequality-and-its-impact-on-economic-growth_5jxrjncwxv6j-en.

30. Anna Valero and John Van Reenen, "The Economic Impact of Universities: Evidence from Across the Globe," Working Paper Series (National Bureau of Economic Research, 2016), http://www.nber.org/papers/w22501.

31. Jason Owen-Smith, *Research Universities and the Public Good: Discovery for an Uncertain Future* (Stanford, CA: Stanford University Press, 2018).

32. Edward L. Glaeser, Giacomo A. M. Ponzetto, and Andrei Schleifer, "Why Does Democracy Need Education?," *Journal of Economic Growth* 12, no. 2 (May 31, 2007): 77–99.

33. "An Investment That Pays Off for Society" (Teacher's College, Columbia University, July 14, 2018), last modified July 14, 2018, https://www.tc.columbia.edu/arti cles/2018/july/americans-believe-in-higher-education-as-a-public-good-a-new -survey-finds/.

34. Lyndon B. Johnson, "Special Message to the Congress on Education: 'The Fifth Freedom,'" February 5, 1968, https://www.presidency.ucsb.edu/documents/spe cial-message-the-congress-education-the-fifth-freedom.

35. Sarah Pingel, "Free College and Adult Student Populations," Education Commission of the States, June 7, 2018, https://www.ecs.org/free-college-and-adult-student -populations/.

36. Benjamin Vermund, "The Red State That Loves Free College: How Tennessee Is Making Bernie Sanders' Favorite Education Idea a Reality," Politico, January 16, 2019, https://www.politico.com/agenda/story/2019/01/16/tennessee-free-college -000867/.

37. US Congress, Senate, *S. 1947 To Amend the Higher Education Act of 1965 to Ensure College for All*, 116th Cong., 1st sess., June 24, 2019, https://www.congress.gov/116 /bills/s1947/BILLS-116s1947is.pdf; Mark Paul, "Campaign Challenge: Fix the African American Student Loan Crisis," *American Prospect*, March 15, 2016, https:// prospect.org/power/campaign-challenge-fix-african-american-student-loan -crisis/.

38. Nick Gass, "Clinton Knocks Sanders' College Plan: Trump's Kids Shouldn't Get Free Ride," Politico, October 5, 2015, https://www.politico.com/story/2015/10 /hillary-clinton-criticize-bernie-sanders-college-plan-214424.

39. Danielle Kurtzleben, "Who Should Get Free College? Buttigieg Ad Inflames Key Divide among Democrats," NPR, December 6, 2019, https://www.npr.org/2019 /12/06/785167895/who-should-get-free-college-buttigieg-ad-inflames-key -divide-among-democrats.

40. Joe English, "Free College Is the Wrong Answer," Politico, October 17, 2019, https:// www.politico.com/agenda/story/2019/10/17/free-college-is-the-wrong-answer -001289/.

41. Conor Friedersdorf, "Universal Free College Would Be a Regressive Scandal," *The Atlantic*, July 30, 2013, https://www.theatlantic.com/politics/archive/2013/07/universal-free-college-would-be-a-regressive-scandal/278201/.

42. Friedersdorf.

43. AEI Archives, S1, E9, "Social Security: Universal or selective? (1971)—with Milton Friedman and Wilbur Cohen," YouTube, 58:50, June 3, 2018, https://www.youtube.com/watch?v=gr-_nRnMh2E.

44. Andrew Kelly, "High Costs, Uncertain Benefits: What Do Americans without a College Degree Think about Postsecondary Education?," American Enterprise Institute, April 2015, 1–16, https://files.eric.ed.gov/fulltext/ED557611.pdf.

45. K. N. Lohr, *Medicare: A Strategy for Quality Assurance*, vol. 1, 2 vols. (Washington, DC: National Academies Press, 1990), https://www.ncbi.nlm.nih.gov/books/NBK23 5450/; Susan Dynarsky et al., "Closing the Gap: The Effect of Reducing Complexity and Uncertainty in College Pricing on the Choices of Low-Income Students," *American Economic Review* 111, no. 6 (June 2021): 1721–56, https://www.aeaweb.org/articles?id=10.1257/aer.20200451.

46. Wesley Whistle and Tamara Hiler, "Why Free College Could Increase Inequality," Third Way, March 19, 2019, https://www.thirdway.org/memo/why-free-college-could-increase-inequality.

47. This debate has also played out when it comes to canceling student debt. For more on the distributional and macroeconomic effects of student debt cancellation, see Fullwiler et al., "The Macroeconomic Effects of Student Debt Cancellation"; Charlie Eaton et al., "Student Debt Cancellation IS Progressive: Correcting Empirical and Conceptual Errors," Roosevelt Institute, June 8, 2021, https://rooseveltinstitute.org/publications/student-debt-cancellation-is-progressive/.

48. Paul and Wilson, "Profiting Off Debt"; Mark Paul, Alan Aja, Darrick Hamilton, and William Darity, Jr., "Making College Free Could Add a Million New Black and Latino Graduates," *Dissent*, March 21, 2016, https://www.dissentmagazine.org/online_articles/bernie-sanders-free-college-plan-black-latino-graduates; Erin Dunlop Velez, National Center for Education Statistics (NCES), US Department of Education, "Baccalaureate and Beyond (B&B:16/17): A First Look at the Employment and Educational Experiences of College Graduates, 1 Year Later," https://nces.ed.gov/pubs2019/2019241.pdf.

49. J. W. Mason, "Why College Should Be Free," *Jacobin Magazine*, January 16, 2020, https://jacobinmag.com/2020/01/free-universal-college-education-means-testing.

50. Richard Vedder, "The Case against Free College Tuition," *Forbes*, April 12, 2018, https://www.forbes.com/sites/richardvedder/2018/04/12/the-free-tuition-craze-now-new-jersey/?sh=438fe6e61b2a; Davies and Harrigan, "The High Cost of Free Education."

51. Michael Mitchell, Michael Leachman, and Matt Saenz, "State Higher Education Funding Cuts Have Pushed Costs to Students, Worsened Inequality," Center on Budget and Policy Priorities, October 24, 2019, https://www.cbpp.org/research/state-budget-and-tax/state-higher-education-funding-cuts-have-pushed-costs-to-students; Robert Hiltonsmith, "Pulling Up the Higher Ed Ladder: Myth and Reality in the Crisis of College Affordability," Demos.org, May 5, 2015, https://www.demos.org/sites/default/files/publications/Robbie%20admin-bloat.pdf.

52. "Educational Attainment of 25–64 Year Olds," OECD Education Statistics, Organisation for Economic Cooperation and Development, 2021, accessed October 30, 2021, https://stats.oecd.org/index.aspx?queryid=93190.

53. Fullwiler et al., "The Macroeconomic Effects of Student Debt Cancellation."
54. "Child Care Costs in the United States," last updated October 2020, https://www
.epi.org/child-care-costs-in-the-united-states/; Nancy L. Cohen, "Why America
Never Had Universal Child Care," *New Republic*, April 23, 2013, https://newrepub
lic.com/article/113009/child-care-america-was-very-close-universal-day-care.
55. "Education at a Glance: Enrollment Rate by Age," OECD Education Statistics,
Organisation for Economic Cooperation and Development, 2021, https://www
.oecd-ilibrary.org/education/data/education-at-a-glance/enrolment-rate-by-age
_38c5b2d2-en; Cynthia Koons, "The U.S. Child-Care Crisis Is Torturing Parents
and the Economy," *Bloomberg*, December 10, 2020, https://www.bloomberg.com
/news/articles/2020-12-10/u-s-economy-could-get-a-boost-from-expanded
-child-care; Lillian Mongeau, "Oklahomans Have Embraced Free, Universal Early
Education—And It's Working," *PBS News Hour*, February 2, 2016, https://www.pbs
.org/newshour/education/
oklahomans-have-embraced-free-universal-early-education-and-its-working.
56. Nancy Folbre, "Children as Public Goods," *American Economic Review* 84, no. 2
(May 1994), https://www.jstor.org/stable/2117807; Robert Lynch and Kavya Vaghul,
"The Benefits and Costs of Investing in Early Childhood Education: The Fiscal,
Economic, and Societal Gains of a Universal Prekindergarten Program in the United
States, 2016–2050," Washington Center for Equitable Growth, December 2, 2015,
https://equitablegrowth.org/research-paper/the-benefits-and-costs-of-investing
-in-early-childhood-education/?longform=true. To be clear, the focus of this chapter is education. I argue that the right to a public education should be expanded
to cover college and pre-K; however, assisting families with childcare in general
requires additional policy action, which is beyond the scope of this chapter. For
an excellent proposal to aid families and work toward accepting children as public
goods and thus socializing many of the costs associated with having children, see
Matt Bruenig, "Family Fun Pack: People's Policy Project," People's Policy Project,
2019, https://www.peoplespolicyproject.org/projects/family-fun-pack/.
57. Benjamin Franklin, Constitutions of the Academy of Philadelphia, November 13,
1749, https://founders.archives.gov/documents/Franklin/01-03-02-0167.

Chapter Seven

1. Kirstin Downey, *The Woman Behind the New Deal: The Life of Frances Perkins, FDR's
Secretary of Labor and His Moral Conscience* (New York: Anchor Books, 2009).
2. https://www.ssa.gov/history/reports/health.html.
3. Committee on Economic Security, Social Security Administration, "The Unpub-
lished 1935 Report on Health Insurance & Disability," 1935, https://www.ssa.gov
/history/reports/health.html; Committee on Economic Security, "Report of the
Committee on Economic Security" https://www.ssa.gov/history/reports/ces
.html#:~:text=The%20President's%20Committee%20on%20Economic,he%20
expected%20the%20CES%20to; Beatrix Hoffman, *Health Care for Some: Rights
and Rationing in the United States since 1930* (Chicago: University of Chicago Press,
2012).
4. Roosevelt, "State of the Union Message to Congress," January 11, 1944.
5. Downey, *The Woman Behind the New Deal*, 349.
6. Paul Starr, *Remedy and Reaction: The Peculiar American Struggle over Health Care
Reform* (New Haven, CT: Yale University Press, 2013); S. Steinmo and J. Watts, "It's

the Institutions, Stupid! Why Comprehensive National Health Insurance Always Fails in America," *Journal of Health and Political Policy Law*, no. 2 (1995): 329–72.

7. "CMS Fast Facts," Centers for Medicare and Medicaid Services, last modified August 20, 2020, https://www.cms.gov/research-statistics-data-systems/cms-fast -facts/cms-fast-facts-mobile-site.

8. Wilbur J. Cohen, "Reflections on the Enactment of Medicare and Medicaid," *Health Care Financ Review* (December 1985): 3–11, https://www.ncbi.nlm.nih.gov /pmc/articles/PMC4195078/.

9. Robin Cohen, Amy Cha, Michael Martinez, and Emily Terlizzi, "Health Insurance Coverage: Early Release of Estimates from the National Health Interview Survey, 2019," National Center for Health Statistics, https://www.cdc.gov/nchs/data/nhis /earlyrelease/insur202009-508.pdf; Sarah Collins, Munira Gunja, and Gabriella Aboulafia, "U.S. Health Insurance Coverage in 2020: A Looming Crisis in Afford-ability," Commonwealth Fund, August 19, 2020, accessed September 27, 2021, https://www.commonwealthfund.org/publications/issue-briefs/2020/aug/loom ing-crisis-health-coverage-2020-biennial.

10. Theodore Marmor, "The Right to Health Care: Reflections on Its History and Poli-tics," in *Rights to Health Care: Philosophy and Medicine*, ed. Thomas Bole and Wil-liam Bondeson (Dordrecht: Springer, 1991), https://link.springer.com/chapter/10 .1007/978-0-585-28295-4_2.

11. "National Health Expenditure Data," Centers for Medicare and Medicaid Ser-vices, last modified August 20, 2020, https://www.cms.gov/Research-Statistics -Data-and-Systems/Statistics-Trends-and-Reports/NationalHealthExpendData /NationalHealthAccountsProjected. The CMS notes that Medicare, in contrast to the private health care system, has been much more effective at controlling costs, with spending per enrollee rising at just 1.5 percentage points per year from 1970 to 2016.

12. "Health Spending," Organisation for Economic Co-operation and Development, 2020, https://data.oecd.org/healthres/health-spending.htm#indicator-chart.

13. Steffie Woolhandlers, Terry Campbell, and David Himmelstein, "Cost of Health-care Administration in the United States and Canada," *New England Journal of Medicine*, no. 349 (2003): 768–75.

14. Bonnie B. Blanchfield, James L. Heffernan, Bradford Osgood, Rosemary R. Shee-han, and Gregg S. Meyer, "Saving Billions of Dollars—and Physicians' Time—by Streamlining Billing Practices," *Health Affairs* 29, no. 6 (2010): 1248–54.

15. "Health Insurance Coverage of the Total Population," Kaiser Family Foundation, accessed September 29, 2021, https://www.kff.org/other/state-indicator/total -population/?currentTimeframe=0&sortModel=%7B%22colId%22:%22Loca tion%22,%22sort%22:%22asc%22%7D; Chris Fleming, "New *Health Affairs*: U.S. Docs Spend Four Times More on Payer Interactions than Canadians," *Health Affairs*, August 5, 2011, https://www.healthaffairs.org/do/10.1377/hblog20110805 .012845/full/.

16. Gerard F. Anderson, Uwe E. Reinhardt, Peter S. Hussey, and Varduhi Petrosyan. "It's the Prices, Stupid: Why the United States Is So Different from Other Coun-tries," *Health Affairs* 22, no. 3 (2003): 89–105.

17. "Average General Annual Health Plan Deductibles for Single Coverage, 2006–2017 9060," Kaiser Family Foundation, accessed September 29, 2021, https://www.kff .org/report-section/ehbs-2017-section-7-employee-cost-sharing/attachment /figure%207_10-11/; Anna Porretta, "How Much Does Individual Health Insurance

Cost," *eHealth*, November 24, 2020, https://www.ehealthinsurance.com/resources /individual-and-family/how-much-does-individual-health-insurance-cost.

18. Tal Gross and Matthew J. Notowidigdo, "Health Insurance and the Consumer Bankruptcy Decision: Evidence from Expansions of Medicaid," *Journal of Public Economics* 95, nos. 7–8 (2011): 767–78.

19. Pilar García-Gómez, Hans van Kippersluis, Owen O'Donnell, and Eddy van Doorslaer, "Long-Term and Spillover Effects of Health Shocks on Employment and Income," *Journal of Human Resources* 48, no. 4 (2013): 873–909.

20. "Report on the Economic Well-Being of U.S. Households in 2019," Board of Governors of the Federal Reserve System, last modified May 21, 2020, https://www .federalreserve.gov/publications/2020-economic-well-being-of-us-households -in-2019-dealing-with-unexpected-expenses.htm; David Himmelstein, Robert M. Lawless, Deborah Thorne, Pamela Foohey, and Steffie Woolhandler, "Medical Bankruptcy: Still Common Despite the Affordable Care Act," *American Journal of Public Health* 109, no. 3 (March 1, 2019): 431–33, https://ajph.aphapublications.org /doi/10.2105/AJPH.2018.304901.

21. OECD (2022), Infant mortality rates (indicator). doi: 10.1787/83dea506-en (accessed on 11 April 2022).

22. "Gross Domestic Product," Organisation for Economic Co-operation and Development, accessed September 29, 2021, https://data.oecd.org/gdp/gross-domestic -product-gdp.htm; "Health Status: Life Expectancy," Organisation for Economic Co-operation and Development, accessed September 29, 2021, https://stats.oecd .org/index.aspx?queryid=30114/.

23. https://www.rwjf.org/en/library/research/2021/09/marketplace-pulse--covid-19 -and-the-coverage-gap.html.

24. Justin M. Feldman and Mary T. Bassett, "Variation in COVID-19 Mortality in the US by Race and Ethnicity and Educational Attainment," *JAMA network open* 4, no. 11 (2021): e2135967–e2135967.

25. Sam Dickman, David Himmelstein, Danny McCormick, and Steffie Woolhandler, "Opting Out of Medicaid Expansion: The Health and Financial Impacts," *Health Affairs*, January 30, 2014, https://www.healthaffairs.org/do/10.1377/hblog2014 0130.036694/full/; Stan Dorn and Rebecca Gordon, "The Catastrophic Cost of Uninsurance: COVID-19 Cases and Deaths Closely Tied to America's Health Coverage Gaps," FamiliesUSA, March 2021, accessed September 29, 2021, https:// familiesusa.org/wp-content/uploads/2021/03/2021-37_Loss-of-Lives_Report _AnalysisStyleB_Final.pdf.

26. https://www.nytimes.com/2018/04/11/magazine/black-mothers-babies-death -maternal-mortality.html.

27. Adam Gaffney, "What Obamacare Can't Do: Single-Payer Is Still the Best Way to Achieve Universal Health Care," *Jacobin Magazine*, February 11, 2016, accessed September 29, 2021, https://www.jacobinmag.com/2016/02/gaffney-single-payer -sanders-healthcare-obamacare-aca-clinton/.

28. "Depression," World Health Organization, September 12, 2021, https://www.who .int/en/news-room/fact-sheets/detail/depression; "Depression Is the No. 1 Cause of Ill Health and Disability Worldwide," World Economic Forum, accessed November 17, 2021, https://www.weforum.org/agenda/2018/05/depression-prevents -many-of-us-from-leading-healthy-and-productive-lives-being-the-no-1-cause -of-ill-health-and-disability-worldwide/.

29. Helen-Maria Vasiliadis, Alain Lesage, Carol Adair, Philip S. Wang, and Ronald C. Kessler, "Do Canada and the United States Differ in Prevalence of Depression and Utilization of Services?," *Psychiatric Services* 58, no. 1 (January 2007): 63–71, doi:10 .1176/ps.2007.58.1.63. For more information, see "America's Mental Health 2018— Cohen Veterans Network," https://www.cohenveteransnetwork.org/Americas MentalHealth/.

30. Kristin Ray, "Disparities in Time Spent Seeking Medical Care in the United States," *Journal of the American Medical Association*, October 5, 2015, https://jamanetwork .com/journals/jamainternalmedicine/fullarticle/2451279.

31. Sarah Kliff, "Private Health Insurance Exist in Europe and Canada. Here's How It Works," Vox, February 12, 2019, https://www.vox.com/health-care/2019/2/12 /18215430/single-payer-private-health-insurance-harris-sanders.

32. Alison P. Galvani, Alyssa S. Parpia, Eric M. Foster, Burton H. Singer, and Meagan C. Fitzpatrick, "Improving the Prognosis of Health Care in the USA," *The Lancet*, no. 10223 (2020): 524–33, https://www.thelancet.com/article/S0140-6736(19)330 19-3/fulltext.

33. "How CBO Analyzes the Costs of Proposals for Single-Payer Health Care Systems That Are Based on Medicare's Fee-for-Service Program: Working Paper 2020-08," Congressional Budget Office, n.d., https://www.cbo.gov/publication/56811.

34. https://www.rand.org/pubs/research_reports/RRA788-1.html.

35. Ryan Nunn, Jana Parsons, and Jay Shambaugh, "A Dozen Facts about the Economics of the US Health-Care System," Hamilton Project (2020), https://www.brook ings.edu/wp-content/uploads/2020/03/HealthCare_Facts_WEB_FINAL.pdf.

36. The CBO provides five options, with option 3, "lower payment rates, lower cost sharing," being the closest. This option purports to save $650 billion; however, long-term support and services are absent for this option. Thus I deduct the difference between options 4 and 5, which are both "higher payment rates, lower cost sharing" but with and without long-term support and services, to gain an estimate for the costs associated with long-term support and services. This provides a reasonably conservative estimate as to option 3 with long-term support and services added in.

37. For more, see Matt Bruenig, "How to Approach Medicare for All Financing," People's Policy Project, October 30, 2019, https://www.peoplespolicyproject.org/2019 /10/30/how-to-approach-medicare-for-all-financing/.

38. It's true that some providers may opt out of the single-payer system. While private health insurance wouldn't be allowed, people could privately pay providers directly for services out of pocket under current Medicare for All legislation. See Section 303 of Sanders's S. 1129.

39. US Department of Labor, Bureau of Labor Statistics, *Number of Jobs, Labor Market Experience, Marital Status, and Health: Results from A National Longitudinal Survey*, August 31, 2021 (Washington, DC), https://www.bls.gov/news.release/pdf/nlsoy .pdf; US Department of Labor, Bureau of Labor Statistics, *Job Openings and Labor Turnover Summary*, September 8, 2021 (Washington, DC), https://www.bls.gov /news.release/jolts.nr0.htm.

40. "How Long Are Waiting Times across Countries?," Organisation for Economic Co-operation and Development, 2020, https://www.oecd-ilibrary.org/sites/242 e3c8c-en/1/3/2/index.html?itemId=/content/publication/242e3c8c-en&_csp _=e90031be7ce6b03025f09a0c506286b0&itemIGO=oecd&itemContentType =book.

41. Sarah Kliff, "Medicare X: The Democrats' Supercharged Public Option Plan, Explained," Vox, October 20, 2017, https://www.vox.com/health-care/2017/10 /20/16504800/medicare-x-single-payer.

42. US Congressional Budget Office, *Budget Options*, November 13, 2013 (Washington, DC), https://www.cbo.gov/budget-options/2013/44890.

43. Matt Bruenig and Jon Walker, "An Exchange Public Option Could Save $170 Billion," People's Policy Project, April 16, 2021, https://www.peoplespolicyproject .org/2021/04/16/an-exchange-public-option-could-save-170-billion/; Matt Bruenig, "Bidencare System Will Kill 125,000 through Uninsurance," People's Policy Project, July 15, 2019, https://www.peoplespolicyproject.org/2019/07/15/biden care-system-will-kill-125000-through-uninsurance/.

Chapter Eight

1. Laura Wheaton, Linda Giannarelli, and Ilham Dehry, "Poverty Projections: Assessing the Impact of Benefits and Stimulus Measures" (Urban Institute, Washington, DC, 2021), https://www.urban.org/sites/default/files/publication/104603/2021 -poverty-projections_0_0.pdf.

2. For more details on the three rounds of payments, see "What to Know about All Three Rounds of Coronavirus Stimulus Checks" (Peter G. Peterson Foundation, March 15, 2021), https://www.pgpf.org/blog/2021/03/what-to-know-about-all -three-rounds-of-coronavirus-stimulus-checks.

3. Note that official poverty calculations do not include tax credits or stimulus payments. Thus official poverty went up while the supplemental poverty measure declined. For more, see Michael C. Cook, "Income, Poverty, and Health Insurance: 2020 Live News Conference," September 14, 2021, https://www.census.gov /content/dam/Census/newsroom/press-kits/2021/iphi/20210914-slides-iphi -plotpoints.pdf.

4. Due to space constraints, I am not able to discuss necessary reforms to the unemployment insurance system. For a well-thought-out proposal, see Arindrajit Dube, *A Plan to Reform the Unemployment Insurance System in the United States* (Washington, DC: Hamilton Project, Brookings Institution, 2021), https://www.hamilton project.org/papers/a_plan_to_reform_the_unemployment_insurance_system_in _the_united_states.

5. Wheaton, Giannarelli, and Dehry, "Poverty Projections: Assessing the Impact of Benefits and Stimulus Measures."

6. "A Poverty Reduction Analysis of the American Family Act" (Center on Poverty and Social Policy at Columbia University, January 25, 2021), https://www.poverty center.columbia.edu/publication/2021/poverty-reduction-analysis/american -family-act.

7. "3.7 million More Children in Poverty in Jan 2022 without Monthly Child Tax Credit" (Center on Poverty and Social Policy at Columbia University, February 17, 2022), https://www.povertycenter.columbia.edu/news-internal/monthly-poverty-janu ary-2022.

8. Frances Perkins, *The Roosevelt I Knew* (New York: Viking Press, 1947), 324.

9. Social insurance in the United States, from Social Security to welfare, has always been racialized, intentionally excluding people of color from benefits. For an excellent overview of the history of welfare in the United States, see Jason DeParle, ed.,

American Dream: Three Women, Ten Kids, and a Nation's Drive to End Welfare (New York: Penguin Books, 2005).

10. Anne Alstott, "What We Owe to Parents," *Boston Review*, June 30, 2014, https://bostonreview.net/forum/anne-l-alstott-what-we-owe-parents/.

11. Kathryn Edin and H. Luke Shaefer, *$2.00 a Day: Living on Almost Nothing in America* (Boston: Houghton Mifflin Harcourt, 2015).

12. United States 2018 Disability Status Report, Yang-Tan Institute on Employment and Disability at the Cornell University ILR School, https://www.disabilitystatistics.org/StatusReports/2018-PDF/2018-StatusReport_US.pdf.

13. These are 2018 poverty statistics. Author calculations of the Current Population Survey Annual Social and Economic Supplement. US Census Bureau, "Current Population Survey, 2018 Annual Social and Economic (ASEC) Supplement," https://www.census.gov/data/datasets/2018/demo/cps/cps-asec-2018.html.

14. J. E. King and John Marangos, "Two Arguments for Basic Income: Thomas Paine (1737–1809) and Thomas Spence (1750–1814)," *History of Economic Ideas* 14, no. 1 (2006): 55–71, https://www.jstor.org/stable/23723271.

15. Warren Weaver Jr., "President's Welfare Plan Passes House, 243 to 155," *New York Times*, April 17, 1970, sec. Archives, https://www.nytimes.com/1970/04/17/archives/presidents-welfare-plan-passes-house-243-to-155-nixon-terms-the.html.

16. President's Commission on Income Maintenance Programs, "Poverty Amid Plenty: The American Paradox," (November 12, 1969), US Federal Documents, HathiTrust Digital Library, https://babel.hathitrust.org/cgi/pt?id=uc1.b4317301&view=1up&seq=5&skin=2021.

17. Peter Passell and Leonard Ross, "Daniel Moynihan and President-Elect Nixon: How Charity Didn't Begin at Home," *New York Times*, January 14, 1973, https://archive.nytimes.com/www.nytimes.com/books/98/10/04/specials/moynihan-income.html. Numerous studies were conducted at the time to investigate the supposed problem of work incentives. See, e.g., Karl Widerquist, "A Failure to Communicate: What (If Anything) Can We Learn from the Negative Income Tax Experiments?," *Journal of Socio-Economics* 34, no. 1 (February 1, 2005): 49–81, doi: 10.1016/j.socec.2004.09.050; Ioana Marinescu, "No Strings Attached: The Behavioral Effects of US Unconditional Cash Transfer Programs," Roosevelt Institute, 2018, https://rooseveltinstitute.org/publications/no-strings-attached-behavioral-effects-us-unconditional-cash-transfer-ubi/.

18. For an overview of Nixon's failed welfare reform, see Brian Steensland, "Understanding the Failed Welfare Revolution," in *The Failed Welfare Revolution: America's Struggle over Guaranteed Income Policy* (Princeton, NJ: Princeton University Press, 2008), 1–27.

19. Andrew Yang, "The Freedom Dividend," Yang2020—Andrew Yang for President, https://www.yang2020.com/policies/the-freedom-dividend/.

20. Nancy Folbre, "Children as Public Goods," *American Economic Review* 84, no. 2 (1994): 86–90, https://www.jstor.org/stable/2117807.

21. Committee on Building an Agenda to Reduce the Number of Children in Poverty by Half in 10 Years et al., *A Roadmap to Reducing Child Poverty*, ed. Greg Duncan and Suzanne Le Menestrel (Washington, DC: National Academies Press, 2019), doi: 10.17226/25246. Exclusions were initially implemented in an attempt to encourage adults to enter the paid labor market, though a major review by economists and sociologists for the National Academy of Science found that a child cash benefit of

$3,000 per year would have minimal effects on paid work hours. Further, it is not at all clear that reducing paid work hours and increasing unpaid care work would be socially undesirable.

22. UNICEF and ODI, "Universal Child Benefits: Policy Issues and Options," June 2020, https://www.unicef.org/media/70416/file/Universal-child-benefits-Briefing -2020.pdf.

23. Paul Krugman, "Opinion | Why Not Make the Kids Alright?," *New York Times*, September 21, 2021, sec. Opinion, https://www.nytimes.com/2021/09/21/opinion /child-tax-credit-poverty.html.

24. Irwin Garfinkel, Laurel Sariscsany, Elizabeth Ananat, Sophie Collyer, and Christopher Wimer, "The Costs and Benefits of a Child Allowance," Center on Poverty & Social Policy at Columbia University, February 23, 2021, https://static1.square space.com/static/5743308460b5e922a25a6dc7/t/605974a4e582be283a097c27 /1616475326656/Child-Allowance-CBA-discussion-paper-CPSP-2021.pdf, 1–64.

25. This draws from the work of Naomi Zewde and co-authors and the work of Matt Bruenig. For more, see, for example, Naomi Zewde et al., "A Guaranteed Income for the 21st Century" (The New School Institute on Race and Political Economy, May 2021), https://kirwaninstitute.osu.edu/sites/default/files/Guaranteed%20 Income%20for%20the%2021st%20Century.pdf; Matt Bruenig, "What Could Have Been for the Child Benefit," People's Policy Project, July 15, 2021, https:// www.peoplespolicyproject.org/2021/07/15/what-could-have-been-for-the-child -benefit/; People's Policy Project, "The Family Fun Pack," 2019, https://peoples policyproject.org/projects/family-fun-pack.

26. Economists have long fought over the proper phase-out rate, with their chief concern being maintaining strong paid employment incentives. In general, I believe this discussion has been too narrow, prioritizing paid employment over broader care work; however, a lower rate of phase-out, at for instance 25% or 33%, may be desirable. For a traditional review of the literature as it applies to a negative income tax, see Jessica Wiederspan, Elizabeth Rhodes, and H. Luke Shaefer, "Expanding the Discourse on Antipoverty Policy: Reconsidering a Negative Income Tax," *Journal of Poverty* 19, no. 2 (April 3, 2015): 218–38, doi:10.1080/10875549.2014 .991889.

27. OECD, "Basic Income as a Policy Option: Technical Background Note Illustrating Costs and Distributional Implications for Selected Countries," 2017, https://www .oecd.org/els/soc/Basic-Income-Policy-Option-2017-Brackground-Technical -Note.pdf.

28. Kaiser Family Foundation, "2021 Employer Health Benefits Survey," 2021, https:// www.kff.org/report-section/ehbs-2021-summary-of-findings/.

29. Matt Bruenig, "New Child Tax Credit Is Not Reaching the Poorest Families," People's Policy Project, October 13, 2021, https://www.peoplespolicyproject.org/2021 /10/13/new-child-tax-credit-is-not-reaching-the-poorest-families/.

30. For an in-depth look at how excessive fees exacerbate inequality, see Devin Fergus, *Land of the Fee: Hidden Costs and the Decline of the American Middle Class* (New York: Oxford University Press, 2018).

31. For a review of how credit cards are structured to benefit the well-to-do at the expense of the poor, see Aaron Klein, "How Credit Card Companies Reward the Rich and Punish the Rest of Us," Brookings Institution, December 23, 2019, https:// www.brookings.edu/opinions/how-credit-card-companies-reward-the-rich-and -punish-the-rest-of-us/.

32. Economists would point out that this isn't exactly "free money," as credit card points are in part financed by fees charged to merchants, which in turn can contribute to higher prices paid by consumers.

33. FDIC, "How America Banks: Household Use of Banking and Financial Services," October 2020, https://www.fdic.gov/analysis/household-survey/2019report.pdf.

34. Frank Bass and Dakin Campbell, "Bank Branches Disappear from Poor Neighborhoods Like Longwood, Bronx," *Bloomberg*, May 9, 2013, https://www.bloomberg.com/news/articles/2013-05-09/bank-branches-disappear-from-poor-neighborhoods-like-longwood-bronx.

35. Dan Murphy, "Economic Impact Payments: Uses, Payment Methods, and Costs to Recipients," Brookings Institution, 2021, https://www.brookings.edu/wp-content/uploads/2021/02/20210216_Murphy_ImpactPayments_Final-3.pdf; Consumer Financial Protection Bureau, "What Is a Payday Loan?," June 2, 2017, https://www.consumerfinance.gov/ask-cfpb/what-is-a-payday-loan-en-1567/.

36. https://slate.com/news-and-politics/2014/08/postal-banking-already-worked-in-the-usa-and-it-will-work-again.html.

37. Thomas Herndon and Mark Paul, "A Public Banking Option as a Mode of Regulation for Household Financial Services in the US," *Journal of Post Keynesian Economics* 43, no. 4 (October 1, 2020): 576–607, doi:10.1080/01603477.2020.1734462. See also Mehrsa Baradaran, "It's Time for Postal Banking," *Harvard Law Review* 174, no. 4 (February 24, 2014): 165–75, https://harvardlawreview.org/2014/02/its-time-for-postal-banking/. Others have also written extensively on the idea of a public option, though at times from a moderately different angle. See Morgan Ricks, J. Crawford, and L. Menand, "FedAccounts: Digital Dollars," *George Washington Law Review* 89, no. 113 (January 28, 2021): 114–72.

Chapter Nine

1. Roy Popkin, "Two 'Killer Smogs,'" *EPA Journal* 12, no. 10 (1986): 27–29.

2. "500% Rise in Emphysema Mortality Rate in Last Decade Reported for City," *New York Times*, March 12, 1970, 27, https://www.nytimes.com/1970/03/12/archives/500-rise-in-emphysema-mortality-rate-in-last-decade-reported-for.html.

3. Rebekkah Rubin, "Oral Histories of the 1969 Cuyahoga River Fire," *Belt*, June 3, 2019, https://beltmag.com/cuyahoga-river-fire-1969/.

4. John Kenneth Galbraith, *The Affluent Society* (New York: Houghton Mifflin, 1998), 13.

5. Kate Wheeling and Max Ufberg, "'The Ocean Is Boiling': The Complete Oral History of the 1969 Santa Barbara Oil Spill," *Pacific Standard*, April 18, 2017, last modified November 7, 2018, https://psmag.com/news/the-ocean-is-boiling-the-complete-oral-history-of-the-1969-santa-barbara-oil-spill; Lila Thulin, "How an Oil Spill Inspired the First Earth Day," *Smithsonian Magazine*, April 22, 2019, https://www.smithsonianmag.com/history/how-oil-spill-50-years-ago-inspired-first-earth-day-180972007/.

6. Gladwin Hill, "One Year Later, Impact of Great Oil Slick Is Still Felt," *New York Times*, January 25, 1970, https://www.nytimes.com/1970/01/25/archives/one-year-later-impact-of-great-oil-slick-is-still-felt.html.

7. Earlier popular ecological works had touched on themes similar to Carson's. For example, William Vogt's *Road to Survival* and Fairfield Osborn's *Our Plundered Planet* were both printed in 1948, but neither coincided with the expansion of the environmental movement in the same way.

8.   Adam Rome, "'Give Earth a Chance': The Environmental Movement and the Sixties," *Journal of American History* 90, no. 2 (September 2003): 525–54, https://www.jstor.org/stable/3659443?seq=1#metadata_info_tab_contents.

9.   "Issue of The Year: The Environment," *Time*, January 4, 1971, accessed October 7, 2021, https://time.com/vault/issue/1971-01-04/page/27/.

10.   Richard M. Nixon, "January 22, 1970: State of the Union Address," Miller Center, University of Virginia, January 22, 1970, https://millercenter.org/the-presidency/presidential-speeches/january-22-1970-state-union-address.

11.   Congressional Record, US Senate, transcript, Edmund S. Muskie Archives and Special Collections Library, Bates College, April 23, 1974, http://abacus.bates.edu/muskie-archives/ajcr/1974/Earth%20Day.shtml.

12.   Nixon, State of the Union Address.

13.   It is worth noting that while the 1970s were a watershed moment in environmental policy and law, both the New Deal and the Great Society included many environmental provisions. Some environmental advocates saw these protections—these rights—as extending the New Deal and the Great Society. For more, see https://lpeproject.org/blog/understanding-environmental-law-as-public-provision/.

14.   James Boyce, "Let Them Drink Pollution?," Institute for New Economic Thinking, January 26, 2016, https://www.ineteconomics.org/perspectives/blog/let-them-drink-pollution.

15.   Andrew Goodkind, Christopher W. Tessum, Jay S. Coggins, Jason D. Hill, and Julian D. Marshall, "Fine-Scale Damage Estimates of Particulate Matter Air Pollution Reveal Opportunities for Location-Specific Mitigation of Emissions," *Proceedings of the National Academy of Sciences of the United States of America*, April 8, 2019, https://www.pnas.org/content/pnas/116/18/8775.full.pdf.

16.   In a number of papers Nordhaus maps the 3.5°C pathway as "optimal." See, e.g., William Nordhaus, "Climate Change: The Ultimate Challenge for Economics," *American Economic Review* 109, no. 6 (2019): 1991–2014, doi:10.1257/aer.109.6.1991. By contrast, companies with a real relationship to the economy have taken a different view, with private entities like Deloitte and McKinsey urging trillions of dollars a year in upfront spending to avert the economic calamity of runaway climate change—and to ensure ongoing economic prosperity. See https://www.bloomberg.com/news/articles/2022-01-28/the-cost-to-reach-net-zero-by-2050-is-actually-a-bargain?sref=eeq6exxF; https://www.bloomberg.com/news/articles/2022-01-28/the-cost-to-reach-net-zero-by-2050-is-actually-a-bargain?sref=eeq6exxF.

17.   Milton Freidman and Rose Friedman, *Free to Choose: A Personal Statement* (New York: Houghton Mifflin Harcourt, 1979).

18.   D. R. Reidmiller et al., "Fourth National Climate Assessment, Volume II: Impacts, Risks, and Adaptation in the United States," US Global Change Research Program (2018), https://nca2018.globalchange.gov/downloads/NCA4_2018_Full Report.pdf.

19.   Thankfully, degrees of warming to this extent are becoming increasingly unlikely, though economists making these arguments were doing so with the understanding that these ranges were well within the realm of the possible, and in fact Nordhaus again models 4°C by 2150 as "optimal."

20.   For more on this, see Anders Fremstad and Mark Paul, "Neoliberalism and climate change: How the free-market myth has prevented climate action," *Ecological Economics* 197, no. July (2022), https://www.sciencedirect.com/science/article/abs/pii/S0921800922000155?dgcid=author.

21. Valérie Masson-Delmotte et al., "Climate Change and Land: An IPCC Special Report on Climate Change, Desertification, Land Degradation, Sustainable Land Management, Food Security, and Greenhouse Gas Fluxes in Terrestrial Ecosystems," 2019, Intergovernmental Panel on Climate Change, https://www.ipcc.ch /site/assets/uploads/2019/11/SRCCL-Full-Report-Compiled-191128.pdf.

22. The idea of a Green New Deal existed long before it caught on in the United States. For examples of earlier writing on a Green New Deal, which had always been associated with an investment- and justice-led decarbonization effort, see https://new economics.org/uploads/files/8f737ea195fe56db2f_xbm6ihwb1.pdf; and Robert Pollin, *Greening the Global Economy* (Cambridge, MA: MIT Press, 2016), https:// doi.org/10.7551/mitpress/9780262028233.001.0001.

23. To clarify, the IPCC does not propose timelines for decarbonization; instead it issued a special report that looked at what it would take to limit global warming to 1.5°C. https://www.ipcc.ch/sr15/.

24. The purely technocratic approach to climate policy was tried with the 2009 Waxman-Markey bill, which passed the House but failed in the Senate in 2010. According to the sociologist Theda Skocpol, the Obama administration's pursuit of an elite compromise on climate policy and failure to engage grassroots environmental groups contributed substantially to the bill's failure. Theda Skocpol, "Naming the Problem: What It Will Take to Counter Extremism and Engage Americans in the Fight against Global Warming" (Harvard University, January 2013), https://scholars .org/sites/scholars/files/skocpol_captrade_report_january_2013_0.pdf.

25. "Jemez Principles for Democratic Organizing," Southwest Network for Environmental and Economic Justice (SNEEJ), December 1996, https://www.ejnet.org /ej/jemez.pdf.

26. US Bureau of Labor Statistics, "All Employees, Coal Mining", last modified October 8, 2021, https://fred.stlouisfed.org/series/CEU1021210001.

27. US Bureau of Labor Statistics, Occupational Outlook Handbook, *Fastest Growing Occupations*, last modified September 8, 2021, https://www.bls.gov/ooh/fastest -growing.htm.

28. Kate Aronoff, Alyssa Battistoni, Daniel Aldana Cohen, and Thea Riofrancos, *A Planet to Win: Why We Need a Green New Deal* (New York: Verso, 2019).

29. The Labor Network for Sustainability is a nongovernmental organization that was launched to bring the labor and climate movements together. For more on the importance of centering justice in the energy transition, see J. Mijin Cha, Dimitris Stevis, Todd E. Vachon, Vivian Price, and Maria Brescia-Weiler, "A Green New Deal for All: The Centrality of a Worker and Community-Led Just Transition in the US," *Political Geography* 95 (2022).

30. In what follows, I offer a *policy framework* for delivering the right to a healthy environment. While some of my recommendations track with those of GND advocates— for example, my emphasis on an investment-forward approach—others do not: I, contra many GND advocates, believe carbon pricing and supply-side policies that keep fossil fuels in the ground are absolutely necessary. That is to say, what follows is neither a rehash of the most frequently discussed policies to realize the GND's aims nor my attempt at the "ideal" policy mix for the GND. Although I hope some of these measures are indeed taken up by GND sponsors and supporters—because I believe them essential and effective—the exact policies that will comprise the GND, like the policies that comprised the New Deal, will be decided democratically and iteratively over time.

31. Garett Hardin's impactful 1968 essay for *Science*, published under the title "The Tragedy of the Commons," should have been titled "The Tragedy of Open Access." A commons is governed by a community, which establishes a set of rules and guidelines. Instead, Harding was really talking about the problem of open access, where resources are not managed.

32. The United States does have the Clean Air Act, which has been a powerful tool in reducing air pollution. However, there is a long way to go in order to sufficiently reduce air pollution across the nation.

33. For a more in-depth look at the economics of deep decarbonization, see Mark Paul, Anders Fremstad, and J. W. Mason, "Decarbonizing the US Economy: Pathways toward a Green New Deal," Roosevelt Institute, 2019, https:// rooseveltinstitute .org/wp-content/uploads/2019/06/Roosevelt-Institute_GreenNew-Deal_Digital -Final.pdf.

34. For a wonderful analysis of the government's role in mobilization around World War II, see Andrew Bossie and J. W. Mason, "The Public Role in Economic Transformation: Lessons from World War II," Roosevelt Institute, 2020, https://roose veltinstitute.org/publications/the-public-role-in-economic-transformation-lessons -from-world-war-ii/.

35. Mark Paul and Daniel Aldana Cohen, "The Green New Deal's Public Infrastructure Should Be Funded by the Public," *Dissent Magazine*, September 21, 2020, https://www.dissentmagazine.org/online_articles/the-green-new-deals-public -infrastructure-should-be-funded-by-the-public.

36. Paul, Fremstad, and Mason, "Decarbonizing the US Economy"; Mariana Mazzucato, *Mission Economy: A Moonshot Guide to Changing Capitalism* (New York: Harper Business, 2021).

37. Mark Paul and Nina Eichacker, "Why We Should Be Funding More Solyndras," *MIT Technology Review*, November 19, 2020, https://www.technologyreview.com /2020/11/19/1012302/solyndra-climate-change-industrial-policy-opinion/.

38. Goksin Kavlak, James McNerney, and Jessika E. Trancik, "Evaluating the Causes of Cost Reduction in Photovoltaic Modules," *Energy Policy* 123, no. 1 (December 2018): 700–710, https://www.sciencedirect.com/science/article/pii/S03014215 18305196.

39. International Energy Agency, "Net Zero by 2050," May 2021, https://www.iea.org /reports/net-zero-by-2050; State of California, Office of Governor Gavin Newsom, "Governor Newsom Announces California Will Phase Out Gasoline-Powered Cars & Drastically Reduce Demand for Fossil Fuel in California's Fight Against Climate Change," September 23, 2020, https://www.gov.ca.gov/2020/09/23/governor -newsom-announces-california-will-phase-out-gasoline-powered-cars-drastically -reduce-demand-for-fossil-fuel-in-californias-fight-against-climate-change/.

40. Some jurisdictions, such as the Northeast under the Regional Greenhouse Gas Initiative, and California, do have modest positive carbon pricing programs currently in place.

41. Janet Redman, "Dirty Energy Dominance Dependent on Denial: How the U.S. Fossil Fuel Industry Depends on Subsidies and Climate Denial" (Oil Change International, Washington, DC, October 2017), http://priceofoil.org/content/uploads /2017/10/OCI_US-Fossil-Fuel-Subs-2015-16_Final_Oct2017.pdf; Ian Parry, Simon Black, and Nate Vernon, *Still Not Getting Energy Prices Right: A Global and Country Update on Fossil Fuel Subsidies*, Working Paper no. 2921/236, International Monetary Fund, September 24, 2021, https://www.imf.org/en/Publications/WP/Issues

/2021/09/23/Still-Not-Getting-Energy-Prices-Right-A-Global-and-Country-Update
-of-Fossil-Fuel-Subsidies-466004.

42. This draws on earlier work done by Peter Barnes and James K. Boyce, as well as joint work I did with Anders Fremstad. See Peter Barnes, *With Liberty and Dividends for All: How to Save Our Middle Class When Jobs Don't Pay Enough* (n.p.: Berrett-Koehler, 2014); James K. Boyce, *The Case for Carbon Dividends* (New York: John Wiley & Sons, 2019). For detailed modeling on the distributional impacts, see Anders Fremstad and Mark Paul, "The Impact of a Carbon Tax on Inequality," *Ecological Economics* 163 (2019): 88–97; James K. Boyce and Mark Paul, "Does Biden's Insurance Policy for the Climate Go Far Enough?," *The Hill*, February 16, 2021, https://thehill.com/opinion/energy-environment/538938-does-bidens
-insurance-policy-for-the-climate-go-far-enough.

43. "Plummeting Solar, Wind and Battery Costs Can Accelerate Our Clean Electricity Future," University of California, Berkeley, Goldman School of Public Policy, June 2020, https://www.2035report.com/wp-content/uploads/2020/06/2035-Report
.pdf?hsCtaTracking=8a85e9ea-4ed3-4ec0-b4c6-906934306ddb%7Cc68c2ac2
-1db0-4d1c-82a1-65ef4daaf6c1.

44. Saul Griffith and Sam Calisch, "Mobilizing for a Zero Carbon America: Jobs, Jobs, Jobs, and More Jobs," Rewiring America, July 29, 2020, https://content.rewiring america.org/reports/mobilizing-for-a-zero-carbon-america-technical-white paper.pdf.

45. Eric Larson et al., "Net-Zero America: Potential Pathways, Infrastructure, and Impacts," Princeton University, December 15, 2020, https://netzeroamerica.prince ton.edu/img/Princeton_NZA_Interim_Report_15_Dec_2020_FINAL.pdf.

46. Chris Hayes, "The New Abolitionism," *The Nation*, April 22, 2014. To be sure, there are other ways to neutralize the political capital of fossil fuel corporations and executives who have long stood in the way of climate action. The government, for instance, could simply nationalize the industry. See Mark Paul, Carla Santos Skandier, and Rory Renzy, "Out of Time: The Case for Nationalizing the Fossil Fuel Industry," People's Policy Project and the Next System's Project (2020), https://www.peoplespolicyproject.org/project/the-case-for-nationalizing-the-fossil-fuel
-industry/.

47. Anders Fremstad, Mark Paul, and Anthony Underwood, "Work Hours and CO_2 Emissions: Evidence from U.S. Households," *Review of Political Economy* 31 no. 1 (2019): 42–59.

Chapter Ten

1. The US dollar is the global reserve currency. This gives the United States special privileges with respect to international financial markets and trade, easing the nation's ability to transform economic rights from an idea into a reality. Other countries will face more challenging constraints in pursuit of an economic bill of rights. For many other nations to successfully adopt the policies discussed here on a global scale would require a substantial retooling of the international financial architecture. This could take place along the lines recommended by Keynes at Bretton Woods: a new global currency, the "bancor." In the meantime, the United States could work within the current international financial system to ease constraints on other nations, by at least supporting the use of capital controls to limit capital flight in other nations. For more on Keynes's proposal, see Joseph E. Stiglitz,

The Stiglitz Report: Reforming the International Monetary and Financial Systems in the Wake of the Global Crisis (New York: New Press, 2010); Yanis Varoufakis, *And the Weak Suffer What They Must? Europe, Austerity and the Threat to Global Stability* (New York: Random House, 2016).

2. Although less so recently. For example, economists associated with the Committee for a Responsible Federal Budget have long thought the deficit a central problem, but they've recently relaxed their position to a degree, now arguing that the government debt is more of a *long-run* problem.

3. There's also a moral component to critiques of the US deficit. Deficit hawks describe the US government's profligacy over the past fifty years as an "intergenerational injustice." https://www.bushcenter.org/catalyst/federal-debt/peterson-national -debt-an-inter-generational-injustice.html.

   In 2010, Obama declared that "just as families and businesses across the nation have tightened their belts, so must the federal government." This, despite unemployment hovering around 10%. Jack Lew, "Tightening Our Belts," November 29, 2010, https://obamawhitehouse.archives.gov/blog/2010/11/29/tightening-our -belts.

4. Although the PAYGO rule can be suspended by a vote, it nevertheless erects additional hurdles to deficit financing. For a brief review of the bad economics of PAYGO, see https://www.epi.org/blog/the-bad-economics-of-paygo-swamp-any-strat egic-gain-from-adopting-it/.

5. https://apnews.com/article/joe-biden-congress-budget-08d7ca3ffc7f438148570 b04bc61ded0.

6. Valerie A. Ramey, "The Macroeconomic Consequences of Infrastructure Investment," National Bureau of Economic Research, July 2020, https://www.nber.org /papers/w27625; https://www.imf.org/en/Publications/WP/Issues/2019/05/31 /U-S-46942.

7. Ricardo J. Caballero, Emmanuel Farhi, and Pierre-Olivier Gourinchas, "The Safe Assets Shortage Conundrum," *Journal of Economic Perspectives* 31, no. 3 (2017): 29–46; Nell Abernathy, Mike Konczal, and Katy Milani, "Untamed: How to Check Corporate, Financial, and Monopoly Power," Roosevelt Institute, 2016, http:// rooseveltinstitute.org/untamed-how-check-corporate-financial-and-monopoly -power/.

8. This view is shared by the CBO, which provides the official "score"—that is, the economic and budgetary impact—of legislation. Any number of progressive proposals have been dead on arrival at CBO because of this assumption, despite the ample evidence contradicting it. Jonathan Huntley, "The Long-Run Effects of Federal Budget Deficits on National Saving and Private Domestic Investment" (Congressional Budget Office, Washington, DC, February 2014), https://www.cbo .gov/sites/default/files/cbofiles/attachments/45140-NSPDI_workingPaper.pdf.

9. There are many studies that demonstrate how public investment provides large returns to the economy. See Robert Lynch and Kavya Vaghul, "The Benefits and Costs of Investing in Early Childhood Education," Washington Center for Equitable Growth, https://equitablegrowth.org/research-paper/the-benefits-and-costs -of-investing-in-early-childhood-educati on/?longform=true; Alfredo M. Pereira, "Is All Public Capital Created Equal?," *Review of Economics and Statistics* (2000): 82, https://doi.org/10.1162/rest.2000.82.3.513; George Psacharopoulos and Harry Anthony Patrinos, "Returns to Investment in Education: A Decennial Review of the Global Literature," World Bank, https://openknowledge.worldbank.org/handle

/10986/29672; Valerie A. Ramey, "The Macroeconomic Consequences of Infrastructure Investment," National Bureau of Economic Research, July 2020, https://
www.nber.org/papers/w27625.

10.   Olivier Blanchard, "Public Debt and Low Interest Rates," *American Economic Review*
109, no. 4 (2018): 1197–1229, doi: 10.1257/ aer.109.4.1197; https://www.aeaweb.org
/aea/2019conference/program/pdf/14020_paper_etZgfbDr.pdf; Jason Furman
and Lawrence H. Summers, "Who's Afraid of Budget Deficits?," *Foreign Affairs*,
March–April 2019, https://www.foreignaffairs.com/articles/2019-01-27/whos
-afraid-budget-deficits?cid=soc-tw-rdr.

11.   J. W. Mason, "The Fed Doesn't Work for You," *Jacobin Magazine*, https://jacobin
mag.com/2016/01/federal-reserve-interest-rate-increase-janet-yellen-inflation
-unemployment/.

12.   This is true to an extent. For instance, when Federal Reserve chair Jerome Powell
was asked about recent rate hikes, he bluntly, and honestly, admitted that the
mechanism through which the rate hikes were intended to slow the speed of the
economy, and therefore in theory inflation, was by "moving down the number
of job openings" which would result in "less upward pressure on wages, less of a
labor shortage." Transcript of Chair Powell's Press Conference, March 16, 2022,
https://www.federalreserve.gov/mediacenter/files/FOMCpresconf20220316.pdf.

13.   Though it has indeed mitigated their damage. A comparison of recessions before
and after the Fed's creation in 1913—and particularly before and after Roosevelt
ordered the Fed to abandon the gold standard in 1933—demonstrates its long-term
stabilizing effect on the US economy. See "Historical Nonfarm Unemployment
Statistics," *Grasping Reality by Brad DeLong*, https://www.bradford-delong.com
/2019/05/historical-nonfarm-unemployment-statistics.html.

14.   Daniel Gabor's work on credit policy, where the Federal Reserve engages in work
to direct real economic activity rather than simply supporting financial stability,
has been influential in my thinking here. Daniel Gabor, "Revolution without Revo-
lutionaries: Interrogating the Return of Monetary Financing," https://transforma
tive-responses.org/wp-content/uploads/2021/01/TR_Report_Gabor_FINAL.pdf.

15.   While the Fed's primary job is to assist the financing side of the "pay for it" question, it also has a sizable role in directing credit, which will aid in relaxing real
resource constraints.

16.   For more on alterations to Federal Reserve policy, see Mike Konczal and J. W. Mason,
"A New Direction for the Federal Reserve: Expanding the Monetary Policy Toolkit,"
Roosevelt Institute, December 2017, https://rooseveltinstitute.org/wp-content
/uploads/2020/07/RI-Monetary-Policy-Toolkit-201711.pdf, and Gerald Epstein,
"Central Banks as Agents of Economic Development," Political Economy Research
Institute Working Paper No. 2014, https://scholarworks.umass.edu/peri_working
papers/103/.

17.   The Harvard economists Carmen Reinhart and Kenneth Rogoff published a paper
in 2010 in the *AEA Papers and Proceedings*, arguing that excessive government borrowing, which was seen as a debt-to-GDP ratio above 90%, would substantially
slow economic growth. This was a key argument pushing the austerity following
the 2008 crisis, austerity that drastically prolonged the recession and weak recovery. Recovering the jobs lost during the crisis took seven painful years (not accounting for population growth), and it took another two to reach the pre-recession unemployment rate—a time frame that could have been significantly shortened had
government kept its foot on the gas pedal rather than prematurely tapping the

brakes. While the paper garnered much attention, it was ultimately shown to be fallacious, with the supposed key findings disappearing once a spreadsheet error in their work was accounted for. Carmen M. Reinhart and Kenneth S. Rogoff, "Growth in a Time of Debt," *American Economic Review* 100, no. 2 (May 1, 2010): 573–78, doi:10.1257/aer.100.2.573; Thomas Herndon, Michael Ash, and Robert Pollin, "Does High Public Debt Consistently Stifle Economic Growth? A Critique of Reinhart and Rogoff," *Cambridge Journal of Economics* 38, no. 2 (March 1, 2014): 257–79, doi:10.1093/cje/bet075.

18. Emanuel Kopp, Daniel Leigh, Susanna Mursula, and Suchanan Tambunlertchai, "U.S. Investment Since the Tax Cuts and Jobs Act of 2017," International Monetary Fund Working Paper, 2019.

19. For a primer on MMT, see Stephanie Kelton, *The Deficit Myth: Modern Monetary Theory and How to Build a Better Economy* (New York: Public Affairs, 2020).

20. J. W. Mason, "What Recovery? The Case for Continued Expansionary Policy at the Fed," Roosevelt Institute, July 25, 2017, https://rooseveltinstitute.org/wp-content/uploads/2020/07/RI-What-Recovery-report-201707.pdf.

21. Diego Anzoategui, Diego Comin, Mark Gertler, and Joseba Martinez, "Endogenous Technology Adoption and R&D as Sources of Business Cycle Persistence," *American Economic Journal: Macroeconomics* 11, no. 3 (2019): 67–110; Regis Barnichon, Christian Matthes, and Alexander Ziegenbein, "The Financial Crisis at 10: Will We Ever Recover?," FRBSF Economic Letter, Federal Reserve Bank of San Francisco, 2018, https://www.frbsf.org/economic-research/publications/economic-letter/2018/august/financial-crisis-at-10-years-will-we-ever-recover/.

22. US Bureau of Labor Statistics, "Labor Force Participation Rate," FRED, Federal Reserve Bank of St. Louis, https://fred.stlouisfed.org/series/CIVPART; US Bureau of Labor Statistics, "Labor Force Participation Rate—25–54 Yrs.," FRED, Federal Reserve Bank of St. Louis, https://fred.stlouisfed.org/series/LNS11300060; https://data.oecd.org/emp/employment-rate-by-age-group.htm#indicator-chart.

23. In fact, the economist Adam Hersh and I found that the cost of insufficient US fiscal policy following the 2008 crisis cost the nation millions of jobs, and at least $8.2 trillion in GDP when you add up the damages from 2010 to 2019. Adam Hersh and Mark Paul, "Room to Run: America Has Ample Fiscal Space—And Should Use It to Tackle Pressing Economic and Climate Challenges," Groundwork Collaborative, April 2021, https://groundworkcollaborative.org/wp-content/uploads/2021/04/GroundworkCollaborative_RoomToRun.pdf.

24. Sushant Acharya, Julian Bengui, Keshav Dogra, and Shu Lin Wee, "Slow Recoveries and Unemployment Traps: Monetary Policy in a Time of Hysteresis," Staff Report, No. 831, Federal Reserve Bank of New York, 2016, https://www.newyorkfed.org/medialibrary/media/research/staff_reports/sr831.pdf.

25. Indeed, the vast bulk of inflation above the core 2% target can be attributed to energy prices, which are global and greatly influenced by geopolitical events such as the war in Ukraine, and used and new cars. This is different from widespread inflation, which would be indicative of an economy that was overheating; instead, inflation was largely a phenomenon of very specific pricing problems arising from supply chain bottlenecks and international conflict, neither of which would be eased by an increase in rates set by the Fed.

26. Paul Krugman, "Inflation Is about to Come Down—but Don't Get Too Excited," *New York Times*, April 12, 2022, https://www.nytimes.com/2022/04/12/opinion/inflation-consumer-prices.html.

27. As the economist Isabella Webber has argued, price controls have historically been thought of as a crucial tool to manage the economy and were even supported in a strongly worded letter to the *New York Times* in 1946 by leading economists of the era. Isabella Webber, "Could Strategic Price Controls Help Fight Inflation?," *The Guardian*, December 29, 2021, https://www.theguardian.com/business/comment isfree/2021/dec/29/inflation-price-controls-time-we-use-it.

28. For more on price controls, see Todd Tucker, "Price Controls: How the US Has Used Them and How They Can Help Shape Industry," Roosevelt Institute Issue Brief, November 2021, https://rooseveltinstitute.org/wp-content/uploads/2021/11/RI _Industrial-Policy-Price-Controls_Brief-202111.pdf; John Kenneth Galbraith, *A Theory of Price Control* (Cambridge, MA: Harvard University Press, 1980).

29. "Policy Basics: Where Do Our Federal Tax Dollars Go?," Center on Budget and Policy Priorities, April 9, 2020, https://www.cbpp.org/research/federal-budget /where-do-our-federal-tax-dollars-go .

30. Congressional Budget Office, "Budgetary Effects of H.R. 3, the Elijah E. Cummings Lower Drug Costs Now Act," December 10, 2019, https://www.cbo.gov/system /files/2019-12/hr3_complete.pdf.

31. Or less, as the case may be, if people were to decide to reduce work hours (as the United States did when it led the world in creating the forty-hour workweek and as other nations like Finland and France have done).

32. For a concise summary of financing an expansion of the public sector, see J. W. Mason, "Fiscal Rules for the 21st Century: How to Pay for the Public Sector," Roosevelt Institute, March 27, 2019.

33. To help address the issue of tax havens, an agreement was reached among the G7 nations in June 2021 to implement a global minimum corporate tax. https://www .nytimes.com/2021/06/05/us/politics/g7-global-minimum-tax.html.

34. https://stats.oecd.org/Index.aspx?DataSetCode=REV.

35. Mark Paul, David Rosnick, and Emily Stephens, "Vox's Tax Calculator Is Wildly Misleading—So We Made a Better One," April 6, 2016, https://www.thenation.com /article/archive/voxs-tax-calculator-is-wildly-misleading-so-we-made-a-better-one/.

36. Ronald Reagan, news conference, August 12, 1986, https://www.reaganfoundation .org/ronald-reagan/reagan-quotes-speeches/news-conference-1/.

37. Robert Pollin, James Heintz, and Thomas Herndon, "The Revenue Potential of a Financial Transaction Tax for US Financial Markets," *International Review of Applied Economics* 32, no. 6 (2018): 772–806.

38. Emmanuel Saez and Gabriel Zucman, *The Triumph of Injustice: How the Rich Dodge Taxes and How to Make Them Pay* (New York: Norton, 2022), https://wwnorton.com /books/the-triumph-of-injustice.

39. Tax Foundation, "Federal Individual Income Tax Rates History," https://files.tax foundation.org/legacy/docs/fed_individual_rate_history_adjusted.pdf.

40. Elliot Smilowitz, "Sanders: I'm 'Not That Much of a Socialist' Compared to Eisen-hower," Text, *The Hill*, November 14, 2015, https://thehill.com/blogs/ballot-box /dem-primaries/260186-sanders-im-not-that-much-of-a-socialist-compared-to -eisenhower.

41. Veronica Stracqualursi, "Ocasio-Cortez Suggests 70% Tax for Wealthy to Fund Climate Change Plan," CNN, January 4, 2019, https://www.cnn.com/2019/01/04 /politics/alexandria-ocasio-cortez-tax-climate-change-plan/index.html.

42. Aaron Rupar, "The Conservative Response to Ocasio-Cortez's Tax Proposal Has Been Embarrassingly Deceptive," *Vox*, January 7, 2019, https://www.vox.com

/policy-and-politics/2019/1/7/18171803/ocasio-cortez-70-percent-marginal-tax
-rate-scalise-norquist-spin.

43.   https://www.vox.com/2021/10/15/22723457/build-back-better-poll-democrats
-bill-infrastructure-taxes.

44.   Peter A. Diamond and Emmanuel Saez, "The Case for a Progressive Tax: From
Basic Research to Policy Recommendations," *SSRN Electronic Journal*, 2011, doi:
10.2139/ssrn.1915957; Thomas Piketty, Emmanuel Saez, and Stefanie Stantcheva,
"Optimal Taxation of Top Labor Incomes: A Tale of Three Elasticities," *American
Economic Journal: Economic Policy* 6, no. 1 (February 1, 2014): 230–71, doi:10.1257
/pol.6.1.230.

45.   Franklin D. Roosevelt, "Message to Congress on an Economic Stabilization Program," April 27, 1942, https://www.presidency.ucsb.edu/documents/message
-congress-economic-stabilization-program.

46.   Atra Taylor, "Idea: Create a Maximum Wage," https://politico.com/interactives
/2019/how-to-fix-politics-in-america/inequality/create-a-maximum-wage/.

47.   Emmanuel Saez and Gabriel Zucman, *The Triumph of Injustice*.

48.   "John Maynard Keynes: How Much Does Finance Matter?," *Grasping Reality by
Brad DeLong*, https://www.bradford-delong.com/2020/05/john-maynard-keynes
-how-much-does-finance-matter.html.

Conclusion

1.   Political and civil rights have come under increasing attack in recent, culminating
in the repeal of crucial freedoms, including the overturning of Roe V. Wade by the
US Supreme Court.

2.   Mike Konczal, "Citizen Coupon," *Dissent*, December 12, 2012, https://www.dissent
magazine.org/online_articles/citizen-coupon.

3.   Joe Deaux, Matthew Boesler, and Katia Dmitrieva, "Fattest Profits Since 1950
Debunk Wage-Inflation Story of CEOs," Bloomberg, November 30, 2021, https://
www.bloomberg.com/news/articles/2021-11-30/fattest-profits-since-1950-debunk
-inflation-story-spun-by-ceos.

4.   Democratic Socialists of American (DSA), "DSA Political Platform,"https://www
.dsausa.org/dsa-political-platform-from-2021-convention/.

Index

Adams, John, 154
Adams, Samuel, 51
Advanced Research Projects Agency
    (ARPA), 218
AFDC (Aid to Families with Dependent
    Children), 36, 192
Affordable Care Act. *See* Patient
    Protection and Affordable Care Act
AFL-CIO, 100–101
aggregate demand, 55–56, 125, 237
Agrarian Justice (Paine), 78–79, 195
Agricultural Adjustment Act, 88, 115
Aid to Families with Dependent Children
    (AFDC), 36, 192
Airline Deregulation Act, 33
Alaska Permanent Fund, 220
alcohol, 20, 244
Allais, Maurice, 62
Alston, Philip, 1–3, 5
amendments: Bill of Rights, 2 (*see also* Bill
    of Rights); Fifteenth, 84; Fourteenth,
    84, 154; legal issues and (*see under*
    legal issues); Nineteenth, 249;
    Reagan and, 48; Thirteenth, 84; US
    Constitution and, 2, 48, 51, 68, 76, 84,
    154, 249
American Crisis papers, 77
American dream: Black people and, 31;
    death of, 28–32; hard work and, 29;
    preferences of, 30; scarcity and, 24;
    wealth and (*see under* wealth)
American Dream Is Not Dead, The (Strain),
    29–30

American Enterprise Institute, 29–30
American Medical Association, 177
American Mortgage, 140
American School, 79–80
American Trends Panel Survey, 37
Anderson, John B., 69
Anti-Federalists, 52
antitrust enforcement, 52
Ariely, Dan, 37
austerity: budget issues and, 229, 239,
    301n17; healthy environment and,
    209, 212, 217
Austin, TX, 16

Baker, Dean, 31
balanced budgets, 48, 50, 69, 229
Ball, Robert, 178
bancor, 299n1
bankruptcy, 115, 180, 184, 229, 235
Baradaran, Mehrsa, 203–4
Barber, William, II, 107
basic income, 9–10; Biden and, 191;
    Black people and, 191, 202, 204;
    budget issues and, 243; CARES Act
    and, 190, 202; children and, 191–
    94, 197–201; citizenship and, 195,
    197; conservatives and, 190, 196;
    COVID-19 pandemic and, 189;
    Democrats and, 192, 197, 200, 229, 235,
    246; economic rights and, 195–201,
    253; electricity and, 200; eligibility for,
    197–98; floors and, 194, 203; food and,
    190, 195–96, 200; Friedman and, 199;

basic income (*cont.*)
GDP and, 190; Great Depression and, 189; homelessness and, 194; housing and, 193–94, 198–200; inequality and, 202; insurance and, 190, 192, 202–3; interest rates and, 202; King on, 189; labor and, 189, 193–96, 200; Medicare and, 197; mortgages and, 190, 204; New Deal and, 192; Nixon and, 195–96; Paine and, 195; phase-out of, 196, 198–99, 294n26; poverty and, 189–99, 204, 292n3, 293n13; profit and, 203; public good and, 197, 199; racial issues and, 193; reform and, 192–96, 292n4; Republicans and, 195; right amount of, 197; Roosevelt and, 192; scarcity and, 194; SNAP and, 190–91, 193; Social Security and, 192–93, 197, 200; taxes and, 191–93, 196–201; timing for, 200–201; unemployment and, 189–96, 292n4; US Congress and, 191–92, 195, 203; wealth and, 193, 204; welfare and, 192–93, 196, 199; well-being state and, 191–92, 197, 204; women and, 194

Bell, Robert, 77
Berlin, Isaiah, 3
Bernanke, Ben, 40
Bernstein, Jared, 124
Beveridge, William, 58, 275n6
Bezos, Jeff, 17–18
Biden, Joe: basic income and, 191; budget issues and, 229; Build Back Better and, 229; Council of Economic Advisers, 124; economic rights and, 254; education and, 159; health care and, 187–88; housing and, 140, 147; interest rates and, 159; right to work and, 124–25, 130
Bill of Rights, 1, 249; capitalism and, 73; economic, 4, 10–11, 41, 76 (*see also* economic bill of rights); influence of, 2; Jefferson and, 4, 48, 51, 76–77, 80; Roosevelt and, 4, 10, 90
Black Belt, 82
Black Lives Matter, 106–7, 255
Blackmon, Douglas A., 28
Black people: access to credit and, 31; American dream and, 31; basic income and, 191, 202, 204; capitalism and, 66; civil rights and, 66 (*see also* civil

rights); COVID-19 pandemic and, 41; Dixiecrats and, 95, 97, 116; earnings gap and, 32, 39, 158; economic rights and (*see under* economic rights); education and (*see under* education); Emancipation Proclamation, 52; Executive Order 8802 and, 100; Freedmen's Bureau Act, 83; Freedom Budget and, 75, 101–4; Friedman and, 66; getting ahead and, 31; GI Bill, 164; Great Society and, 28; health care and, 181; healthy environment and, 209; housing and, 16, 22, 136; integration and, 22, 83, 156–57; Jim Crow rule and, 84, 95–97, 101, 156; Johnson and, 28; Lincoln and, 52, 83; lynching of, 95–96; mobility and, 31–32; mortality gap and, 21, 181; NAACP, 156; right to banking and, 202; right to work and, 121, 124, 131, 275n13; Roosevelt and, 28; southern segregationists and, 28, 95, 273n40; Special Field Orders No. 15 and, 82; unemployment and, 31, 124
Blanchard, Olivier, 232
Booth, John Wilkes, 83
Bowman, Jamaal, 109
Boyce, James K., 42
Bretton Woods, 35, 299n1
Brinkley, Alan, 97
British National Health Service, 58
Brotherhood of the Sleeping Car Porters (BSCP), 99–100
budget issues: aggregate demand and, 55–56, 125, 237; austerity and, 229, 239, 301n17; balanced budgets, 48, 50, 69, 229; Biden and, 229; Build Back Better and, 229; ceilings and, 246; citizenship and, 228, 242, 246; conservatives and, 228, 243; constraints, 235–42; COVID-19 pandemic, 231; deficits, 25, 33, 50, 54, 56, 89, 163, 228–36, 242, 264n28, 300nn2–4; democracy and, 246, 250, 255; economic bill of rights and, 10, 227–35, 239, 241–44, 299n1; economic expansion, 18, 231; education and, 243; electricity and, 227, 236, 240; Federal Reserve and, 229–34, 237, 301n12, 301n14; floors and, 241, 246; food and, 236; Freedom Budget and,

75, 101–4; Friedman and, 69, 228–29; full employment and, 18, 238; GDP, 228, 234, 243, 246; government debt, 10, 228–35, 300n2; Great Depression and, 229; growth, 230–38; health care, 235–36; housing, 227, 230–32, 235–36, 239–42; hysteresis, 123, 237; inequality, 231, 235, 240, 244; inflation, 238–41, 302n25; interest rates, 228–29, 232–34, 238; Keynes and, 10, 227, 235, 247–48; 299n1; labor and, 231, 237; liberals and, 238; Medicare and, 227, 240–41; mortgages, 232–33; neoliberalism and, 235, 238–39; Nixon and, 240; PAYGO rule, 229; pollution and, 241, 246; poverty, 249, 255; price controls, 238–41, 303n27; public good and, 229; reallocation, 241–42; real resources, 235–42; reform and, 246; Republicans and, 229–30, 242, 245; resource approach to, 227–28; revenue, 82, 171, 186, 215, 220, 229–30, 246–47; Roosevelt and, 246–47; Sanders and, 245–47; socialism and, 245, 250; Social Security, 229; student debt, 243; subsidies and, 241; supply and, 238–40, 302n25; surpluses, 115, 231; taxes, 227–35, 238–48; Trump and, 235; unemployment and, 231, 237–38, 300n3, 301n17; US Congress and, 16, 18, 27, 122, 171, 185, 188, 191, 229–31, 236–37, 241, 275n13, 291n36, 300n8; wealth and, 229–31, 243–47; welfare, 227; well-being state and, 243; World War II era and, 234, 240, 245, 247

Build Back Better, 229
Bureau of Labor Statistics (BLS), 118, 158, 275n7
Bush, Cori, 109
Bush, George H. W., 71
Bush, George W., 147
business cycles, 125
Buttigieg, Pete, 166
Byrd amendment, 281n19

Caldwell, Tiana, 135–36, 140
Canada, 179–85
cancer, 135
capital gains, 244–46

Capital in the Twenty-First Century (Piketty), 38
capitalism: affluence and, 16, 23–28, 201; Black people and, 66; children and, 52, 70; citizenship and, 52, 58; conservatives and, 49, 57–61, 67–70, 268nn21–22; Declaration of Independence and, 51, 68; deficits and, 50, 54, 56; democracy and, 52, 54, 62, 67; Democrats and, 70–73, 84, 96–97, 104–7; economic bill of rights and, 48, 69, 73; fascism and, 53, 57–59; Founders and, 47, 51–52, 72–73; free market and, 49, 51, 53–54, 58, 60, 65–68; full employment and, 56–58, 71; golden age of, 23–24, 28, 34, 54; Great Depression and, 53, 63; Great Financial Crisis of 2008 (*see* Great Financial Crisis of 2008); Great Society and, 51, 67, 71; growth and, 49, 55, 69–72; Hamilton and, 51; Hayek and, 57–66, 69, 71; homelessness and, 53; inequality and, 44–46, 71; inflation and, 70, 94; labor and, 30, 40, 48, 53, 55, 68–69, 117, 121, 123, 231; liberals and, 54–58, 63–67, 71; Medicare and, 66; negative freedom and, 51–53, 58–59, 65–66, 72–73; neoliberalism and, 44–46, 49, 51–53, 61–65, 69–73, 105–6, 250, 269n24; New Deal and, 48, 51, 53–59, 63, 66–67, 71; Nixon and, 71; political economy and, 53, 56, 62; positive freedom and, 58, 73, 267n3; poverty and, 55, 59, 66; price controls and, 64, 68; property and, 52–61, 64; racial issues and, 24, 28; reform and, 53, 56; Republicans and, 68–71, 80, 83–85, 105; Roosevelt and, 48, 53, 56–58, 63, 73, 268n9; saving, 87–88; socialism and, 53–54, 57–63, 66, 268n21; as solving social problems, 24; taxes and, 49–52, 56, 64–71; Trump and, 71; unemployment and, 55–56, 59, 65, 70; unions and, 48; US Congress and, 48–51, 68–70; US Constitution and, 48, 51, 68; wealth and, 56; welfare and, 58–59, 65, 67; World War II era and, 23
Capitalism and Freedom (Friedman), 47, 65–68

carbon: cap for, 220–21; climate issues and (*see under* climate issues); decarbonization (*see* decarbonization); Green New Deal and, 9, 210, 213–17, 220, 222, 298n33; pricing of, 217–21, 298n40; tax on, 43, 210, 216, 220

CARES Act, 190, 202

Carson, Rachel, 207

Carter, Jimmy, 33, 69

Carter, Zach, 54

Case, Anne, 20–21

CCC: Civilian Conservation Corps (*see* Civilian Conservation Corps [CCC]); "new" (Civilian Climate Corps), 130–31, 278n40

ceilings: budget issues and, 246; economic rights and, 86–87; health care and, 188; housing and, 5, 146; inequality and, 10; labor and, 5, 124

Center for Infectious Disease Modeling and Analysis, 184

Center on Poverty and Social Policy, 198

Centers for Medicare and Medicaid Services (CMS), 179

"Century of the Common Man" (Wallace), 97

Charles River, 208

Cheek, Cord, 96

Chicago school of economics, 146

child labor, 53, 69, 155, 175–76

children: AFDC, 36, 192; basic income and, 191–94, 197–201; capitalism and, 52, 70; childcare, 15–16, 44, 71, 88n56, 118, 131, 171, 236, 239; climate issues and, 42; Comprehensive Child Development Act, 171; economic rights and, 78, 88, 103; education and (*see under* education); Elementary and Secondary Education Act and, 27; food and, 23, 36, 88; health care and, 180–82; healthy environment and, 208; homelessness and, 17, 135–36, 194; housing and, 135–37, 148; old-age benefits and, 192; poverty and, 5, 191, 194, 197–98; as public good, 172, 181, 197, 199, 288n56; TANF, 36

child tax credit (CTC), 191, 198, 200

citizenship: basic income and, 195, 197; budget issues and, 228, 242, 246;

capitalism and, 52, 58; economic rights and (*see under* economic rights); education and, 154, 157, 162; healthy environment and, 19, 207; human rights and, 1; right to work and, 114–15

Civilian Climate Corps, 130–31, 278n40

Civilian Conservation Corps (CCC), 25, 31, 88, 126, 129, 277n29, 278n41

civil rights: Bill of Rights, 1–2, 41, 73, 76, 90, 249; economic rights and (*see under* economic rights); Freedom Budget and, 75, 101–4; Jim Crow rule and, 84, 95–97, 101, 156; New Deal and, 6, 10, 28, 51, 101, 216, 249, 253; *Roe v. Wade*, 304n1

Civil Rights Act, 27, 32, 99, 249, 271n10

Civil Works Administration (CWA), 25, 114–16, 121, 126, 129

Civil Works Service, 115

Clean Air Act, 71, 208

Clean Water Act, 208

climate issues, 39; carbon, 9, 41–43, 125, 141–42, 206, 209–22, 227, 236, 297n23, 297n30, 298n40; children and, 42; Civilian Climate Corps and, 130–31, 278n40; cold winters, 136; drought, 42; economic rights and, 109; education and, 163; fossil fuels, 41, 209–10, 215, 219, 221, 241, 297n30, 299n46; GHGs, 210, 218, 221; global warming (*see* global warming); healthy environment and, 9, 205, 208–22, 297n24, 297n29, 299n46; hurricanes and, 213; inequality and, 41–43; IPCC, 209, 214, 297n23; Keynes and, 221–22; Paris Climate Accords, 212–14; pollution (*see* pollution); rapid mobilization against, 221–22; seriously addressing, 255; smog, 206, 208; threat multipliers and, 42; wildfires, 41–42, 208, 213

Clinton, Bill, 63, 71, 137, 177, 192, 231

Clinton, Hillary, 166

coal, 2, 215, 219

Cohen, Daniel Aldana, 144

Cohen, Wilbur, 167

Colm, Gerhard, 101

Color of Law, The (Rothstein), 22

Columbia University, 198

Committee on Economic Security, 176

"Common Sense" (Paine), 77–79
Commonwealth Club Address, 85
communism, 61, 72
Community Action Agencies, 27
Comprehensive Child Development Act, 171
Compromise of 1877, 84
Confederacy, 84
Congressional Budget Office (CBO): funding issues, 18, 122, 185, 188, 236–37, 275n13, 291n36, 300n8; health care and, 185, 188, 291n36; right to work and, 122, 275n13
conservatives, 27; American dream and, 28–32; American Enterprise Institute and, 29–30; basic income and, 190, 196; budget issues and, 228, 243; capitalism and (see under capitalism); economic rights and, 97, 270n9; education and, 162–66; health care and, 291n36; housing and, 282n42; King and, 274n59; right to work and, 116, 118, 127, 133, 274n59; unions and, 7, 35, 116
Constitutional Convention, 51
Consumer Financial Protection Bureau (CFPB), 203
cost of living, 16
Council of Economic Advisers, 19, 124, 147
COVID-19 pandemic: basic income and, 189; Black people and, 41; budget issues and, 231; deaths from, 20, 40–41, 189, 290n25; economy before, 18, 20; education and, 160; food and, 23, 279n44; Great Reshuffling and, 30; health care and, 181; increased wealth from, 17–18; inequality and, 40–41; racial issues and, 32; right to work and, 117–23, 275n9, 279n44; supply and, 239; unemployment and (see under unemployment); vaccines and, 40, 253
Cowen, Tyler, 30
credit cards, 18, 38, 200–201, 294n31, 295n32
Cuyahoga River, 206
CWA. See Civil Works Administration (CWA)

Darity, William, Jr., 31–32, 82, 127
DDT, 207
Deaton, Angus, 20–21
Debs, Eugene, 53
decarbonization: climate issues and, 9, 41, 141, 210–17, 221–22, 297n23, 298n33; Green New Deal and, 9, 213–17; healthy environment and, 210–17, 221–22, 297n23, 298n33
Declaration of Independence: capitalism and, 51, 68; economic rights and, 77, 79, 82; Jefferson and, 4, 51, 77; "life, liberty, and the pursuit of happiness," 4, 19, 48, 76, 85, 117, 249, 255, 270n9; negative freedoms and, 2
deficits: budget issues and (see under budget issues); capitalism and, 50, 54, 56; economic rights and, 89; education and, 163; government debt and, 10, 228–34, 300n2; New Deal and, 25, 56, 89, 264n28; spending and, 33, 89, 228–31, 234–35, 242, 264n28; surplus and, 115, 231
demand: affluence illusion and, 23–25, 28; aggregate, 55–56, 125, 237; budget issues and, 229–30, 233–40; carbon products and, 220; education and, 153–55, 157; healthy environment and, 220, 222; housing and, 18, 146, 282n35; public goods and, 153–54; right to work and, 122, 125, 132
democracy: budget issues and, 246, 250, 255; capitalism and, 52, 54, 62, 67; Dewey on, 43; economic rights and (see under economic rights); education and, 154, 162; Founders and, 43; inequality and, 10, 44, 255; in the balance, 43–44; protecting, 10; Reconstruction and, 154; right to work and, 113; wealth and, 5, 44, 137, 229, 246
Democratic Socialists, 7, 26, 107–8, 214, 254–55
Democrats: basic income and, 192, 197, 200; budget issues and, 229, 235, 246; capitalism and (see under capitalism); conservative, 70, 97, 116; education and, 11, 167; Eighty-Ninth Congress and, 27; free college and, 11; full

Democrats (*cont.*)
  employment and, 7; health care and,
    178; healthy environment and, 213-14;
    liberal, 27; northern, 28; right to work
    and, 7, 116, 130, 133. *See also specific
    officials*
Department of Housing and Urban
  Development, 16
Department of Labor, 124, 127, 175, 196
depression, 183
deregulation: airlines, 33; Bill Clinton and,
    71; neoliberalism and, 6, 34, 37, 71;
    Reagan and, 6, 33-34, 68
Desmond, Matthew, 17
developmentalist state, 79-80, 82, 270n8
Dewey, John, 43
Diamond, Peter, 245
diplomas, 155-56
"Dirty Water" (Standells), 208
disabled people, 90, 176, 178, 192-94
discrimination, 27, 32, 99-100, 108, 129,
    169, 277n29
disposable income, 242
Dixiecrats, 95, 97, 116
Donahoe Act, 164-65
"Double V," 96
Douglass, Frederick, 82
Dow Jones Industrial Average, 18
Dream Defenders, 107
drought, 42
drugs, 2, 20, 66, 185, 241
Du Bois, W. E. B., 28, 39, 83, 264
DuPont, 207

Earned Income Tax Credit (EITC), 128,
    168, 193, 200
earnings gap, 32, 39, 158
Earth Day, 207-8
Eccles, Marriner, 57
economic bill of rights: budget issues and
    (*see under* budget issues); capitalism
    and, 48, 69, 73; Democrats and, 11;
    education and, 166; effects of, 251-55;
    financing, 10; health care and, 177;
    King and, 4, 104; national debate on,
    251; Reagan and, 48, 69; reform and,
    11; Roosevelt and, 4, 48, 76-77, 80, 91-
    97, 102, 104, 108-9, 177, 273n34
economic expansion, 18, 231

Economic Opportunity Act, 27
Economic Policy Institute, 33
economic rights: basic income and, 195-
    201, 253; Biden and, 254; Black people
    and, 82-84, 93-107, 249, 255, 271n10;
    ceilings and, 86-87; children and, 78,
    88, 103; citizenship and, 2, 4, 52, 58, 75-
    81, 84, 87, 96, 106, 271n10; civil rights
    and, 4-7, 98-104, 270n8, 273n40;
    climate issues and, 109; conservatives
    and, 97, 270n9; Declaration of
    Independence and, 77, 79, 82; deficits
    and, 89; democracy and, 77-78, 86-91,
    94, 97; economic bill of rights and, 48,
    69, 73 (*see also* economic bill of rights);
    education and, 251; fascism and, 10,
    76-77, 90-91, 94, 96; floors and,
    86-87; food and, 85, 88, 91-92, 97,
    102, 104, 107; Founders and, 6, 85, 98,
    249, 257; four freedoms and, 91-97;
    free college and, 255; Freedom Budget
    and, 75, 101-4; free market and, 79,
    85-86, 88, 95, 103-5, 270n9; Friedman
    and, 250; full employment and, 89, 94,
    101-2, 107; Great Depression and, 84,
    89, 93; Great Financial Crisis of 2008
    and, 253; Great Society and, 99, 103;
    Green New Deal and, 222; growth and,
    77-80, 91-92, 102, 105, 109; Hamilton
    and, 77-80, 84, 101, 270n8; Hayek
    and, 86, 250-51; housing and, 85, 101,
    104, 107-8, 251, 255; human rights and,
    108; inequality and, 8, 76-79, 86-87,
    95, 99, 102, 105, 255; insurance and,
    78, 87, 252, 254; Jefferson and, 76-77,
    80, 270nn8-9; King and, 77; labor
    and, 80, 88, 94, 100, 103, 105; liberals
    and, 90, 106; living wage and, 7, 78,
    89, 101, 107-8; mobility and, 28-32, 35,
    70, 146; negative freedom and, 7, 85,
    90; New Deal and, 6, 76, 80, 84-91,
    95-97, 101, 104-5, 249, 253, 273n34,
    273n40; Nixon and, 105; Paine and,
    77-80, 84; political economy and,
    250; positive freedom and, 3, 6, 76;
    poverty and, 76-79, 94, 99, 101-3,
    107, 109; profit and, 106, 253; property
    and, 83, 270n9; racial issues and,
    93, 99, 106-8; Radical Republicans

and, 81–84; reform and, 83, 85, 88, 93, 95, 98-101, 105; reviving, 104–9; Roosevelt and, 75–80, 84–109, 272n21, 273n24, 273n34; Sanders and, 104–9; scarcity and, 249; socialism and, 98, 107-8; Social Security and, 76, 79, 87; subsidies and, 250; supply and, 253; taxes and, 78, 89, 105, 109; Trump and, 254; unemployment and, 84, 87–92, 99, 102, 104–5, 109; unions and, 76, 88–89, 100, 107, 252; US Congress and, 76, 81–84, 87–90, 94, 105, 107; US Constitution and, 75–76, 79, 84; wealth and, 85–86, 99, 107; welfare and, 79–80, 92, 104, 108–9; well-being state and, 78, 87, 252, 257; World War II era and, 76, 84, 97

Edin, Kathryn J., 192–93

education: Adams and, 154; Biden and, 159; Black people and, 156–57, 161, 164, 168–69; BLS, 158; budget issues and, 243; children and, 22, 27, 42, 156, 167, 171–72, 288n56; citizenship and, 154, 157, 162; climate issues and, 163; Comprehensive Child Development Act, 171; conservatives and, 162–66; COVID-19 pandemic and, 160; deficits and, 163; demand and, 153–55, 157; democracy and, 154, 162; Democrats and, 11, 167; diplomas, 155–56; Donahoe Act, 164–65; earnings gap and, 158; economic bill of rights and, 166; economic rights and, 251; Elementary and Secondary Education Act, 27; Federal Reserve and, 158; food and, 171, 285n23; Fourteenth Amendment, 154; Franklin and, 173; free college and, 8, 10–11, 158, 161–71, 227, 255; Freedom Budget and, 101–4; Friedman and, 162; GED, 165; GI Bill, 164; Great Society and, 167; growth and, 159, 162, 170, 172; high school, 8, 32, 62, 154–58, 161, 164–65, 168; homelessness and, 167; human rights and, 154; inequality and, 162–63, 169; inflation and, 170; integration and, 156–57; interest rates and, 159; Jefferson and, 154; Johnson and, 164; Keynes and, 154;

labor and, 155–58, 160, 163; liberals and, 164; means-tested programs, 168; middle class and, 160; Morrill Act, 81–82; NAACP and, 156; National Center for Education Statistics, 159; neoliberalism and, 161, 172; New Deal and, 167; Paine and, 78; profit and, 160–61; as public good, 153–58, 161–63, 169–72; racial issues and, 154–57, 284n11; reform and, 155, 163; Republicans and, 165; revenue and, 82, 171; right to college, 161–71; right to early childhood, 171–73; Roosevelt and, 164; Sanders and, 163; student debt and, 11, 21, 38, 158–61, 169–70, 243, 276n16, 287n47; subsidies and, 162, 168, 171; supply and, 153–54, 166; taxes and, 155, 161, 163, 166–68, 171; Trump and, 166; tuition costs and, 131, 160–61, 164–70, 285n23; unemployment and, 158; US Congress and, 171; US Constitution and, 154; wealth and, 153–59, 167–71; welfare and, 173; well-being state and, 163; women and, 161, 171

EEOC (Equal Employment Opportunity Commission), 66

Eisenhower, Dwight, 71

EITC. *See* Earned Income Tax Credit (EITC)

electricity: basic income and, 200; budget issues and, 227, 236, 240; healthy environment and, 42, 210, 217–21; housing and, 150, 156; regulated rates of, 150

electric vehicles, 15, 217–18, 227

Elementary and Secondary Education Act, 27

Emergency Banking Act, 87

emphysema, 206

"End of Laissez-Faire, The" (Keynes), 54

"End of the New Deal, The" (Hart), 105

Environmental Protection Agency (EPA), 66, 70–71, 208-9, 211

Equal Employment Opportunity Commission (EEOC), 66

Evicted: Poverty and Profit in the American City (Desmond), 17

Eviction Lab, 17

evictions, 17, 135
Executive Order 6420B, 114

Fair Employment Practice Committee,
    100
Fannie Mae, 139–40
fascism: capitalism and, 53, 57–59;
    economic rights and (*see under*
    economic rights); Hoover and, 53;
    modern rise of, 254–55
Federal Deposit Insurance Corporation
    (FDIC), 202
Federal Emergency Relief Act, 87–88
Federal Emergency Relief
    Administration, 114
Federal Home Loan Bank (FHLB) Act, 138
Federal Housing Authority, 139
Federal Labor Relations Authority, 34
Federal Reserve, 34, 211; Bernanke, 40;
    budget issues and (*see under* budget
    issues); capacity utilization and, 123;
    as central planer, 232–33; education
    and, 158; FOMC statement, 123;
    Greenspan, 105; health care and, 180;
    housing and, 138; interest rates and
    (*see under* interest rates); Powell, 120,
    123; right to work and (*see under* right
    to work); Volcker, 34
Federal Water and Pollution Control Act,
    208
FHLB (Federal Home Loan Bank) Act, 138
FICO credit scores, 18
Fight for $15, 106
Finland, 144
Flint, MI, 209
floors: basic income and, 194, 203; budget
    issues and, 241, 246; economic rights
    and, 86–87; health care and, 188;
    housing and, 5, 144–46; labor and, 5,
    116, 129, 194; right to work and, 5, 116,
    129
food: AFDC and, 36, 192; basic income
    and, 190, 195–96, 200; budget issues
    and, 236; children and, 23, 36, 88; cost
    of, 16, 22–23, 171, 255, 276n22, 285n23;
    COVID-19 pandemic and, 23, 279n44;
    dictatorships and, 76; economic rights
    and (*see under* economic rights);
    education and, 171, 285n23; Freedom

Budget and, 101; healthy environment
    and, 206–8, 214; housing and, 136;
    insecurity in, 2, 18, 22–23, 250; laissez-
    faire and, 85; means-tested programs
    and, 168; Poor People's Campaign
    and, 103; quality, 45; right to work and,
    115, 117, 126; Roosevelt and, 24, 26;
    SNAP and, 190–91, 193
Food and Drug Administration (FDA), 66
Food Stamp Act, 27
food stamps, 7, 29, 36, 168, 190, 196, 250
Ford, Gerald, 69
fossil fuels: climate issues and (*see under*
    climate issues); coal, 2, 215, 219;
    revenue from, 215
Foundation for Economic Education,
    161–62
Founders: Alston report and, 2; capitalism
    and (*see under* capitalism); democracy
    and, 43; economic rights and (*see
    under* economic rights); Locke and, 51
four freedoms: economic rights and,
    91–97; freedom from fear, 91; freedom
    from want, 91; freedom of religion,
    91; freedom of speech, 91; Moyn and,
    273n34; Roosevelt and, 6, 91–97, 105,
    273n34
Francis (pope), 205
Franklin, Benjamin, 173
free college: Buttigieg on, 166; Hillary
    Clinton on, 166; economic rights
    and, 255; education and (*see under*
    education); federal-to-state
    match program and, 166; healthy
    environment and, 227; means-tested
    programs, 168; Pell grants and, 166
Freedmen's Bureau Act, 83
Freedom Budget, 75, 101–4
"Freedom Budget" for All Americans, A
    (A. Philip Randolph Institute), 101
Freedom Papers (Dream Defenders), 107
freedom to work, 48–49
free market: capitalism and (*see under*
    capitalism); economic rights and (*see
    under* economic rights); Friedman
    and, 6, 63–72, 146, 211, 250; Greenspan
    and, 105; growth and, 37, 49, 70, 105,
    211; Hayek and, 6, 58–60, 63, 65, 71,
    250; housing and, 145–46; labor and, 6,

53, 68, 250; laissez-faire and, 53; New Deal and, 88–89; as synonymous with freedom, 6, 250, 261n7
Free to Choose (M. Friedman and R. Friedman), 68
free will, 4
French Revolution, 78
Friedman, Gerald, 180–81
Friedman, Milton: background of, 62–63; basic income and, 199; budget issues and, 69, 228–29; *Capitalism and Freedom*, 47, 65–68; compromise system of, 64; economic rights and, 250; education and, 162; free market and (*see under* free market); *Free to Choose*, 68; growth and, 69; Hayek and, 6, 45, 61–65, 69, 71, 250; health care and, 180–81; healthy environment and, 211; housing and, 146; John Bates Clarke Medal and, 65; Keynes and, 63; labor and, 72, 120; laissez-faire and, 63, 65–67; NAIRU and, 120; narrowness and, 66–67; neoliberalism and (*see under* neoliberalism); New Deal and, 63, 66–67, 71; Nobel Prize and, 62; Reagan and, 6, 63, 68–71, 269n34, 269n39; rent control and, 146; right to work and, 120; state provisioning and, 64; subsidies and, 64; wages and, 69; welfare and, 65
Friedman, Rose, 62, 68
"Friedman Debunked the Gospel of Keynes" (Pearlstein), 63
Fukuyama, Francis, 6
full employment: Beveridge on, 275n6; budget issues and, 18, 238; capitalism and, 56–58, 71; Democrats and, 7; economic rights and (*see under* economic rights); expanded public employment, 124–26; federal job guarantees and, 126–32; healthy environment and, 222; housing and, 151; industrial policy and, 253; Keynes on, 124; New Deal and, 25; right to work and (*see under* right to work); running a full-capacity economy, 122–24
Full Employment and Balanced Growth Act, 277n24, 278n35

Gabor, Daniel, 301n14
Galbraith, John Kenneth, 206
Gallup polls, 97, 157
GDP. *See* gross domestic product (GDP)
GED, 165
General Motors, 209
General Theory of Employment, Interest, and Money, The (Keynes), 56, 124
Georgetown University, 158
GHGs. *See* greenhouse gases (GHGs)
GI Bill, 164
Globalists (Slobodian), 62
global warming, 41, 211–13, 219, 241, 297n23
GND advocates, 297n30
Goldin, Claudia, 155
gold standard, 301n13
Goldwater, Barry, 27, 63, 67
Great Compression, 25–26, 32, 54, 264n29
Great Depression: basic income and, 189; budget issues and, 229; capitalism and, 53, 63; economic rights and, 84, 89, 93; housing and, 139; inequality and, 38; right to work and, 113–14, 129; Roosevelt and, 24–26, 53
Great Financial Crisis of 2008, 253; budget issues and, 231–32, 235, 239; education funding cuts and, 170; faith in market and, 105; right to work and, 122
Great Recession, 17, 19, 40, 117, 122–23
Great Reshuffling, 30
Great Society: Black people and, 28; capitalism and, 51, 67, 71; Civil Rights Act and, 27, 32, 99, 249, 271n10; economic rights and, 99, 103; education and, 167; healthy environment and, 296n13; Johnson and, 5, 27–28, 51, 67, 71, 99, 103, 167, 296n13; King and, 99; redistribution and, 5; Vietnam War and, 27
Green, T. H., 261n7
greenhouse gases (GHGs), 210, 218, 221
Green New Deal: carbon and (*see under* carbon); coal and, 215, 219; economic rights and, 222; healthy environment and (*see under* healthy environment); Jemez Principles and, 214–15; Markey and, 214, 216; Ocasio-Cortez and, 214, 216; Paris Climate Accords and,

Green New Deal (*cont.*)
213–14; Sunrise Movement and, 213, 255
Greenspan, Alan, 105
Gregory, David, 96
Griffith, Saul, 221
gross domestic product (GDP): basic income and, 190; budget issues and, 228, 234, 243, 246; future effects of, 123; growth of, 18, 92, 162; healthy environment and, 212, 217, 223; housing and, 179–80, 185; labor and, 35; limitations of as indicator, 6, 19; postwar, 32; redistribution of, 15; war mobilization and, 92
growth: aggregate demand and, 55–56, 125, 237; before COVID-19, 18; budget issues and, 230–38; capitalism and, 49, 55, 69–72; divergent patterns in, 36–37; economic expansion, 18, 231; economic rights and (*see under* economic rights); education and, 159, 162, 170, 172; equitable, 172, 250, 288n56; Freedom Budget and, 102; free market and, 37, 49, 70, 105, 211; Friedman and, 69; Full Employment and Balanced Growth Act, 278n35; GDP and, 18, 92, 162; government borrowing and, 301n17; great expansion and, 19, 84; healthy environment and, 207, 211–12; housing and, 148; hysteresis, 123, 237; inequality and, 32, 36, 40, 71, 105, 162, 231, 235; inflation and, 35; Keynes and, 55, 70, 72; labor and, 32, 34–35, 44–45, 55, 105, 121, 123, 237; National Commission on Technology, Automation, and Economic Progress and, 44–45; neoliberalism and, 35–37, 44, 49, 70–71, 105, 211; New Deal and, 25, 33, 35, 71, 80, 105; non-stop, 18; poverty and, 19, 25, 32, 43, 55, 77, 213; powers of, 44; reliant trust in, 32–37; right to work and, 121–23; taxes and, 32–37, 43, 49, 70–71, 105, 211, 230, 235; Trump and, 19; wages and, 19, 25, 32–33, 35, 40, 44, 55, 71, 92, 121, 123, 231; Washington Center for Equitable Growth and, 172, 288n56
Guterres, António, 41

Hamilton, Alexander: capitalism and, 51; central state and, 80; economic rights and, 77–80, 84, 101, 270n8; Jefferson and, 80; "means proper" and, 79–80; right to work and, 127; as sage of development, 79–80, 270n8
Hamilton, Darrick, 31, 265n47
Harlem, 26
Harrington, Michael, 26
Harris/HillTV poll, 133
Hart, Gary, 105
Harvard University, 209
Haslam, Bill, 165
Hayek, Friedrich: capitalism and, 57–66, 69, 71; economic rights and, 86, 250–51; free market and (*see under* free market); Friedman and, 6, 45, 61–65, 69, 71, 250; "High Road to Servitude" and, 58; Keynes and, 57–62, 86; laissez-faire and, 60, 63, 65; London School of Economics, 58; MPS and, 61–63; neoliberalism and, 6, 61–62, 65; Nobel Prize and, 62; personal freedom and, 58–59; Presidential Medal of Freedom and, 71; *The Road to Serfdom*, 47, 58–61, 64, 268n21
Hayes, Rutherford B., 84
Head Start, 66
health care: Biden and, 187–88; British National Health Service and, 58; budget issues and, 235–36; cancer and, 135; ceilings and, 188; children and, 180–82; conservatives and, 291n36; COVID-19 pandemic and, 181; Democrats and, 178; depression and, 183; economic bill of rights and, 177; Federal Reserve and, 180; Freedom Budget and, 101–4; Friedman and, 180–81; GDP and, 179–80, 185; housing and, 185–86; inequality and, 20–21; insurance and, 10, 29, 127, 150, 176–87, 215–16, 252, 254, 291n38; labor and, 175–77; life expectancy and, 20–21, 180–81; loss of meaning and, 20–21; Medicaid, 27, 66, 127, 172, 179, 181, 240; Medicare (*see* Medicare); medicine, 16, 185, 188, 235; middle class and, 186; mortality gap and, 21, 181; New Deal and, 175; Nixon and,

177–78; Obama and, 178; Patient Protection and Affordable Care Act, 178, 180, 188, 229, 254; Perkins and, 175–77, 188; pollution and, 41–42, 206–10, 220, 241, 246, 298n32; public good and, 182; Reagan and, 49; Republicans and, 10; revenue and, 186; Roosevelt and, 175–77, 184; skinny coverage and, 183; Social Security and, 176–78; subsidies and, 187; supply and, 10; taxes and, 186; unemployment and, 175–77, 183; universal, 9–10, 71, 128, 176–88, 222, 227, 255, 257, 291n38; US spending on, 179–80; vaccines and, 40, 253; wealth and, 180; welfare and, 58; well-being state and, 176–77

healthy environment: austerity and, 209, 212, 217; Black people and, 209; carbon and, 9, 41–43, 125, 141–42, 206, 209–22, 227, 236, 297n23, 297n30, 298n40; Carson on, 207; children and, 208; citizenship and, 19, 207; Civilian Climate Corps and, 130–31, 278n40; Clean Air Act, 71, 208; Clean Water Act, 208; climate issues and (*see under* climate issues); coal and, 2, 215, 219; demand and, 220, 222, 229–30, 233–40; Democrats and, 213–14; Earth Day and, 207–8; electricity and, 42, 210, 217–21; environmental dissonance and, 205–6; EPA, 66, 70–71, 208–9, 211; food and, 206–8, 214; fossil fuels, 41, 209–10, 215, 219–21, 241, 297n30, 299n46; free college and, 227; Freedom Budget and, 101–4; Friedman and, 211; full employment and, 222; GDP and, 212, 217, 223; GHGs, 210, 218, 221; global warming and, 41, 219, 241, 297n23; Great Society and, 296n13; Green New Deal and, 9–10, 213–17, 222, 255, 297n22; growth and, 207, 211–12; housing and, 212–16, 222; inequality and, 214–15, 220; insurance and, 215–16, 220; Jemez Principles and, 214–15; Keynes and, 221; labor and, 217, 222; litter, 206; neoliberalism and, 211–12; New Deal and, 213–17, 222, 296n13, 297n30; Nixon and, 207–8; oil spills,

206; Paris Climate Accords, 212–14; Pigouvian taxes and, 244; political economy and, 221; pollution, 41–42, 206–10, 220, 241, 246, 298n32; poverty and, 209, 222; profit and, 221, 240; public obliviousness to, 205; racial issues and, 209; Republicans and, 220; revenue and, 215, 220; scarcity and, 212; sewers and, 1, 115, 206, 232, 250; smog, 206, 208; smoking and, 206; socialism and, 214; subsidies and, 219; taxes and, 210–11, 216–20; threat multipliers and, 42; unemployment and, 210–12, 222; unions and, 215, 218; US Congress and, 207–8, 214; wealth and, 210, 220–21; wildfires, 41–42, 208, 213; World War II era and, 207, 217

Henderson, Vivian, 101
Herndon, Thomas, 204
Hersh, Adam, 276n16
Hill, Galdwin, 207
hill folks, 26
Hispanics, 41, 98, 161, 202
Hitler, Adolph, 89
HIV/AIDS, 21
HOLC. *See* Homeowner Loan Corporation (HOLC)
homelessness: basic income and, 194; Caldwell on, 135–36; capitalism and, 53; children and, 17, 135–36, 194; chronic, 136; conventional wisdom on, 149; demographics on, 17; education and, 167; ending, 141, 151; evictions, 17, 135; Finland and, 144; food and, 136; Harrington on, 26; healthy environment and, 212, 222; high US rate of, 8, 17; loneliness of, 135; numbers of, 136; paralysis of, 135–36; policies manufacturing, 6; scarcity and, 45; shelter and, 2, 45, 83, 88, 91, 126, 136, 145, 250; Skid Row and, 1–3, 8, 251; Utah and, 283n43
Homeowner Loan Corporation (HOLC), 139–40, 280n12
homes guarantee: origins of, 140–42; rent control and, 144–51; social housing and, 142–44
Homestead Act, 81, 271n10

Hoover, Herbert, 69; budget issues and, 247; economic rights and, 84–87; FHLB Act and, 138; New Deal and, 53, 84–87; right to work and, 113

Hopkins, Harry: background of, 113; CWA and, 114–16, 121, 126, 175; Federal Emergency Relief Administration and, 114; Roosevelt and, 57, 113–17, 121–22, 126, 134, 175; WPA, 126

household income, 16, 18–19, 143, 201, 203, 220

housing: affordable, 15–17, 107, 137, 142–45, 148, 236, 239, 281n19; basic income and, 193–94, 198–200; Biden and, 140, 147; Black people and, 16, 22, 136; budget issues and (*see under* budget issues); Byrd and, 281n19; care worker wages and, 20; ceilings and, 5, 146; children and, 135–37, 148; conservatives and, 282n42; demand for, 18, 146, 282n35; Department of Housing and Urban Development, 16; economic rights and (*see under* economic rights); electricity and, 150, 156; evictions and, 17, 135; Federal Housing Authority and, 139; Federal Reserve and, 138; FHLB Act and, 138; fire protection and, 169–70; floors and, 5, 144–46, 188; food and, 136; Freedom Budget and, 101–4; free market and, 145–46; Friedman and, 146; full employment and, 151; as fundamental need, 7–8; Great Depression and, 139; Great Recession and, 17; Green on, 261n7; growth and, 148; health care and, 185–86; healthy environment and, 214–16, 222; homelessness and, 135 (*see also* homelessness); home ownership, 21–22, 31, 137–40, 202, 210; homes guarantee, 140–51; human rights and, 140; inequality and, 148; inflation and, 145, 178–79; insurance and, 139; Johnson and, 177–78; labor and, 141, 144; laissez-faire and, 85; landlords, 17, 137, 142–50, 241, 252, 282n34, 282n36; liberals and, 144; middle class and, 139, 143; millennials and, 21; mortgages, 8, 18, 22, 31, 38, 87, 137–40, 151, 190, 204, 232–33; National

Homeownership Strategy and, 137; neoliberalism and, 140, 145; New Deal and, 138–39, 150; ownership rate, 137; Poor People's Campaign and, 103; poverty and, 138, 281n19; price controls and, 146–50; profit and, 8, 17, 22, 135, 142, 145–48; property and, 138–39, 146; public (*see* public housing); racial issues and, 22, 108, 141; reform and, 141, 151, 182, 187, 282n37; rent burden, 16, 145, 137–38, 148 (*see also* renters); Republicans and, 144; right to work and, 276n21; Roosevelt and, 24, 26, 140, 145; Sanders and, 146; scarcity and, 15–16; Section 8, 140–41; security through, 166; segregated, 22, 143; shelter and, 2, 45, 83, 88, 91, 126, 136, 145, 250; shortage in, 15–16, 142, 239; social (*see* social housing); stability in, 22; starts, 18–19, 148; supply and, 18, 142, 145–48, 282n34, 282n37; taxes and, 142; tenants' rights and, 140–41; tenements, 138; Wagner and, 283n42; wealth and, 8, 22, 137–40; World War II era and, 145

Housing Act, 283n42

How Much Does Finance Matter? (Keynes), 247–48

Hughes, Langston, 15, 93

human rights: Alston and, 1, 5; Bill of Rights, 1–2, 41, 73, 76, 90, 249; citizenship and, 1; economic rights and, 108; education and, 154; housing and, 140; "life, liberty, and the pursuit of happiness," 4, 19, 48, 85, 117, 249, 255, 270n9; "naming and shaming," 2; right to work and, 134; UN Universal Declaration of Human Rights, 279n49

Hume, David, 59

Humphrey-Hawkins Act, 277n24, 278n35

Hurricane Harvey, 213

Hurricane Irma, 213

hysteresis, 123, 237

In Defense of Housing (Madden and Marcuse), 135

inequality: basic income and, 202; budget issues and, 231, 235, 240, 244; capitalism and, 44–46, 71; Case and

Deaton on, 20; ceilings and, 10; CEO
compensation and, 19; choosing,
44–46; climate issues and, 41–43;
COVID-19 pandemic and, 40–41;
democracy and, 10, 44, 255; Dixiecrats
and, 95, 97, 116; earnings gap and, 32,
39, 158; economic rights and (*see under*
economic rights); education and, 162–
63, 169; Emancipation Proclamation
and, 52; equal distribution and, 15;
Great Depression and, 38; growth and
(*see under* growth); health care and,
20–21; healthy environment and, 214–
15, 220; housing and, 148; labor and,
25, 38, 40, 42, 45, 105, 231; middle class
and, 28, 46; neoliberalism and, 5, 36,
38, 44–46, 71, 105; redistribution and,
15, 36, 72, 81, 89, 220, 250; runaway,
25; segregation and, 22 (*see also*
segregation); Sen on, 1; structural, 30;
wages and (*see under* wages); wealth
and (*see under* wealth)
inflation: budget issues and, 238–41,
302n25; capitalism and, 70, 94;
education and, 170; growth and, 35;
housing and, 145, 178–79; maximum
employment and, 123; rent, 16; right
to work and, 120–24; runaway, 45;
Volcker and, 34
Initiative on Global Markets, 147
insurance: basic income and, 190, 192,
202–3; economic rights and, 78, 87,
252, 254; health (*see under* health
care); healthy environment and,
215–16, 220; labor and, 78, 87, 176;
mortgage, 139; social, 60, 78, 87,
292n9; unemployment (*see under*
unemployment)
integration, 22, 83, 156–57
intentional policy choices, 5
interest rates: basic income and, 202;
budget issues and (*see under* budget
issues); Federal Reserve and, 123–24,
232–34, 276n21; mortgages and, 18;
regulation of, 150; student loans and,
159
Intergovernmental Panel on Climate
Change (IPCC), 209, 214, 297n2
International Energy Agency, 219

International Monetary Fund (IMF), 219,
232
IPCC. *See* Intergovernmental Panel on
Climate Change (IPCC)

Japan, 89
Japanese American internment camps, 96
Jayapal, Pramila, 109
Jefferson, Thomas: American School and,
80; Bill of Rights and, 4, 48, 51, 76–77,
80; Declaration of Independence and,
4, 51, 77; economic rights and (*see
under* economic rights); education
and, 154; Hamilton and, 80; "life,
liberty, and the pursuit of happiness,"
4, 19, 48, 76, 85, 117, 249, 255, 270n9;
Locke and, 51; Paine and, 4, 77;
property and, 270n9; Roosevelt and,
48
Jeffersonian Revolution, 80
Jefferson Memorial, 47, 75
Jemez Principles, 214–15
Jewish refugees, 96
Jim Crow rule, 84, 95–97, 101, 156
job loss, 17, 39–40, 105
John Bates Clarke Medal, 65
Johnson, Lyndon B.: Civil Rights Act and,
27, 32, 99, 249, 271n10; education and,
164; Goldwater and, 27, 67; Great
Society and (*see under* Great Society);
health care and, 177–78; Medicare
and, 178; National Commission
on Technology, Automation, and
Economic Progress, 44–45; poverty
and, 27–28; reform and, 27, 99; taxes
and, 33; US Congress and, 27; Vietnam
War and, 27, 103; war on poverty, 27
Jones, Mondaire, 109
*Journal of the American Medical Association
Network Open*, 41

Kahn, Tom, 101
Kaiser Family Foundation, 199
Kalecki, Michal, 118–19
Katz, Lawrence, 155
Katznelson, Ira, 28
Kaye, Harvey J., 78
Kelton, Stephanie, 235, 302n19
Kennedy, John F., 25–27, 32–33

Keyersling, Leon, 101
Keynes, John Maynard: background of, 54; budget issues and (see under budget issues); critique of, 57–62; education and, 154; "The End of Laissez-Faire," 54; Friedman and, 63; full employment and, 124; *The General Theory of Employment, Interest, and Money*, 56, 124; growth and, 55, 70, 72; Hayek and, 57–62, 86; healthy environment and, 221; *How Much Does Finance Matter?*, 247–48; laissez-faire and, 54–57, 60; New Deal and (see under New Deal); property and, 54–55, 57; right to work and, 113, 124–25; Robinson on, 113; Roosevelt and, 56–58, 86, 247, 268n13; triumph of, 53–57
King, Coretta Scott, 129
King, Martin Luther, Jr.: assassination of, 103, 129; basic income and, 189; Civil Rights Act and, 99; conservatives and, 274n59; economic rights and, 4, 77, 98–99, 104, 109; Freedom Budget and, 101–4; Great Society and, 98–99; housing and, 8; "I Have a Dream," 100–101; Poor People's Campaign and, 103; Sanders and, 109; shortcomings of, 274n59; SCLC and, 98–99, 103; Voting Rights Act and, 99
Kissinger, Henry, 219
Klein, Naomi, 205
Knight, Frank, 61, 63
Krugman, Paul, 238

labor: American dream and, 29 (see also American dream); basic income and, 189, 193–96, 200; BLS, 158; budget issues and, 231, 237; capitalism and (see under capitalism); Carter and, 33; CCC and, 25, 126, 129, 277n29, 278n41; ceilings and, 5, 124; COVID-19 pandemic and, 30, 40, 117, 121, 123, 231; CWA, 25–26, 114–16, 121, 126, 129; Department of Labor and, 124, 127, 175, 196; disabled, 90, 176, 178, 192–94; earnings gap and, 32, 39, 158; economic rights and (see under economic rights); education and,

155–56, 158, 160, 163; Emancipation Proclamation and, 52; Executive Order 6420B and, 114; Executive Order 8802 and, 100; expanded public employment, 124–26; Fair Employment Practice Committee, 100; Federal Emergency Relief Administration and, 114; federal job guarantee, 126–32; floors and, 5, 116, 129, 194; Freedmen's Bureau Act, 83; Freedom Budget, 101–4; free market and, 6, 53, 68, 250; Friedman and, 72, 120; full employment, 7 (see also full employment); GDP, 35; good jobs, 107, 118, 125, 185, 215; growth and (see under growth); health care and, 175–77; healthy environment and, 217, 222; housing and, 141, 144; inequality and (see under inequality); insurance and, 78, 87, 176, 190, 192, 275n9, 292n4; maximum employment, 123; mobility and, 28–32, 35, 70, 146; NAIRU and, 120–24; National Labor Relations Act, 25, 88; neoliberalism and, 6, 14, 34, 44, 105, 132; New Deal and, 34–35, 53, 88, 105, 222; organized, 34, 48–49; participation rate, 117, 237; pensions, 49, 78–79, 176; power of, 35; PRO Act, 125, 252; Reagan and, 6, 33–34, 48, 68; retirement, 18, 107–8, 128; right to work, 116–34; Roosevelt and, 25, 88, 94, 105, 116, 121, 175–77, 277n29; segregation and, 28, 40; slavery (see under slavery); strikes, 88, 100, 116, 255; Task Force on Worker Organizing and Empowerment, 125; underemployment, 5, 12, 31, 117, 230, 236 (see also unemployment); unions, 7 (see also unions); US Congress and, 26, 68, 94, 107, 116, 123, 124–25, 133, 231, 252; Wagner and, 25, 88, 150–51, 283n42; war effort and, 76; WPA and, 25, 126–30
Labor Network for Sustainability, 297n29
laissez-faire: failures of, 84; free markets and, 53; Friedman and, 63, 65–67; Great Depression and, 84; Hamilton and, 80; Hayek and, 60, 63, 65–66; Hoover and, 84; Keynes and, 54–57,

60; Reagan and, 50; Roosevelt and, 53, 86, 89

Lancet, The (journal), 184

Land-Grant College Act, 81–82

landlords: evictions and, 17, 135; renters and (*see under* renters); right to housing and, 137, 142–50

Latinx, 16, 131, 169, 204, 275n13

legal issues, 55, 267n7; amendments, 2, 48–51, 68–69, 76, 84, 154, 229, 249, 281n19; basic income and, 192, 198; Bill of Rights, 1–2, 41, 51–52, 73, 76, 90, 249; Civil Rights Act, 27, 32, 99, 249, 271n10; Full Employment and Balanced Growth Act, 278n35; *Plessy v. Ferguson*, 84; *Roe v. Wade*, 304n1; US Supreme Court, 52, 84, 88, 156

LGBTQ+ community, 129

liberals: budget issues and, 238; capitalism and (*see under* capitalism); declining faith in, 255; Democrats, 27; economic rights and, 90, 106; education and, 164; housing and, 144; neoliberalism, 5 (*see also* neoliberalism); social, 261n7

life expectancy, 20–21, 180–81

Lincoln, Abraham, 43, 52, 77, 80–84, 98

Lind, Michael, 270n8

litter, 206

living wage. *See under* economic rights; right to work

Lochner era, 52–53

Locke, John, 51, 53, 59, 270n9

London School of Economics, 58

loss of meaning, 20–21

lynching, 95–96

MacArthur "Genius Grant," 221

Macy's Thanksgiving Day Parade, 205

Madden, David J., 135

Madison, James, 51

Mankiw, Gregory, 45, 147

March on Washington Movement, 100

Marcuse, Peter, 135

Markey, Ed, 214, 216

Marmor, Theodore, 178–79

Marshall Plan, 24

Mason, J. W., 169

Mason, Patrick, 32

Massachusetts Constitution, 153

Massachusetts Institute of Technology (MIT), 147, 245

Master Plan, 164–65

McCarthy, Mary, 24

McGovern, George, 105

Medicaid, 27, 66, 127, 172, 179, 181, 240

Medicare: Ball on, 178; basic income and, 197; budget issues and, 227, 240–41; capitalism and, 66; Centers for Medicare and Medicaid Services, 179; Democratic Socialists and, 255; design goal of, 9; eligibility age for, 181; for all, 9–10, 178, 181–88, 227, 255, 291n38; Johnson and, 177–78; Nixon and, 178; out-of-pocket expenses and, 291n38; Sanders on, 10; Social Security Act, 27; universal nature of, 167–68

medicine, 16, 185, 188, 235

Metcalf, Gilbert, 146–47

middle class: education and, 160; Great Recession and, 40; health care and, 186; housing and, 139, 143; inequality and, 28, 46; New Deal and, 25, 28, 139, 186; as policy choice, 24; White, 21, 28

millennials, 29

MIT (Massachusetts Institute of Technology), 147, 245

mobility, 28–32, 35, 70, 146

modern monetary theory (MMT), 235, 302n19

Mont Pelerin Society (MPS), 61–63

Moore, Freddy, 96

Moral Mondays, 106

Morrill, Justin, 153

Morrill Act, 81–82

mortality rates, 5, 21, 180–81

mortgages: American Mortgage, 140; basic income and, 190, 204; budget issues and, 232–33; economic rights and, 87; Fannie Mae and, 139–40; FHLB Act and, 138; HOLC and, 139–40, 280n12; housing and (*see under* housing); interest deduction for, 137; interest rates and, 18; Veterans Administration and, 139

Moyn, Samuel, 273n34

MPS (Mont Pelerin Society), 61–63

Mullen, A. Kirsten, 82

Musk, Elon, 18, 43

Muskie, Edmund, 207–8
Mussolini, Benito, 72, 89

NAIRU (nonaccelerating inflation rate of unemployment), 120–24
National Association for the Advancement of Colored People (NAACP), 156
National Center for Education Statistics, 159
National Commission on Technology, Automation, and Economic Progress, 44–45
National Emergency Council, 115
National Environmental Policy Act, 208
National Homeownership Strategy, 137
National Industrial Recovery Act (NIRA), 53, 88–89
National Labor Relations Act, 25, 88
Nazis, 76, 90, 96, 254
negative freedom: Berlin on, 3; Bill of Rights and, 2, 51–52; capitalism and (*see under* capitalism); citizenship and, 52; Declaration of Independence and, 2, 51; economic rights and, 7, 85, 90; Jefferson and, 51; Lincoln and, 52; Locke and, 51; vs. positive freedom, 261n3, 267n3; radicalization of, 5
negative income tax (NIT), 196, 198–99
neoliberalism: budget issues and, 235, 238–39; capitalism and (*see under* capitalism); collective action and, 44; decline of, 253; deregulation and, 6, 34, 37, 71; education and, 161, 172; Friedman and, 6, 61–65, 70–72, 211; Great Financial Crisis of 2008 and, 253; growth and (*see under* growth); Hayek and, 6, 61–62, 65; healthy environment and, 211–12; housing and, 140, 145; inequality and (*see under* inequality); labor and (*see under* labor); market fundamentalism and, 5; New Deal and, 5, 10, 34–35, 38, 51, 71, 105; origins of, 6; price controls and, 121; property and, 44; questioning, 10; right to work and, 132, 277n23
"Neo-Liberalism and Its Prospects" (Hayek), 63
New America, 270n8

New Deal: basic income and, 192, 203; breaking of, 105; capitalism and (*see under* capitalism); civil rights and (*see under* civil rights); Commonwealth Club Address, 85; CWA and, 26, 114–16, 121, 126, 129; deficit spending and, 25, 56, 89, 264n28; dismantlement of, 35; economic rights and (*see under* economic rights); education and, 167; free market and, 88–89; Friedman and, 63, 66–67, 71; full employment and, 25; goal of, 24–25; Green, 9–10, 213–17, 222, 255, 297n22; growth and (*see under* growth); health care and, 175; healthy environment and (*see under* healthy environment); Hoover and, 53, 84–87; housing and, 138–39, 150; in action, 87–89; Keynes and, 54, 56–58, 86, 264n28; labor and (*see under* labor); middle class and, 25, 28, 139, 186; neoliberalism and (*see under* neoliberalism); political economy and, 10, 51, 56, 86; Rauchway on, 264n28; redistribution and, 5, 139; reform and, 27, 56, 85, 105, 273n34; renters and, 150–51; right to banking and, 203; right to work and, 126; southern segregationists and, 28; stability of, 35; taxes and, 9–10, 33–35, 56, 105, 167, 186; unemployment and, 25; welfare and, 58, 67, 80
New Yorker, 207
New York Times, 20, 22, 56, 60, 67, 195, 207, 238
New York Tribune, 93
NIMBYism, 148
Nirenberg, Ron, 23
Nixon, Richard M.: basic income and, 195–96; budget issues and, 240; capitalism and, 71; Comprehensive Child Development Act and, 171; economic rights and, 105; health care and, 177–78; healthy environment and, 207–8; Medicare and, 178; reform and, 194–95, 293n18; State of the Union, 207; welfare and, 293n18
Nobel Prize, 31, 50, 62, 211
nonaccelerating inflation rate of unemployment (NAIRU), 120–24

Nordhaus, William, 211–12
Norquist, Grover, 245

Obama, Barack: deficits and, 300n3; Patient Protection and Affordable Care Act, 178, 180, 188, 229, 254; Skocpol on, 297n24; Summers and, 63; universal health insurance and, 177; "Yes We Can," 106
Ocasio-Cortez, Alexandria, 109, 214, 216, 245
Occupational Safety and Health Administration (OSHA), 66
Occupy Wall Street, 106–7
Office of Price Administration and Civilian Supply, 145
oil shock, 35
oil spills, 206
Omar, Ilhan, 109
Organization for Economic Cooperation and Development (OECD), 118, 162, 172, 179–80, 199
Organization of the Petroleum Exporting Countries (OPEC), 219
OSHA (Occupational Safety and Health Administration), 66
Other America, The (Harrington), 26

Pacific Railroad Act, 81
Paine, Thomas: Agrarian Justice, 78–79, 195; basic income and, 195; "Common Sense," 77–79; economic rights and, 77–80, 84; education and, 78; Jefferson and, 4, 77; Rights of Man, 78–79
Parenti, Christian, 79
Paris Climate Accords, 212–14
participation rates, 117, 168, 237
patents, 49
Patient Protection and Affordable Care Act, 178, 180, 188, 229, 254
PAYGO rule, 229
Pearl Harbor, 89–90
Pell grants, 166
Pelosi, Nancy, 213, 229
pensions, 49, 78–79, 176
people of color, 40, 43, 129, 136–37, 166, 181, 194, 292n9
People's Action, 140

Perkins, Frances, 175–77, 188–89, 192, 277n29
Pew Research Center, 37, 159, 161
phase-out rate, 196, 198–99, 294n26
Pigouvian taxes, 244
Piketty, Thomas, 35, 38, 245
Pinochet, Augusto, 63
Plessy v. Ferguson, 84
"Political Aspects of Full Employment" (Kalecki), 118–19
political economy: capitalism and, 53, 56, 62; economic rights and, 250; Hayes and, 221; healthy environment and, 221; intentional policy choices and, 5; Locke and, 53; New Deal and, 10, 51, 56, 86; Radical Republicans and, 81–84
pollution: budget issues and, 241, 246; global warming and, 41, 219, 241, 297n23; healthy environment and (see under healthy environment)
Poor People's Campaign, 103
populism, 70, 254
positive freedom: capitalism and, 58, 73, 267n3; economic rights and, 3, 6, 76; ensuring for all, 6; free will and, 4; negative freedom and, 2–3, 261n3, 267n3; Sen and, 261n7
poverty: AFDC and, 36, 192; Alston on, 1; basic income and, 189–204, 292n3, 293n13; budget issues and, 249, 255; by design, 281n19; capitalism and, 55, 59, 66; child (see under children); democracy and, 44; economic rights and (see under economic rights); education and, 156; eradication of, 3, 9, 27, 194, 197–98, 255; eviction and, 17; food stamps and, 7, 29, 36, 168, 190, 196, 250; Freedom Budget and, 101–4; growth and, 19, 25, 32, 43, 55, 77, 213; Harrington and, 26; have-nots, 15, 18–23, 30, 40, 44–45, 209, 217; healthy environment and, 209, 222; homelessness and, 1 (see also homelessness); housing and, 138, 281n19; Johnson and, 27–28; Kennedy and, 25; line of, 2, 190, 194, 196–200; mobility and, 28–32, 35, 70, 146; persistence of, 1; policy

poverty (*cont.*)
manufacturing of, 6, 281n19; right to work and, 113–14, 117, 123, 128, 275n7; scarcity and, 43, 45, 194; Skid Row and, 1–3, 8, 251; TANF, 36; Trump and, 19; unemployment and, 5, 7, 10, 19, 45, 55, 59, 99, 102, 109, 128, 190–96, 222, 275n7; wages, 7, 10, 19, 32, 55, 78, 107, 123, 128, 193–94; war on, 27, 66
Poverty amid Plenty: The American Paradox (report), 195
Powell, Jerome, 120, 123, 277n23
Presidential Medal of Freedom, 71
Presley, Ayanna, 109
price controls: budget issues and, 238–41, 303n27; capitalism and, 64, 68; housing and, 146–50; right to work and, 121; Webber on, 303n27
Professional Air Traffic Controllers Organization, 34
profit: basic income and, 203; budget issues and, 240; economic rights and, 106, 253; education and, 160–61; healthy environment and, 221; housing and, 8, 17, 22, 135, 142, 145–48; people after, 106; people over, 3; right to work and, 116, 119; short-term, 9
Progressive Era, 53
progressivism, 79, 255
property: capitalism and, 6, 49–61, 64; economic rights and, 83, 270n9; Hayek and, 47; Homestead Act, 81, 271n10; housing and, 138–39, 146; inheritance rights and, 77; Jefferson and, 270n9; Keynes and, 54–55, 57; neoliberalism and, 44; patents, 49; private rights and, 6; public good and, 50; Reagan and, 6, 49–50; taxes and, 155
Protecting the Right to Organize (PRO) Act, 125, 252
public good: basic income and, 197, 199; budget issues and, 229; children as (*see under* children); education as (*see under* education); health care and, 182; as nonexcludable, 153; property and, 50; supply and demand and, 153–54; universal, 71
public housing, 104, 140–44, 216, 239, 281n19

quality of life, 21, 115

Race between Education and Technology (Goldin and Katz), 155
Race for Profit (Taylor), 22
racial issues: basic income and, 193; Black people, 32 (*see also* Black people); capitalism and, 24, 28; civil rights, 66 (*see also* civil rights); COVID-19 pandemic and, 32; discrimination (*see* discrimination); Dixiecrats and, 95, 97, 116; earnings gap, 32, 39, 158; economic rights, 93, 99, 106–8; education, 154–57, 284n11; Emancipation Proclamation, 52; Executive Order 8802 and, 100; Freedom Budget, 101–4; getting ahead and, 31; GI Bill, 164; healthy environment and, 209; Hispanics, 41, 98, 161, 202; housing, 22, 108, 141; integration, 22, 83, 156–57; Japanese American internment camps, 96; Jim Crow rule, 84, 95–97, 101, 156; Latinx, 16, 169, 204, 275n13; lynching, 95–96; military and, 93; mortality gap and, 21, 181; Nineteenth Amendment, 249; people of color (*see* people of color); right to banking, 202; segregation (*see under* segregation); slavery (*see* slavery); Social Security and, 292n9; Special Field Orders No. 15, 82; structural, 6, 32; unemployment, 31; unions, 21, 100, 107, 121, 255; welfare and, 292n9
Radical King, The (West), 100–101
Radical Republicans, 6, 80–84
Raghuveer, Tara, 140–41
Randolph, A. Philip, 99–101
Rauchway, Eric, 264n28
Reader's Digest, 60
Reagan, Ronald: amendment of, 48, 75; Carter defeat and, 69; charisma of, 47–48; deregulation and, 68; economic bill of rights, 48, 69; freedom to property, 49; freedom to work, 48–49; Friedman and, 6, 63, 68–71, 269n34, 269n39; health care and, 49; labor and, 6, 33–34, 48, 68; laissez-faire approach of, 50; property and,

6, 49–50; right to work and, 48–49; Screen Actors Guild and, 48; taxes and (*see under* taxes); unions and, 33–34, 48; US Congress and, 48, 50, 70; US Constitution and, 48

Reagan Revolution, 6, 68, 106

Reconstruction, 154

redistribution, 15, 36, 72, 81, 89, 220, 250

reform: basic income and, 192–96, 292n4; budget issues and, 246; capitalism and, 53, 56; economic bill of rights and, 11; economic rights and (*see under* economic rights); education and, 155, 163; health care and, 182, 187; housing and, 141, 151, 282n37; Johnson and, 27, 99; Lincoln and, 83; New Deal and (*see under* New Deal); Nixon and, 194–95, 293n18; Progressive Era, 53; right to work and, 125, 132; Roosevelt and, 25, 27, 56, 85, 93, 95, 105, 192, 273n34; tax, 56, 105, 246; unemployment insurance, 292n4; unified vision for, 11; welfare, 293n18

Reinhart, Carmen, 301n17

rent burden, 16, 137–38, 145, 148

renters, 22; affordable, 137; Austin, 16; Detroit, 16; Friedman and, 146; homes guarantee and, 144–51; landlords and, 17, 137, 142–50, 241, 252, 282n34, 282n36; Metcalf on, 146–47; New Deal and, 150–51; New York City, 145–46; number of, 136–37; Office of Price Administration and Civilian Supply and, 145; public housing and (*see* public housing); rent control policies and, 144–51; Roosevelt and, 145; Sanders and, 146; social housing and (*see under* social housing); Stigler on, 146; tenants' rights and, 140–41

"Report on the Subject of Manufacture" (Hamilton), 80

Republicans: basic income and, 195; budget issues and, 229–30, 242, 245; capitalism and (*see under* capitalism); economic rights and, 270n9; education and, 165; health care and, 10; healthy environment and, 220; housing and, 144; Radical, 6, 80–84; right to work and, 133, 278n41; wealth and, 10, 37, 229. *See also specific officials*

retirement, 18, 107–8, 128

revenue: budget issues and (*see under* budget issues); carbon dividend and, 220; corporate, 246; education and, 82, 171; fossil fuel, 215; health care and, 186; healthy environment and, 215, 220; linking policies to specific, 230; maximization of, 247; US Revenue Act, 33; wealth tax and, 247 (*see also* taxes)

Revolutionary War, 30, 77, 80

Rewire America, 221

Rights of Man (Paine), 78–79

right to banking, 201–4

right to work: Biden and, 124–25, 130; Black people and, 121, 124, 131, 275n13; ceilings and, 124; citizenship and, 114–15; conservatives and (*see under* conservatives); COVID-19 pandemic and, 117–23, 275n9, 279n44; CWA and, 26, 114–16, 121, 126, 129; demand and, 122, 125, 132; democracy and, 113; Democrats and, 7, 116, 130, 133; Executive Order 6420B, 114; Federal Emergency Relief Administration and, 114; federal job guarantee, 126–32; Federal Reserve and, 119–20, 123–25, 130, 133, 275n13, 276n21, 278n35; floors and, 5, 116, 129; food and, 115, 117, 126; Friedman and, 120; full employment and, 118, 122–34, 275n6, 276n16, 276n19, 277n23, 278n35; Great Depression and, 113–14, 129; growth and, 121–23; Hamilton and, 127; Hopkins and, 57, 113–17, 121–22, 126, 134, 175; housing and, 276n21; human rights and, 134; inflation and, 120–24; insurance and, 78, 87; interest rates and, 123; Keynes and, 113, 124–25; labor and, 116–34; Latinx and, 131; living wage and, 7, 117, 127, 128, 134; NAIRU and, 120–24; neoliberalism and, 132, 277n23; New Deal and, 126; poverty and (*see under* poverty); profit and, 116, 119; Reagan and, 48–48; reform and, 125, 132; Republicans and, 133, 278n41; Roosevelt and, 92, 113–17, 121, 126, 279n49; Sanders and, 133; scarcity of good jobs, 118; subsidies

right to work (*cont.*)
and, 128, 130, 277n31; taxes and, 128; Trump and, 123; unemployment and, 113, 116–24, 127–28, 130, 275n7, 275n9, 275n13, 277n29, 279n44, 279n49; unions and, 116, 119, 121–22, 125, 132, 275n14; United Nations and, 279n49; US Congress and, 116, 123, 125, 133, 278n40; wages and, 7 (*see also* wages); wealth and, 116; women and, 115, 118, 129, 131, 277n29

Riis, Jacob, 138

Road to Serfdom, The (Hayek), 47, 58–61, 64, 268n21

Robbins, Lionel, 61

Roberts, Dorothy E., 192

Robinson, Joan, 113

Roe v. Wade, 304n1

Rogoff, Kenneth, 301n17

Romney, Mitt, 254

"Roofs or Ceilings? The Current Housing Problem" (Friedman and Stigler), 146

Roosevelt, Eleanor, 277n29

Roosevelt, Franklin D.: arrogated power of, 272n21; basic income and, 192; Black people and, 28; budget issues and, 246–47; capitalism and (*see under* capitalism); CCC and, 25, 31, 88, 126, 129, 278n41; Commonwealth Club Address, 85; CWA, 25–26, 114–16, 121, 126, 129; deregulation and, 6, 33–34; economic bill of rights and (*see under* economic bill of rights); economic rights and (*see under* economic rights); education and, 164; Executive Order 6420B, 114; Executive Order 8802, 100; Federal Emergency Relief Administration, 114; "First Hundred Days" of, 87–88, 113; food and, 24, 26; four freedoms, 6, 91–97, 105, 273n34; gold standard and, 301n13; Great Depression and, 24–26, 53; Hart and, 105; health care and, 175–77, 184; Hopkins and, 57, 113–17, 121–22, 126, 134, 175; housing and, 24, 26, 140, 145; Jefferson and, 48; Keynes and, 56–58, 86, 247, 268n13; labor and (*see under* labor); laissez-faire and, 53,

86, 89; maximum income and, 246; Moyn and, 273n24; New Deal and, 6, 84–87 (*see also* New Deal); Office of Price Administration and Civilian Supply, 145; Pearl Harbor attack, 89–90; reform and (*see under* reform); renters and, 145; right to work and (*see under* right to work); security and, 76; southern segregationists and, 28, 95, 273n40; State of the Union (*see under* State of the Union); subsidies and, 49; taxes and (*see under* taxes); US Congress and (*see under* US Congress); welfare and, 58, 67, 80, 268n9; WPA and, 25, 126–30

Roosevelt, Teddy, 177

Röpke, Wilhelm, 61

Rothstein, Richard, 22

Rouse, Cecilia, 147

Rustin, Bayard, 100

Rutgers University, 62

Saez, Emmanuel, 35, 38, 245, 247

Samuel DuBois Cook Center on Social Equity, 39

San Antonio Food Bank, 23

Sanders, Bernie, 10; budget issues and, 245–47; economic rights and, 104–9; education and, 163; housing and, 146; rent control and, 146; right to work and, 133; and the "Squad," 109; Twenty-First-Century Economic Bill of Rights, 108

Scalise, Steve, 245

scarcity: American dream and, 24; basic income and, 194; distribution and, 45; economic rights and, 249; Freedom Budget and, 102; of good jobs, 118; healthy environment and, 212; mistaken view of, 43; as policy choice, 102; right to work and, 118

Schmalensee, Richard, 147

Schoofs, Greg, 160

Science Advances (journal), 41

SCLC (Southern Christian Leadership Conference), 98, 103

Screen Actors Guild, 48

Second Continental Congress, 51

segregation: housing and, 22, 143; labor and, 28, 40; racial issues and, 12, 24, 27–28, 40, 84, 93, 95, 143, 273n40, 277n29, 281n19; Roosevelt and, 28, 95, 273n40; southern segregationists and, 28, 95, 273n40

Sen, Amartya, 1, 156, 261n7

sewage, 1, 115, 206, 232, 250

sexism, 6, 108, 193

Shaefer, H. Luke, 192–93

Sherman, William T., 82–83

Sierra Club, 207

Silent Spring (Carson), 207

Simone, Nina, 205

60 Minutes (TV show), 245

Skid Row, 1–3, 8, 251

Skocpol, Theda, 297n24

slavery: Emancipation Proclamation, 52; Freedmen's Bureau Act, 83; labor and, 28, 52, 82–84, 97, 181, 245, 249, 270nn8–9; Lincoln and, 52, 83; Special Field Orders No. 15 and, 82

Slavery by Another Name (Blackmon), 28, 84

Slobodian, Quinn, 44, 62

Smith, Adam, 51, 54

smog, 206, 208

smoking, 206

SNAP. *See* Supplemental Nutrition Assistance Program (SNAP)

social housing: cost of, 144; homes guarantee and, 142–44; neighborhood diversity and, 143; vs. public housing, 143; renters and, 5, 8, 21, 141–45, 150, 198, 222, 227; tax credits and, 142; Vienna and, 144

socialism: budget issues and, 245, 250; capitalism and (*see under* capitalism); democratic, 7, 26, 107–8, 214, 254–55; economic rights and, 98, 107–8; Harrington and, 26; healthy environment and, 214; King on, 8; liberal, 261n7; wealth and, 10

Social Security: basic income and, 192–93, 197, 200; budget issues and, 229; economic rights and, 76, 79, 87; health care and, 176–78; Medicaid and, 27, 66, 127, 172, 179, 181, 240; Medicare and (*see* Medicare); racial issues and, 292n9; Trump's defunding of, 254; universal, 167

Social Security Act, 25, 27, 92, 176

Sons of Liberty, 51

Southern Christian Leadership Conference (SCLC), 98, 103

southern segregationists, 28, 95, 273n40

Special Field Orders No. 15, 82

Special Rapporteur on Extreme Poverty and Human Rights for the United Nations, 1

Springfield, Dusty, 205

stagflation, 27, 35

standard of living: basic income and, 193; economic rights and, 94, 102; golden age of capitalism and, 24; Hayek on, 58; healthy environment and, 210, 217, 222; housing and, 145; inflation and, 145

Standells, 208

Standing Rock, 214

Stanton, Elizabeth Cady, 52

State of the Union: Carter and, 33; Nixon and, 207; Roosevelt and, 4, 75, 84, 90, 94, 257

Steinbaum, Marshall, 160

Steinbeck, John, 93–94

Stevens, Thaddeus, 83

Stigler, George, 61–63, 146

Stiglitz, Joseph E., 31, 299n1

stock market, 6, 18–19

Strain, Michael, 29–30

strikes, 88, 100, 116, 255

student debt: education and (*see under* education); free college and, 8, 10, 11, 158, 161–71, 227, 255

subsidies: budget issues and, 241; economic rights and, 250; education and, 162, 168, 171; Friedman and, 64; Hamilton and, 79; health care and, 187; healthy environment and, 219; Pacific Railroad Act, 81; Reagan and, 49; right to work and, 128, 130, 277n31

suicide, 20, 29, 41

Summers, Larry, 45, 63, 232

Sunrise Movement, 213, 255

Supplemental Nutrition Assistance Program (SNAP), 190–91, 193 supply: budget issues and, 302n25; carbon pricing and, 297n30; constraints of, 222, 236–42; COVID-19 pandemic and, 239; economic rights and, 253; education and, 153–54, 166; food, 207 (see also food); health care and, 10; housing and (see under housing); Office of Price Administration and Civilian Supply, 145; public goods and, 153–54; public investment and, 238–40; taxes and, 71, 235; water, 209

surpluses, 115, 231

TANF (Temporary Assistance for Needy Families), 36
Task Force on Worker Organizing and Empowerment, 125
Tax Cuts and Jobs Act, 235, 269n40
taxes: basic income and, 191–93, 196–201; budget issues and, 227–35, 241–48; capital gains, 244–46; capitalism and, 49–52, 56, 64–71; carbon, 43, 210, 216, 220; child tax credit (CTC), 191, 198, 200; corporate, 5, 33, 229, 231, 244–47, 253, 303n33; credits, 128, 142, 168, 191, 193, 198, 200–201, 292n3; cuts in, 6, 8, 32–34, 37, 66, 70–71, 227, 231, 235, 243; economic rights and, 78, 89, 105, 109; education and (see under education); EITC, 128, 168, 193, 200; free market and, 250; growth and (see under growth); havens for, 242, 244, 303n33; health care and, 186; healthy environment and, 210–11, 216–20; housing and, 142; income, 9, 35–36, 64, 128, 166, 168, 191, 193, 196–201, 243–47; on job creators, 33; Johnson and, 33; Kennedy and, 32–33; Lochner era and, 52–53; low rate of, 243; marginal rates of, 33–34, 70, 244–46, 304n42; midcentury code for, 245; negative, 196, 198–99; New Deal and (see under New Deal); number of brackets for, 244–46; payroll, 23, 128, 186; Pigouvian, 244; progressive code for, 5, 32, 198–99, 244; property, 155; Reagan and, 6, 33–34, 49–50, 68–71, 243; reform and, 56, 105, 246;

regressive code for, 5, 37; right to work and, 128; Roosevelt and, 9–10, 33–35, 56, 89, 105, 167, 246; supply-side cuts, 235; top marginal rate of, 33–34, 70, 245–46; unemployment and, 253; US Revenue Act and, 33; wealth and, 6, 10, 33, 167, 229–31, 243–47

Taylor, Keeanga-Yamahtta, 22
Tcherneva, Pavlina, 128
Teamsters, 88
Tea Party, 71
Temporary Assistance for Needy Families (TANF), 36
tenants' rights, 140–41
Ten Commandments, 2
tenements, 138
Tesla, 17–18
threat multipliers, 42
Time magazine, 207
Tlaib, Rashida, 109
tobacco, 244
"To Fulfill These Rights" conference, 101
Treaty of Versailles, 76
Truman, Harry S., 177
Trump, Donald: budget issues and, 235; capitalism and, 71; Council of Economic Advisers, 19; economic rights and, 254; education and, 166; poverty and, 19; right to work and, 123; wealth distribution and, 37
Tugwell, Rexford, 85, 95
$2.00 a Day: Living on Almost Nothing in America (Edin and Shaefer), 192–93

"Umbrellas Don't Make it Rain" (Hamilton et al.), 31
underemployment, 5, 12, 31, 117, 230, 236
unemployment: basic income and, 189–96, 292n4; before COVID-19, 18; Black people and, 31, 124; budget issues and (see under budget issues); capitalism and (see under capitalism); COVID-19 pandemic and, 17–18, 117, 121, 189, 253, 275n9, 279n44; as economic indicator, 19; economic rights and (see under economic rights); education and, 158; full employment and, 25, 56–58 (see also full employment); have-nots and,

18–19; health care and, 175–77, 183; healthy environment and, 210–12, 222; industrial policy and, 253; insurance and, 176, 190, 192, 275n9, 292n4; job loss and, 17, 39–40, 105; level playing field and, 252; Musk's threats of, 18; NAIRU and, 120–24; New Deal and, 25; persistent, 5, 116–22; poverty and (*see under* poverty); racial issues and, 31; rate of, 18, 25, 120–21, 124, 158, 237–38, 301n17; reform and, 292n4; right to work and (*see under* right to work); scarcity and, 45; Skid Row and, 1–3, 8, 251; taxes and, 253; U-3 measurement of, 121; U-6 measurement of, 117
Union Army, 82
Union Oil, 206
unions: capitalism and, 48; conservatives and, 7, 35, 116; economic rights and (*see under* economic rights); evading, 7; healthy environment and, 215, 218; longshoremen, 88; PRO Act, 125, 252; racial issues and, 21, 100, 107, 121, 255; Reagan and, 33–34, 48; right to work and (*see under* right to work); sense of belonging from, 20; strikes and, 88, 100, 116, 255; Task Force on Worker Organizing and Empowerment, 125; US Congress and, 94, 107, 116, 125, 252; wages and, 7, 20–21, 25, 89, 107, 116, 119–22, 132, 218, 255. *See also specific unions*
United Nations: Alston and, 1–3, 5; Article 23 of, 279n49; Guterres and, 41; IPCC, 209, 214, 297n23; right to work and, 279n49; Secretary General, 41; Special Rapporteur on Extreme Poverty and Human Rights, 1; Universal Declaration of Human Rights, 279n49
University of Chicago, 63, 160
University of Florida, 164
US Bureau of Labor Statistics (BLS), 118, 158, 275n7
US Census Bureau, 190
US Civil War, 28, 81–82, 84, 154
US Congress: basic income and, 191–92, 195, 203; budget issues and (*see under* budget issues); capitalism and, 48–51,

68–70; economic rights and (*see under* economic rights); education and, 171; Eighty-Ninth, 27; healthy environment and, 207–8, 214; Johnson and, 27; labor and (*see under* labor); Reagan and, 48, 50, 70; right to work and (*see under* right to work); Roosevelt and, 4, 25, 87, 90, 94, 116; Thirty-Seventh, 81; unions and, 94, 107, 116, 125, 252. *See also* Congressional Budget Office (CBO)
US Constitution: amendments (*see* amendments); Anti-Federalists and, 52; Bill of Rights, 2 (*see also* Bill of Rights); capitalism and, 48, 51, 68; Constitutional Convention, 51; economic rights and, 75–76, 79, 84, 91–92; education and, 154; free speech and, 3; Reagan and, 48; segregation and, 84; 200th anniversary of, 48
US dollar, 299n1
US Postal Service, 204
US Revenue Act, 33
US Supreme Court, 52–53, 84, 88, 156
US Treasury, 63, 79, 127, 130, 228, 232–33

vaccines, 40, 253
Veterans Administration (VA), 139
Vietnam War, 27, 35, 103–4
Volcker Recession, 34
Von Mises, Ludwig, 61
voting rights, 44, 98–99, 108, 249

wages: average, 19; care worker, 20; CEO compensation and, 19; cost of living and, 16; distribution, 35; earnings gap, 32, 158; Fight for $15, 106; Freedom Budget and, 102; Friedman on, 69; growth and (*see under* growth); household income and, 16, 18–19, 143, 201, 203, 220; inequality and, 24, 29–30, 32, 40, 45, 86, 108, 231; living, 7, 78, 89, 101, 107–8, 117, 127, 128, 134; millennials and, 29; poverty and (*see under* poverty); rise of, 19–20; service workers, 20; standard of living and, 24, 58, 94, 104, 145, 193, 210, 217, 222;

wages (*cont.*)
  teachers, 20; unions and (*see under* unions)
Wagner, Robert F., 25, 88, 150–51, 283n42
Walker, Frank, 115–16
Wallace, Henry, 57, 96–97
Wall Street, 94, 97, 101, 106
Warner, Lloyd, 96
Warren, Elizabeth, 246
Washington Center for Equitable Growth, 172, 288n56
Washington Post, 63, 215
"Washington Should End Its Debt Obsession" (Summers), 232
water supplies, 209
wealth: affluence and, 16, 23–28, 201; American dream and, 22, 24, 28–32, 37, 45, 70, 157; basic income and, 193, 204; budget issues and, 229–31, 243–47; capitalism and, 56; CEO compensation and, 19; COVID-19 pandemic and, 17–18; democracy and (*see under* democracy); disposable income and, 242; earnings gap and, 32, 39, 158; economic rights and, 85–86, 99, 107; education and, 153–59, 167–71; free market and, 6, 99; gaps in, 37–39; Great Financial Crisis of 2008 and, 105, 122, 170, 231–32, 235, 239, 253; Great Reshuffling and, 30; haves, 15, 18–23, 30, 40, 44–45; health care and, 180; healthy environment and, 21, 210, 220–21; household income and, 16, 18–19, 143, 201, 203, 220; housing and, 8, 22, 137–40; illusion of affluence, 23–28; immense US, 2, 15, 18–19, 251; inequality and, 5, 30, 37–39, 44–45, 99, 231; insecurity multipliers and, 39–43; longevity and, 21; pandemic increases of, 17–18; power of, 251; redistribution of, 15, 36, 72, 81, 89, 220, 250; Republicans and, 10, 37, 229; right to work and, 116; as shield from suffering, 253; socialism and, 10; standard of living and, 24, 58, 94, 104, 145, 193, 210, 217, 222; taxes and (*see under* taxes); trickle-down theory and, 229; women and, 39

wealth gap, 21, 32, 39, 158
wealth tax, 10, 167, 246–47
Webber, Isabella, 303n27
welfare: AFDC and, 36, 192; American School and, 79; basic income and, 192–93, 196, 199; Beveridge report and, 58; British National Health Service and, 58; budget issues and, 227; capitalism and, 58–59, 65, 67; childcare and, 15–16, 44, 71, 88n56, 118, 131, 171, 236, 239; Bill Clinton and, 192; economic rights and (*see under* economic rights); education and, 173; food stamps and, 7, 29, 36, 168, 190, 196, 250; Friedman on, 65; Hayek on, 59; health care and, 58; New Deal and, 58, 67, 80; Nixon and, 293n18; racial issues and, 292n9; reform and, 293n18; Roosevelt and, 58, 67, 80, 268n9; Social Security and (*see* Social Security); TANF, 36
well-being state: basic income and, 191–92, 197, 204; budget issues and, 243; economic rights and, 78, 87, 252, 257; education and, 163; health care and, 176–77
"We Need an Economic Bill of Rights" (King), 104
West, Cornel, 100–101
Whigs, 80
wildfires, 41–42, 208, 213
women: basic income and, 194; Bill of Rights and, 52; Civil Works Service and, 115; democracy and, 43, 52, 97; education and, 161, 171; Homestead Act and, 271n10; job losses and, 40; military and, 93; right to vote and, 52, 249; right to work and (*see under* right to work); Stanton and, 52; wealth of, 39
Works Progress Administration (WPA), 25, 126–30
World Bank, 63
World Economic Forum, 183
World Health Organization (WHO), 175, 183
World War I, 20, 145
World War II: budget issues and, 234, 240, 245, 247; capitalism and, 23; deaths from, 90; defeat of Axis powers,

270n8; economic rights and, 76, 84,
97; healthy environment and, 207, 217;
housing and, 145; Japanese American
internment camps and, 96; Jewish
refugees and, 96; Pearl Harbor attack,
89–90; as war for freedom, 89–91
WPA. *See* Works Progress Administration
(WPA)
W-2 income, 244

Yale University, 184
Yang, Andrew, 197, 199
"Yes We Can" (Obama),
106

Zewde, Naomi, 294n25
Zuccotti Park, 106
Zucman, Gabriel, 35, 38,
247